# Miami

**timeout.com/miami**

**Time Out Digital Ltd**
Universal House
251 Tottenham Court Road
London W1T 7AB
United Kingdom
Tel: +44 (0)20 7813 3000
Fax: +44 (0)20 7813 6001
Email: guides@timeout.com
www.timeout.com

**Published by Time Out Digital Ltd**, a wholly owned subsidiary of Time Out Group Ltd.
Time Out and the Time Out logo are trademarks of Time Out Group Ltd.

10 9 8 7 6 5 4 3 2 1

**This edition first published in Great Britain in 2013 by Ebury Publishing.**
A Random House Group Company
20 Vauxhall Bridge Road, London SW1V 2SA

**Random House Australia Pty Ltd** 20 Alfred Street, Milsons Point, Sydney, New South Wales 2061, Australia

**Random House New Zealand Ltd** 18 Poland Road, Glenfield, Auckland 10, New Zealand

**Random House South Africa (Pty) Ltd** Isle of Houghton, Corner Boundary Road & Carse O'Gowrie,
Houghton 2198, South Africa

Random House UK Limited Reg. No. 954009

Distributed in the US and Latin America by Publishers Group West (1-510-809-3700)

**For further distribution details, see www.timeout.com.**

ISBN (UK): 978-1-84670-214-3

ISBN (US): 978-1-84670-298-3

A CIP catalogue record for this book is available from the British Library.

Printed and bound by Butler Tanner & Dennis Ltd, Frome, Somerset.

The Random House Group Limited supports the Forest Stewardship Council® (FSC®), the leading international forest-certification organisation. Our books carrying the FSC label are printed on FSC®-certified paper. FSC is the only forest-certification scheme supported by the leading environmental organisations, including Greenpeace. Our paper procurement policy can be found at www.randomhouse.co.uk/environment.

# Contents

# Arts & Entertainment 158

# Escapes & Excursions 202

# In Context 236

# Essential Information 258

# Maps 276

# Introduction

Miami's reputation as a world capital of flash is certainly well deserved – and regularly represented in the many novels, movies and TV shows set amid the city's bright neon lights. Created as a warm-weather playground for America's social elite, it has long been a magnet for dreamers and hedonists. Critics snipe that it's plastic, but the fact that a tropical paradise has been created out of a swamp is a modern miracle – it's the American dream with palm trees thrown in.

For visitors used to European cities that have grown organically around some central feature, Miami can be disorientating. For the fact is that it has no centre at all. Instead, it's made up of a collection of enclaves. While the same could be said of London, Paris or Madrid, the difference with Miami is that its neighbourhoods tend to be separated by vast swathes of no man's land. In keeping with its unflattering distinction of being one of the poorest cities in the US, Miami has a highly visible degree of urban decay and poverty. It's not quite Johannesburg, but it's definitely not a city for exploring on foot. Of course, this is not an issue if you decide, as many people do, to spend all your holiday time on glamtastic South Beach (by day it's got the beaches and cafés; by night it's buzzing with restaurants, bars and clubs).

Detractors claim that South Beach has lost its individuality (yes, even with all that glamorous art deco architecture), as pioneering hipsters have been replaced by visiting hordes. Yet the SoBe backlash is ultimately good for the city, as coolhunting locals are forced to broaden their horizons and spread the wealth. Attracted by low rents, hoteliers, restaurateurs and bar owners are now setting up shop away from the beach in once-shady neighbourhoods such as Brickell, Wynwood and the Design District. The booming art scene has helped. Spurred on by the global creative extravaganza known as Art Basel, galleries in Wynwood proliferate and the neighbourhood even has its own outdoor street art park, Wynwood Walls. The culinary scene is heating up too, and not just for the week that some of the world's most famous foodies come to town for the South Beach Wine & Food Festival. Plenty of top chefs – José Andrés, Jean-Georges Vongerichten and Daniel Boulud among them – have opened up permanent outposts in Magic City.

One thing is clear. These days, Miami is much more than a beach. As revered Miami architect Morris Lapidus put it so succinctly: 'Less is not more… If you like ice-cream, why stop with one scoop? Have two. Have three. Too much is never enough.' Enjoy.

*Jennifer M Wood, Editor*

# About the Guide

## GETTING AROUND

The back of the book contains street maps of Miami, as well as overview maps of the city and its surroundings. The maps start on page 278; on them are marked the locations of hotels (❶), restaurants and cafés (❶), and bars and pubs (❶). Many businesses listed in this guide are located in the areas we've mapped; the grid-square references in the listings refer to these maps.

## THE ESSENTIALS

For practical information, including visas, disabled access, emergency numbers, lost property, useful websites and local transport, please see the Essential Information. It begins on page 258.

## THE LISTINGS

Addresses, phone numbers, websites, transport information, hours and prices are all included in our listings, as are selected other facilities. All were checked and correct at press time. However, business owners can alter their arrangements at any time, and fluctuating economic conditions can cause prices to change rapidly.

The very best venues in the city, the must-sees and must-dos in every category, have been marked with a red star (★). In the Explore chapters, we've also marked venues with free admission with a FREE symbol.

## PHONE NUMBERS

Miami has two area codes: 305, which the vast majority of Miami numbers take, and the newer 786. All local phone numbers in this guide are prefaced by a 1 and an area code. Always dial the 11-digit number as listed, including the 1, even if you're calling from a phone in the same area code.

From outside the US, dial your country's international access code (00 from the UK) or a '+' symbol, followed by the number as listed in this guide; here, the initial '1' serves as the US country code. So, to reach the Miami Art Museum, dial +1-305 375 3000. For more on phones, see p268.

## FEEDBACK

We welcome feedback on this guide, both on the venues we've included and on any other locations that you'd like to see featured in future editions. Please email us at guides@timeout.com.

## Time Out Guides

Founded in 1968, Time Out has grown from humble beginnings into the leading resource for anyone wanting to know what's happening in the world's greatest cities. Alongside our influential weeklies in London, New York and Chicago, we publish more than 20 magazines in cities as varied as Beijing and Beirut; a range of travel books, with the City Guides now joined by the newer Shortlist series; and an information-packed website. The company remains proudly independent, still owned by Tony Elliott four decades after he launched *Time Out London*.

Written by local experts and illustrated with original photography, our books also retain their independence. No business has been featured because it has advertised, and all restaurants and bars are visited and reviewed anonymously.

### ABOUT THE EDITOR

Jennifer M Wood came to Miami by way of New York City in 2010. She is the former Editor-in-Chief of *MovieMaker Magazine* and the author of seven books, including the best-selling *Mr Cheap's New York* and *Mr Cheap's Chicago*. Her writing appears in *Condé Nast Traveler*, *Time Out New York*, *Relish*, *Complex* and *Mental Floss*.

A full list of the book's contributors can be found on page 11.

## LINCOLN ROAD MALL

South Beach's most popular pedestrian thoroughfare is a mile-long stretch of boutiques, bars, cafés and clubs. Whether you're looking for a designer bikini or a mojito, you'll find it at this outdoor retail mecca. See p39.

## HAULOVER BEACH

Naturists (and those after a quick thrill) head straight for the northern end of Haulover Beach, Miami's only official 'clothing optional' stretch of sand. See p43.

## WYNWOOD WALLS

The centrepiece of the Wynwood Arts District, this eye-popping street-art park features bold creations by artists taking graffiti beyond the spray-paint can, including Shepard Fairey, Kenny Scharf and Ron English. See p67.

Golden Beach
Sunny Isles
Haulover Beach
Bal Harbour
Surfside
Aventura Mall
Loehmann's Fashion Island
Intracoastal Mall
Bal Harbour Shops
Bay Harbour Islands
Aventura
N. Miami Beach
To Fort Lauderdale, Palm Beach
To Orlando
To Naples
To Lake Okeechobee
COLLINS AVENUE
BISCAYNE BOULEVARD
N MIAMI BEACH
Monastery
Museum of Contemporary Art
North Miami
7TH AVENUE
27TH AVENUE
Design District
Dr. Martin Luther King Jr.
Liberty City
Earlington Heights
Northside
Tri-Rail
Hialeah Park Race Track
Opa-Locka City Hall
Opa-Locka
Opa-Locka Airport
PALMETTO EXPRESSWAY
FLORIDA'S TURNPIKE
Hialeah
Okeechobee
Miami Springs
Brownsville
Allapattah
JULIA TUTTLE CAUSEWAY

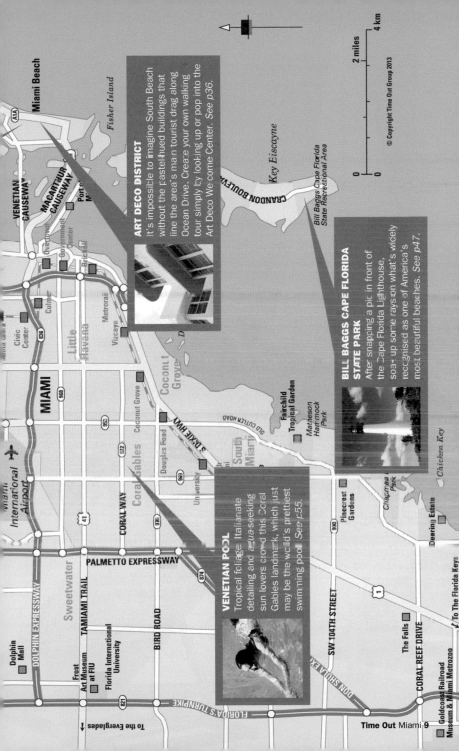

**Miami Beach**

Fisher Island

VENETIAN CAUSEWAY
MACARTHUR CAUSEWAY

## ART DECO DISTRICT

It's impossible to imagine South Beach without the pastel-hued buildings that line the area's main tourist drag along Ocean Drive. Create your own walking tour simply by looking up or pop into the Art Deco Welcome Center. *See p36.*

Key Biscayne

CRANDON BOULEVARD

Bill Baggs Cape Florida
State Recreational Area

© Copyright Time Out Group 2013

0 —— 2 miles
0 —— 4 km

Port of
M

Overtown
Government
Center
Brickell

Civic
Center

836

Little
Havana

Vizcaya

D

**MIAMI**

968

Coconut
Grove

Coconut Grove

95

Fairchild
Tropical Garden

Matheson
Hammock
Park

## BILL BAGGS CAPE FLORIDA STATE PARK

After snapping a pic in front of the Cape Florida Lighthouse, soak up some rays on what's widely recognised as one of America's most beautiful beaches. *See p47.*

Chicken Key

Coral Gables

Douglas Road

S Dixie Hwy

University

962

South
Miami

OLD CUTLER ROAD

Chapman F
Park

Pinecrest
Gardens

990

Deering Estate

CORAL WAY

212

## VENETIAN POOL

Tropical foliage, Italianate detailing and aqua-seeking sun lovers crowd this Coral Gables landmark, which just may be the world's prettiest swimming pool. *See p55.*

PALMETTO EXPRESSWAY

874

SW 104TH STREET

1

To The Florida Keys

Miami
International Airport

Dolphin
Mall

DOLPHIN EXPRESSWAY

Sweetwater

TAMIAMI TRAIL

Frost
Art Museum
at FIU

Florida International
University

41

BIRD ROAD

976

DON SHULA EX

FLORIDA'S TURNPIKE

821

To the Everglades ↑

The Falls

CORAL REEF DRIVE

Goldcoast Railroad
Museum & Miami Metrozoo

# TimeOut Miami

## Editorial
**Editor** Jennifer M Wood
**Consultant Editor** Lisa Ritchie
**Deputy Editor** Dominic Earle
**Proofreader** Tamsin Shelton
**Indexer** Holly Pick

**Editorial Director** Sarah Guy
**Management Accountant** Margaret Wright

## Design
**Senior Designer** Kei Ishimaru
**Group Commercial Senior Designer** Jason Tansley

## Picture Desk
**Picture Editor** Jael Marschner
**Picture Researcher** Ben Rowe
**Freelance Picture Researcher** Lizzie Owen

## Advertising
**Sales Director** St John Betteridge

## Marketing
**Senior Publishing Brand Manager** Luthfa Begum
**Head of Circulation** Dan Collins

## Production
**Production Controller** Katie Mulhern-Bhudia

## Time Out Group
**Chairman & Founder** Tony Elliott
**Chief Executive Officer** Aksel Van der Wal
**Editor-in-Chief** Tim Arthur
**UK Chief Commercial Officer** David Pepper
**International Managing Director** Cathy Runciman
**Group IT Director** Simon Chappell
**Group Marketing Director** Carolyn Sims

## Contributors
**Introduction** Jennifer M Wood. **Miami Today** Fred Grimm. **Miami Crime Lit** Andrew Humphreys. **Diary** Lesley Abravanel, Gretchen Schmidt, Jennifer M Wood. **Tour Miami** Jennifer M Wood. **Explore** Judy Cantor, Wendy Doescher Smith, Hugh Graham, Nina Korman, Michael Sasser, Anne Tschida, Jennifer M Wood. **Restaurants & Cafés** Lesley Abravanel, Hugh Graham, Jennifer M Wood. **Bars & Pubs** Lesley Abravanel, Andrew Humphreys, Jennifer M Wood. **Shops & Services** Lesley Abravanel, Judy Cantor, Brett Graff, Nina Korman, Anne Tschida, Jennifer M Wood. **Hotels** Lissette Fernandez, Hugh Graham, Jennifer M Wood. **Children** Brett Graff, Gretchen Schmidt. **Film** Geoff Andrew, Judy Cantor, Tom Huddleston, Anne Tschida. **Gay & Lesbian** James Cubby, Hugh Graham, Tony Miro, Jennifer M Wood. **Nightlife** Lesley Abravanel, Judy Cantor, Hugh Graham, Anne Tschida, Jennifer M Wood. **Performing Arts** James Cubby, Mia Leonin, Jennifer M Wood. **Sport & Fitness** Jacquelynn Powers, Courtney Recht. **Getting Started** Lesley Abravanel, Andrew Humphreys. **Fort Lauderdale & Palm Beach** Lesley Abravanel, Hugh Graham, Gretchen Schmidt. **The Everglades** Lesley Abravanel, Michael Sasser. **Florida Keys** Lesley Abravanel, Hugh Graham, Andrew Humphreys. **History** Lesley Abravanel, Hugh Graham, Tony Thompson. **Architecture** Hugh Graham, Andrew Humphreys. **Essential Information** Mary Green, Andrew Humphreys, Anne Tschida.

**The Editor would like to thank** Karen Barofsky, Matt Brooke, Lauren Busch Ginger, Larry Camino, Omar DeWindt, Brooke Hoffman, Ellen Marchman, James Menzies, Richard Murry, Kara Rosner, Robin Schwartz and all contributors to previous editions of *Time Out Miami*, whose work forms the basis for parts of this book.

**Maps** john@jographics.co.uk

**Cover photograph** James Ravilious; Beaford Archive/CORBIS
**Back cover photography** Alys Tomlinson

**Photography** Alys Tomlinson, except pages 6, 8 (top), 14, 34, 42, 47, 200, 232, 235, 251, 252, 253, 254 (top) Shutterstock; 22 Deborah Rodriguez; 24 (top) Cristian Lazzari; 24 (bottom) Carlos Ilano; 25 Melanie Dunea; 26 Mike Coppola/Getty Images; 0 (middle), 22, 43, 46, 51, 59, 67 (bottom), 70, 71, 168 Greater Miami Convention & Visitors Bureau; 35 (top) Maria Veras/Shutterstock; 35 (bottom) Steve Heap/Shutterstock; 36 Greg Schneider; 38 (top) Dan Forer; 45 Florida State Parks; 57 Florida Department of Environmental Protection; 67 (top) Martha Cooper; 79 Skott Snider; 80 Noah Fecks; 85 (top) Felipe Cuevas; 85 (bottom) Michael Pisarri; 89 Greg Clark; 90 Troy Robertson; 91 Gesi Schilling; 92, 100 Simon Hare; 96 (top) Andres Aravena; 96 (bottom) Michael Pisarri; 103 (top) Mark Roskams; 103 (bottom) Andrew Meade; 137, 139 Moris Moreno; 142, 152 Elan Fleisher; 148, 149 Adrian Gaut; 169 Moviestore Collection/Rex Features; 170 Denis Largeron; 186 Mark Elias; 188 (top) Emilio Collavino; 188 (bottom), 189 Rui Dias-Aidos; 194 Jorg Hackemann/Shutterstock.com; 197 Domenic Gareri/Shutterstock.com; 205 Dariush M/Shutterstock; 209 David Warren; 210 John Wollwerth/Shutterstock; 220 Bob Care/Florida Keys News Bureau; 223 Bob Krist/Florida Keys News Bureau; 225, 227 Andy Newman/Florida Keys News Bureau; 232 Chuck Wagner/Shutterstock.com; 239, 246, 248 Getty Images; 241 behindlens/Shutterstock; 243 Time & Life Pictures/Getty Images; 256 meunierd/Shutterstock.com.

The following images were supplied by the featured establishments/artists: 17, 21, 23, 27, 31, 37, 38 (bottom), 39, 50, 54, 58, 63, 73, 74, 75, 78, 81, 83, 84, 88, 93, 94, 95, 99, 101, 102, 107, 108, 110, 111, 114, 115, 119, 122, 136, 140, 144, 145, 151, 160, 167, 172, 175, 178, 181, 183, 184, 187, 190, 191, 193, 195, 207, 208, 211, 212, 257.

In Focus

# Miami Today

*Miami Herald columnist Fred Grimm delves beneath the city's shiny façade and shatters a few illusions along the way.*

Miami is a city that was founded on fantasy, and it remains engulfed in shimmering illusions. Hordes of tourists (an estimated 12 million each year) still seek tropical days and neon nights, despite a slowly recovering economy and tentative spending. Movie stars and hero athletes, some of them has-beens, still bask in the South Beach spotlight – and SoBe grants them the pretence that their lives really do glitter. The celebs and their entourages part the velvet ropes, pass queues of mortals waiting outside joints such as LIV and head for the VIP room, trading their notoriety for complimentary champagne. With luck, a tabloid photographer will happen to pass by and boost their egos a little further.

But even the glamour palaces have noticed some unhappy economic signs. Waiters at chi-chi clubs complain that sales of $1,000 bottles of Cristal are down, and customers no longer try to stifle their shock at tabs the size of the national debt.

Meanwhile, miles away from the shore, Miami's teeming immigrants cling to their own particular illusion: that they've never left home. More than half of Miamians were born outside the US and only a quarter of them list English as their first language. Migrant workers flee poverty in Mexico, Guatemala and El Salvador to work around Homestead. Argentinians have been coming in droves ever since their economy foundered in the early part of the new millennium. Colombians make up one of the largest Hispanic groups, and affluent Venezuelans began arriving en masse after Hugo Chávez took office in 1999. Brazilians, Peruvians and Nicaraguans in search of a better life have also established communities here, but it's the Haitians and Cubans who are the most prominent exiles. In shops in Little Havana and Little Haiti, the only languages you'll hear are Spanish or Creole, with English frowned upon.

Miami's Cubans, even after dominating local politics and business for more than 50 years, still refer to themselves as 'exiles'. As if, when the old villain dies, they'll abandon Miami and return en masse to reclaim their island. This is the most enduring of the city's illusions. On the island, the fading Fidel Castro may be retired from power. But in Miami, he remains an iconic obsession.

In a city so preoccupied with foreign policy, problems at home are roundly ignored. Nobody has much to say about the poor. They're like rumours in Miami – consigned to the rough neighbourhoods beyond that dazzling skyline. Miami ranks third in the nation for accumulated wealth, but the struggling out-of-sight districts attest to the city's more ignominious ranking: about 28 per cent of Miami's residents live on incomes below the poverty level. As the city boasts about skyscrapers and luxury hotels, it hides its woes in forsaken neighbourhoods haunted by gangs. Drive-by shootings in Liberty City and Opa-Locka have become routine. In late 2012, a car opened fire on two police officers serving a search warrant in Little Haiti, and the officers were forced to return fire amid a crowd of onlookers. The Miami Police Department, complaining that officers with their meagre pistols are being outgunned, has begun equipping patrol cars with military assault rifles.

Even convicts are obliged to pay homage to Miami's illusions. From 2006 to 2010, after serving out their prison sentences, more than 100 convicted sex offenders were forced to live under the Julia Tuttle Causeway. A bizarre county ordinance barred them from residing within 2,500 feet of a school, church, playground or daycare centre, or anywhere children might congregate – leaving literally nowhere for them to go.

This dank, stinking existence contrasts strongly with the gleaming condominium towers – 40 storeys tall with million-dollar apartments and glorious views – that have risen in the old Downtown core. But these towers have been constructed on what were once some of the most desolate and dangerous tracts in the city. A decade ago, these were the haunts of crack addicts, winos and the mentally ill, who slept on the pavements in cardboard boxes. But south Florida's builders are gamblers. Local suckers might lose a few bills at the Indian casinos on the other side of town, but these guys are making million-dollar bets. In a few years, some 25,000 new condo units have been built in Downtown, the beaches and the Design District – the latest slum gone chic.

Some 20 miles to the north, developers have razed the old spring break hotels in Fort Lauderdale and spent billions of dollars building beachfront luxury hotels. Seemingly overnight, room rates have jumped from $70 to $700. Out go the college kids, in come the big spenders from Europe and Latin America – or so the developers hope.

There was a pervading sense in the early noughties – maybe it was mass insanity – that Miami's building spree would last forever. The illusion was that the banking capital of Latin America was somehow recession-proof. But those who drove past the new Downtown condos noticed something unnerving: they were dark. In a 45-storey tower, perhaps only six apartments were lit. It was another Miami illusion; few of the owners were actual residents. Most were speculators, who bought with the intention of flipping them for a quick profit, selling to another tier of speculators. It was madness, a pyramid scheme. In residential districts, houses were being built and flipped in the same crazed manner.

The trouble was, there were never enough solid, dependable, real-life home-buyers to go around. The average cost of a home in Miami-Dade County inflated to more than $300,000 at the peak of the bubble – beyond the means of 85 per cent of the county's population.

No one seemed to mind lending money to speculators, who snatched up five or six new units at a time. Nor were banks and mortgage brokers worried about lending money to buyers with poor credit or low income. They doled out dodgy subprime loans to anyone, then bundled them and resold the packages to hedge funds and investment banks. Miami's loans spread like a disease through the international banking system. More than 547,000 Florida properties were purchased with subprime loans.

Banks kept lending. Builders kept building. It was as if Miami in 2006 had returned to the mentality of Miami in 1926, the other time in the city's history when real estate speculators went berserk. In the spring of 1926, the boom fizzled and a brutal hurricane that summer knocked Miami into a depression three years ahead of the rest of the world. In autumn 2006, the modern boom fizzled out. As the number of defaults soared, Miami was among the first dominoes to fall in a global calamity. In the first three months of 2008, Florida led the nation in foreclosures with 77,000 – 22,000 of those in Miami-Dade and adjacent Broward counties. Over a third of Florida's 547,000 subprime loan holders were past due or already in foreclosure.

Yet, Miami retained a dogged optimism – and perhaps rightly so. After all, it had

come through worse. Miami survived the 1926 real estate bust and the hurricane that killed 1,000 people and destroyed much of the city. The city survived the 1980 race riot when black Miamians exploded in rage, an uprising that left 18 people dead, 120 buildings burned and $100 million in property damage. That same year, Fidel Castro unleashed the Mariel boatlift and 120,000 Cuban refugees flooded the city, among them 5,000 convicts and mental patients. Against this volatile backdrop, Cuban and Colombian drug gangs waged a murderous war in the city over control of the cocaine trade. Miami became the murder capital of America and *Time* magazine ran a 1980 cover story with the headline 'Paradise Lost'.

In 1988, economist and futurist TD Allman famously wrote: 'Never again will Miami Beach be the American ideal of a winter resort.' He was wrong. A decade later, Miami Beach defied Allman's prediction and became a mecca for fashion, music and art. Celebrities snapped up property. And the hipsters flocked to South Beach, sparking a spike in mainstream tourism.

Miami now has the busiest cruise ship port in the world and 35 million people a year pass through Miami International Airport. And it's not just tourism that is flourishing: the city now rivals New York in terms of the number of international banks with offices here. The city's real estate industry is on the rise again too. Between 2011 and 2012, property values rose 19 per cent – despite an economy that still sees many US homeowners upside down on their mortgages.

Viewed from across the water, Miami looks as beautiful and prosperous as any of the world's great cities. Yet the alluring waterfront masks a still recovering economy, ethnic tensions and urban poverty. This dark side is as difficult to contemplate as the notion that a beautiful actress sipping Cristal at the Delano might suffer from insecurities, depression or other human frailties. Intellectually, you know the city has troubles. But in Miami, reality has always been trumped by shimmering illusions.

# Miami Crime Lit

*Behind its sunny façade, Miami has murder on its mind.*

New York boasts Paul Auster, Bret Easton Ellis, Jay McInerney and Tom Wolfe. San Francisco has Dave Eggers, Armistead Maupin and Amy Tan. And Miami? Try Edna Buchanan, James W Hall, Carl Hiaasen, John D MacDonald, Charles Willeford and Jeff Lindsay. If none of these names raises a glimmer of recognition, that's hardly surprising. Aside from Carl Hiaasen, whose books regularly feature on the bestseller lists, and Jeff Lindsay, whose *Dexter* book series is the basis of Showtime's hit show, these are writers who rarely trouble the literary pages of the world's newspapers. It's not that their work isn't deserving of attention (on the contrary, it's read plenty in the studio lots of LA, where books by Buchanan, Hiaasen, MacDonald and Willeford have all been made into movies), it's just that there's a certain literary prejudice against the kind of fiction they write: genre fiction, or – to be more specific – crime fiction.

Crime writing is Miami's greatest contribution to the American literary scene. There's no doubt that these days Miami supports more crime, thriller and mystery writers per capita than any other US city, yet the genre didn't begin here. The greatest early exponents of the field, Raymond Chandler and Dashiell Hammett, were both southern Californian writers who had their gumshoes treading leather and trading bruises in the canyons around Los Angeles and valleys of San Francisco. But over the last three decades, no city has done crime writing as well as Miami. The reasons for this aren't hard to fathom: over the last four decades, no city has done crime as well as Miami.

Since the 1970s, the city has virtually made an art of murder. Its recent history is as a late 20th-century frontier town with an explosive mix of immigrants from all 50 states and the whole of Latin America. The resulting violent racism, political unrest, drug trafficking and organised crime – combined with the hedonistic lifestyle of the wealthy and the desperation of the poor – make for a volatile combination. Add tropical heat, step back and wait for it to explode.

Whenever it did explode, the first one on the scene to witness the aftermath was often a big-haired, fast-talking lady named **Edna Buchanan**. A native of New Jersey, but a life-long convert to the charms of south Florida, Buchanan spent most of her working career covering the crime beat for the *Miami Herald*, winning a Pulitzer Prize along the way. Her autobiographical account of those years, *The Corpse Had a Familiar Face*, makes for lurid and sensational reading: the Haitian who was knitted to death in a Hialeah factory. The father who murdered his comatose daughter in her hospital bed. The naked man who threw his girlfriend's severed head at a young cop – who threw it back. During Buchanan's time on the paper, Miami broke all prior records for violence, and from 1980 to 1981 its murder rate soared to number one in the nation. Killings in one particular nightclub became such a fixture that staff just dumped the bodies out in the parking lot with the trash. Police beatings set off

riots that burned whole neighbourhoods. Bodies were stacked so high at the Jackson Memorial Hospital morgue that it had to rent a refrigerated trailer from Burger King to cope with the overflow.

Since quitting the newsroom in the late '80s, Buchanan has taken up mystery writing, penning a series of novels starring Britt Montero, who is – what else? – a spunky lady crime reporter. The trouble is that Buchanan's fiction can't begin to compete with Miami's reality.

The city's turbulent times were illustrated by an incident that made worldwide headlines on 11 April 1986. That morning, FBI agents were staking out a traffic corridor off US 1 in upscale Pinecrest, looking for a gang of bank robbers. Spotting the suspects driving by, the agents forced them to stop, but the thieves came out firing. For several minutes, a dramatic shootout erupted at the intersection of SW 183rd Street and SW 22nd Avenue, just feet from South Miami's major artery. Hundreds of rounds of ammunition were expended on both sides. Despite being badly wounded, the two bandits staggered up to FBI special agents Jerry Dove and Benjamin Grogan and callously executed them at close range.

With that kind of communal exchange going on in the 'burbs, most sane people's reaction would be '*adiós*'. But when, shortly before his death in 1988, **Charles Willeford** was asked by the *Miami Herald* why he preferred to live in Miami, he replied: 'because of the high crime rate'. Willeford was the writer who launched the modern era of Miami crime fiction, yet it was another writer, **John D MacDonald** (author of *Cape Fear*), who had put the city on the mystery map far earlier with his Travis McGee books. That was back in the 1960s, when south Florida was older and sleepier. Willeford sparked off the whole weird crime thing with his own peculiar brand of fiction, which isn't so much hard-boiled as just plain crotchety. A former flea circus barker, professional boxer, soft-porn writer and decorated tank commander, he knew how to grab people's attention. Take the provocative titles of his books:

*Kiss Your Ass Goodbye, The Way We Die Now, The Shark-Infested Custard*. But his breakthrough came with a simply named book: *Miami Blues*.

Published in 1984, the title was chosen by his publishers, who hoped to get a free ride on the coat tails of hit TV show *Miami Vice*. In contrast to that slick programme, it starred a cop with ill-fitting false teeth and a poor dress sense named Hoke Moseley, adrift in a Miami in transition. '*Miami Blues* launched the modern era of crime fiction,' says Mitch Kaplan, owner of Miami's popular mini-chain of independent bookstores, Books & Books. Willeford was big on absurdities. In the opening scene of *Miami Blues* (made into a 1990 film), Freddy Frenger, a haiku-writing psychopath, wards off a Hare Krishna at Miami International Airport by casually breaking his finger; the Krishna collapses in shock and dies of a heart attack. The hard-living Willeford himself died of a heart attack, although in his case it was largely brought on by drinking and smoking.

If Charles Willeford pioneered a particularly skewed Miami take on crime writing, it was sold to the mainstream by **Carl Hiaasen**. Another former *Miami Herald* crime reporter, now its star columnist, Hiaasen has what has been described as a 'gleefully wicked mind'. A twisted Mark Twain, he writes satires that paint the Sunshine State as a paradise screwed (which is, incidentally, the title of a volume of his collected *Herald* columns). The screwing in his view has been done by a toxic mix of rapacious developers, hand-in-the-till councillors, craven administration and toss-the-trash out-the-window tourists. For Hiaasen, writing is a way of getting his own back at the devastation of Florida's natural environment. He will write about a blue-haired retiree getting eaten by a crocodile and have you rooting for the crocodile. In May 2006, the film version of Hiaasen's *Hoot*, a fun slice of crime fiction aimed at a teen crowd, was released. Producers included Jimmy Buffett, and the film was shot in Fort Lauderdale: it seems Hiaasen likes to keep his stuff firmly in the south Florida family.

Fellow author **James W Hall**, originally from Kentucky but a long-time Florida resident, began his thriller writing (with 1986's *Under Cover of Daylight*) in the same vein as Hiaasen, mixing conservation battles with ruthless semi-competent hitmen and a healthy dose of thinly disguised authorial outrage at the destruction he saw around him. However, over the course of ten or so books, Hall has mellowed and his thrillers are now more straightforward tales of local psychos on the loose. But Hall doesn't come close to Hiaasen when it comes to upping the ante on the wackos. The hitman in Hiaasen's 1989's *Skin Tight*, for example, is a six-foot nine-inch victim of plastic surgery gone wrong left with a face that looks like it's covered in Rice Krispies. He also has a rotor-stripper attached to the stump of his right hand.

> '*Florida is the super-kingdom for bad behaviour. Frankly, it's hard for a novelist to stay ahead of the weirdness curve.*'

But what appears in his fiction to be political farce often turns out to be grounded in political fact. Hiaasen admits that much of what seems like the product of a warped imagination comes out of the newspapers. 'Florida is the super-kingdom for bad behaviour; frankly, it's hard for a novelist to stay ahead of the weirdness curve. There are times when I've written something that I think is really sick; the next day the *Miami Herald* has a headline that makes me weep that I didn't think of it first.' Case in point: in 2012, following a bizarre incident in which a nude man chewed the face off a homeless man in broad daylight along one of the city's major causeways, Hiaasen responded with an opinion piece entitled 'Nude face-eating cannibal? Must be Miami'.

Hiaasen, like many other crime writers, is one of the most astute chroniclers of America today and his novels make for a first-class primer to Miami. In fact, his first novel, *Tourist Season* (1986), was named by *GQ* magazine as 'one of the ten best destination reads of all time'. Hiaasen, though, would disagree: he once said that the best book ever written about Miami is *La Brava* by **Elmore Leonard**. You've certainly heard of Leonard. According to online magazine *Salon*, he's the 'world's coolest crime writer'. Even people who don't read have heard of Leonard, thanks to a string of highly successful movies, including *Get Shorty* (1995), *Jackie Brown* (1997) and *Out of Sight* (1998), and the hit television show *Justified*, all adapted from his books.

## 'You can read Elmore Leonard with a map of Miami spread open, plotting the action.'

Unlike the writers already mentioned who, if not Miami born and bred, at least have called the city home, Leonard has lived in the northern state of Michigan for most of his life. His first crime novels (he wrote westerns early in his career) were set in and around Detroit. Yet, like so many Americans, he grew up holidaying down south. He was quick to see the potential in the freakiness of south Florida and spread some of the action of 1980's *Gold Coast* down to Fort Lauderdale. He followed up with a string of novels all utilising Sunshine State locales. His breakthrough came with *Stick* (1983), which assembled the combination that caught the public's attention of Miami, Marielitos, movies and drugs. Leonard's characters are supremely suited to Miami life. The people on the right side of the law (cops, judges, lawyers) are frequently dirty themselves, while the criminals are often smart talkers full of bullshit and charm – John Travolta's hustling enforcer Chili Palmer in *Get Shorty* is a classic

Leonard character and, at the same time, the kind of guy you might run into at News Café on Ocean Drive.

Leonard's research is meticulous. Characters drop by (the now-defunct) Wolfie's on North Beach for takeout Jell-O; they lunch on claws at Joe's Stone Crab in South Beach; they size up their prey from the front porch of Ocean Drive's Cardozo Hotel. You can read Leonard with a map of Miami spread open, plotting the action.

If it seems odd that the best-known practitioner of Miami crime lit has never lived in the city, consider this: Miami's most famous crime writer has never written about Miami. **Thomas Harris**, the man who has scared the bejesus out of millions courtesy of his fictional creation Hannibal Lecter (presented to the public in the novels *Red Dragon*, *The Silence of the Lambs* and *Hannibal*), is a resident of the exclusive enclave of Golden Beach in north Miami Beach.

Harris is a permanent fixture on the South Beach A-list, sporting his trademark straw hat and a beard that may disguise his inner demons. We have a theory about why he's never set any of his writing in the weirder-than-fiction city in which he lives: if dear old Hannibal were to venture down to the South Beach of Willeford, Hiaasen, Leonard et al, the freaks down there would eat him alive.

It's no shock that some experts consider crime lit Miami's only real genre of fiction. 'Right now this is a wide-open, wild and woolly town. Anybody who's writing about this place and who we are would rightfully be talking about crime and punishment,' said Les Standiford, author of several Miami crime lit books including *Raw Deal* and *Deal with the Dead*. He's right. In October 2012, Tom Wolfe released his latest novel, a Miami-set thriller called *Back to Blood*, featuring a journalist on the trail of a mobster and a Cuban police officer. Three decades after *Miami Vice* and *Scarface*, it seems that Miami and crime still go hand in hand. 'Imagine trying to put out *New Times* every week in Kansas City,' adds Standiford. 'What the hell would you write about?' Scary, but true.

# Diary

*Plan your perfect trip with our guide to the year ahead.*

Miami needs absolutely no excuse to party: from the traditional to the tacky, film to flowers, the city is fast on its feet when it comes to putting on a show. While some of the best-known annual events – such as Art Basel, the South Beach Wine & Food Festival, Art Deco Weekend and the Coconut Grove Arts Festival – attract revellers from all over the planet (and put a squeeze on the city's hotel capacity), many of the city's smaller neighbourhood events are worth checking out too. Miami's social calendar is as quirky as its denizens.

## SPRING

### Miami International Film Festival
*Gusman Center for the Performing Arts, 174 E Flagler Street, at SE 2nd Avenue, Downtown & other locations (1-305 237 3456, www.miamifilmfestival.com).* **Date** early Mar. **Map** p282 D3.
Run by Miami Dade College, MIFF showcases the best of world cinema. Some 70,000 people attended the 2013 festival – the 30th edition – including scores of award-winning writers, directors and actors. There's a special focus on Ibero American cinema, and prizes are handed out for documentary and dramatic categories. *Photo p22.*

### WGC-Cadillac Championship
*Doral Golf Resort & Spa, 4400 NW 87th Avenue, at NW 41st Street, Doral (www.world golfchampionships.com/cadillac-championship. html).* **Date** mid Mar.
Once host to the PGA's Ford Championship, the swanky Doral's Blue Monster course is now home to the WGC-Cadillac Championship, featuring top professional male golfers from across the globe. Case in point: Tiger Woods took home the top prize at the 2013 event.

### Winter Party Week
*On the beach at Ocean Drive, at 14th Street, South Beach (www.winterparty.com).* **Date** early Mar. **Map** p280 D3.
A benefit for the local gay community, this week-long bash attracts celebrity DJs and thousands of revellers, and includes music, dance, art, film and comedy at South Beach nightclubs and hotels. It all culminates with a beach dance party. As with the White Party (*see p24*), you're best off booking tickets in advance.

### ★ Carnaval Miami/Calle Ocho
*Throughout Miami-Dade County (1-305 644 8888, www.carnavalmiami.com).* **Date** mid Mar.
Each spring, Latino Miami struts its stuff to the max with a full slate of beauty pageants, sports activities, domino competitions, food events and concerts. The grand finale is Calle Ocho, a 23-block street festival in Little Havana – the largest block party in the world. More than a million revellers watch live entertainment on 30 stages featuring salsa, merengue and Caribbean music. *Photo p23.*

## THE BEST EVENTS

For foodies
**Food Network South Beach Wine & Food Festival.** *See p27.*

For art aficionados
**Art Basel Miami Beach.** *See p24.*

For speed freaks
**Ford Championship Weekend.** *See p24.*

For architecture buffs
**Art Deco Weekend.** *See p26.*

For bibliophiles
**Miami Book Fair International.** *See p24.*

For Cuban culture
**Carnaval Miami/Calle Ocho.** *See above.*

**Miami International Film Festival.** *See p21.*

### ★ Miami Music Week
### Throughout Miami

*Various venues (www.miamimusicweek.com).*
**Date** mid Mar.

Miami gets melodic during March when a series of events, including the Ultra Music Festival (www.ultramusicfestival.com) and the Winter Music Conference (www.wintermusicconference. com), bring first-class concerts, special events, demonstrations, educational workshops and the rock 'n' roll lifestyle to Magic City.

### Miami Beach International
### Fashion Week

*Miami Beach Convention Center, 1901 Convention Center Drive, South Beach (www. miamifashionweek.com). Bus A, M, R, S.*
**Date** late Mar. **Map** p280 C3.

South Florida's answer to Bryant Park, Miami Beach International Fashion Week takes place over three days in late March, when a global gaggle of designers converge for one enormous event, with a focus on Hispanic hemlines.

### Miami Taste of Brickell
### Food & Wine Festival

*Various venues (1-305 200 8892, www.taste ofbrickell.com).* **Date** late Mar.

Created in 2010 to accommodate Brickell's bustling culinary scene, more than 40 Downtown restaurants and bars now take part in this gourmet showcase, which includes tastings, demonstrations and shopping, plus live music and art exhibitions.

### Dade Heritage Days

*Throughout Miami-Dade County (1-305 358 9572, www.dadeheritagetrust.org).* **Date** Mar-Apr.

Miami-Dade County celebrates its history with eight weeks of events, including open houses, lectures, and guided walking and canoe tours of sights such as the Deering Estate *(see p73)* and Barnacle site *(see p58).*

### Miami-Dade County Fair & Exposition

*Tamiami Park, SW 24th Street & SW 112th Avenue, West Dade (1-305 223 7060, www. fairexpo.com). Bus 24.* **Date** Mar-Apr.

One of the largest county fairs in the US, this 18-day event features rides, food, entertainment and lots of exhibits. Food ranges from all-American corn on the cob and barbecues to Hispanic treats.

### Sony Open Tennis

*Crandon Park Tennis Center, 7300 Crandon Boulevard, Key Biscayne (1-800 725 5472, www.sonyopentennis.com). Bus B.* **Date** Mar-Apr.

This prestigious two-week tennis tournament is one of the world's largest, in terms of players, prize money and attendance, with 200 of the world's top competitors taking part.

### South Beach Comedy Festival

*Various venues (www.southbeachcomedyfestival. com).* **Date** mid Apr.

South Beach hosts world-famous jokesters, plus newbies, during this four-day event presented by Comedy Central.

# SUMMER

## Miami/Bahamas Goombay Festival
*Throughout Coconut Grove (www.goombayfestival coconutgrove.com). Bus Coconut Grove Circulator.*
**Date** early June.
No need to jet off to the Bahamas – just head to this raucous two-day festival for authentic food and music. It celebrated its 37th anniversary in 2013.

## International Mango Festival
*Fairchild Tropical Garden, 10901 Old Cutler Road, at SW 101st Street, South Miami (1-305 667 1651, www.fairchildgarden.org). Bus 65.*
**Date** 2nd wknd in July. **Map** p279.
Indulge in mango smoothies, chutney, sweets and even a mango-themed brunch made by celeb chefs (must be booked online in advance).

## Mercedes-Benz Fashion Week Swim
*Raleigh hotel, 1775 Collins Avenue, at 17th Street, South Beach (www.miami.mbfashion week.com). Bus C, G, H, L, M, S.* **Date** late July. **Map** p280 C3.
There are few better places than sun-soaked South Beach to show off what's hot in bikinis, tankinis and beyond. The Raleigh's world-famous art deco swimming pool makes the perfect backdrop for this annual fashion extravaganza.

## Miami Spa Month
*Throughout Miami (www.miamispamonth.com).*
**Date** July-Aug.

Experience Miami's happening spa scene with a tempting array of discounted treatments and days of glorious pampering at some of the city's most serene relaxation spots.

## Miami Spice Restaurant Month
*Throughout Miami (www.ilovemiamispice.com).*
**Date** Aug-Sept.
Dinner at Mr Chow for less than $40? Yep. To spice up business during the summer doldrums, many top Miami restaurants offer upscale meals at reasonable prices. Three-course lunches cost $19-$23 and dinner will set you back $33-$39.

# AUTUMN

## Festival Miami
*University of Miami, Gusman Concert Hall, 1314 Miller Drive, at San Amaro Drive, Coral Gables (1-305 284 4940, www.festivalmiami.com).*
**Date** Oct-Nov. **Map** p284 F1.
The University of Miami provides the stage for a five-week festival of world premières, symphonic concerts, masterclasses and lectures.

## Junior Orange Bowl
*Throughout Miami-Dade County (1-305 662 1210, www.jrorangebowl.com).* **Date** Oct-Jan.
This popular youth festival combines a range of sports tournaments and cultural workshops. The Junior Orange Bowl Parade, with floats and bands, marches through Coral Gables between Christmas and New Year.

**Carnaval Miami/Calle Ocho.** *See p21.*

Miami Book Fair International.

### Columbus Day Regatta

*Biscayne Bay (www.columbusdayregatta.net).* **Date** mid Oct.

To commemorate Christopher Columbus's voyage in 1492, 200 sailing boats race around Biscayne Bay, off Coconut Grove. A rowdy party off Elliott Key concludes the weekend.

### ★ Miami Book Fair International

*Miami Dade College, 401 NE 2nd Avenue, Suite 4102, at NE 3rd Street, Downtown (1-305 237 3258, www.miamibookfair.com). Metromover Government Center.* **Date** mid Nov. **Map** p282 D3.

Miami a cultural backwater? You must be kidding. Half a million people turn out each year for this literary event, with 250 renowned writers giving lectures and readings. There's a street fair too.

### Ford Championship Weekend – NASCAR

*Homestead-Miami Speedway, 1 Speedway Boulevard, between SW 132nd & 137th Avenues, at SW 336th Street, Homestead, South Miami (1-305 230 5000, www.homesteadmiami speedway.com).* **Date** mid Nov.

Three days of racing on the track, plus beer, excitement, car-racing celebs and more beer.

### White Party

*Various locations on South Beach (1-305 576 1234, www.whiteparty.org).* **Date** late Nov.

This renowned HIV/AIDS benefit, which celebrates its 29th anniversary in 2013, attracts an estimated 12,000 people for a week of events and parties. Highlights include the legendary White Party itself and the Muscle Beach open-air dance party bash (dress code: swimsuits and shorts). Expect DJs and gay celebs aplenty.

## WINTER

### ★ Art Basel Miami Beach

*Miami Beach Convention Center & various venues (www.artbasel.com).* **Date** 1st wk Dec.

*See p26* **Well Hung**.

### Design Miami/

*Various venues in the Design District (www.design miami.com).* **Date** 1st wk Dec.

The design equivalent of the fabulous Art Basel (*see above*). Expect a great range of talks, exhibitions, international dealers and parties.

### Art Miami

*Wynwood Arts District, 3101 NE 1st Avenue, at NE 31st Street, Miami (1-305 515 8573, www.art-miami.com). Bus C, G, H, K, L, S, W, South Beach Local.* **Date** early Dec. **Map** p280 C3.

Celebrating its 23rd year in 2013, this is one of south Florida's major art fairs. More than 125 international galleries participate, with a strong Hispanic flavour.

# Interview Lee Brian Schrager

*Cooking up a storm on South Beach.*

Back in 2000, few people would have guessed that the world's culinary elite could be persuaded to head south to Miami for four days each February. No, not even Lee Brian Schrager, founder and executive director of the Food Network South Beach Wine & Food Festival (www.sobefest.com; *see p27*), as well as the five-year-old New York version (www.nycwineandfoodfestival.com), which takes place in the Big Apple each autumn. But what started as a one-day, college-based event called Florida Extravaganza has morphed into one of the world's most prestigious food festivals, with hundreds of the world's best-known chefs descending on South Beach to show off their skills, taste some grub and mingle with more than 50,000 food-lovin' locals.

IN FOCUS

**The South Beach Wine & Food Festival celebrated its 12th anniversary in 2013. Did you ever imagine it would be as large as it is today?**
No. It was probably the end of the second year when we said: 'Hey, this is bigger than we thought and has a lot more to it than we ever dreamed.' I don't think we had a lot of plans or expectations going into it. It was seeing the response from consumers, sponsors and talent who wanted to be here that we realised we were on to something.

**Was there a specific event or turning point that you can identify?**
No. I just think that when you combine the talent we have and the diverse calendar of events, and put it all together on a beautiful beach in the dead of winter in most places in the world, it's not a hard sell. Talk about location. Champagne on the beach while eating a barbecue? What could be better?

**What are the biggest changes you've noticed on the Miami food scene since the festival started?**
Firstly, consumers are much more educated now – not just in Miami, but generally. Also, if you looked at our first Best of the Best event – which is one of our highlights with 50 restaurants involved – we had to bring in 43 chefs from outside Miami because we didn't have more than a handful of great homegrown chefs. Now the ratio is more like 50/50.

**Do you attribute the current food culture to hosting such a world-class event here?**
We can't take credit for the rise of the food culture down here. I think what we can take credit for is bringing down world-renowned chefs and encouraging the media to kind of zoom in and want to visit all the great local restaurants while they're down here, which in turn has got these guys a lot of attention.

**In what ways do you think the culinary scene is unique in Miami?**
I think it's a very supportive industry. Chefs want to help each other and see people do well. It's a small world; there's six degrees of separation like nowhere else. The person you work with today could be your boss tomorrow – or vice versa.

**Although people often highlight the star-studded nature of the festival, it exists to benefit Florida International University's School of Hospitality. What changes have you been able to make with the money the festival has raised over the years?**
Next year, for the first time, we'll have a teaching restaurant at FIU. We've used almost $10 million that we've managed to raise over the years, and it makes all the effort seem worthwhile.

### King Mango Strut

*Begins at Main Highway & Commodore Plaza,
Coconut Grove (1-305 582 0955, www.king
mangostrut.org). Bus Coconut Grove Circulator.*
**Date** late Dec. **Map** p285 B2.
What began as a parody of the old Orange Bowl
Parade continues to poke tasteless fun at the year's
events and newsmakers. Its tagline is 'Putting the
NUT back in CocoNUT Grove since 1982'.

### Art Deco Weekend

*Ocean Drive, South Beach (1-305 672 2014,
www.artdecoweekend.com). Bus C, H, K, W,
South Beach Local.* **Date** mid Jan.

Organised by the Miami Design Preservation
League (*see p254* **Walk**), the Art Deco Weekend
is a massively popular event that celebrates the
city's tropical art deco and Mediterranean deco
heritage. Events include walks, bicycle and boat
tours, lectures, movies, street theatre and live music
on the beach.

### Beaux Arts Festival of Art

*University of Miami, Lowe Art Museum, 1301
Stanford Drive, at Ponce de León Boulevard,
Coral Gables (1-305 668 8499, www.beauxarts
miami.org). Bus 52, 56.* **Date** 3rd wknd Jan.
**Map** p284 F2.

# Well Hung

*Art Basel Miami-style.*

**IN FOCUS**

Miami Beach is better known for
interminable kitsch than cutting-edge art,
so it seemed odd when the organisers
of Switzerland's annual sophisticates'
jamboree, **Art Basel** (*see p24*), chose
Miami for its first American sortie in 2001.
Despite widespread initial cynicism, by its
tenth year the fair was pulling in 50,000
collectors and there were more than 250
galleries across the main fair. Art world
figures from as far afield as New York,
Berlin and Tokyo had quickly discovered
the joys of schmoozing over cocktails on
the sand and alfresco power dining, not
to mention a pre-work swim. Now dealers
could go home boasting a profit and a tan.

This being Miami, showbiz culture and
celebrities are also part of the equation.
Spotting stars buying up art, and then
spotting them again at exclusive galas,
is all part of the fun. The South Beach
clubs get in on the act by hosting art
parties, and even restaurants offer Art
Basel specials. And then there's the art
itself. Lots of it, from installations set up
in cargo containers along the beach to all
the satellite fairs that have sprouted in the
Wynwood Arts District. These side shows
– such as Pulse in a tent in Wynwood,
and Design Miami/ in the Design District
– now garner almost as much attention as
the main event.

A family-friendly weekend affair featuring work from more than 200 artists, to view and purchase, in more than ten types of media. Admission is free.

### International Chocolate Festival

*Fairchild Tropical Garden, 10901 Old Cutler Road, at SW 101st Street, South Miami (1-305 667 1651, www.fairchildgarden.org). Bus 65.* **Date** late Jan. **Map** p279.

Everyone's favourite sweet gets the royal treatment at this festival. Expect to learn about, cook with and taste plenty of cacao.

### ING Miami Marathon

*Throughout Miami (www.ingmiamimarathon. com).* **Date** early Feb.

Test your stamina or just watch as some of the fittest folks on the planet compete in this 26.2-mile marathon. The race kicks off at AmericanAirlines Arena and ends back in Bayfront Park.

### ★ Food Network South Beach Wine & Food Festival

*Various locations in South Beach (1-877 762 3933, www.sobefest.com).* **Date** late Feb.

Serious foodies and wine connoisseurs should book early for this festival, which attracts superstar chefs such as Alain Ducasse, Bobby Flay, Nigella Lawson, Jamie Oliver and Emeril Lagasse. Expect tastings, culinary seminars, parties, parties and more parties. *See also p25* **Interview**.

### Miami International Boat Show & Strictly Sail

*Miamarina at Bayside, 401 Biscayne Boulevard, Downtown & other locations (1-954 441 3220, www.miamiboatshow.com).* **Date** mid Feb.

Here's your chance to see what a $7m aqua juggernaut looks like. This popular event showcases the latest in powerboats, yachts, engines, electronics and accessories. There's also a Sunset Celebration with street performers, contests and drinks specials. The show takes place at three enormous venues, including the Miami Beach Convention Center.

### Coconut Grove Arts Festival

*Throughout Coconut Grove (1-305 447 0401, www.cgaf.com). Coconut Grove Circulator.* **Date** mid Feb.

This immense beer — sorry, arts — festival attracts more than 120,000 people to view the works of 350-plus artists and craftspeople. Take public transport shuttles from Metrorail to avoid traffic.

### South Miami Art Festival

*Along SW 72nd Street, off US 1, South Miami (1-305 769 5977). Metrorail South Miami.* **Date** late Feb.

Music, food and art from 150 juried artists around the country take over Sunset Drive (the nicest bit of South Miami) during this two-day festival.

Food Network South Beach Wine & Food Festival

**IN FOCUS**

Explore

# Tour Miami

*Explore Magic City any which way you choose.*

Whether you fancy gawking at the art deco architecture on the beach, stuffing your face full of classic Cuban fare in Little Havana, off-roading through the Everglades or soaring above the action in a seaplane, Miami offers a vast menu of sightseeing activities. A range of local companies run expert-led tours to help you make sense of this wild subtropical terrain – whatever your chosen pace or interest. So hop aboard or polish your most comfortable shoes and get an inside look at Magic City.

## TOURS

### By air

**Miami Seaplane Tours**
*3401 Rickenbacker Causeway, Key Biscayne (1-305 361 3909, www.miamiseaplane.com). Bus 102.* **Open** 9am-5pm Tue-Sun. **Tours** $135-$350. **Credit** AmEx, MC, V. **Map** p279.
It doesn't take long to be amazed by an unobstructed view of Miami's coastline, which explains the popularity of the 15-minute SoBe Seaplane Tour ($135). It begins with an exhilarating water take-off in Key Biscayne and includes photogenic views of more than two dozen Miami landmarks, including Fisher and Star Islands, the Fontainebleau hotel and buzzing Ocean Drive. Travellers with deeper pockets and more time to kill can opt for the Grand South Florida & Beaches Tour ($350), during which you'll fly by all of Miami's key sights before making your way up the coast to see what bird's-eye treasures Fort Lauderdale has to offer.

### By bike

**Bike and Roll**
*210 10th Street, at Collins Avenue, South Beach (1-305 604 0001, www.bikemiami.com). Bus C, H, K, W, South Beach Local.* **Open** 9am-7pm daily. **Tours** $25-$59. **Credit** AmEx, MC, V. **Map** p280 D3.
Culture, fresh air and pedestrian-dodging combine at Bike and Roll, Miami's leading bike tour company for more than a decade. The five-mile Art Deco South Beach trek departs twice daily, with additional stops at the (decidedly non-deco) Versace Mansion, Holocaust Memorial and Miami Beach Botanical Garden. For those less inclined to physical activity, the same tour can be taken on a Segway. There's another office at Bayside Marketplace, 410 Biscayne Boulevard, Downtown (same phone).

### By boat

**Thriller Miami Power Boat Tours**
*Bayside Marketplace, 401 Biscayne Boulevard, Downtown (1-305 371 3278, www.thrillermiami.com). Metromover College or Bayside.* **Open** 11am-5pm daily (call ahead to confirm schedule). **Tours** $22-$45. **Credit** AmEx, MC, V. **Map** p282 C4.
Adrenaline junkies will love watching the world whip by at speeds of up to 50mph on a 45-minute sightseeing tour aboard a power catamaran (what they like to refer to as *Miami Vice*-style). Tours leave at least five times daily from Bayside Marketplace and will have you seeing stars in no time as you cruise along the celebrity-strewn shores of South Beach, Star Island and Miami's Gold Coast.

### By bus

**HistoryMiami**
*101 W Flagler Street, at NW 1st Avenue, Downtown (1-305 375 1621, www.history miami.org). Metromover Government Center.* **Open** 10am-5pm Tue-Fri; noon-5pm Sat, Sun. **Tours** $25-$55. **Credit** AmEx, MC, V. **Map** p282 D1.
As part of its dedication to celebrating the city's fascinating past, HistoryMiami (*see p49*) offers a variety of themed walking, boat, bike and bus tours. The tone turns somewhat sinister during the ever-popular Mystery, Mayhem and Vice ($35-$45) tour,

a three-hour bus ride that guides you through the city's storied mobsters, smugglers and murderers.

## Weird Miami

*Bas Fisher Invitational, 100 NE 11th Street, at NE 1st Avenue, Downtown (www.basfisher international.com). Metromover 11th Street.* **Open** times vary. **Tours** $15 **Credit** AmEx, Disc, MC, V. **Map** p282 B2.

Popular with locals and visitors alike, Weird Miami's artist-led bus tours offer a true insider's look at the city's creative side. Expect the unexpected: recent offerings have included a look behind the glitz of South Beach and an up-close guide to the stranger parts of Cuban culture, led by local artist/curator/art activist César Trasobares.

## By Hummer

### Everglades Hummer Adventures

*10355 SW 109 Road, at SW 112th Street, South Miami (1-888 637 4448, www.everglades hummeradventures.com). No public transport.* **Open** times vary. **Tours** $99-$249. **Credit** AmEx, Disc, MC, V. **Map** p279.

Yes, it may seem politically incorrect to explore one of Mother Nature's most delicate eco-systems from the backseat of a Hummer. But given the difficult terrain, it makes sense. Bring the whole family along on this private four-hour off-roading, air-conditioned escapade. For an extra fee you can add in hotel pick-up and drop-off, an airboat ride, tickets to an alligator show or a visit to the panther reserve.

## On foot

### Art Deco Walking Tour

*Art Deco Welcome Center, 1001 Ocean Drive, at 10th Street, South Beach (1-305 672-2014, www.mdpl.org). Bus C, H, K, W, South Beach Local.* **Open** times vary. **Tours** $15-$20. **Credit** AmEx, MC, V. **Map** p280 D3.

It makes sense that the Miami Design Preservation League is behind the city's most popular art deco walking tours. But don't let the deco moniker fool you: the MDPL's knowledgeable team of guides also take in Mediterranean Revival and Miami Modern (aka MiMo) structures during this 90-minute jaunt past the neighbourhood's most iconic hotels, restaurants and public buildings. Tours depart daily at 10.30am (plus 6.30pm Thur).

### Miami Culinary Tours

*1000 5th Street, at Michigan Avenue, South Beach (1-786 942 8856, www.miamiculinary tours.com). Bus C, K, M, South Beach Local.* **Open** noon-6pm daily (call ahead for schedule). **Tours** $59. **Credit** AmEx, MC, V. **Map** p280 E2.

Eating and exercise combine during one of Miami Culinary Tours' two daily extravaganzas: the two-and-a-half-hour South Beach Food Tour includes up to eight stops, with tastings including everything from classic French to artisanal Colombian. Alternatively, explore the history and tastes of Cuba as part of the two-hour Little Havana Food Tour, which wends its way through Calle Ocho's must-visit dining spots. Bus tours are also available.

**EXPLORE**

**Miami Seaplane Tours.**

# The Beaches

*Billion Dollar Sandbar.*

Separated from the mainland by Biscayne Bay, which is bridged by several causeways, Miami Beach is made up of a tiny cluster of barrier islands. Three miles from the city itself, it actually spans several waterfront neighbourhoods, from the sandy bacchanalia of South Beach to the ultra-exclusive Golden Beach (which counts Bill Gates among its residents) to the north. Locals and pleasure-seekers congregate among palm trees, warm sands and balmy sea breezes, but the beaches don't naturally look this good. The city's founders dredged sand from the bottom of Biscayne Bay to embellish the shoreline. To this day, the coastal communities fight a never-ending battle with Mother Nature to maintain those famous sandy shores. The massive expenditure required to keep the sand attached to land is why cynics call Miami Beach the 'Billion Dollar Sandbar'.

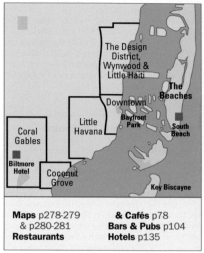

| Maps p278-279 | & Cafés p78 |
| & p280-281 | Bars & Pubs p104 |
| Restaurants | Hotels p135 |

## South Beach

Contemporary yet historic, tiny but diverse, South Beach commands hyperbole. It is the Miami stereotype come alive. The action centres on Ocean Drive and Collins Avenue between 5th Street to the south and Lincoln Road to the north. Every Miami scene ever filmed in any movie seems to have been shot here. Like wheeled, thong-clad Mercuries, hyper-tanned rollerbladers glide along the beach down

Ocean Drive past whimsical, pastel-hued art deco buildings. Seven-foot, eight-stone models saunter past four-foot, ten-stone geriatrics. Eurotrash and celebs rub oiled shoulders with artists, hipsters and a sprinkling of local stock in the sidewalk cafés, designer boutiques, lounge bars and dusk-to-dawn clubs. Then there's the turquoise ocean, the waving palm trees and the delicious blue skies.

The whole place would be almost beyond perfect were it not for South Beach's pervasive seediness. The *m'as-tu-vu* scenes at the likes of Nikki Beach Club and Mansion (for both, *see pp178-179*) are brought back down to earth with a bump by the scattering of beach bums with their possessions piled high in supermarket trolleys, and crack-addled homeboys and prostitutes prowling Washington Avenue after dark. Add in the stubbornly egalitarian nature of good ol' redneck Florida, and you end up with the startling juxtaposition of world-class hotels next door to grungy tattoo parlours and sex shops. It's little wonder that the place lends itself so perfectly to lurid TV and cinema.

### INSIDE TRACK GET LOCAL

South Beach is compact enough to get around on foot, but there's also a handy shuttle bus, the **South Beach Local** (1-305 770 3131, www.miamidade.gov/transit) that trundles up and down Washington Avenue (every 13-20mins, 7.40am-1.20am Mon-Sat, 10am-1am Sun). The route is marked on the Miami Beach map (*see p280*) and the fare's 25¢.

## SOUTH OF 5TH STREET

The lower swathe of South Beach below 5th Street (known as South of Fifth Street or, more cutely, SoFi) is quietly hip, tucked off the tawdry main drag. But it's either in trouble or in a state of repair, depending on who you speak to. The culprit? Development, or – as detractors would have it  avarice  The boundaries protecting the Beach's architectural heritage stop at 5th Street, so while small condos and refurbished art deco apartment buildings fill most of the area, a growing number of mega-monolith towers mar the overall atmosphere. The 26-storey South Pointe Tower, itself grossly out of scale with the neighbourhood, is now dwarfed by the adjacent Portofino, a controversial 44-storey condo built by real estate developer Thomas Kramer, nemesis of local preservationists (and a fixture on the *Real Housewives* reality TV franchise).

Still, there remains some old-school flair You'll find one of the Beach's best restaurants here in **Joe's Stone Crab** (*see p83*), known worldwide for its succulent crab claws and creamy key lime pie. For a cheaper bill and a dress code that leans towards sandy feet and beach wraps, head to **Big Pink** (*see p81*) for enormous portions of diner food, including excellent cakes and pies (it's open late too).

A wonderful respite from the urban madness is **South Pointe Park**, a verdant spot on the very tip of Miami Beach. Surrounded by the Atlantic Ocean and Government Cut channel, the aquatic highway for cruise ships, it provides wonderful views (*see right* **Inside Track**).

(*see right* **Inside Track**)

### INSIDE TRACK
### CRUISE SHIP ALLEY

With more than four million cruise passengers passing through the Port of Miami each year, the city is worthy of its 'Cruise Capital of the World' title. Land-bound folk can enjoy a front-row view of all the transatlantic action at the southern tip of Miami Beach: **South Pointe Park** (*see left*) overlooks Government Cut, the main aquatic highway. Watching these massive floating cities set sail is a thrilling sight, and it's even better with a cocktail at alfresco bar Smith & Wollensky, which is located within the park.

Or, for a little culture, duck into the **Jewish Museum of Florida** (*see below*), which tells the story of Miami's large Hebrew community. A popular 'only in South Beach' stop is the **World Erotic Art Museum** (*see p39*), which houses a huge collection of erotic art, including a sizeable collection of antique penises.

### Jewish Museum of Florida-FIU

*301 Washington Avenue, at 3rd Street (1-305 672 5044, www.jmof.fiu.edu). Bus South Beach Local.* **Open** 10am-5pm Tue-Sun. **Admission** $6; $5 reductions; free under-6s & all Sat. **Credit** AmEx, MC, V. **Map** p280 E3.
Housed in a beautifully restored art deco former synagogue, this Florida International University-run museum documents the Jewish experience in Florida

**EXPLORE**

**South Pointe Park.**

# Life's a Beach

*The best spots to spread out your towel.*

These are a few of our favourite beaches (all open daily). There are public parking lots and metered street parking, but most spaces will be full by 10am.

## MIAMI BEACH

### South Pointe Park
*1 Washington Avenue, South Beach.* **Map** p280 F3.
Part of a 17-acre park with picnic areas, a playground, a fishing pier and great views of cruise ships. *See p33.*

### Lummus Park Beach
*Ocean Drive, between 5th & 15th Streets, South Beach.* **Map** p280 D3/E3.
Volleyball, thatched huts and people-watching. There's also a gay beach at 12th Street. *See p37.*

### 21st-35th Street Beach
*Collins Avenue, Mid Beach.* **Map** p280 A4/B4.
Small stretch of sand, with boardwalk and snacks. *See p37.*

### 53rd-63rd Street Beach
*Collins Avenue, Mid Beach.* **Map** p281 C4/D4.
Pleasant, not too crowded and very family-oriented, with a play area at 53rd. *See p37.*

### Pelican Island
*Free weekend-only boat taxi from the marina at 79th Street Causeway, Belle Meade (1-305 754 9330).*
A small island reachable by private boat or, on weekends, a free 35-seat public boat. Expect barbecue grills, picnic tables, volleyball nets, horseshoe pits and – of course – pelicans.

### North Shore Open Space Park
*Collins Avenue, between 79th & 86th Streets, Surfside.* **Map** p281 inset.
Boardwalks, pavilions, barbecue grills and a Vita course. *See p43.*

### Surfside
*Collins Avenue, between 88th & 96th Streets, Surfside.* **Map** p281 inset.
Few facilities besides the lifeguards. *See p43.*

### Bal Harbour
*Beach Collins Avenue, at 96th Street, Bal Harbour.* **Map** p281 inset.
A small beach with a Vita course. *See p43.*

### Haulover Beach
*10600 Collins Avenue, Bal Harbour.* **Map** p281 inset.
A dozen miles of white sand, ocean surf, landscaped dunes and shaded picnic

**Lummus Park Beach**.

Sunny Isles Beach.

## ESSENTIAL TIPS

Umbrellas and loungers are available at many beaches; if you don't see an attendant, claim a chair and one will soon show up to collect the fee. Topless sunbathing is permitted on Miami Beach, and there are a few places that allow nude sunbathing (notably Haulover Beach; *see p43*). Sun here is subtropical, and you can get burned even on overcast days. Use a sunscreen with an SPF of at least 15 (30 for children) year round, and take a hat.

Pay attention to official warnings about beach conditions. Lifeguards post warning flags and signs by their stations. Green means it's safe to swim. 'No swimming' (red) means just that. 'Caution' (yellow) means hazardous conditions such as riptides – ask the lifeguard what dangers exist. Riptides, which occur on days with strong onshore winds, can carry even experienced swimmers out to sea. If it happens to you, aim to swim parallel to the shore until you're out of the rip's hold, then turn to swim towards shore. A purple flag means 'dangerous marine life', usually referring to Portuguese men-of-war, jellyfish-like sea creatures that look like blue bubbles floating in the water or washed up on the seaweed. Their long tentacles pack a nasty sting and can cause allergic reactions. If you get stung, head for the lifeguard, who will treat the stings. You'll smart for a few hours, but that's usually all. Sea lice are more annoying than dangerous. They latch on to your swimsuit and cause itching. To relieve itching, shower with soap and water. For information on conditions, call Miami Beach Patrol (1 305 673 7714).

areas. There's a nude beach (between the two northernmost parking lots) and a gay nude beach (north of the lifeguard tower). *See p43*.

### Sunny Isles Beach
*Collins Avenue, between 163rd & 192nd Streets, Sunny Isles.* **Map** p278. Two miles of public beaches, souvenir shops and hotels. *See p43*.

## KEY BISCAYNE & VIRGINIA KEY

### Hobie Beach
*Virginia Key.* **Map** p279. Windsurf, jet-ski and sailing boat rentals. *See p45*.

### Crandon Park
*4000 Crandon Boulevard, Key Biscayne.* **Map** p279. Pristine sand, calm shallow water, a winding boardwalk and convenient parking. *See p47*.

### Bill Baggs Cape Florida State Recreation Area
*1200 S Crandon Boulevard.* **Map** p279. A popular spot, with many activities on offer. *See p47*.

## SOUTH MIAMI

### Matheson Hammock Park Beach
*9610 Old Cutler Road, between SW 93rd & 101st Streets, South Miami.* **Map** p279. Scenic park with a man-made atoll pool that's flushed by the tidal action of Biscayne Bay.

Bill Baggs Cape Florida
State Recreation Area.

**EXPLORE**

since 1763. In addition to its travelling exhibitions, its core exhibition, Mosaic: Jewish Life in Florida, presents 500 photos and artefacts, two films and a timeline of local Jewish history.

## THE DECO DISTRICT

A compact grid of streets easily navigable on foot, the Deco District stretches from 5th Street north to Dade Boulevard and from the Atlantic Ocean west to Biscayne Bay. Three north–south streets – Ocean Drive, Collins Avenue and Washington Avenue – are home to the highest concentration of pastel-painted,

neon-lit bars, restaurants, clubs and shops. For all the self-importance, snobbishness and preening vanity, this is the beating heart of Miami Beach.

More than 800 buildings in the fanciful art deco style give the district its title – the architecture not only lends its name to the area, it more or less defines it. Immortalised in millions of postcards, it's the one image the outside world has of Miami Beach. It's a good one to have, too: without it, the Beach's tourist industry would struggle. Such glamorous architecture has in turn helped to spawn a suitably glamorous nightlife scene.

# Miami on the Med

*Española Way serves up a charming slice of old-world Europe.*

Café Nuvó.

Havana 1957.

Decked out in art deco pastels and portholes, **Española Way** channels old-world Europe across a charming, six-block swathe of South Beach. Conceived as a 'Historic Village' in 1925, the area was intended to serve as a meeting place for the city's elite, with a Mediterranean village vibe. And while it did succeed in becoming a hotspot for the city's A-listers, it also attracted its fair share of nefarious types, including Golden Age gangster Al Capone, who often used to gamble at the Clay Hotel (*see p148*).

As with Miami Beach in general, the popularity of Española Way has ebbed and flowed over the years. But its distinctive European flair in an area known for its deco designs has made it a popular film and TV backdrop; both the pilot and final episodes of *Miami Vice* were filmed here, as was a recent episode of *Burn Notice*.

While it's just a few short steps from the heart of South Beach's party scene with its

cobbled streets, outdoor cafés, galleries and boutiques, Española Way feels worlds away. Sit below the white twinkling lights and choose from one of more than a dozen mojitos at Café Nuvó (412 Española Way, 1-305 534 5822), indulge in some Cuban food at Havana 1957 (405 Española Way, 1-305 503 3828), get Gallic at A la Folie Café (*see p79*) or head south of the border at Oh Mexico (1440 Washington Avenue, at Española Way, 1-305 532 0490).

Oh Mexico.

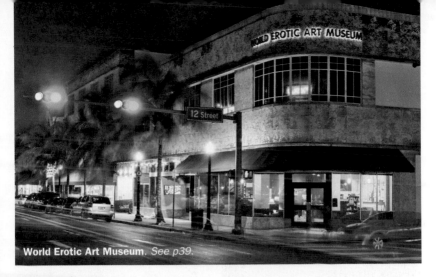

**World Erotic Art Museum.** *See p39.*

For a suggested walking tour taking in the best of South Beach deco (and a listing for the informative Art Deco District Welcome Center), *see p254* **Walk**.

## Ocean Drive

The ten-block strip of Ocean Drive from 5th to 14th Streets is the epicentre of South Beach. On the eastern side of the street, the dunes and beach volleyball courts of **Lummus Park** front the Atlantic Ocean and the white sandy beaches. Six funky lifeguard stands punctuate the beach: a mod antenna spikes the stand at 10th Street, 12th Street's looks like a purple mobile home, and the one at 14th Street sports a circular roof crowned with AstroTurf.

The western side of the street is home to one sidewalk café or bar after another, many of them attached to deco hotels. Let whim guide you or bank on the ever-popular **News Café** (*see p85*); occupying the corner of 8th Street and Ocean Drive, its tables are sardined with trendies 24 hours a day. This was the last halt on earth for Gianni Versace, who breakfasted here almost daily, including on 15 July 1997 – the day Andrew Cunanan followed the famed fashion designer for three blocks before shooting him dead at the gates of his home. The **Versace Mansion** itself (1114 Ocean Drive, at 11th Street), aka the Amsterdam Palace, is a flashy (of course) three-storey Italianate palace built in 1930, which was supposedly modelled on Christopher Columbus's home in Genoa. Since Versace's murder, the house has been sold and turned into the **Villa by Barton G** (*see p80*), a luxury hotel, restaurant and event space. But even with the bloodstains long gone, its front steps are still the most photographed spot in town.

## Collins Avenue

Collins is one block inland from Ocean and boasts a similar mix of deco hotels, cafés and bars – minus the crassness, at least to some degree. In addition to the same old shops selling tourist tat, Collins boasts a number of high-end boutiques such as Nicole Miller, Barneys and the Webster. Amid the gloss is **Puerto Sagua** (*see p87*), a Cuban restaurant where meals arrive on plates larger than Long Island and often cost less than $10.

Several blocks north, on the corner of 12th, is the photogenic **Marlin** hotel. A couple more blocks up is **Jerry's Famous Deli** (*see p83*); built in 1939 as Hoffman's Cafeteria, it became a ballroom, then a nightclub. It's now a wonderful diner, open 24 hours for quick-fill reubens, burgers and authentic New York cheesecake.

Above 14th Street, the buildings rise. Whereas lower Collins is all three and four storeys, suddenly we're up to ten, 15 and 20 or more floors. Most of these contain beds for visitors and the neon signs denote some of the ritziest spots in town, including the **Delano** (*see p135*), **Raleigh** (*see p137*), **SLS** (*see p140*) and the **Setai** (*see p138*). Each has had millions poured into renovation and restyling, and boy does it show. Suck in your gut and put some purpose into your stride as you make a brazen entrance, pretending you 'belong', in order to check out the lobbies and bars. And curse the humble heritage that has bequeathed you nights at the Days Inn.

## Washington Avenue

A further block inland from Collins Avenue is Washington Avenue, where pizza-by-the-slice joints, all-night grocers and cheque cashiers are interspersed with one-of-a-kind boutiques selling retro houseware, faddish club gear and $500 sunglasses. Despite being only two blocks from the beach, it can be seedy: after dark, it's frequented by wandering homeless and some seriously substance-enhanced streetfolk, so take care. The elegant **Angler's** (*see p135*) and the glam art deco **Hotel Astor** (*see p142*) are trying to raise the tone.

Diagonally across from the Astor is the **Wolfsonian-FIU** (*see p39*), a shamefully undervisited design museum and a place we can't recommend highly enough. On the same block and just a few doors north is another design classic in the sleek and chrome form of the **11th Street Diner** (*see p78*) – a real beauty to look at, and the food's pretty good too. There are no spotlights to guide you there, but if you walk another block north, you'll find

the **Miami Beach Cinematheque** (*see p168*), home to the best indie and classic films on the beach, and HQ for the prestigious Miami International Film Festival. Come prepared for a touch of culture and class, just slightly out of place on SoBe.

There's more noteworthy architecture on the corner of 13th Street with the **Miami Beach Post Office** (no.1300), which deviates from the art deco norm with nods towards Depression Moderne style, including a rotunda with exquisite acoustics.

A couple of blocks further north is **Española Way**, a sweet – if overly contrived – block-long cluster of Spanish Mediterranea: the buildings come in peach and orange, ornamented with awnings and balconies. Originally designed in the 1930s as an artists' colony, it is now given over to twee galleries, boutiques and

## Parking Fine

*Even the garages are glam in Magic City.*

**Ballet Valet Parking Garage**.

It doesn't take long to realise that Miami is a car-loving kind of town. But forget BMW and Mercedes – Ferrari, Lamborghini, Maserati and Bentley are the favoured rides here. Of course, such prestigious marques require a suitably smart place to park, and in the past few years the city has hired a slew of star architects to build a series of stunning garages.

In 1996, legendary local design firm Arquitectonica completed the Ballet Valet Parking Garage (630 Collins Avenue, at 6th Street), a six-level mix of garage and topiary that takes up an entire South Beach block. The same company has taken a much more industrial approach to its second car park project, the soon-to-open Sunset Harbour Garage (1900 Bay Road, at 20th Street) – more mesh and metal than flora and fauna.

When renowned architect Frank Gehry was hired to bring new cultural life to the corner of 17th Street and Washington

Avenue with the building of the New World Center, the campus of the New World Symphony, he also agreed to design its attached six-level Pennsylvania Avenue Parking Garage with parking for nearly 600 vehicles. Gehry chose to highlight his sleek, durable mesh construction with a dynamic LED lighting scheme, creating a stunning 3D effect come nightfall.

Just two blocks to the west, on Meridian Avenue, the City Hall Annex Parking Garage, designed by Perkins+Will, uses acres of glass and strategically placed metal blades to mimic the flow of the nearby ocean. Finally, less than half a mile to the west, 1111 Lincoln Road is an art deco-inspired garage and – believe it or not – in-demand special event space, which is hired out for as much as $15,000 a night. Created by Herzog & de Meuron – the design team behind London's Tate Modern – the garage has hosted an assortment of A-list soirées and black-tie weddings.

**Sunset Harbour Garage**.

cafés, although **A la Folie** (*see p79*) adds a welcome bit of Gallic bite. The **Clay Hotel** (*see p148*), which occupies most of the south side of the street, was formerly the home of Desi '*I Love Lucy*' Arnaz. The building was also at one time the headquarters of Al Capone's gambling syndicate.

### World Erotic Art Museum

*1205 Washington Avenue, at 12th Street, South Beach (1-305 532 9336, www.weam.com). Bus C, H, K, W, South Beach Local.* **Open** 11am-10pm Mon-Thur; 11am-midnight Fri-Sun. **Admission** $15; $13.50-$14 reductions. **Credit** AmEx, MC, V. **Map** p280 D3.

The world's capital of hedonism now has its own museum dedicated to erotic pleasures. At 12,000sq ft, the collection of sex toys, paintings and artefacts is the second largest of its kind in the world, spanning all periods (ancient Rome, Victorian, art deco) and ethnicities (from Chinese to African). The penis collection is the highlight – a mind-boggling array of phalluses in all shapes, colours and sizes. If you're not overwhelmed by the giant penis (over 6ft) then you'll be blown away (pun intended) by the wooden four-poster bed, where the four posts are, you guessed it, shaped like giant penises. Unsurprisingly, under 18s are not admitted. What is surprising is that the museum's owner/curator, Naomi Wilzig, is a near-octogenarian grandmother. *Photo p37.*

### ★ Wolfsonian-FIU

*1001 Washington Avenue, at 10th Street (1-305 531 1001, www.wolfsonian.org). Bus C, H, K, W, South Beach Local.* **Open** noon-6pm Mon, Tue, Thur, Sat, Sun; noon-9pm Fri. **Admission** $7; $5 reductions. **Credit** AmEx, MC, V. **Map** p280 D3.

Housed in a finely restored 1927 storage facility, this museum and research centre explores how design shapes and reflects the human experience. If that sounds a bit stuffy, it's not. The artefacts include some real treats – a deco postbox from New York's Central Station, a stained-glass window by fey Irish illustrator Harry Clarke, and Cuban cinema posters, as well as lots of attractively displayed furniture, ceramics, metalwork, paintings and architectural drawings. The permanent exhibits are supplemented by touring exhibitions, lectures and films.

## LINCOLN ROAD MALL

The Lincoln Road Mall – or, in local shorthand, 'the Road' – had its heyday in the 1950s, when it was designed by iconic architectural guru Morris Lapidus and dubbed the 'Fifth Avenue of the South'. And just as Lapidus went through an unpopular period before coming back into fashion in the 1990s, so Lincoln Road waned before experiencing a resurgence as a prime South Beach spot, especially for locals jaded with the preening crowds on Ocean Drive.

Gussied up in 1997 with a $16 million facelift, the mall sits between 16th and 17th Streets and stretches from Washington Avenue to Alton Road. It's wall-to-wall sidewalk cafés, clubs, boutiques, restaurants, cultural venues and galleries. After the renovation, rents soared and today most of the shops and cafés are chains – it now has more Starbucks than some entire cities in America's Midwest.

Busiest time is late evening, when the café and restaurant sidewalk tables fill up with the bridge and tunnel crowd. Choice venues include the Van Dyke Café and

**EXPLORE**

Wolfsonian-FIU.

the sun-soaked outpost of pink London fave **Balans** (*see p79*). The Road also has popular glam gay nightspot **Score** (*see p173*). An upscale steak house can be found at the dinner-only **Meat Market** (*see p85*). SoBe outposts of popular NYC sweet factories are here, too, including **Dylan's Candy Bar** (*see p129*) and **Serendipity3** (*see p86*); save room for its world-famous frozen hot chocolate. Sundays are popular for the antiques and farmers' market.

Cultural venues on Lincoln include **ArtCenter/South Florida** (*see p126*), a collection of artists' studios and gallery space, and the **Colony Theatre** (*see p167*), a deco gem that hosts film, theatre, dance and music performances. At the mall's western end is the vast **Regal South Beach** cinema (*see p167*).

## NORTH OF LINCOLN ROAD

Immediately north of Lincoln Road is the civic centre of Miami Beach; on or just off 17th Street, you'll find **City Hall**, the **Miami Beach Convention Center**, the **Fillmore Miami Beach at Jackie Gleason Theater** (*see p182*), the Frank Gehry-designed **New World Center** (*see p187*) and the Beach's most prominent place of worship, **Temple Emanu-El** (1701 Washington Avenue, 1-305 538 2503, www.tesobe.org), an historic synagogue that aggressively holds sway over the junction with Washington Avenue.

Directly across from the Miami Beach Convention Center is the **Miami Beach Botanical Garden** (2000 Convention Center Drive, at Dade Boulevard, 1-305 673 7256, www.mbgarden.org), a charming three-acre green space featuring an impressive collection of flowering trees, palms, cycads, orchids, bromeliads and native plant species. Among all the fronds and flora lurks a highly emotive **Holocaust Memorial** (1945 Meridian Avenue, at Dade Boulevard, 1-305 538 1663, www.holocaustmmb.org, open 9am-sunset daily, free). Created by artist Kenneth Treister, the memorial takes the form of a 42-foot upraised beckoning hand, tattooed with an Auschwitz serial number and anchored by a writhing mass of death camp victims.

A short walk east of the Convention Centre, between Washington and Collins Avenues, is the excellent **Bass Museum of Art** (*see below*) and the sexily curvaceous home of the **Miami City Ballet** (*see p194*).

### ★ Bass Museum of Art

*2100 Collins Avenue, at 21st Street (1-305 673 7530, www.bassmuseum.org). Bus C, G, H, L, S.* **Open** noon-5pm Wed-Sun. **Admission** $8; $6 reductions; free under-6s. **Credit** AmEx, MC, V. **Map** p280 B3.

The Bass is the centrepiece of Miami Beach's 'cultural campus'. The core of the building is the old Miami Beach public library, originally built in 1930. After an $8m renovation it now boasts vastly expanded facilities. In addition to pieces from the museum's own permanent collection (including European Old Masters, rococo court paintings, 18th-century English portraits, Flemish tapestries and Chinese woodblock prints), it hosts world-class travelling exhibitions – everything from folk art to photography and video installations. There are also talks, workshops and a decent little gift shop.

## Mid Beach

In the 1950s, the kitschy oversized hotels on mid-Miami Beach – or Mid Beach – defined the stereotypical vacation here. Grandes dames such as the **Eden Roc** and **Fontainebleau** (*see p150*) went all out for a campy interpretation of glamour. In the decades that followed, the icons became ironic and benign, catering mostly to Latin American visitors and conventioneers instead of the starlets and movie moguls who once headed here. But all that has changed in recent years as both of the aforementioned hotels have had spectacular makeovers aimed at attracting a younger, hipper crowd. Still, the hotels get larger, the crowds get older and the pace gets slower as you head north out of South Beach.

West of Collins Avenue, Mid Beach is a mix of golf courses and palatial private homes, with sprawling estates fronting **Indian Creek**, a narrow waterway west of Collins where yachts bob and the University of Miami rowing club practises at dawn. If ogling grand homes intrigues, try old-money La Gorce and Pine Tree Drives on the west side of the creek for mixed imitation architecture behind imposing gates. Collins is the only street of consequence, but even Collins becomes a soulless collection of bland condos beyond 50th Street.

A public beach just north of the Eden Roc has ample parking, while a wooden boardwalk popular with joggers, elderly couples and orthodox Jewish families runs behind the hotels and allows visitors to peer into beachfront bars.

## North Beach

North Beach is local slang; you won't find the name on official cartography. Extending north of the condo canyon, this working- and middle-class residential area stretches roughly from 63rd Street to 79th Street. The two smatterings of commercial activity are on 71st Street, where the JFK Causeway spans the bay, and Collins Avenue, where slightly seedy restaurants, cafés

# View from the Bridge

*The city's causeways are worth crossing for the vistas alone.*

Rickenbacker Causeway.

Four causeways span the three miles of Biscayne Bay between mainland Miami and Miami Beach, while two more cross its waters further north, providing the sort of vistas that make Miami worthy of its Magic City moniker.

The busiest one, **MacArthur Causeway** (I-395), crosses north of Downtown, spilling three lanes of traffic on to South Beach's 5th Street. On weekend evenings, traffic goes bumper to bumper as suburban clubgoers make a pilgrimage across the bay. Seen from MacArthur, the Downtown skyline is splendid, with 40 permanently illuminated buildings.

The MacArthur also provides access to Watson Island, a once-scruffy bit of shore that's being redeveloped. It's now home to the Miami Children's Museum and Jungle Island (for both, *see p161*). Watson Island's waterside park benches are ideal for ogling the giant cruise ships docked across the Government Cut channel at the Port of Miami. The port itself consumes Dodge and Lummus islands, the sole working-class islands in a bay of wealth. Three small bridges lace off the MacArthur's north side to a trio of exclusive residential islands, each with its own stars: Palm, the former home of Al Capone; Hibiscus, one-time residence of Damon Runyon; and Star, where you'll find Gloria Estefan's abode.

At the Beach end of the MacArthur is the ferry dock for Fisher Island, a well-manicured private island clustered with Mediterranean-style condos, visible just across the channel. Originally the southernmost tip of Miami Beach, Fisher was created in 1905 when the well-named Government Cut was dredged to improve access to the port. Today, the island is home to the impossibly exclusive Fisher Island Club (if you have to ask, you can't afford to stay here).

South is the **Rickenbacker Causeway** in the Key Biscayne area (*see p45*), which provides superb vantage points over the city and its waterfront.

Just over a mile north of MacArthur on the Beach side (it's considerably closer on the mainland) is the **Venetian Causeway**. The first of the crossings to be built, it's a slow, two-lane street that stretches from the northern edge of South Beach to Downtown. The causeway bisects several residential islands (Belle Isle, San Marino, Biscayne Isle and Dilido – signs for the latter invariably have the second 'i' painted out by local wags) – and it's a popular cycling and jogging trail.

North again, the **Julia Tuttle Causeway** (also known as I-195) feeds into I-95, the freeway that acts as south Florida's Main Street. On the Beach side, the Tuttle becomes 41st Street, the commercial hub of Mid Beach. Finally, furthest north, the **JFK Causeway** and **Broad Causeway** form the last major physical links to the mainland, although Miami Beach will always maintain the firm belief that it's hundreds of miles from the rest of the US – in attitude, if nothing else.

# Sand Grab

*Miami Beach looks to stem the tide of erosion.*

Quick, grab your towel – Miami Beach is running out of sand. That's right, the ten-mile stretch of wide white sand – the one that attracts millions of tourists and generates billions of dollars in revenue – is being washed out to sea. It's no great surprise, though: Miami Beach has always been something of an illusion. Like almost everything in this manufactured paradise, the beach is man-made and maintained by army engineers at a cost of some $3 million a year.

Nor is erosion a new phenomenon. Back in the 1960s, the name Miami Beach had become a misnomer, as the wide sands had been reduced to a sliver. In front of certain hotels, there was no beach left: you had to use a ladder to climb into the sea. For a time, breakwaters were constructed to stop the sand from haemorrhaging. By the late 1970s, there were so many bulwarks along the beach that critics said it resembled a military obstacle course.

Tourists deserted Miami and luxury hotels teetered on the brink – until the army took action. In a huge $64 million operation, between 1976 and 1980, the Army Corps of Engineers dredged sand from the bottom of the ocean floor and pumped it on to the shore. The result was spectacular: a 300-foot wide beach made up of 13 million cubic yards of sand – equal to 600,000 dump-truck loads.

But after 30 years of dredging, the army says there's no more usable sand left on the ocean floor. And the glorious beach is dwindling again – in some parts of Mid Beach, it's now just 20 feet wide. The army has asked for permission to scoop sand from other cities on Florida's east coast, but the idea has been flatly rejected – sand is the bread and butter of every resort along this stretch.

As a temporary solution, the county is spending millions trucking in prehistoric sand from a commercial mine inland near the Everglades. But this is a logistical – and financial – nightmare. Then there is the idea of using recycled glass bottles to make sand. Fort Lauderdale is testing the idea, but only time will tell whether it works.

Now, in true US imperialist style, Miami is trying to buy sand in from small foreign countries. Dade County has asked the Federal Government to help pay for imported sand from cash-poor, sand-rich countries such as Mexico, Panama, Turks and Caicos, the Dominican Republic and the Bahamas. There are several obstacles. For one thing, there is a federal law that forbids importing sand. If that law is overturned, naturalists worry that foreign sand could wreak havoc on domestic flora and fauna – sea turtles, for instance, are fussy about the type of sand in which they nest. The state law also requires that replacement sand conforms to a certain grain size and colour. Finally, to maintain a ten-mile stretch of sand for 25 years, at a width of 200 feet, engineers need 12 million cubic yards of sand – and $120 million dollars. But Miami will undoubtedly find a way. It has to. As local politician Ileana C Ros-Lehtinen put it: 'If we don't have beautiful beaches... we might as well be in Nebraska.'

Oleta River State Recreation Area. *See p43.*

and shops intersperse with hotels that cater to budget-minded South Americans. Not as chic as South Beach nor as residential as Mid Beach, North Beach nonetheless has a few hidden charms, among them the wildly popular **Café Prima Pasta** and **Café Ragazzi** (for both, *see p92*), where the queues outside say it all.

## Surfside to Golden Beach

Just north of North Beach, on a seedy two-block stretch of Collins Avenue around 85th Street, is **North Shore Open Space Park**. The park is a lovely, underused stretch of pristine beach lined with sea grape trees, sand dunes, a boardwalk, a Vita exercise course and amenities such as changing rooms, picnic tables and barbecue pits. The park forms the southern border of **Surfside**, a sleepy residential enclave less than a mile square, clotted with two- and three-storey apartment buildings and boasting little to entice visitors save the promise of less crowded beaches.

You don't need to see a city limits sign to know you've arrived in **Bal Harbour**, the elegant town just north of Surfside. The landscape sports an expensive topiary manicure, luxury cars ply the streets, chauffeurs in caps keep the motor idling and the A/C on while madam shops: there's a distinct whiff of money in the air. In Bal Harbour, crime is low (the local police are notoriously zealous about dispensing speeding tickets), property prices are high and the median age is at least 30 years older than anywhere on the southern half of the sandbar. There are said to be more millionaires per capita in Bal Harbour than in any other city in the US, and it shows. You need to be one to hang out here for long. **Bal Harbour Shops**

(*see p118*) is an oppressively top-end mall where the concession list reads like a *Who's Who* of haute couture. Security guards in faux-colonial uniforms and Styrofoam pith helmets prowl around its parking lots in golf carts.

**Haulover Beach Park**, just north of Bal Harbour, scores big points as one of the area's most scenic stretches of beachfront. Worth the drive or straightforward bus journey from South Beach (take the S from Lincoln Road), the beach is fringed with dense vegetation that blocks out the visual pollution of nearby high-rises. Known primarily for its section of nude beach, Haulover also has a 1,100-foot fishing pier, picnic tables, concession stands and a kayak rental outfit for jaunts into the nearby Oleta River, a pristine waterway that wends its way westwards through the **Oleta River State Recreation Area** (*see below*).

Beyond Haulover Beach Park lies **Sunny Isles Beach**, where architectural kitsch and older tourists once prevailed. In an effort to change its reputation forever, the place has undergone a luxury beachside condo boom, irritating most residents but pleasing city fathers with the massively expanding tax base. These days, Sunny Isles Beach resembles more the condo canyon of mid-Miami Beach than the low-rent beach community it was from World War II until just a few years ago. And there are plenty of high-priced restaurants and resorts – including **Acqualina** and **Trump International Beach Resort** (for both, *see p153*) – popping up as a result.

### Oleta River State Recreation Area

*3400 NE 163rd Street, between Biscayne Boulevard & Collins Avenue, Sunny Isles Beach (1-305 919 1846, www.floridastateparks.org/ oletariver). Bus E, S, V.* **Open** *8am-sundown daily.* **Admission** *Per vehicle $4-$6. On foot/ bicycle $2; free under-8s.* **Credit** *MC, V.*

**EXPLORE**

# Swimming with Sharks

*Just when you thought it was safe to go back in the water.*

Florida has been declared the world's shark attack capital, beating the likes of Australia and South Africa. There were 25 attacks in 2012, up from 11 in 2011.

Shark attacks are nothing new in Florida – the first recorded fatality was in 1882. But the media feeding frenzy began in the summer of 2001, when *Time* magazine ran a cover story with the headline 'The Summer of the Shark'. It was triggered by an attack straight out of a horror film: at the end of a summer's day on 6 July, eight-year-old Jessie Arbogast was splashing in knee-high water with his cousins near Pensacola, on Florida's panhandle. Suddenly, the water turned blood red and the cry 'Shark!' rang out across the beach.

Vance Flosenzier, Jessie's uncle, arrived at the scene to find a seven-foot bull shark with his teeth clenched around his nephew's arm. He grabbed the shark by the tail and wrestled him to the beach. But in the process, the shark bit off the young boy's arm. A park ranger had to shoot the shark with a rifle and wrench open his jaws to retrieve it. Jessie lived to tell the tale – and the media lapped it up.

Following the attack, some marine biologists claimed that Florida's sharks were becoming more aggressive because of shark-feeding tours. To give tourists a thrill, boats bait the water with bloody fish to attract man-eaters, but in the process they condition sharks to associate food with people. The practice was banned in 2002, but several tour operators circumvented the law by taking passengers offshore into international waters. And sure enough, shark-baiting was back in the headlines in February 2008 when Markus Groh, an Austrian lawyer, was killed by a bull shark while scuba diving off the coast of Fort Lauderdale without a cage. Groh, 49, had joined a day cruise with Scuba Adventures, a local company that ran 'swimming with sharks' expeditions. He had his arm ripped off and was airlifted to a Miami hospital, where he died.

As Florida waters go, Miami is a safe haven. The last fatal shark attack in Dade County occurred in June 1961, when a diver was killed off Key Biscayne. And there are relatively few surfers – the most common shark bait – in Miami. But the east coast of Florida, a few hours north

of the city, is like something out of *Jaws*. Volusia County, home to Daytona and New Smyrna beaches, is the shark-bite capital of Florida, with around 250 bites (and counting). Palm Beach County, which ranks third out of 26 counties in the number of shark attacks, is 90 minutes up the coast from Miami. And every time someone goes swimming in south Florida, there is probably a shark 'within a few dozen yards', according to a 2001 *Miami Herald* article. 'Just get aboard one of those planes that tows the suntan lotion signs over Haulover Beach and you'll see lots of them, right where people are swimming,' said Robert Hueter, then director of the Center for Shark Research at the Mote Marine Laboratory in Sarasota.

Statistically speaking, the riskiest time to swim is between June and October, peaking in September – sharks stray closer to the shore in summer. On 13 September 2007, for instance, 14-year-old Brandon Chapman was standing in three feet of water at Lauderdale-by-the-Sea when a four-foot lemon shark clamped on to his abdomen with its teeth. It took a team of firefighters to prise the shark's mouth open and rescue the boy.

But the sharks responsible for the majority of attacks in Florida are aggressive bull sharks, followed by blacktips, spinners and hammerheads. In late March, hundreds of blacktips and spinners congregate 300 feet off south Florida's east coast as part of a seasonal migration northwards in pursuit of mackerel and bluefish. But local papers have run stories about sharks coming in closer – just 100 feet off Key Biscayne or Haulover Beach.

To be safe, don't swim out too far, avoid swimming at dusk, near fishermen or in murky water, don't swim if you're bleeding, and don't wear flashy jewellery or splash around. In the extremely unlikely event that you're attacked, experts say you should fight back. Hit the shark in the eyes, gills or snout, or hug the shark so it can't sever your limbs. If you cover its gills, it will have trouble breathing and might let you go.

But, above all, don't cancel your trip to Florida. You're far more likely to be struck by lightning than you are to be attacked by a shark. In Miami, you should be more worried about the sharks on land.

The largest urban park in the state, covering around 1,000 acres, Oleta River is another of those splendid natural wonders that manages to exist in the shadows of condo canyons and metropolitan mayhem. Once home to the Tequesta Indians, who camped along its shores, the river is a habitat for manatees, waterbirds and dolphins. Visitors can explore the river by canoe or kayak, and there is a popular fishing pier. The park is well known for its mountain bike trails, all graded at varying levels of difficulty. A concession offers kayak, canoe and bicycle rentals.

# Key Biscayne

The **Rickenbacker Causeway** arcs from just south of Downtown on to two sleepy and physically striking islands: Key Biscayne and its silent partner, Virginia Key. The ratio of models to grains of sand may be smaller here than on Miami Beach, but what the islands lack in superficial beauty is compensated for with serenity and lack of pretension. You can get to Key Biscayne by taking bus B from the Downtown bus terminal.

## VIRGINIA KEY

Just over the causeway on Virginia Key are **Hobie Beach**, **Windsurfer Beach** and **Jet Ski Beach**, each named after its most popular watersport. Rental stands for windsurfers, kayaks, sailboats and jet skis dot the white-sand shoreline, and the azure water of Biscayne Bay forms a wide, relatively shallow pan with steady winds. If you need to amuse the kids, you can take them to the **Miami Seaquarium** (4400 Rickenbacker Causeway, 1-305 361 5705, www.miamiseaquarium.com), but the venue has seen better days.

On the northern side of the causeway as it hits Virginia Key sits the recently renovated **Rusty Pelican** (3201 Rickenbacker Causeway, 1-305 361 3818, www.miami.therustypelican. com), a seafood restaurant with a modern nautical motif, decent fare and stunning views back towards the city, particularly at sunset.

## KEY BISCAYNE

The Key, as locals call Key Biscayne, is the northernmost island in the Florida Keys. Its life as an exclusive resort began in the early 1900s, when sea captain William Commodore dredged the bay, zealously planted tropical foliage and built yacht basins for his pals. Locals feared the worst – the invasion of riffraff – in the late 1940s, when flamboyant flying ace Eddie Rickenbacker opened the toll bridge; indeed, construction went into a frenzy and the condos that cluster to the west of the island were built.

**Bill Baggs Cape Florida State Recreation Area.** *See p47.*

**EXPLORE**

EXPLORE

Still, the Key remained an unknown, affluent hangout until former US president Richard Nixon bought a home here in the 1970s.

Nixon may have, in a twisted way, helped push up property prices and put the Key on the map, but the mendacious president did little to liven it up. With minimal nightlife, shopping and culture, the lure for visitors is nature: beaches, two waterfront parks, a cycling path and absurdly photogenic views of Miami.

Crossing to Key Biscayne, the causeway is renamed Crandon Boulevard. The prime attractions are **Crandon Park** on the east and **Bill Baggs Cape Florida State Recreation Area** (*see right*), the 400-acre park at the tip of the island. Palm trees line Crandon, and shallow waters, barbecues and picnic tables make it a favourite destination for families. Bill Baggs, too, offers good swimming. The shoreline is softened by sand dunes, and boardwalks lead to the picturesque **Cape Florida Lighthouse**, built

in 1825. On the horizon, half a dozen brightly coloured houses sit in the water on wooden legs, like oversized grasshoppers.

### ★ Bill Baggs Cape Florida State Recreation Area

*1200 S Crandon Boulevard (1-305 361 5811, www.floridastateparks.org/capeflorida). Bus B.* **Open** 8am-sundown daily. **Admission** *Per vehicle* $4-$8. *On foot/bicycle* $2. **Credit** MC, V. Occupying the southern tip of Key Biscayne, this park's wide beaches regularly make the national top ten lists. But this is more than just a place to catch some rays: there's history, wildlife and plenty of activities too. You can tour the Cape Florida Lighthouse, the oldest building in south Florida; explore native wildlife planted in the aftermath of 1992's Hurricane Andrew; and try your hand at shoreline fishing, ocean kayaking, windsurfing, cycling and in-line skating. Covered pavilions are available for picnics, and the Lighthouse Café offers good food. *Photo p43.*

# Invasion of the Iguanas

*The night it rained reptiles.*

Forget about cats and dogs – in Miami, it rains iguanas. On the night of 2 January 2008, lizards began falling from the sky on the island of Key Biscayne and residents woke up to find the island's bike paths, pavements and parks strewn with the reptiles – some living, some not. The bizarre spectacle was caused by a freak twist of nature: on the previous night, Miami was hit by a rare cold snap and the temperature plunged to 4°C (39°F). Being cold-blooded creatures, iguanas go into a comatose state when the mercury dips below 5°C and as a result are unable to cling on to tree branches, hence the reptile rainstorm.

Native to Latin America, iguanas are thought to have arrived in the Miami area in the 1960s, stowed away on cargo ships. Prolific breeders – females breed twice a year and lay 50 eggs at a time – they flourish in Florida, where they have no natural predators, and there are now thought to be 100,000 in Florida.

Tourists love them, of course – they look like mini-dinosaurs – but locals can't stand them. They foul the pavements, mess up pools and are public enemy number one for gardeners: iguanas love to munch on hibiscus and other tropical flowers.

Over on the mainland, Fairchild Tropical Garden (*see p73*) fights an ongoing war with the creatures – there are thought to be as many as 20 living in any given tree – and are forced to fence off some plants. But in Key Biscayne's Crandon Park (*see above*), where there are believed to be up to 1,000 iguanas, authorities have given up the battle. The tourists couldn't be happier – Crandon Park golf course often resembles a scene from *Jurassic Park* in miniature, and at the Key Biscayne Library (299 Crandon Boulevard, 1-305 361 6134, www.mdpls.org) children have far more fun playing spot the iguana in the garden than they do reading *Where's Waldo* inside.

For a truly brazen display, check out the sea wall in front of the Boater's Grill (1200 Crandon Boulevard, 1-305 361 0080, www.lighthouserestaurants.com), a waterfront restaurant in Bill Baggs State Park. The reptiles like to bake there on hot sunny days. It's surely better than baking in an oven – iguana is a delicacy in South America, but one that has yet to catch on in Florida. It might do in the future, though, as the only surefire way to control the burgeoning population.

**EXPLORE**

# Downtown

*The formerly faded city centre is on the up.*

Downtown Miami's once-modest gathering of skyscrapers continues to multiply, as the architecture evolves from colourful, campy 1980s to post-millennium sleek. Not long ago, the scene at ground level was largely characterised by an assortment of tacky discount electronics stores, pawn shops, seedy immigration lawyers and 99¢ emporiums. However, the past decade has seen a major residential migration and today more than 70,000 people call the neighbourhood home – almost twice as many as in 2000. The Downtown property boom has brought plenty of other benefits with it, too, from first-rate restaurants and bars to vibrant cultural centres.

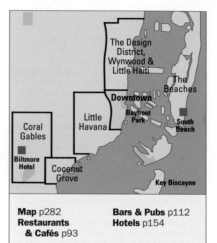

**Map** p282      **Bars & Pubs** p112
**Restaurants**      **Hotels** p154
  **& Cafés** p93

## AROUND FLAGLER STREET

**Flagler Street** is the main drag, lined with shops catering mainly to South Americans. About the only one without a 'Todo Ten Dollars' sign is **Macy's**, which occupies a fine 1936 streamline Depression Moderne building at 22 E Flagler. A little way east, the **Seybold Building** (36 NE 1st Street, at N Miami Avenue, www.seyboldjewelry.com) is the heart of one of the largest jewellery districts in the country: there are more than 280 jewellers here. If you need a glittery rock, this is the place.

Further along Flagler is the 1926 **Gusman Center for the Performing Arts**, easily

### INSIDE TRACK TOBACCO ROAD

It may be considered a dive bar, but **Tobacco Road** (*see p113*) is a dive bar with some serious history. Opened in 1912, it has been slaking Downtowners' thirst for more than 100 years (yes, even during Prohibition). Al Capone, John Lee Hooker and Buddy Guy have all hit the bottle at this former speakeasy, which is now an impressive music venue.

recognisable by the restored marquee and charming box office kiosk at the front. Both Rudy Vallee and Elvis Presley played this Mediterranean Revival stunner, which features extravagant plaster details, twinkling ceiling lights and 12-foot crystal chandeliers.

Across the street, the **Alfred I DuPont Building** (169 E Flagler Street, at NE 2nd Avenue) is an elegant example of Depression Moderne style, with ornately wrought gates and exquisite brass elevator doors, while the lobby of the 1927 **Ingraham Building** (25 SE 2nd Avenue, at E Flagler Street) has a beautiful vaulted ceiling. On the corner is the **Historic Gesu Church** (*see p49*).

Despite the recent residential influx, the area is still mostly known as a business district, but it's also home to a thriving college campus. Some 27,000 students dodge the vagrants on NE 2nd Avenue to attend **Miami Dade College Wolfson Campus** (300 NE 2nd Avenue, at NE 3rd Street). Tourists, however, will be more interested in the campus's third-floor **Centre Gallery** (*see p49*); the annual book fair (*see p24*) is also a delight, drawing literary names to Miami from far and wide.

One block west is the distinctive ziggurat-roofed 1928 **Miami-Dade County Courthouse** (73 W Flagler Street, at NW 1st Avenue), once

the tallest building south of Washington, DC. West again is the bunker-like **Miami-Dade Government Center** (111 NW 1st Street, at NW 1st Avenue), a modern administrative and transport hub; the severity of its architecture is softened by a fanciful public sculpture, *Dropped Bowl with Scattered Slices and Peels* (1990), by Claes Oldenburg and Coosje van Bruggen.

A large nouveau Mediterranean complex comprises the **Miami-Dade Public Library** (*see p264*), HistoryMiami and **Miami Art Museum** (for both, *see right*), all set around an elegant courtyard. In December 2013, the art museum will reopen as Pérez Art Museum Miami (PAMM), part of the 29-acre Biscayne Bay-fronted Museum Park. Until then, the finest way to experience Downtown is a night view from either the Rickenbacker or MacArthur Causeways. Seen from one of these vantage points, it's one of the finest illuminated skylines in the US, notable for the curved **Miami Tower** (100 SE 2nd Street, at SE 1st Avenue), often bathed in white light but sometimes aqua and orange (the Miami Dolphins football team colours) or snowflakes for Christmas; the **Southeast Financial Center** (200 S Biscayne Boulevard, at SE 2nd Street); and the **Freedom Tower** (*see p50*).

### FREE **Historic Gesu Church**
*118 NE 2nd Street, at NE 1st Avenue (1-305 379 1424, www.gesuchurch.org). Metromover 1st Street. Services English & Spanish 8.15am Mon-Sat; 8.30am, 11.30am Sun. Spanish 10am, 1pm Sun.* **Map** p282 D2.

This Venetian-style building, which was constructed in 1922, is the oldest church in Miami still on its original site. The main part rises to four storeys, with a belfry and a large stained-glass rose window above the main entrance, while the interior has 16 additional stained-glass windows, several large painted murals, and intricately carved marble altar screens and railings.

### ★ **HistoryMiami**
*101 W Flagler Street, at NW 1st Avenue (1-305 375 1492, www.historymiami.org). Metromover Government Center.* **Open** 10am-5pm Tue-Fri; noon-5pm Sat, Sun. **Admission** $8; $5-$7 reductions; free under-6s. **Credit** AmEx, MC, V. **Map** p282 D1.

It's young, but south Florida does have a past and a lively one at that. Tracing the history of the region, from early Indians to rafting Cubans, HistoryMiami succeeds in educating while entertaining. The exhibits on the wreckers of Key West and Henry Flagler both merit an extended look, as does the section on photographer Ralph Middleton Munroe.

### **Miami Art Museum (MAM)**
*101 W Flagler Street, at NW 1st Avenue (1-305 375 3000, www.miamiartmuseum.org). Metromover Government Center.* **Open** 10am-5pm Tue-Fri; noon-5pm Sat, Sun. **Admission** $8; $4 reductions; free under-12s. **Credit** AmEx, MC, V **Map** p282 D1.

With a permanent collection of works from artists such as Marcel Duchamp, George Segal, Frank Stella and Ana Mendieta, not to mention high-calibre temporary exhibitions, this museum is worth a look. In December 2013, the museum will relaunch as the Perez Art Museum Miami (PAMM), a brand-new, cultural institution that will become an anchor of Downtown's still-in-progress Museum Park.

### FREE **Miami Dade College Centre Gallery**
*300 NE 2nd Avenue, at NE 3rd Street (1-305 237 7700, ww.mdc.edu/arts). Metromover Government Center.* **Open** 1-6pm Mon-Fri. **Admission** free. **Map** p282 D3.

Of the handful of public galleries maintained by the community college, the Centre Gallery on the Downtown campus is the most frequented. Shows focus exclusively on contemporary works by international artists and cover a broad range of themes, from performance art to new technological works.

Bayside Marketplace.

## BISCAYNE BOULEVARD & AROUND

Biscayne Boulevard divides Downtown from the waterfront green of **Bayfront Park** (301 N Biscayne Boulevard, www.bayfrontparkmiami. com), a busy venue for concerts, ethnic festivals and huge Independence Day, New Year's Eve and Winter Holiday celebrations. A 100-foot white metal pipe tower commemorates the 1986 Challenger space shuttle disaster. North is a plaza marked by the **JFK Torch of Friendship** and adorned with statues of Christopher Columbus and Juan Ponce de León, along with plaques representing Caribbean, South and Central American countries (except Cuba, naturally). Close by is touristy **Bayside Marketplace** (*see below*) and its often-packed marina. A pedestrian bridge conveniently links Bayside to the **AmericanAirlines Arena**, home of local pro basketball team Miami Heat. The arena is also a concert venue and hosts assorted temples to consumerism, such as Gloria Estefan's Bongos Cuban Café.

### FREE **Bayside Marketplace**

*401 Biscayne Boulevard, at NE 4th Street (1-305 577 3344, www.baysidemarketplace.com). Metromover College or Bayside.* **Open** 10am-10pm Mon-Thur; 10am-11pm Fri, Sat; 11am-9pm Sun. **Map** p282 C3.

The local tourist industry cites Bayside Marketplace as proof that Downtown is on the up. The increased safety and accessibility of the area is clear, but if Bayside is 'up', what was 'down'? It's little more than a mall, and a high-priced one at that. A Hard Rock Café here, a Gap there, a food court yonder, none of it very unusual or exciting. Sightseeing cruises from the marina are pleasant enough, though.

## NORTH OF NE 5TH STREET

Some of the dodgier bits of Downtown lie north of NE 5th Street. The best way to visit may be via the Omni extension of the Metromover (see, it does have its uses after all). From the relative comfort of the train, you'll get a good look at the baroque **Freedom Tower** (600 Biscayne Boulevard, at NE 6th Street), designed in 1925 and modelled on Seville's Giralda. It was once home to the old *Miami News* but its current name came from its use in the 1960s as a processing centre for refugees. It's now a memorial to Miami's Cuban immigrants.

To the west is the troubled **Overtown** district, one of the earliest settlements of Miami's black population. It has historically been plagued by poverty, drugs and, in the 1970s and '80s, rioting. City officials had the pink **Miami Arena** built here nearly two decades ago, believing it would spur economic development. The plan failed and, with the opening of the AmericanAirlines Arena, the Miami Arena became testament to grand plans gone wrong. It was demolished in 2008.

As the Metromover crosses the Miami Beach-bound MacArthur Causeway, to the right lies the bayfront **Miami Herald Building**, and to the left, the **Adrienne Arsht Center for Performing Arts** (*see p190*).

East of the Omni International (an old shopping mall that's now part of the Miami International University School of Art & Design) is the neo-Romanesque **Trinity Episcopal Cathedral** (464 NE 16th Street, at N Bayshore Drive, 1-305 374 3372, www. trinitymiami.org). The current building was completed in 1924, but the church itself is the oldest in Miami, having opened a month before the city was incorporated in 1896.

It's worth strolling a couple more blocks north to lunch at the 75-year-old **S&S Diner** (1757 NE 2nd Avenue, at NE 17th Street, 1-305 373 4291), one of the city's oldest eateries. Afterwards, press on to NE 21st Street for a look at the extraordinary Latin Moderne architecture of the **Bacardi Building**, the former American headquarters of the world's best-known brand of rum. The striking eight-storey tower was built in 1963, its sides adorned with ceramic tile murals in Spanish blue and white, and a smaller square building decorated with glass 'tapestries' was added in 1973.

## SOUTH OF THE RIVER

Despite its brevity, the four-mile **Miami River** is swampy south-east Florida's main stream. It was first used by a tribe of Native Americans called the Tequesta, whose village near the north shore was discovered by Ponce de León in 1513. It was a fateful discovery: less than 200 years on, the Tequesta were wiped out by wars and disease brought by the European explorers. The drawbridge carrying NE 2nd Avenue over the water is crowned with a bronze sculpture of a Tequesta Indian firing his arrow in the sky; it all but has an inscription that says: 'Sorry, sorry, sorry'. The best way to see the river is by boat. **HistoryMiami** (*see p49*) organises tours, as does the **Dade Heritage Trust**.

South of the river is an area known as **Brickell**: this is Miami's financial district, home to some of the city's 120-odd national and international banks. It's estimated that about 60 per cent of all US trade with Central America starts here. Conveniently enough, some of the

newest and most upscale business hotels are located here (*see below* **Rebuilding Brickell**), including the Mandarin Oriental and the 70-storey Four Seasons, which became the tallest building south of Atlanta when it was completed in 2002. But it's getting some competition now; currently under construction, the Panorama Tower at 1101 Brickell Avenue will soar to 849 feet. Dubbed Mary Brickell Village, the area has a lively after-hours scene, particularly around S Miami Avenue and SE 10th Street, which is home to several popular after-work hangouts such as **Gordon Biersch**, **Oceanaire** and **Perricone's**. Also not to be missed are the riverside ambience and great seafood at **Garcia's**. For more details, *see pp93-95.*

# Rebuilding Brickell

*This nondescript business district is being reinvented as a hipster hub.*

Until recently, the term Downtown Miami was something of an illusion: as Gertrude Stein wrote of Oakland, California: 'There is no there there.' Anonymous, depressing and lonely, it was the sad result of a total lack of planning in the city's heyday.

In healthy US cities, the Downtown area combines office, commercial and residential space, but such a balance wasn't considered in Miami's early days. Back then, the focus was landmark buildings for big companies, and not much else. The few shops and restaurants that did exist only served local workers. At the end of the business day, Downtown rolled up the carpet, security bars were put in place and every living soul took off for the safety of the suburbs.

But for Miami to be a truly great city it had to kick some life into the ghost town at its heart. In 2005, then Mayor Manny Diaz released a manifesto entitled 'The New Destiny', which offered his grand visions of a vibrant, bustling Downtown. The first step was the much-anticipated opening of the Adrienne Arsht Center for the Performing Arts (*see p190*). Unveiled in October 2006, it has already achieved the unthinkable and livened up a dodgy district of Downtown after dark. Designed by César Pelli, it's a postmodern showpiece of limestone and glass. As home to the city's key cultural groups (including the Florida Grand Opera and Miami City Ballet), it has brought a cultural buzz to the mean streets.

The regeneration scheme also includes the development of an 'entertainment district'. This is well under way: the restaurants and bars of Mary Brickell Village are heaving on a Saturday night, and the condos along Brickell Avenue are also a success. With its growing number of upscale, high-rise residential buildings – including three Philippe Starck-designed ICON buildings – Brickell is becoming known as the 'Manhattan of the South', largely colonised by young hipsters who are drifting away from South Beach. The sign that an area has actually arrived? Celebrity residents. Jennifer Lopez, Marc Anthony, Luis Miguel and José José are just a few of the boldface names who have recently conducted property deals in the 'hood.

EXPLORE

# Coral Gables

*Where Miami meets the Med.*

There is substance behind the boast of this self-ordained 'City Beautiful'. Coral Gables residents enjoy a peachy habitat of terracotta roofs, jewel-like colours and (mostly) lush vegetation. Once a tiny Miami suburb, founded in 1925 as one of the country's first planned communities, the city is now a spotless home for more than 175 multinational companies and a score of consulates and trade offices. A smattering of upscale commercial galleries, theatres and restaurants all contribute to the air of affluence. But for visitors, the main draw is the picturesque appeal of its Mediterranean Revival architecture, reflected in such landmarks as the Venetian Pool and the Biltmore Hotel.

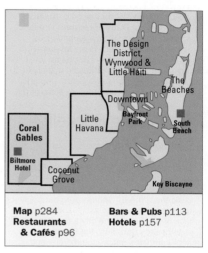

**Map** p284          **Bars & Pubs** p113
**Restaurants**       **Hotels** p157
**& Cafés** p96

**Map** p284      **Bars & Pubs** p113  
**Restaurants**      **Hotels** p157  
**& Cafés** p96

**EXPLORE**

## PARADISE RESTORED

Located a few miles south-west of Downtown, Coral Gables was the brainchild of quixotic developer George Merrick. The son of a prominent citrus farmer, Merrick returned to Miami from college in 1911 to find his home town in disarray, growing rapidly with no particular sense of either purpose or direction. As a man who disliked disorder, Merrick

### INSIDE TRACK
### BILTMORE HOTEL

The **Biltmore Hotel** (*see p157*) has been a prime destination for the holidaying elite since 1926. But it's a cultural centre for south Florida locals, too, hosting some of the area's don't-miss social events, including a weekly outdoor movie night, live music by the pool and wine tastings. The hotel is also home to the Biltmore Culinary Academy, North America's only hotel-based recreational cooking school, offering classes and workshops for kids and adults alike. Visit the website for a calendar of events.

managed to convince his uncle, artist Denman Fink, and landscape architect Frank Button to help him create a newer, prettier version of the town, drawing inspiration from the Garden City and City Beautiful movements of the late 19th and early 20th centuries, and the architectural styles of 16th-century Spain and Italy.

By the mid 1920s, the group had created one of the nation's first planned communities, a strange little town of tranquil loveliness with wide streets and lush greenery, full of gabled and tiled rooftops capping dainty buildings coloured in delicate pastel shades. Its streets were even given exotic names such as Valencia and Giralda, and adorned with fountains, plazas and arched entrance gateways.

But then, in 1926, a hurricane demolished thousands of homes and left Merrick's dream in tatters. While much of the Gables survived the storm, the local economy was destroyed. Suddenly, Merrick couldn't pay his bills; by 1928, in a final ignobility, the Coral Gables Commission removed him from the council of the community he had created, and he slunk off into a life of anonymity.

In the modernisation movement that swept the country after World War II, much of Merrick's work was disfigured. Some of his Downtown structures were demolished, while others had their original character disguised by ham-fisted renovations. Thankfully, though, things have changed.

In 1973, Coral Gables was one of the first cities in Florida to adopt a Historic Preservation Ordinance. Since then, most of the district's buildings have been designated as landmarks and are protected. The current civic zeal for preserving Coral Gables' bucolic character can, in fact, border on the obsessive. A hefty list of official 'dos and don'ts' applies to everything from replacing windows to how many guests can park their cars in front of a home for a dinner party without the host having to rent an off-duty police officer to supervise. Even the size of real estate 'For Sale' signs is regulated.

## MIRACLE MILE & AROUND

Coral Way is the major east–west street through the Gables. The section that runs down the central business district, from SW 37th to 42nd Avenues (Douglas to Le Jeune), is known as the **Miracle Mile** – somewhat exaggeratedly, given that it's actually no more than half a mile long. Once a bustling shopping zone full of local boutiques, nowadays it's just another Disneyfied US neighbourhood with all the requisite chains: Barnes & Noble, Starbucks, Einstein Bros Bagels et al. At least the very good **Actors' Playhouse** (280 Miracle Mile) maintains some semblance of the creative Gables days of old.

**Merrick House**. See p54.

A number of interesting spots have also survived in the streets immediately north of Miracle Mile. One is the old John M Stabile building at 265 Aragon Avenue, now the home of **Books & Books** (see p120), Miami's finest independent bookstore. Built in 1924, it was one of the area's first commercial structures. The diminutive building has a red barrel-tiled roof that is characteristic of the Mediterranean Revival style, and retains its tiled floor, beamed ceilings and fireplace. Across the street stands the **Old Fire House & Police Station** (285 Aragon Avenue, at Salzedo Street), now part of the Coral Gables Museum (1-305 603 8067, www.coralgablesmuseum.org). Combining simple Depression-era architecture with Mediterranean Revival accents, it's not a Merrick building; rather, it was constructed out of coral rock by the federal Works Progress Administration (WPA) in 1939.

A block north-west of the old station is the **Dream Theatre** (2308 Ponce de León Boulevard, at Giralda Avenue). Originally an outdoor silent-movie theatre built in 1926 and designed to emulate a Spanish bullring, it now houses the offices of Bank of America. Some of the original details remain, including the tower where the film projector once stood.

Across Alhambra Circle is the tiny **Hotel St Michel** (162 Alcazar Avenue; see p157). Used as an office after it was built in 1926, in the 1960s it was converted into the Hotel Seville and defaced with dropped ceilings, fluorescent lighting and Danish modern furniture. Then, in 1979, it was transformed into the ultra-quaint hotel it is today.

## ALONG CORAL WAY

Some of the Gables' most interesting residences lie on Coral Way, between Le Jeune (SW 42nd Avenue) and Granada Boulevard. The eastern end of this stretch is marked by **City Hall** (405 Biltmore Way, at S Le Jeune Road), a building that exemplifies Merrick's love of Spanish Renaissance style, although it was actually loosely based on the historic Philadelphia Exchange building. The stately edifice is encircled by 12 majestic columns and topped off with a three-tiered clock tower. Inside, there are paintings, photographs and advertisements from the town's early days.

Heading west beneath the massive banyan trees, Coral Way intersects with three other roads at **Balboa Plaza**, a typical example of a Gables plaza, featuring fountains, cisterns, gates and pergolas. South-west down De Soto Boulevard is the **Venetian Pool** (see p55), while sticking with Coral Way brings you to one of the oldest houses in the area, **Merrick House** (see p54), which is usually open to

**EXPLORE**

visitors; **Poinciana Place** (937 Coral Way, at Toledo Street) is another early structure, built by George Merrick for his wife, Eunice Peacock.

Two blocks further along is **Doc Dammers' House** (1141 Coral Way, at Columbus Boulevard), constructed in 1924 by Merrick for Edward 'Doc' Dammers, the city's first mayor and Merrick's major huckster when it came to selling Gables real estate. **Casa Azul** (1254 Coral Way, at Madrid Street), as its name implies, has a striking blue element: to be specific, a blue-glazed tile roof. Built in 1924, it was once the home of architect H George Fink, Merrick's cousin and the designer of many Gables buildings between 1921 and 1928.

### ★ Merrick House

*907 Coral Way, at Toledo Street (1-305 460 5361). Bus 24, Coral Gables Trolley. Tours* 1pm, 2pm, 3pm Wed, Sun. **Admission** $5; $1-$3 reductions; free under-6s. **No credit cards**. **Map** p284 C2.

The boyhood home of city founder George Merrick was designed by his mother, Althea, and built between 1900 and 1906. It offers a charming glimpse into 1920s Coral Gables, a colourful era when the City Beautiful that Merrick lovingly envisioned was starting to grow. Note the use of oolitic limestone (commonly called coral rock) quarried from the nearby Venetian Pool, the Dade County Pine and the gracious veranda. Inside, the house is filled with Merrick family artwork, photographs, furniture and memorabilia. Tours last 45 minutes. *Photo p53.*

## COUNTRY CLUB GABLES

Some of the town's oldest buildings, and Merrick's masterpieces, are located in the area known as the Country Club. This is the area on either side of the nine-hole **Granada Golf Course**, one of the first parts of Coral Gables to be completed. The main **Country Club Building** (997 North Greenway Drive, at Granada Boulevard) was originally intended to house guests who came to visit the development in search of homes. It's one of the best places to see Merrick's original architecture: the homes here are among the finest still standing. His attention to detail can be seen at 709 North Greenway Drive, while his obsession with Mediterranean Revival style is displayed further along the same road at nos.737, 803 and 1251.

Along the way is the impressive **Granada Plaza** (Granada Boulevard and Alhambra Circle), with its walls and pillars made of rough-cut rock, stucco and brick; vine-covered pergolas complement the matching pools situated at opposite ends of the plaza. At the far end of the golf course is Alhambra Circle and its striking 1924-built **Alhambra Water Tower** (2000 Alhambra Circle, at Ferdinand Street). Though it looks like a landlocked lighthouse, it is just another of Merrick's fanciful ideas: a steel tank that once supplied locals with drinking water.

One of the most beautiful elements of the Gables can be found at the far north-western end of the Country Club district, in the glorious

Lowe Art Museum.

**Country Club Prado Entrance** (SW 57th Avenue/Red Road and SW 8th Street/Tamiami Trail). This elaborate gateway (one of four such fancy entrances) has 20 elliptically arranged columns, all topped with vine-covered trellises. In the centre is a Spanish-style fountain that's surrounded by a reflecting pool.

## SOUTH OF CORAL WAY

From Balboa Plaza (*see p53*) on Coral Way, De Soto Boulevard angles south-west towards the Gables' other two golf courses, the Biltmore and the Riviera. En route is the spectacular **Venetian Pool** (*see below*), a former rock quarry converted in 1924 into a freshwater pool in the style of a Venetian lagoon.

A block west of the pool is the **De Soto Plaza** (at Sevilla Avenue, Granada and De Soto Boulevards), where three roads meet at a stepped fountain built of rough-cut rock. A column encircled by wrought-iron light fixtures rises majestically from the circular pool, and a steady stream of water gurgles from four sculptured faces. From here it's a short stroll on to the astonishing Mediterranean-style **Biltmore Hotel** (*see p157*) and the neighbouring **Coral Gables Congregational Church** (*see below*). To reach Coral Gables' other worthwhile sight, the **Lowe Art Museum** (*see below*), catch a southbound 56 bus from Le Jeune Road (SW 42nd Avenue).

### FREE Coral Gables Congregational Church

*3010 De Soto Boulevard, at Malaga Avenue (1-305 448 7421, www.coralgablescongregational. org). Metrorail Douglas Road, then 72 bus.* **Services** 11am Sun. **Map** p284 C2.

The first church in Coral Gables (and today one of the most liberal), this Mediterranean Revival building, with its lovely baroque belfry and sculpture over the main entrance, was designed as a replica of a church in Costa Rica and completed in 1924. In the summer it hosts a popular concert series that includes well-known names in jazz, classical and folk music, along with the odd barbershop quartet.

### Lowe Art Museum

*University of Miami, 1301 Stanford Drive, off Ponce de León Boulevard (1-305 284 3535, www.lowemuseum.org). Bus 52, 56.* **Open** 10am-4pm Tue-Sat; noon-4pm Sun. **Admission** $10; $3-$5 reductions. **Credit** (shop only) AmEx, MC, V. **Map** p284 F2.

The only museum in the area with a notable collection of Egyptian, Greek and Roman antiquities, the Lowe also features the Kress Collection of Renaissance and baroque art, plus galleries of pre-Columbian, Asian, African, Native American, European and American work. The European collection includes pieces by

**Venetian Pool.**

Monet and Gauguin; the South West Indian art collection contains textiles, baskets and other utilitarian objects; and the Art of Asia gallery has objects from China, Korea, Japan and South Asia.

### ★ Venetian Pool

*2701 De Soto Boulevard, at Toledo Street (1-305 460 5306, www.coralgables.com). Bus 24, 72, Coral Gables Trolley.* **Open** call for details. **Admission** $11.50; $6.60 reductions; under-3s not allowed in pool. **No credit cards. Map** p284 C2. Possibly the most beautiful swimming pool in the world, even if it *is* jammed on hot days. It combines an impossibly idyllic setting (tropical foliage, waterfalls, Italian architectural touches) with fresh water, replenished nightly in the summer months from a subterranean aquifer. Once a quarry, it was built in the 1920s as an exotic locale for swimming and entertainment. Back in the day, there were gondolas and orchestras, and movie stars such as Esther Williams and Johnny Weissmuller serenaded poolside dancers. Luckily for Joe Public, it's open to the masses seven days a week (but perhaps best avoided at weekends when it's heaving).

# Coconut Grove

*Miami's oldest enclave offers lush gardens and eclectic architecture.*

Once a bastion for free-thinking wheeler-dealers who enjoyed its serene bay setting, Coconut Grove still attracts free spirits and creative types, though they are increasingly overrun by their press agents and marketing teams. Still, the Grove continues to enjoy a reputation as a cultural (and cultured) enclave, even if chain stores reign supreme. Beyond the malls and boutiques, it's a pretty little neighbourhood with a few pockets that are full of character. This may not be immediately evident, given that this is a living, working community with all the concomitant symptoms: snarled traffic, a lack of cohesion and even elements of seediness. But that's Coconut Grove, and locals wouldn't have it any other way.

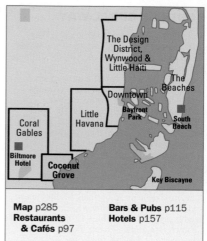

| | |
|---|---|
| **Map** p285 | **Bars & Pubs** p115 |
| **Restaurants** | **Hotels** p157 |
| **& Cafés** p97 | |

## ROOTS OF THE GROVE

Coconut Grove was originally settled by Bahamian seafarers and pioneer families. One of these early residents was Dr Horace P Porter. He was only around for a year (1873), but in that time he established a post office, which he named, rather lyrically, 'Cocoanut Grove'.

Porter moved on, the post office closed, and that might have been the end of it. But around the same time, an English pioneer, 'Jolly' Jack Peacock, settled in the area, and was so taken that he persuaded his brother Charles to join him. In one of those fortuitous moments that define south Florida's history, Commodore Ralph Munroe, visiting from New England, met the Peacocks. Munroe assured the brothers that if they built an inn, he would spread the word up north. In 1882, Charles, his wife Isabella and their three sons opened the Bay View House, later called the Peacock Inn, the first local hotel. On one of his many return visits, Munroe reopened the post office and repainted its sign, dropping the letter 'a' from its name. Quirky little Coconut Grove began to flower.

In 1886, Munroe moved here permanently, as did a community of sea enthusiasts, writers and intellectuals. Many migrant families from the Bahamas also arrived to work at the Peacock

Inn, and so Miami's earliest black settlement was founded. With its mix of white intellectuals and poor, uneducated islanders, the Grove gained a reputation for tolerance.

Part of the reason locals were able to avoid the kind of racial tensions that gripped the rest of the US was that residents were unified in fighting exploitation by outsiders. In 1919, the Groveites incorporated, hoping to fend off annexation by the growing city of Miami. They never stood a chance, and Miami consumed the Grove in 1925. Since then, independent-minded locals have banded together in repeated attempts to secede from Miami, each of which has failed. More recent attempts at secession have been hamstrung by the small matter of Miami City Hall being located in the Grove.

In the 1960s, the area was the heart of Miami's counterculture, a southern cousin to San Francisco's Haight-Ashbury and New York's Greenwich Village. In 1963, residents launched the Coconut Grove Arts Festival (*see* p27), which is now recognised as one of the leading arts events in the US.

Rising property prices in the 1980s and '90s forced most of the artists out, and since that time the Grove has changed considerably, much to the consternation of long-time residents. Squabbles between die-hard Groveites and newbie developers often make the headlines; though there are plenty of big box stores to be found (such as Home Depot), they haven't been built there without a good deal of resistance.

## CENTRAL COCONUT GROVE

Coconut Grove's centre of activity is focused on the intersection of Grand Avenue, McFarlane Road and Main Highway. It's an area busy with shops, offices and restaurants, and it has the benefit of being one of the best sections of Miami for walking – aside from South Beach's Lincoln Road, the Grove is just about as pedestrian-friendly as south Florida gets.

Along Grand Avenue, between Mary and Virginia Streets, is **Mayfair in the Grove** (*see p118*), once a fortress-like shopping mall, now a lovely open-air shopping centre. At the busy intersection of Grand Avenue, McFarlane Road and Main Highway is **CocoWalk** (*see p118*), a huge and hugely successful open-air mall that helped revitalise the Grove in the early 1990s. Like any American mall, the shops are more brand name than boutique; Gap, Victoria's Secret, Starbucks and the Cheesecake Factory are among the more than two dozen shopping and dining merchants you'll find here. If you want to dabble in local fashion, pay a visit to **Guayabera World** (1-305 477 4600) for a wide selection of its famed shirts for men, women and kids (*see also p62* **Get Shirty**).

When walking west on Grand Avenue, don't go too far inland, as beyond McDonald Street (aka SW 32nd Avenue) things can get a bit hairy. Instead, head south on vegetation-lined Main Highway. Two short blocks down, its chairs and tables crowding the junction with Commodore Plaza, is one of the Grove's most popular meeting places, the **GreenStreet Cafe** (*see p97*). A further block along, hidden behind a thicket of plants and trees, is the **Barnacle Historic State Park** (*see p58*), the original residence of pioneer Ralph Munroe.

Back on Main Highway is the now-shuttered **Coconut Grove Playhouse** (3500 Main Highway). Built as a movie house in the 1920s, the Spanish-style building became a theatre in the '50s. Samuel Beckett's *Waiting for Godot* had its US premiere here in 1956, but many in the battled audience left at the interval or queued at the box office to ask for refunds. The Playhouse is currently closed due to financial reasons but campaigners are trying to revive it.

About two blocks south, on Devon Road, is the Mission-style **Plymouth Congregational Church** (3400 Devon Road, at Main Highway), which dates back to 1917, and Dade County's first public schoolhouse. Built in 1887 out of lumber salvaged from shipwrecks, the schoolhouse was originally located across from the Peacock Inn and used as a Sunday school. It was moved to its present site in 1970.

Back on Main Highway, Bryan Memorial Church (3713 Main Highway, at Devon Road), built in the 1920s as a memorial to orator, politician, salesman and attorney William Jennings Bryan, is an unusual Byzantine-style building. Nearby is El Jardin at Carrollton School (3747 Main Highway). Constructed in 1917, it's the earliest-known complete Mediterranean Revival structure left in Miami.

**Barnacle Historic State Park**. *See p58*.

**EXPLORE**

Miami Science Museum.

Continue on Main Highway and you'll reach the end of Coconut Grove at the **Kampong** (4013 Douglas Road, at Bay Breeze Avenue), a seven-acre botanical garden that was once the home of botanist Dr David Fairchild, who went on to found the **Fairchild Tropical Garden** (*see p73*). As chief of the Seed Section of the US Department of Agriculture in the early 20th century, Fairchild travelled the world collecting plant specimens and bringing them back here. One of only two tropical plant research sites in the country, it's a stunning place, with an Indonesian-inspired house set by a lagoon. Scientists and world leaders such as Winston Churchill, Henry Ford, Thomas Edison and Dwight Eisenhower have all visited, as did Fairchild's father-in-law Alexander Graham Bell, who invented a device for extracting fresh water from sea water while staying here. To this day, botanists and horticulturalists come to the Kampong, now part of the Hawaii-based National Tropical Botanical Garden, to conduct research. It's open to the public for guided tours on Wednesdays and Saturdays at 10.30am from September to June. Self-guided tours are possible from Monday to Friday, by appointment only. Call 1-305 442 7169 or visit www.ntbg.org/gardens/kampong-tours.php for more information.

### Barnacle Historic State Park

*3485 Main Highway, at Charles Avenue (1-305 442 6886, www.floridastateparks.org/thebarnacle). Coconut Grove Circulator.* **Open** *9am-5pm Mon, Fri-Sun. Guided tours 10am, 11.30am, 1pm, 2.30pm Mon, Fri-Sun.* **Admission** *$2; free under-6s.* **No credit cards. Map** *p285 B2.*

Built in 1891 and named after the distinctive shape of its roof, Ralph Munroe's 'Barnacle' is the oldest home in Miami to remain on its original site. It was designed as a one-storey house facing Biscayne Bay. Three verandas and a skylight, which could be opened with a pulley, provided ventilation. The Munroe family continued to live at the Barnacle until 1973, when they sold the house and its furnishings to the state of Florida to be used as a museum. The pristine beauty of this bayfront pioneer home and its grounds is even more apparent now that it has been tragically sandwiched between two cramped luxury condo developments. You can tour the house and the grounds, or catch one of the regularly scheduled concerts on the lawn. *Photo p57.*

## ALONG S BAYSHORE DRIVE

Back at Grove ground zero (that is, the intersection of Grand Avenue and Main Highway), McFarlane Avenue slopes away south-east, down towards the waters of Biscayne Bay. Between MacFarlane and the water is **Peacock Park**, the original site of Bay View House, torn down in 1926. In the 1960s, hippies hung out here, getting stoned and playing frisbee. Now a new generation does the same, albeit only on weekends. Just across the street is the **Coconut Grove Public Library** (2875 McFarlane Road, at Peacock Park), the grounds of which contain the oldest marked grave in Dade County: that of Ralph Munroe's first wife, Eva, who died in 1882.

From McFarlane, **S Bayshore Drive** runs north parallel to the shoreline. Just a little way along is what used to be the old Pan American seaplane base and terminal (3500 Pan American

Drive, at S Bayshore Drive), the nation's busiest during World War II, when it was used as a US naval base. The building has now been home to **Miami City Hall** for nearly 60 years.

Beyond City Hall, check out the boats docked at **Dinner Key Marina**, the city's largest. If you're in the mood for a bayside frosty margarita or pina colada, check out **Monty's** (2550 S Bayshore Drive; *see p115*).

A little further up S Bayshore Drive, near the junction with the delightfully named Treasure Trove Lane, are the **Coral Reef Yacht Club** (no.2484) and the very exclusive **Biscayne Bay Yacht Club** (no.2540). The former is housed in a Mediterranean-style mansion built in 1923; the latter, Dade County's oldest social institution (founded by Ralph Munroe in 1887), is in a 1932 bungalow designed by prominent Miami architect Walter DeGarmo. There are more architecturally interesting historic homes just ahead (the 1600-2100 blocks), in an area known as Silver Bluff because of the large oolitic limestone formation beside the road.

Continue north, or hop on a no.48 bus, for the swankiest historic home of them all: **Vizcaya Museum & Gardens** (*see right*). Across from Vizcaya is the **Miami Science Museum** (*see below*), an affiliate of the Smithsonian Institution that just keeps growing. In March 2011, local entrepreneur Phillip Frost donated $35 million to the museum, allowing them to add a new structure – the Patricia and Phillip Frost Museum of Science – which is scheduled to open in Downtown Miami in 2015.

If you want to continue walking, switch a block east to beautiful **Brickell Avenue**. This last vestige of residential bayfront property before Downtown kicks in is part of what was once known as Millionaires' Row. It's still home to loaded folks: the rich businessmen have now been joined by a smattering of celebs, although the two most famous residents – Sylvester Stallone (100 SE 32nd Road, at Brickell Avenue) and Madonna (3029 Brickell Avenue, at Alice Wainwright Park) – have both moved out.

## Miami Science Museum

*3280 S Miami Avenue, at SW 32nd Road (1-305 646 4200, www.miamisci.org). Bus 48/Metrorail Vizcaya.* **Open** 10am-6pm daily. **Admission** $14.95; $10.95 reductions; free under-3s. **Credit** AmEx, MC, V. **Map** p283 F3.

It may not be the most technologically advanced museum, but where else are you greeted by a giant concrete sloth? The permanent exhibits are of mixed quality, while the displays compiled in association with the Smithsonian Institution are educational and occasionally fascinating. The recently opened Energy Playground – which features a range of interactive exhibits, including the Human YoYo and the Giant Lever – are fun for the kids. The adjoining

Planetarium is a bit old-school (it opened in 1966), but benefits from the free observatory viewings on the first Friday of each month (8.30-10pm), a favourite of south Florida teens for decades.

## ★ Vizcaya Museum & Gardens

*3251 S Miami Avenue, at SW 32nd Road (1-305 250 9133, www.vizcayamuseum.org). Bus 48/Metrorail Vizcaya.* **Open** 9.30am-4.30pm Mon, Wed-Sun. **Admission** $15, $5 reductions; free under-6s. **Credit** AmEx, MC, V. **Map** p283 F3.

Incongruous, unlikely and bizarre, Vizcaya is also an utter delight. An Italian Renaissance-style villa and gardens set on Biscayne Bay, it was built by F Burrall Hoffman, Diego Suarez and Paul Chalfin for Chicagoan industrialist and committed Europhile James Deering from 1914 to 1916. And a wildly extravagant spot it is too. Not only architecturally: the place is crammed with European antiques and works of decorative art spanning the 16th to the 19th centuries. All the furnishings at Vizcaya are just as they were in Deering's time, including early versions of such amenities as a telephone switchboard, a central vacuum-cleaning system, elevators and fire sprinklers. The East Loggia looks out on to the bay, the exit guarded by a vast telescope. Off to the south stretch Vizcaya's idyllic gardens, with fountains, pools, greenery, a casino and a maze. Strolling here on a quiet summer's day can be magical (not surprisingly, it's a popular spot for weddings). Another bonus is the café, which offers above-average lunches and, on Sundays, tea for two ($16) from 1pm to 4pm.

Vizcaya Museum & Gardens.

**EXPLORE**

# Little Havana

*Get a taste of Cuban culture.*

If you want to truly experience the sights, sounds and smells of classic Miami, there's no better place than Little Havana (aka La Pequeña Habana). Miami Cubans take great pride in this neighbourhood just west of Downtown – even if they don't live there. SW 8th Street (commonly known as Calle Ocho), the neighbourhood's main drag, and the surrounding area are a testament to the American dream pursued by the hundreds of thousands of Cubans who fled to Miami after Fidel Castro came to power in 1959. Vestiges of the lives they left behind are evident in the many Mediterranean-style coral rock and stucco houses – complete with cane rocking chairs on their pastel-painted front porches – reminiscent of Havana's Vedado and Miramar neighbourhoods.

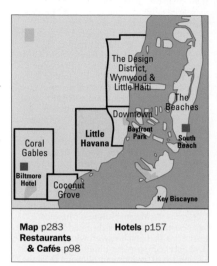

Map p283
Restaurants
& Cafés p98

Hotels p157

## MEMORIAL BOULEVARD

Most of Little Havana's major 'sights' are in the historical district between SW 12th and SW 17th Avenues, on and off Calle Ocho. Start your tour where **Memorial Boulevard** meets SW 13th Avenue. At the entrance to the boulevard is the **Brigade 2506 Memorial**, an eternal flame that burns in memory of those killed in the disastrous Bay of Pigs invasion. Further down, 19th-century Cuban revolutionary heroes José Martí and Antonio Maceo are commemorated for leading the battle for Cuba's independence from Spain. Other monuments include a bronze map of Cuba and a statue of the Virgin Mary, a figure of great importance to the largely Catholic Cuban-American community.

As you walk down the boulevard, you can't miss the large ceiba tree right in the centre. Practitioners of the Santería religion consider it sacred, leaving offerings of chicken bones and cloth bundles for their deities. Santería, a syncretistic religion that originated in the Caribbean, is based on the Yoruba culture of West Africa and incorporates elements of Roman Catholicism. *Botánicas* are stores catering to

Santería followers, selling religious articles, oils and candles and offering spiritualist readings by the local *santero*. **Botánica Negra Francisca** (1323 SW 13th Street, at SW 13th Avenue, 1-305 860 9328) is one of the most popular. A word of advice: be respectful. This is a religion, and its followers take their beliefs very seriously.

## CALLE OCHO

Today, the neighbourhood's classic homes are more likely to be inhabited by families from Central America or more recent and less affluent Cuban immigrants. Most of the early Cuban exiles have moved on to larger houses or more comfortable condos, particularly in Coral Gables, Hialeah, or further south in the suburb of Kendall. But some of their children and grandchildren, particularly those with an artistic bent, have been seduced by the faded charm and cheap prices of the neighbourhood and have started to return. The stretch of Calle Ocho from SW 12th to 16th Avenues is particularly vibrant, with the air of rich tobacco wafting from new cigar shops, and Cuban music coming from the open doors of Latin record stores. Stop by **Little Havana Cigar Factory & Lounge** (1501 SW 8th Street, at SW 15th Avenue, 1-305 541 1035) to smell, purchase and enjoy a wide selection of tobacco products. Although you can't buy an authentic Cuban cigar in the US, Little Havana's tobacco factories sell handmade cigars, many with tobacco grown from Cuban seed. **El Titan de Bronze** (1071 SW 8th Street, at SW 11th Avenue, 1-305 860 1412, www.eltitandebronze.com) hand-crafts its distinguished El Titan brand on-site. Elsewhere, **La Tradición Cubana** (1336 SW 8th Street, at SW 13th Court, 1-305 643 4005) sells premium-blended tobaccos rich in flavour and aroma.

For more souvenirs, wander into **Little Havana to Go** (1442 SW 8th Street, at SW 14th Avenue, 1-305 857 9720) for gifts with a particular Miami Cuban slant. These include a Havana phone book from 1958 (listing the names of many of Miami's exile families), T-shirts with Cuban pride slogans, landscape paintings of Havana and Fidel Castro playing cards (with an X through the image of El Comandante's face).

An informal atmosphere recalling rural Cuba can be found at **Los Pinareños Frutería** (1334 SW 8th Street, at 13th Avenue, 1-305 285 1135), a lush fruit and vegetable stand where you can eat the daily lunch special at a picnic table.

Máximo Gómez Park. *See p62.*

# ¿Hablas Spanglish?

*Tuning into radio bemba.*

You should be able to find someone in every Calle Ocho establishment who speaks some English, but it won't hurt to learn a bit of the lingua franca before you arrive. In this case it's Spanish, of course, in particular the Spanglish-inflected Cuban-American dialect sometimes referred to as Cubonics.

Once you get past the customary greetings – *hola* (hello) or *buenos días* (good day) – you'll have to know how to order the syrupy sweet coffee for which Calle Ocho is famous. The Cuban-American rocket fuel comes in four basic forms: *cafecito*, a shot of black coffee in a thimble-size plastic cup; *colada*, black coffee in a larger Styrofoam cup served with a stack of the thimble-size plastic cups – be warned, this is meant for sharing and drinking the entire *colada* yourself is comparable to mainlining speed); *cortadito*, a *cafecito* with a little milk; and *café con leche*, which is primarily a breakfast drink (though comforting any time), with more milk than coffee and, needless to say, lots of sugar.

Below is a brief glossary of Cuban words that could come in handy in a restaurant,

shop, club or simply hanging with your new Little Havana friends. *See also* p266 **¿Hablas español?**

**bibaporrú** Vicks VapoRub (popular remedy among Cubans)
**conflay** breakfast cereal
**cubanidad** 'Cubanness'; the qualities that make one Cuban; Cuban pride
**guajiro** a peasant or small farmer; someone who's naïve
**jewban** a Cuban of Jewish persuasion
**kenedito** A traitor (ie someone who acts like John F Kennedy. The word has its origins in the Bay of Pigs invasion
**kilo** a penny
**loca** flamboyantly gay
**peso** a dollar
**radio bemba** the grapevine; the means by which gossip spreads through the Cuban community
**rumba** party
**socio** buddy, bro
**tremenda rumba** great party
**windshiwaipers** windscreen wipers
**yuca** upwardly mobile Cuban American

# Get Shirty

*Pull on some Cuban chic.*

Nothing says Havana (Little or otherwise) quite like the *guayabera* shirt. These days, however, the ubiquitous symbol of Cubanismo isn't just the preserve of old men hanging at the *cafecito* stand in Little Havana. No, the shirt has been caught up in a wave of Latin chic. It now shows up on revellers in Berlin nightclubs and covering the torsos of stars such as Marc Anthony.

Today's *guayaberas* come in all colours bright or cool, with extra pockets or elaborate stitching, and tailor-made in linen or off the rack in pure polyester, but plain white is the classic style (and the favourite of tourists coming home from Miami sporting new tans) – practical yet smart and perfect for the intense tropical heat. Originally made of cotton, the shirt can be long- or short-sleeved, is worn loose and untucked, and traditionally features four pockets on the front and vertical embroidery (it has also been noted that the design

of the shirt can hide a *cerveza* belly and make any man look manly).

Like so many things involving Cuba, the shirt has had a long and sometimes controversial history – Mexicans contest the fact that it's a Cuban shirt at all. However, most agree it originated in Cuba about 200 years ago, when it was sewn, depending on which version you believe, either by a poor rural wife who added extra pockets so her husband could carry guavas or *guayabas* (hence *guayabera*), or by a rich landowner's wife who added extra pockets for her husband so he could carry various sundries while checking out his estate by the River Yayabo (hence *yayabera*). Whatever the truth, farm workers began donning the handy lightweight shirt and the style has now spread to include such unlikely spin-offs as tuxedo *guayaberas* and office *guayaberas*, many of them now made in Miami.

At the corner of SW 14th Avenue, the combined clatter of clacking domino tiles and Spanish chatter announces **Máximo Gómez Park** (*photo p61*). Cuban retirees have been gathering on this corner to play dominoes and drink coffee for decades; it was designated a city park in 1976 and is popularly called Domino Park. In the late '80s, due to the presence of numerous vagrants, winos and drug dealers, the park was enclosed and membership rules were enforced. (Note that it is still closed to anyone under 55; proof of age is required.)

The **Tower Theater** (1508 SW 8th Street, at SW 15th Avenue; *see p168*), half a block west of the park, was the only movie theatre in Miami to show English-language films with Spanish subtitles in Little Havana's heyday. These days it is Miami's only theatre dedicated exclusively to foreign language films. Next door to the theatre, stop for a super-sweet Cuban coffee at the window counter of **Exquisito Restaurant** (1510 SW 8th Street, at SW 15th Avenue, 1-305 643 0227, www.exquisitorestaurant.com), a family-run restaurant that has been in the same location for more than 30 years. If you're hungry, order a *palomilla* steak with rice and beans.

As you walk up and down SW 8th Street, you'll notice that the sidewalk is marked with pink marble stars, making up the **Calle Ocho Walk of Fame**. This Little Havana version of the Hollywood attraction began as a way to recognise Cuban celebrities. Cuba's most famous salsa singer, Celia Cruz, who died in 2003, was the first to be immortalised in 1987, and since then singers and soap stars from all over Latin America have been honoured. It's been proven that anyone perceived to show affinity with Castro risks having their star removed.

Another Little Havana shrine can be found a few blocks north; **Casa Elián** (2319 NW 2nd Street, at SW 23rd Avenue; open 10am-6pm Sun; admission free but donations encouraged) is the house formerly belonging to the relatives of Elián González, the six-year-old boy who was rescued from a raft at sea in November 1999 and whose plight became a Cuban exile *cause célèbre*. To the Miami Cubans' chagrin, Elián was sent back to Cuba and his father in 2000. The house is now a museum to what the exiles perceive as the child's martyred fate. Pathos-laden exhibits include Elián's toys, as well as poems dedicated to him and hundreds of collaged photographs of the boy. For a look at another Cuban-American conflict, pay a visit to the **Bay of Pigs Museum** (*see below*).

Cubans everywhere can at least usually manage to agree on one thing: Cuban music. Record stores on Calle Ocho stock albums by pre-revolutionary Cuban legends, as well as contemporary music from the island and the latest by US-Latin pop stars.

Cuban sartorial style really boils down to one item of clothing: the *guayabera* (*see p62* **Get Shirty**). Plenty of places along Calle Ocho sell the shirts, but for the greatest range jump on a no.8 bus and ride way west to **La Casa de las Guayaberas** (5840 SW 8th Street, at SW 58th Avenue, 1-305 266 9683). In addition to classic men's styles and a tailor-made service, the store makes a flattering women's version.

Also out this way, a 15-minute ride from central Little Havana (take the no.8 bus), is the neighbourhood's most famous culinary landmark, **Versailles** (3555 SW 8th Street; *see p98*). This huge, mirror-lined restaurant is packed with loud families on weekends, and during the day older Cuban men hang around the coffee counter outside and talk (Cuban) politics. The food may be forgettable, but, like the rest of Little Havana, at its best this kitschy Cuban exile stalwart is truly memorable.

#### FREE **Bay of Pigs Museum**
*1821 SW 9th Street, at SW 18th Avenue (1-305 649 4719). Bus 8, Little Havana Connection.* **Open** 9am-4pm Mon-Sat. **Admission** free. **No credit cards. Map** p283 C1.
This museum has a small but interesting collection of ephemera and memorabilia relating to the failed Bay of Pigs invasion of 1961, when a small brigade of Cuban exiles in Miami was trained by the CIA as

Frost Art Museum at FIU.

part of a covert operation to invade the island and restore US interests. But the 1,300-strong force, known as Brigade 2506, was met by the Cuban army soon after landing at the Bahía de Cochinos (Bay of Pigs). Almost 100 were killed and the rest – including the father of pop singer Gloria Estefan – were taken prisoner. Perhaps the most notable exhibit is a Brigade 2506 flag held up by President John F Kennedy during a speech at the Orange Bowl in 1962, welcoming the survivors back to Miami.

### TAMIAMI TRAIL

SW 8th Street/Calle Ocho continues arrow-straight out east of the city and all the way across southern Florida, where, as Route 41 – 'the Tamiami Trail' – it bisects the Everglades, before swinging north up the Gulf Coast. As the highway approaches the outskirts of the city, it passes by the Florida International Modesto A Maidique Campus, the location for the **Frost Art Museum** (*see below*). While this is some distance from Little Havana, the campus is the terminus for the main Little Havana bus service, the no.8.

#### ★ FREE **Frost Art Museum at FIU**
*10975 SW 17th Street (1-305 348 2890, www. thefrost.fiu.edu). Bus 8.* **Open** 10am-5pm Tue-Sat; noon-5pm Sun. **Admission** free. **No credit cards. Map** p279.
Known for its Latin American and 20th-century American art, FIU's museum is housed in a striking building designed by Yann Weymouth of HOK, the prestigious architectural firm. An airy, three-storey atrium leads to nine different galleries, which show six to eight exhibitions each year, exploring traditional themes from a contemporary perspective. Past exhibitions include a groundbreaking show on Haitian sculpture, both folk and postmodern, and a study of Florida artists. Adjacent to the main building is the museum's Sculpture Park, where works include major pieces by Anthony Caro, Arnie Zimmerman, Steve Tobin and Jack Henry; it's recognised as one of the country's most important 3D art collections.

EXPLORE

# The Design District, Wynwood & Little Haiti

*Slumming it in style.*

While South Beach is still a destination with a capital D, coolhunters are now also venturing into once-forbidden neighbourhoods across the Julia Tuttle Causeway. Formerly best avoided, the Design District, Wynwood, Little Haiti and now the Upper East Side are enjoying a renaissance. In the first two, reputations as bad-'hoods-made-good add edge to what are otherwise areas for high-end boutique and gallery outings, plus a growing number of hip bars and eateries. Some 20 blocks to the north, Little Haiti is still largely a frontier too far – but give it time. It remains shabby and grittily ethnic, and not in a romantic way: a few bright murals do little to hide the area's poverty and desperation. Intrepid explorers will encounter a strange mix of *botánicas*, Haitian bakeries, a British pub and a working farm. Leave the Armani shades at home or be prepared to lose them.

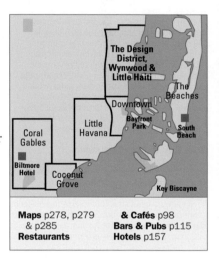

**Maps** p278, p279 & p285
**Restaurants**
**& Cafés** p98
**Bars & Pubs** p115
**Hotels** p157

## THE DESIGN DISTRICT

Vastly out of proportion with its influence on the arts and culture scene, the Design District fills a grid a mere five streets (NE 36th to NE 41st Street) by two (NE 2nd Avenue to N Miami Avenue). The area started as a pineapple grove, and evolved into what became known as Decorators' Row during the building boom of the early 1920s, when home-design stores lined its streets. The neighbourhood fell on hard times in the late '80s, when crime drove many businesses north. It's still not perfectly polished, but it's getting there. Rising retail rents in South Beach have lured an increasing number of high-end luxury retailers to the area: Prada, Cartier, Louis Vuitton, Hermès and Christian Louboutin have all recently set up shop. As its name attests, the area still attracts the type of tenants it enjoyed during its heyday: fine furnishings and kitchen and bathroom showrooms. Until recently, the District catered to 'the trade', open only to interior designers and their clients. These days, though, establishments are open to anyone, usually from 9am to 5pm weekdays and 11am to 4pm Saturday (though some galleries are also closed on Mondays). For more on where to shop and what to buy in the Design District, *see p131* **Shopping by Design**.

Where there's design, there's usually art, and galleries occupy many premises here. **De La Cruz Collection Contemporary Art Space** (23 NE 41st Street, at N Miami Avenue, 1-305 576 6112, www.delacruzcollection.org) shows work by local and international figures.

Thanks to developer and art collector Craig Robins, a South Beach pioneer who also owns about 40 per cent of the Design District's property, a good deal of public art (most of it created by locals) is also on display. Rosario Marquardt and Roberto Behar's zany open-air *Living Room*, complete with couch, lamps and curtains, is on the corner of NE 40th Street and N Miami Avenue. Even the Marc Newson-constructed fence running along NE 2nd Avenue outside the prestigious Design and Architecture Senior High School (DASH) is a work of art; its strategically placed metal slats create a series of changing patterns as you stroll along. The majestic 1921 **Moore Building** (4040 NE 2nd Avenue, at NE 40th Street) is the historic heart of the district. Originally a furniture showroom, it's now the retail home to interior designer and potter extraordinaire Jonathan Adler (1-305 576 0200, www.jonathanadler.com) and a rentable space for special events and parties (many of which happen during Art Basel).

Complementing the art and design are food and drink. Pick of the bunch is sleek foodie favourite **Michael's Genuine Food & Drink** (*see p100*). **South Street** (4000 NE 2nd Avenue, at 40th Street, 1-305 573 5474, www.southstreetmiami.com), a cool new neo-soul food restaurant and bar, is housed in an elegant old post office building. **Crumb on Parchment** (3930 NE 2nd Avenue, at NE 39th Street, 1-305 572-9444) is a cosy café and bakery from local culinary hero Michelle Bernstein (proprietor of Michy's on the Upper East Side; *see p100*).

## WYNWOOD

South of the Design District is Wynwood (which is more clunkily known as the Wynwood Arts District). Running all the way to the northern fringes of Downtown, it's an area roughly bounded by NE 2nd Avenue to the east, I-95 to the west, I-395 to the south and NE 36th to the north. From the Design District you can approach Wynwood by ambling south on traffic-heavy N Miami Avenue, although it might be safer to catch the bus (nos.9 or 10) south down NE 2nd Avenue.

Formerly a working-class area with a large Puerto Rican population, Wynwood is one of the city's newest trendy neighbourhoods. Many of its erstwhile factories and warehouses are now inhabited by creative types – more than 50 galleries, artist's studios, art complexes, private collections and museums call the district home. The proximity of the **Adrienne Arsht Center for the Performing Arts** (*see p190*) can only help to hasten the gentrification process.

Area pioneers include the **Bakehouse Art Complex** (561 NW 32nd Street, at NW 5th Avenue, 1-305 576 2828, www.bacfl.org), a former bread factory converted into studios for painters, sculptors, photographers and printmakers; the **Rubell Family Collection** (*see below*); and the **Margulies Collection** at the Warehouse (*see below*), home to photography, video, sculpture and installations.

### FREE **Margulies Collection**
*591 NW 27th Street, at NW 6th Avenue (1-305 576 1051, www.margulieswarehouse.com). Bus 3, 9, 10, 16, J.* **Open** 11am-4pm Wed-Sat. **Credit** AmEx, MC, V. **Map** p285 F1.
The Margulies Collection is a giant of the scene. It showcases contemporary and vintage photography, video, sculpture and installations from prominent Miami collector Martin Z Margulies. A recent airing of his sculpture collection included pieces by Miró, Andy Warhol and Roy Lichtenstein; photography features the likes of Cindy Sherman and Walker Evans.

### ★ **Rubell Family Collection**
*95 NW 29th Street, at NW 1st Avenue (1-305 573 6090, www.rfc.museum). Bus 2, 9, 10.* **Open** 10am-6pm Wed-Sat. **Admission** $10; $5 reductions. **Credit** MC, V. **Map** p285 E2.
One of the country's top private collections of contemporary art, this is a bold assortment of avant-garde work: conceptual art, photography, sculpture and painting are all represented. Owned by brother and sister Jason and Jennifer Rubell, the collection features important works by Jean-Michel Basquiat, Keith Haring, Cindy Sherman, Jeff Koons, Andy Warhol and Damien Hirst. It's located in a former DEA confiscation centre – something that the late Steve Rubell, founder of Manhattan's infamous Studio 54 and uncle to Jennifer and Jason – would have found hugely amusing.

---

## INSIDE TRACK ART PARTY

Art is always more interesting with a drink in your hand – which is how you'll view the latest exhibitions at the 50-plus galleries, studios, museums and event spaces that open their doors during Wynwood's **Second Saturday Art Walk**. Taking place on the second Saturday of the month, this evening art stroll offers a feast for eyes and gullet. Visit www.wynwoodmiami.com for more information.

**EXPLORE**

## LITTLE HAITI

Little Haiti is 20 blocks north of the Design District, but feels a world away – there are no chi-chi interiors to be found here. Yet some visitors appreciate its rawness. Its official borders are between NE 55th and NE 70th Streets around NE 2nd Avenue. To get from one neighbourhood to the other, ride the no.9 or no.10 bus on NE 2nd Avenue. The bulk of commerce and activity takes place on a few busy streets, notably NE 2nd Avenue and NE 54th Street, both of which can be explored on foot. Be aware that crime is a concern here, so dress down – and don't come calling after dark.

The neighbourhood's history dates back to the late 1890s, when it was the site of citrus groves and strawberry fields, and known as Lemon City. Since the late 1970s it has been home to thousands of Haitians, who fled from the brutal dictatorships of François 'Papa Doc' Duvalier and his son, 'Baby Doc'.

Controversially, there exists in Miami an unspoken distinction between Cuban exiles and other immigrants. There's no question the US government treats Haitian immigrants (seen as fleeing poverty) differently from their Cuban counterparts (who are viewed as fleeing communism). Unlike Cuban refugees, the Haitians – who packed shaky wooden boats and took to the seas in a mass exodus during the early 1980s – weren't welcomed with open arms. It took survivors years to establish a foothold, but this is now a vibrant community.

By day, Little Haiti bubbles with colour and spirit. Bright murals depicting Caribbean landscapes, political leaders and voodoo symbols decorate storefront walls and public buildings, while street names commemorate Haitian heroes. However, there is no disguising the poverty. Little Haiti is plagued by illegal trash-dumping, crack houses and homelessness. Typical dwellings are cramped apartments and shabby wood-frame houses with chickens roaming around the front yards. Inhabitants often hold two menial jobs to make ends meet for both their households, the one in Miami and the one back in Haiti. At night, immigrants fill local school classrooms, learning to speak and write in English. Otherwise, both Creole and French are often spoken in the small record stores, *botánicas* (shops that supply the accoutrements of voodoo and Santería), churches and eateries that line main NE 2nd Avenue.

'Guidebook' sights are few. Instead, satisfy appetites with dishes of *griot* (fried pork), rice, plantains and seafood at the super-cheap **Chez Le Bebe** (114 NE 54th Street, at NE 1st Court, 1-305 751 7639, www.chezlebebe.com). One caveat: you get what you pay for, so expect slow service and cramped quarters.

A failed attempt at celebrating Haitian culture languishes at the shuttered **Caribbean Marketplace** at 5927 NE 2nd Avenue, an erstwhile vendor of Haitian primitive arts and crafts opened in 1990, perhaps before its time. Inspired by Port-au-Prince's century-old Iron Market and winner of a 1991 American Institute of Architects award for its bold design and splashy bright colours, the shopping centre, located in a neighbourhood too many thought of as unsafe, failed to draw tourists.

Still going strong, on the other hand, is **Earth 'n' Us Farm** (7630 NE 1st Avenue, at NE 76th Street, 1-305 754 0000, www.earthnusfarm.org). Founded in the late 1970s by Ray Chasser, this working farm (with goats, chickens and all the trimmings) is the last known address of a lost hippie tribe, and a purveyor of exceptional honey. A variety of rural-themed and New Age social and cultural activities takes place here. It isn't just the hippie nature of Ray's that is out of place here, it's the incongruously rural feel in such an intensely urban environment. Almost as incongruous is the shabby **Churchill's Pub** (*see p115*), a rock venue that serves English beer and shows UK football on satellite.

Attempts to improve the area's reputation and celebrate its culture are on the rise. In 2009, the **Little Haiti Cultural Center** (212-260 NE 59th Terrace, at NE 2nd Avenue; 1-305 960 2969) opened to offer a range of family-friendly arts-focused activities and events. The Cultural Center also recently banded together with events organiser YO Miami and other area advocates to introduce the Little Haiti Sunday Stroll (noon-6pm Sundays; www.yo-miami.com), a weekly street fair presented as an alternative to Wynwood's Second Saturday Art Walk (*see p65* **Inside Track**).

## THE UPPER EAST SIDE

The Upper East Side is a textbook case for gentrification. In parts, it is seedy and slightly scary – the stretch of Biscayne Boulevard between 50th Street and NE 79th Street is overrun with hookers, drug dealers and cockroach motels. But the kitsch retro architecture of said motels, with their playful neon signs, has captivated historians. Thanks to their efforts, the area has recently been declared a historical preservation area, otherwise known as the MiMo District, in reference to the Mid-century Modern architecture. A young, edgy arts crowd is buying up bungalows on the scruffy side streets, and funky shops and restaurants are moving in, led by upscale eaterie **Michy's** (*see p100*), gourmet hot dog joint **Dogma Grill** and cool pizzeria **Andiamo** (for both, *see pp98-99*).

# Profile Wynwood Walls

*Taking art to the streets.*

While Miami is home to Art Basel (*see p24*), arguably one of the world's most highfalutin art fairs, it also harbours its fair share of DIY creative types. Legendary neighbourhood revitaliser Tony Goldman – the man responsible for seeing the cultural potential in once-undesirable areas such as Philadelphia's Midtown Village – recognised this better than anyone. After transforming New York's SoHo from a downtrodden warehouse district to a vibrant loft-lover's paradise in the '70s, he set his sights southwards.

First came Miami Beach: then a hotbed of crime and grime, Goldman saw the covered-up beauty of this oceanfront locale and purchased 18 of its art deco buildings over the course of 18 months, beginning in 1986. He widened the sidewalks on Ocean Drive, opened the Park Central Hotel and the Hotel of South Beach, and helped turn the area into a world-class destination for a slice of (sometimes debauched) fun in the sun.

But Goldman wasn't done with Miami just yet; he next turned his attention across the MacArthur Causeway, to the working-class, warehouse-filled Wynwood district. Like SoHo before it, Goldman saw the neighbourhood's nondescript and decaying storefronts as the perfect blank canvas for the area's artists. In 2009, that vision became a reality with Wynwood Walls.

Launched during Art Basel and located on NW 2nd Avenue between NW 25th and 26th Streets, what began as a few commissioned murals to beautify the area has morphed into the city's only outdoor street art park, featuring more than 40 murals from a roster of world-renowned artists, including Shepard Fairey, Ryan McGinness,

Kenny Scharf, How and Nosm, Faile, Retna, the Date Farmers and Liqen. In late 2012, a major installation was added to the park as a tribute to Goldman, who passed away in September: the Kenny Scharf Garden (2219 NW 2nd Avenue, at NW 22nd Street) features a landscaped garden, fountain, large-scale mural and Scharf's own 1960s-style Airstream trailer, complete with Day-Glo interior. Fairey also reworked his mural outside Goldman's Wynwood Kitchen & Bar (*see p102*) to incorporate an image of the man himself.

Wynwood Walls is open to the public all year round and admission is free (11am-11pm Mon-Sat, noon-6pm Sun, www.wynwoodwalls.com). You can even take home a piece of Wynwood – the GO! Shop features a curated collection of limited edition prints from Wynwood artists.

**EXPLORE**

# North Miami & Beyond

*From grim suburbia to greener pastures.*

It's getting harder and harder to ignore North Miami. That's because, along with Downtown Miami and midtown, the growth here – from both a residential and cultural perspective – is booming. The impressive collection and calendar of special events at the Museum of Contemporary Art of North Miami are luring people out of the city and into 'the suburbs' – quite some feat, especially when you consider the stiff competition from Wynwood. At the same time, Whole Foods is eyeing up the neighbourhood for its next upscale health-food superstore. But the ultimate proof that

North Miami is buzzing may be that it's where famous-for-nothing celeb sisters Kim and Kourtney Kardashian chose to hole up while filming their newest Miami-set reality show. The mayor even gave them the keys to the city.

EXPLORE

## NORTH MIAMI

The development bug has taken a juicy bite out of North Miami. Case in point: after years of false starts, the city's largest piece of real estate, Biscayne Landing on the shores of Biscayne Bay, is poised to finally break ground. The project will feature a vast luxury housing complex made up of more than 3,400 residential units, plus restaurants and shops, from big box stores to no fewer than four car dealerships.

If you go west on the city's main drag, NE 125th Street, you'll pass through the downtown North Miami area. Here, trendy stores have started to pop up, from novelty gift shops to antiques dealers, and – the ultimate mark of mainstream gentrification – a Starbucks. Art galleries are opening too. Downtown North Miami even has a cute nickname: the NoMi Arts, Design and Culture District, bordered by 125th Street between NE 6th and NE 10th Avenues, NE 6th Avenue between NE 123rd and NE 125th Streets, and West Dixie Highway from 123rd Street to NE 135th Street. For North Miami's best galleries, *see pp126-127*.

Greener pleasures can be enjoyed in **Greynolds Park** (17530 West Dixie Highway, 1-305 945 3425, www.miamidade.gov/parks/ parks/greynolds.asp), a haven for picnickers and ornithologists north of Oleta River State Recreation Area (*see p43*).

Further north is **Aventura**, home to many a wealthy woman with a newly sculpted face and bod, multiple black AmEx cards and a propensity for running people off the road with her big, black Caddy Escalade. Some claim that the tiny, congested but well-manicured city of Aventura (also known as 'Oyventura' due to its large New York Jewish population and 'Aventorture' by those who loathe its gridlock) is the only city in America to be named after a mall. Indeed, **Aventura Mall** (*see p117*) is the city's main attraction.

### Ancient Spanish Monastery

*16711 W Dixie Highway, at NE 167th Street (1-305 945 1461, www.spanishmonastery.com). Bus 3, V.* **Open** 10am-4pm Mon-Sat; 11-4pm Sun. **Admission** $5; $2 reductions. **No credit cards. Map** p278.

Built in the mid 1100s near Segovia, Spain, this monastery was occupied by Cistercian monks for 700 years before it was converted to a granary and stable. In 1924, newspaper magnate William Randolph Hearst purchased the cloisters and outbuildings, and had the structure dismantled and shipped to the United States. It was intended for his California coastal mansion, Hearst Castle, but Hearst had financial problems, so most of his collection was sold at auction, and the stones remained in a Brooklyn warehouse for 26 years before finally being purchased and reassembled at a cost of $1.5 million. Today, this Romanesque structure is an anomalous oasis in a noisy area. Things to look out for include a life-size statue of the Spanish king Alfonso VII (the monastery was originally constructed to commemorate one of his victories over the Moors) and a couple of attractive round stained-glass windows. The monastery is a favourite spot for weddings – so much so that it's often closed to the public, especially on Sundays; call in advance before setting out.

### FREE Arch Creek Park & Museum
*1855 NE 135th Street, at Biscayne Boulevard (1-305 944 6111, www.miamidade.gov/parks/parks/arch_creek.asp). Bus 3, 28.* **Open** 9am-5pm Wed-Sun. **Admission** free. **No credit cards.**
Created around a natural limestone bridge formation that was once part of an important Indian trail, this small park has a museum and nature centre containing artefacts left by natives as they passed over the arched bridge. Naturalists are on hand to point out native birds, animals and insects. It's a perfect place for gazing at the natural world around you, and allegedly also a hotspot for supernatural activity; park guides lead nature walks every Saturday and ghost tours each Wednesday (call ahead for reservations). *Photo p70.*

### ★ Museum of Contemporary Art of North Miami
*770 NE 125th Street, at NE 8th Avenue (1-305 893 6211, www.mocanomi.org). Bus 10, 16, G.* **Open** 11am-5pm Tue, Thur-Sat; 1-9pm Wed; noon-5pm Sun; 7-10pm last Fri of mth. **Admission** $5; $3 reductions; free under-12s. **Credit** (over $10) AmEx, MC, V. **Map** p278.
Aiming to be a forward-thinking museum and to discover new artists, MOCA (or, even more cutely, MoCaNoMi) maintains a busy schedule, presenting exhibitions in its Charles Gwathmey-designed structure. MOCA's permanent collection now numbers approximately 600 works from artists such as John Baldessari, Louise Nevelson and Gabriel Orozco. High-profile exhibits and artists' discussions with personalities such as Yoko Ono put MOCA firmly at the forefront of contemporary art on the East Coast. Free outdoor concerts are given at 8pm on the last Friday of each month as part of Jazz at MOCA, a popular music series. *Photo p71.*

## MIAMI SPRINGS

In the 1920s, Glenn Curtiss, a daredevil aviation pioneer who'd won recognition by flying from Albany to New York a decade earlier, parlayed

**Ancient Spanish Monastery.**

EXPLORE

**Arch Creek Park & Museum**.
*See p69.*

**EXPLORE**

fame into fortune by using his celebrity status to attract investors to southern Florida. He and partner James Bright divided their 100,000-acre land grab into three communities: **Hialeah** (*see right*), **Opa-Locka** (*see p71*) and Country Club Estates, now **Miami Springs**.

While heavy industrial traffic surges past, this tiny municipality is largely untouched by the urban behemoth surrounding it. It is a quiet, scenic bedroom community most notable for its collection of homes in the style of the Pueblo Indians, and for the strong history of civic activism among its residents. However, other than for golf-lovers, who may be drawn to the **Miami Springs Golf & Country Club** (650 Curtiss Parkway, at Pinecrest Drive, 1-305 805 5180, www.miamispringsgolfcourse.com),

there is little of note here besides the curiosity of the municipality's ability to maintain its small-town sensibilities.

## HIALEAH

While Little Havana (*see pp60-63*) may be the spiritual home of Miami's Cuban-American community, Hialeah is their residential neighbourhood of choice (Cubans and Cuban Americans account for more than 73 per cent of the city's population). Bordered by the Miami Canal to the south and Le Jeune Road to the east, it's the largest of the outlying Miami communities and is less a structured city than a seemingly endless world of concrete, strip malls, neon signs and eateries. Hialeah's traffic is gridlocked, its politics are incendiary and, for some unknown reason, the district is home to a disproportionately large number of warehouses and manufacturers. Yet there's not one skyscraper within its city limits.

In addition, getting around Hialeah is daunting. Street numbers are out of sync with the rest of the county, and, every year, more and more streets are renamed after obscure figures from Cuban and Latin American history.

The area's past is also bound up in horse racing. Developer Glenn Curtiss laid out **Hialeah Park** (2200 E 4th Avenue, at E 21st Street, 1-305 885 8000, www.hialeahparkracing. com), an elaborate course, in 1925. Covering 230 acres, it was conceived as a resort and modelled after European courses such as Longchamps in France. Hailed as the most beautiful track in the world, it boasts a Mediterranean Revival

### INSIDE TRACK
### ENCHANTED FOREST

True to its name, the **Enchanted Forest Elaine Gordon Park** (1725 NE 135th Street, near NE 17th Avenue, 1-305 895 1119) is a hidden oasis on North Miami's Arch Creek, offering 22 acres of lush greenery, bike paths, hiking trails, pony rides and other activities. The nearby Museum of Contemporary Art North Miami (*see p69*) regularly offers Enchanted with Art classes, with would-be Warhols of all levels using the park as a muse for their masterpieces (check the museum's online calendar for details).

clubhouse, pink-and-turquoise buildings and lush landscaped gardens, complete with lake, islands and flocks of pink flamingos. The racing stopped in 2001, but preservation groups won the fight to save it. A new era of racing began when the park reopened in late 2009.

Hialeah is worth a stroll if you want to soak up the Cuban flavour. There are several inexpensive cafés and *bodegas*, and little shops specialising in authentic pre-Castro Cuban memorabilia and the ubiquitous but Miami-stylish *guayabera* (*see p62* **Get Shirty**).

Bounding the northern edge of Hialeah is **Amelia Earhart Park** (*see p162*), a family-oriented swathe of greenery with five lakes. The park is named after the famous solo flyer who, in 1937, stopped at neighbouring Opa-Locka Airport (then a US Navy airbase) on her ill-fated attempt to fly around the world.

Despite possible first impressions of foreboding – and beyond the language barrier and difficult street names – Hialeah, like Little Havana, is not intimidating at all.

## OPA-LOCKA

Glenn Curtiss saved travel writers everywhere much fishing around for adjectives when he called Opa-Locka the 'Baghdad of Dade County'. A fanciful description, perhaps, but one not a million miles from the truth, at least architecturally speaking. Curtiss had a fascination with the Arabian fantasies of the tales of the *Thousand and One Nights*, and he commissioned his architect, Bernhardt Emil Muller, to build a city around that theme. Boy, did he ever deliver.

When he set out to create his theme park with residents, Curtiss doubtless hoped it would stay fanciful and well off. It hasn't. The Opa-Locka of the 21st century is economically deprived and long gone to seed, with little to offer its largely poor locals. Unsurprisingly, it's a neighbourhood blighted by crime, and real care should be taken by visitors. It goes without saying, you shouldn't hang around after dark.

Despite the efforts of city planners to swamp Curtiss's vision, Opa-Locka retains much of the incongruous pantomime-Arab architecture for which it was initially famed. (The name comes from the Seminole Indian 'Opatishawockalocka' – or 'wooded hummock' – but with the tongue-twisting 'tishawocka' removed to create something that to Curtiss looked and sounded like it might pass as Persian or Arabic.) **Opa-Locka Station** (490 Ali Baba Avenue), with its arched arcades alongside sadly silent tracks, and the **Hurt Building** (480 Opa-Locka Boulevard) are both notable surviving examples of the Curtiss-Muller style, although nothing tops the ridiculous Toytown dome-and-minaret ensemble of **Opa-Locka City Hall** (780 Fisherman Street, 1-305 953 2868), which looks like the set for a low-budget production of *Aladdin*. But, these buildings aside, there is precious little reason to head this far north.

**EXPLORE**

**Museum of Contemporary Art of North Miami.** *See p69.*

# South Miami & Beyond

*Head out on the highway for exotic blooms and eccentric creations.*

South-west of Coral Gables, South Miami is the beginning of true strip-mall suburbia, but it's also the gateway to the rural charms of Miami-Dade County, including the Everglades. The basic rule is the further south-west you travel, the more pleasant (read: less congested, greener and friendlier) it gets. By the time you reach Homestead and the agricultural Redlands (so named because of the colour of the soil), you're in the heart of farming land, though much of the fruit and vegetable crops for which the area is famous have been replaced by plantations for palm trees and ornamental shrubbery.

## THE ROAD SOUTH-WEST

At first sight, the main South Miami monuments seem to be places like the **Dadeland Mall** and the **Shops at Sunset Place** (for both, *see pp118-119*), but the tackiness is countered by the charming small-town feel of Sunset Drive, with its pricey boutiques and cafés frequented by yuppies who've fled the city for the 'burbs. In order to travel south, you'll probably need a car; aside from the few exceptions noted in the listings, public transport doesn't really operate in this area. Head down US 1, the route to the Keys, or along the more scenic Old Cutler Road. Note that distances can be quite significant; attractions such as the **Biscayne National Underwater Park** (*see below*) and the **Coral Castle Museum** (*see right*) are way down in Homestead, which is a good 50 miles from Miami Beach and Downtown. Factor in congested traffic and you're looking at around an hour's driving time each way, so it would make sense to schedule a visit to such places as part of an excursion to the Keys.

★ **FREE** **Biscayne National Underwater Park**
*9700 SW 328th Street, at SW 97th Avenue, Homestead (1-305 230 1100, www.nps.gov/bisc). No public transport.* **Open** 7am-5.30pm

daily. **Park admission** free. *Boat tour* $35. *Scuba diving* $75-$99 (excl equipment). *Snorkelling* $45 (incl equipment). **Credit** AmEx, DC, MC, V. **Map** p204.
Nearly all of this park's 181,500 acres are underwater, so come prepared to explore via glass-bottomed boat tours, canoe or – better yet – snorkelling or scuba diving. Get an introduction to the park's ecosystems and wildlife at the visitors' centre, built in the style of the area's pioneer homes. Of interest are the ecologically important mangrove forest, the abundant birdlife and, of course, the dazzling coral reef filled with brilliantly coloured fish, sea turtles and other marine life. Wildlife-lovers should take a boat trip to the neighbouring keys, full of nesting birds, subtropical forests and nature trails. Note that due to damage caused to the dock by Hurricane Sandy, boat tours had been temporarily suspended at time of writing; call to confirm schedule before visiting.

### Coral Castle Museum
*28655 S Dixie Highway (US 1), at SW 288th Street, Homestead (1-305 248 6345, www.coral castle.com). Metrorail Dadeland North, then bus 38.* **Open** 8am-6pm Mon-Thur, Sun; 8am-8pm Fri, Sat. **Admission** $15; $3 reductions; free under-7s. **No credit cards. Map** p204.
On the day before their wedding Agnes Scuffs jilted her husband-to-be, Latvian Edward Leedskalnin, on the grounds that he was too poor. Traumatised, Ed

Coral Castle Museum.

EXPLORE

left Latvia and, after spells in California and Canada, came to Miami in 1919. It was here that he embarked on a monumental act of lovelorn folly and built this castle of coral. In addition to being a strange and touching testament to one man's inability to just get over it already, Coral Castle is also a miracle of engineering. Secretive Ed built the castle himself between 1920 and 1940 using only hand tools, a feat that is mind-boggling even *before* you learn that Leedskalnin was just five feet tall. The mystery, how did he shift tons of rock from Florida City, where he carved it, to Homestead, where he erected it? Totally bonkers, but also quite beautiful, and certainly worth a detour for anyone driving down to the Keys.

### Deering Estate
*16701 SW 72nd Avenue, at SW 168th Street, South Dade (1-305 235 1668, www.deering estate.org). No public transport.* **Open** 10am-5pm daily. **Admission** $12; $5 reductions; free under-3s. **Credit** AmEx, MC, V. **Map** p279.
No, not the same Deering who built Vizcaya (*see p59*), but close. The Deering Estate was, in fact, set up and built by James's similarly well-off brother Charles, who erected his own winter retreat at about the same time that Vizcaya was constructed. The main building, the Stone House, takes a similarly revivalist tack to Vizcaya: Deering built it to remind himself of his properties in Spain. It's not as grand as his brother's digs, but it's impressive nonetheless. Other buildings on the site include the Richmond Cottage, built at the turn of the 19th century, and three small but delightful utilitarian buildings from 1918. The vast grounds contain all manner of nature, including a mangrove boardwalk, and canoe trips to pleasant Chicken Key are available if you book in

advance. The estate is most notable for its fossil pit of 50,000-year-old animal bones and 10,000-year-old human remains; the latter are Paleo-Indians.

### Everglades Outpost
*35601 SW 192nd Avenue, S of West Palm Drive, Homestead (1-305 247 8000, www.everglades outpost.org). No public transport.* **Open** 10am-5pm Mon, Tue, Fri-Sun. **Admission** $10; $5 reductions. **No credit cards. Map** p204.
This not-for-profit wildlife refuge in the heart of Homestead is home to bears, big cats and exotic creatures of every stripe, and offers a more intimate zoo-like experience. Medical care and treatment for the sick and injured are provided, and whenever possible the animals are released back into their natural habitat. The reptile house is not to be missed.

### ★ Fairchild Tropical Botanic Garden
*10901 Old Cutler Road, at SW 101st Street (1-305 667 1651, www.fairchildgarden.org). Bus 65.* **Open** 7.30am-4.30pm daily. **Admission** $25; $12-$18 reductions; free under-6s. **Credit** AmEx, MC, V. **Map** p279.
One of south Florida's natural jewels, this 83-acre garden, named after renowned botanist and Miami resident David Fairchild, is filled with tropical splendour: a lush rainforest with a stream, sunken garden, dramatic vistas, an enormous vine pergola and a museum of plant exploration. A must-see is the exquisite rare plant conservatory, a stunning showcase of palms, bromeliads, orchids and ferns. Narrated tram rides (given on the hour from 10am to 3pm) give visitors a close-up look at the resident flora. The Richard H Simons Rainforest, a two-acre site dominated by a gurgling 500-foot waterfall,

opened in 2001. In addition to Fairchild's annual events, among them July's International Mango Festival (*see p23*), every five years the garden is home to a rare plant phenomenon: the blooming of the amorphophallus titan, a gigantic single bloom as large as a person, which emits the powerful stench of rotting flesh to attract insects for pollination. Fairchild also has a fun gift shop and associations with well-known artists (sculptures by Dale Chihuly and Roy Lichtenstein have both been displayed here among the greenery).

### Fruit & Spice Park

*24801 SW 187th Avenue, at SW 248th Street, Homestead (1-305 247 5727, www.fruitandspice park.org). No public transport.* **Open** 9am-5pm daily. **Admission** $8; $2 reductions; free under-6s. **Credit** MC, V. **Map** p204.

The name may evoke images of fragrant Florida orange groves with a hint of exoticism, but the reality is more prosaic. Still, it's the only garden of its kind in the US: a 37-acre park exhibiting more than 500 varieties of fruits, vegetables, spices, herbs, nuts and exotic edibles. An old schoolhouse and coral rock building recall south Florida's pioneer life, while the charming gift shop sells spices, jams and jellies, unusual seeds and aromatic teas, plus cookbooks on tropical fruits and vegetables. The park is also the site of the Asian Culture Festival in March, and Blues, Brews and Barbecue in April. There are free guided tours at 11am, 1.30pm and 3pm daily.

### Gold Coast Railroad Museum

*12450 SW 152nd Street, at SW 124th Avenue, South Dade (1-305 253 0063, www.gcrm. org). Metrorail Dadeland North, then Zoobus.*

**Fairchild Tropical Botanic Garden.** *See p73.*

### INSIDE TRACK JUKEBOX HERO

For a serious taste of old-school Americana, wet your whistle at the divey but charming **Fox's Lounge** (6030 S Dixie Highway, at SW 61st Avenue, 1-305 661 9201), a dimly lit restaurant and bar that dates back nearly 70 years. It's home to one of the few remaining and (usually) working coin-operated jukeboxes, featuring more than 200 songs.

**Open** 10am-4pm Mon-Fri; 11am-4pm Sat, Sun. **Admission** $8; $6 reductions. *Rides* $2.50-$12. **Credit** AmEx, MC, V. **Map** p279.

Located across from Zoo Miami (*see p75*), the Gold Coast Railroad Museum is another good one for the kids, with its collection of old trains and carriages. The highlight is the Ferdinand Magellan, a railroad coach used by presidents Roosevelt, Truman, Eisenhower and, for one day during the 1984 election campaign, Ronald Reagan. Kids will enjoy rides on the Edwin Link Children's Railroad (1pm and 3pm on weekends, $3), and for adults it's a pleasant way to wind down for an hour after the zoo.

### FREE Knaus Berry Farm

*15980 SW 248th Street, at SW 160th Avenue, Homestead (1-305 247 0668, www.knausberry farm.com). No public transport.* **Open** Nov-Apr 8am-5.30pm Mon-Sat. **Admission** free. **No credit cards.**

For a taste of the old Homestead, with its abundant fruit orchards and crop fields, visit the family-run Knaus Berry Farm. You can still pick your own strawberries and tomatoes here, but most people come for the quaint bakery – and its hugely addictive cinnamon buns, pineapple upside-down cake and fruit milkshakes.

### Pinecrest Gardens

*11000 Red Road, at SW 110th Street, Pinecrest (1-305 669-6990, www.pinecrest-fl.gov). Metrorail South Miami, then bus 57.* **Open** 9am-5pm daily. **Admission** $3; $2 reductions; free under-2s. **No credit cards. Map** p279.

Jungle Island (*see p161*), which occupied this site for more than 60 years, flew the coop in 2001 to a $50 million complex on Watson Island. Although the owners took their thousand-plus alligators and crocodiles, flamingos, peacocks and parrots, they left the thousands of plants and flowers that now form the basis of this municipal park. As well as being beautiful, the site contains a playground and offers classes and workshops in subjects as varied as chess and photography. It also presents regular jazz and classical music concerts and occasional craft shows, and it plays host to year-round horticulture lectures and classes.

## ★ FREE RF Orchids

*28100 SW 182nd Avenue, at SW 280th Street,*
*Homestead (1-305 245 4570, www.rforchids.com).*
*No public transport.* **Open** 9am-5pm Tue-Sun.
**Admission** free. **Credit** AmEx, DC, MC, V.
South Florida has a thriving orchid industry, and RF
Orchids is its most renowned nursery. In fact, its
owner, Robert Fuchs, was dubbed 'the king of the
orchids' by author Susan Orleans in her book *The
Orchid Thief*. Fuchs has created a lavish kingdom:
an oasis of exotic blooms with winding pathways,
palms and fish ponds. Orchids are available for sale.

## FREE Robert is Here

*19200 SW 344th Street, at SW 192nd Avenue,*
*Homestead (1-305 246 1592, www.robertishere.*
*com).* **Open** Nov-Aug 8am-7pm daily. **Admission**
free. **Credit** AmEx, MC, V.
A throwback to Florida's fruit stands of old, Robert
is Here started in 1959 when the shop's namesake,
then six, began selling his family's cucumbers from
a roadside table. It has since grown into an emporium of exotic fruit and vegetables – and a huge
tourist attraction. Back in the day, all the produce
was grown locally, and there are still workers toiling
in the fields out back. But much of this stuff is
now imported, which mars its authenticity. Still, the
farmland setting is lovely.

## Wings Over Miami Air Museum

*Kendall-Tamiami Executive Airport, 14710 SW*
*128th Street, at SW 143rd Avenue, South Dade*
*(1-305 233 5197, www.wingsovermiami.com).*
*No public transport.* **Open** 10am-5pm Wed-Sat;
noon-5pm Sun. **Admission** $10; $6-$7 reductions;
free under-6s. **Credit** AmEx, DC, MC, V.

For almost 20 years this was known as the Weeks
Air Museum, until founder Kermit Weeks moved his
private collection of planes to Polk City and created
Fantasy of Flight. A group of flight enthusiasts then
reopened the place in 2001 under a different name.
Still loaded with lots of classic and military aircraft,
such as a B-26 that flew in the Bay of Pigs invasion,
the site brands itself a 'living museum' in honour of
aviators and veterans. Translation: these babies can
still fly and often do. Formation flights mainly take
place on weekends; call ahead for information.

## Zoo Miami

*12400 SW 152nd Street, at SW 124th Avenue,*
*South Dade (1-305 251 0400, www.miamimetro*
*zoo.com). Metrorail Dadeland North, then Zoobus.*
**Open** 9.30am-5.30pm daily (last entry 4pm). free
under-2s. **Credit** AmEx, MC, V. **Map** p279.
**Admission** $15.95; $11.95 reductions; free
This zoo was once considered one of the best in the
country, but Hurricane Andrew took its toll in 1992.
It certainly has cred with the animal welfare brigade.
Opened in 1981, it was billed as a 'progressive'
zoo: there are no cages or fences here, with animals
cleverly enclosed by moat-style perimeters. And
there are plenty of animals, too, from kangaroos and
rhinos to crocodiles and flamingos, not to mention
bears, camels, tigers and monkeys. The site covers
740 acres, so the free monorail service comes in
handy. For kids, there's a wildlife-themed carousel
ride and PAWS, a petting zoo with pony rides and
meerkats, along with shows in the amphitheatre and
animal feedings. Other big draws include Dr Wilde's
World, featuring a 500-gallon aquarium, plus
amphibians, reptiles and insects, and the largest
open-air Asian aviary in the western hemisphere.

**Gold Coast Railroad Museum.**

Consume

# Restaurants & Cafés

*Food imitates art.*

Now that Miami is a top destination for the art world, the restaurant scene is aiming higher too. Gone are the days when the city was dismissed as a gastronomical wasteland of early-bird specials and shrimp cocktails served in bland hotel restaurants. Yes, the chic boutique hotels along South Beach are still sometimes a lopsided mix of A-list interiors and C-list cuisine. But there are an increasing number of pleasing exceptions to the rule: the Bazaar by José Andrés (*see p80*) at the SLS, the Dutch (*see p81*) at the W South Beach, Bianca (*see p80*) at the Delano, and BLT Steak (*see p81*) at the Betsy for starters.

## THE LOCAL SCENE

Even on South Beach, you don't need an oceanfront address to make a splash these days, as shown by the buzzing **Yardbird** (*see p90*), **Meat Market** (*see p85*), and the **Pubbelly** (*see p87*) family of eateries, including **Barceloneta** (*see p80*). However, increasing numbers of the best restaurants are now found on the mainland, far from the madding crowd. Critical darling **Michael's Genuine Food & Drink** (*see p100*), which serves high-end comfort food, is located in the Design District. **Michy's** (*see p100*), a fashionably kitsch bistro run by celebrity chef Michelle Bernstein, is breathing new life into the dodgy Upper East Side with the help of fun gastropub the **Federal** (*see p99*). And **Hiro's Yakko-San** (*see p102*), a cheap and wonderful Japanese gem beloved by serious chefs, is hidden in a strip mall in the North Miami suburbs.

Miami may not be New York, despite the arrival of outposts of NYC chains (*see p86* **Manhattan Comes to Miami**), but give it time – increasingly, this city can satisfy wealthy epicureans with spots to eat foie gras and sip Château Lafite Rothschild, while a wealth of unsung gems keeps the chowhounders blogging.

❶ Blue numbers given in this chapter correspond to the location of each restaurant and café as marked on the street maps. *See pp280-285.*

## TIPS AND RESERVATIONS

Reservations are recommended for almost anywhere except cafés and diners. In fact, at most places they're an absolute requirement – unless you turn up before 7pm, in which case you'll probably get the place to yourself.

Miami restaurants are notorious for slow, arrogant service; by the time you finally get your cutting-edge dish of pan-roasted, pan-seared whatever, the trend may well be over. To add insult to injury, many restaurants top up the bill with a 15-18 per cent gratuity 'for your convenience'. Less conveniently, they often neglect to tell you. Ask if service is included, and don't be afraid to insist that the tip be adjusted down, or dropped, if the service hasn't warranted it (and don't mind dirty looks and a bit of attitude). Do note, however, that servers in the US rely largely on tips for their pay and that it's customary to leave 15-20 per cent.

## SMOKING

A law banning lighting up in any establishment whose main profit comes from serving food has forced many eateries to set up outdoor seating and smoking areas for those whose preferred digestif comes in a pack of 20.

## SOUTH BEACH

★ **11th Street Diner**
*1065 Washington Avenue, at 11th Street (1-305 534 6373, www.eleventhstreetdiner. com). Bus C, H, K, W, South Beach Local.*

**Bazaar by José Andrés.** *See p80.*

Open 24hrs daily. **Main courses** $6-$19. **Credit**
AmEx, DC, MC, V. **Map** p280 D3 ❶ American
The best-looking high-carb, high-fat joint in town,
this streamlined, stainless-steel 1946 diner was
shipped in from Wilkes-Barre, Pennsylvania. It's a
popular all-night spot that attracts a regular crew of
locals and club kids, plus curious tourists. The food
is above average (in quality and price), and there's
an outdoor terrace and bar area (until 5am only).

### A La Folie
*516 Española Way, at Pennsylvania Avenue
(1-305 538 4484, www.alafoliecafe.com). Bus
C, H, K, W, South Beach Local.* **Open** 9am-
midnight daily. **Main courses** $6-$20. **Credit**
MC, V. **Map** p280 D3 ❷ Café
Quintessentially French, *avec* the attitude to
prove it, this café is run by a Parisian who brought
a piece of his precious city to Miami, A Euro crowd
gathers to sip on endless cups of *café au lait* (ask
for small, otherwise it arrives in something the
size of a soup bowl). It also serves a mean croque-
monsieur and crêpes.
**Other location** 1701 Sunset Harbour Drive, at
Dade Boulevard, South Beach (1-305 672 9336).

### AltaMare
*1223 Lincoln Road, at Alton Road (1-305 532
3061, www.altamarerestaurant.com). Bus C,
G, H, K, L, M, S, W, South Beach Local.* **Open**
5-10pm Mon-Thur, 5-11pm Fri, Sat. **Main
courses** $19-$54. **Credit** AmEx, DC, MC, V.
**Map** p280 C2 ❸ Seafood
On a forgotten stretch of Lincoln Road, this mom-
and-pop setup is the antithesis to glitzy Miami. But
the fresh, simply prepared seafood – done with an

Italian slant – has earned the restaurant a loyal
following. Typical entrées might be fettuccine with
wild ocean rock shrimp; beer-battered yelloweye
snapper with crispy Yukon gold wedges; or local
grouper with sunchoke purée and cilantro salsa
verde. Softly lit, AltaMare has a warm ambience
that makes up for the humdrum decor.

### Balans
*1022 Lincoln Road, at Michigan Avenue (1-305
534 9191, www.balans.co.uk). Bus C, G, H, K, L,
M, S, W, South Beach Local.* **Open** 8am-1am
Mon-Thur; 8am-2am Fri, Sat, 8am-midnight Sun.
**Main courses** $8-$30. **Credit** AmEx, DC, MC, V.
**Map** p280 C2 ❹ Fusion
A longtime fave of London's pink brunchers, Balans'
first overseas venture is on Lincoln Road. Curiously,
despite the laid-back locale, it's more uptight than
its Anglo counterpart. Wait staff want you to know
that they're only doing this job until the call from
their agent comes through. Still, the food is good (a

**CONSUME**

Dutch.

**CONSUME**

★ **Barton G the Restaurant**
*1427 West Avenue, at 14th Terrace (1-305 672 8881, www.bartongtherestaurant.com). Bus M, S, W.* **Open** 7-10pm Mon-Thur; 6pm-midnight Fri-Sun. **Main courses** $18-$30. **Credit** AmEx, DC, MC, V. **Map** p280 D2 ➏ **American**
Owned by Barton G Weiss, an A-list caterer, this unique restaurant manages to be both plush and cosy. Fabulous American cuisine is funked up with presentations that include popcorn shrimp in a popcorn box and grilled sea bass in a brown paper bag with laundry clips to keep the steam in. A phenomenal caesar salad comes complete with mini cheesegrater and, for the grand finale, a plume of cotton candy reminiscent of Dame Edna's wig. This is one menu that has to be seen and tasted to be believed.

**Bazaar by José Andrés**
*SLS South Beach, 1701 Collins Avenue, at 17th Street (1-305 455 2999, www.thebazaar.com/the-bazaar-south-beach). Bus C, G, H, L, M, South Beach Local.* **Open** 6pm-midnight Mon-Wed, Sun; 6pm-1am Thur-Sat. **Main courses** $12-$50. **Credit** AmEx, Disc, MC, V. **Map** p280 C3 ➐ **Spanish/Latin American**
Everything about the SLS (*see p140*) is painfully hip, including the Bazaar, its house restaurant. Opened in 2012 by culinary giant José Andrés, the Bazaar has already risen to the top of local foodies' must-visit list, earning it the distinction of being the second most-booked restaurant in the city, according to online reservation site OpenTable.com. Perhaps that's because the food and overall vibe of the place are an experiment in decadence, bringing a playful spirit to the old-world glamour that defined the city's art deco era. The menu is lively, combining elements of Spain and Latin America to wind up with dishes like Papas a la Huancaína (Peruvian potatoes with sea urchin) and Cuban coffee-rubbed *churrasco* with passionfruit. If you can snag a reservation, strap on your seatbelt and get ready for a wild ride. *Photo p79.*

★ **Bianca**
*Delano Hotel, 1685 Collins Avenue, at 17th Street (1-305 674 5752, www.delano-hotel.com). Bus C, G, H, L, M, S.* **Open** 7am-4pm, 7-11pm Mon-Thur, Sun; 7am-4pm, 7pm-midnight Fri, Sat. **Main courses** $27-$46. **Credit** AmEx, DC, MC, V. **Map** p280 C3 ➑ **Italian**
With Philippe Starck responsible for the stunning white and billowy surroundings and culinary guru Luciano Sautto in charge of the kitchen, the eyes are as well fed as the stomach. In fact, this is what it must be like to dine in heaven. Don't believe us? Try the slow-braised ossobucco. Entrées are refined and Italian, with home-made pastas and fresh south Florida seafood. Veranda seating and an all-you-can-eat Sunday brunch add further appeal. (Just be warned that all this dreaminess comes with a high price tag.)

mix of Asian and Mediterranean, and keenly priced). And, unlike in London, the umbrellas outside are there to keep the sun off, not the rain.
**Other locations** 6789 Biscayne Boulevard, at NE 68th Street (1-305 534 9191); 901 S Miami Avenue, at SE 9th Street (1-305 534 9191).

★ **Barceloneta**
*1400 20th Street, at Purdy Avenue (1-305 538 9299, www.barcelonetarestaurant.com). Bus 117, 123.* **Open** 6pm-midnight Mon-Sat; noon-4pm, 6-11pm Sun. **Main courses** $5-$22. **Credit** AmEx, MC, V. **Map** p280 C2 ➎ **Tapas**
There's a reason why this Spanish tapas joint is sandwiched next to two members of the Pubbelly (*see p87*) family of restaurants: she's their little sister. Opened in 2011, small plates of well-balanced Catalan classics are the speciality here, and they're served up by an impressive staff of true hospitality professionals (after 24 hours in Miami, you'll understand why this is so noteworthy). Carnivores will appreciate flavourful dishes of tempranillo-braised oxtail with creamy polenta and rabbit rillettes with a cherry brandy compote, while veggie-lovers will want seconds of crispy *patatas bravas*, spicy shishito peppers (topped with a decadent valdeón cheese) and a rich potato and onion omelette. If nothing on the extensive wine list strikes your fancy, opt for an exotic speciality martini (the Cardamomo, made with tequila, lime juice, fresh pineapple and cardamom pods complements much of the menu).

## Big Pink

*157 Collins Avenue, at 2nd Street (1-305 532 4700, www.mylesrestaurantgroup.com). Bus H, M, W, South Beach Local.* **Open** 8am-midnight Mon-Wed, Sun; 8am-2am Thur; 8am-5am Fri, Sat. **Main courses** $8-$20. **Credit** AmEx, MC, V. **Map** p280 F3 **❾ American**

A Miami Beach mainstay, this big square room is studded with big TV screens tuned to sports and big pink menus of all-American favourites – the likes of sandwiches, burgers, pastas, pizzas, all-day breakfasts and even TV dinners on a tray. The family-style table arrangement promotes camaraderie, which, late at night, erupts into full-blown rowdiness. Takeouts are delivered by a fleet of little pink VW Beetles.

## BLT Steak

*The Betsy, 1440 Ocean Drive, at 15th Street (1-305 673 0044, www.e2hospitality.com/blt-steak-miami). Bus C, H, K, W, South Beach Local.* **Open** 8am-2.30pm, 6-10pm Mon-Thur, Sun; 8am-2.30pm, 6-11pm Fri, Sat. **Main courses** $19-$60 **Credit** AmEx, Disc, MC, V. **Map** p280 D3 **❿ Steakhouse**

Opened in 2009, chef Laurent Tourondel's modern steakhouse occupies the ground floor of the Betsy hotel (*see p135*). Mixing creative American ingredients with classic French techniques, the menu offers a half-dozen different slabs of beef, all of them naturally aged and broiled at super-high temperatures. Grab a table on the charming beachfront patio for Miamians' favourite sport: people-watching

## Casa Tua

*1700 James Avenue, at 17th Street (1-305 673 1010, www.casatualifestyle.com). Bus C, G, H, K, L, M, S, W, South Beach Local.* **Open** 7.30-11pm daily. **Main courses** $22-$46. **Credit** AmEx, DC, MC, V. **Map** p280 C3 **⓫ Italian**

One of the city's finest and fussiest big-bucks restaurants, Casa Tua is a sleek and chic country Italian-style establishment set in a refurbished 1925 Mediterranean-style two-storey house. It has several dining areas, including an outdoor garden, comfy Ralph Lauren-esque living room and a communal eat in kitchen. The lamb chops are stratospheric in price ($40), but orgasmic in taste. After dinner, head upstairs to the lounge (if staff let you – the place is technically a members-only club), where the beautiful people commune over $15 cocktails.

## Clarke's

*840 1st Street, at Alton Road (1-305 538 9885, www.clarkesmiamibeach.com). Bus H, M, W, South Beach Local.* **Open** 5pm-midnight Mon; noon-midnight Tue-Sat; 11am-11pm Sun. **Main courses** $13-$19. **Credit** AmEx, MC, V. **Map** p280 F2 **⓬ Irish/International**

An authentic Irish pub in the swank South of Fifth (aka SoFi) area might seem like a mismatch of venue and location, but it's not. The rich wood bar and warm interior separate Clarke's from the other, more down-at heel Irish bars in the area. The food rocks, too, with everything from shepherd's pie to bangers and mash via juicy burgers, fabulous fish and chips and our personal fave, a big, salty New York-style pretzel with a side of mustard. Whatever you eat, it'll wash down nicely with a pint of Guinness on draft, of course.

## Dutch

*W South Beach, 2201 Collins Avenue, at 22nd Street (1-305 938 3111, www.thedutch miami.com). Bus C, G, H, L, M, South Beach Local.* **Open** noon-4pm, 6.30-11.30pm Mon-Wed,

**Florida Cookery.** *See p82.*

Joe's Stone Crab.

**CONSUME**

Sun; noon-4pm, 6.30pm-midnight Thur-Sat. **Main courses** $15-$36. **Credit** AmEx, MC, V. **Map** p280 B3 ⑬ **American**
After wowing critics in Manhattan, Andrew Carmellini has duplicated his popular, roots-inspired American eaterie in Miami by way of the W hotel. Paying tribute to the kind of American culinary traditions you'd witness in neighbourhood taverns and roadside cafés, the menu runs the gamut from chicken wings with pickled ramps to crisp lamb belly with couscous and tomato. The vibe is as laidback as the vintage, beach-house decor.

### ★ Escopazzo
*1311 Washington Avenue, at 13th Street (1-305 674 9450, www.escopazzo.com). Bus C, H, K, W, South Beach Local.* **Open** 6-11pm Tue-Sat; 6-10.30pm Sun. **Main courses** $18-$46. **Credit** AmEx, DC, MC, V. **Map** p280 D3 ⑭ **Italian**
The name may mean 'crazy', but the only sign of insanity at this organic Italian stalwart is the fact that there are only 90 seats – nowhere near enough to accommodate the legion of die-hard escopazzosos. Their continued loyalty is maintained by superb home-made risotto (we recently had one made with dark chocolate and topped with edible gold), excellent pasta, some outstanding wines and doting service. It's pricey but, we have to say, it's worth it.

### Florida Cookery
*James Royal Palm, 1545 Collins Avenue, at 15th Street (1-786 276 0333, www.florida-cookery.com). Bus C, G, H, L, M, South Beach Local.* **Open** 7am-10pm daily. **Main courses** $11-$42. **Credit** MC, V. **Map** p280 C3 ⑮ **American**

If it ain't local, Florida Cookery doesn't want it. The signature restaurant at the James Royal Palm hotel has a passion for fresh, locally sourced produce, meat and seafood, as demonstrated by Kris Wessel's impressive menu, which includes old-school favourites such as a 65-year-old conch chowder recipe and cast iron-cooked Sunshine State frogs' legs. Local culinary hero Lee Brian Schrager, founder of the South Beach Wine & Food Festival (*see p27*), even has a burger named after him, made with Vidalia onions and your choice of fontina, white cheddar, bleu or goat's cheese. *Photo p81.*

### Front Porch Café
*1458 Ocean Drive, at 15th Street (1-305 531 8300, www.frontporchoceandrive.com). Bus C, H, K, W, South Beach Local.* **Open** 7am-11pm daily. **Main courses** $5-$21. **Credit** AmEx, DC, MC, V. **Map** p280 D3 ⑯ **Diner**
One of the quainter and less posey spots on Ocean Drive, the Front Porch is the preferred breakfast and lunch venue of locals who seek good food with no attitude. Expect no-nonsense diner fare, including pancakes, plus fruit salads; the moreish french toast comes with bananas and walnuts.

### Ice Box Cafe
*1657 Michigan Avenue, at Lincoln Road (1-305 538 8448, www.iceboxcafe.com). Bus C, G, H, K, L, M, S, W, South Beach Local.* **Open** 10am-11pm Mon-Thur; 10am-midnight Fri; 9am-midnight Sat; 9am-11pm Sun. **Main courses** $8-$28. **Credit** AmEx, MC, V. **Map** p280 C2 ⑰ **Café**
The Ice Box is a curious mix of industrial space (exposed ducting, hard metallic surfaces), matronly

tearoom (creamy chocolate cakes on frilly stands) and gay bar (beefcake waiters serve a campy crowd). But it's quite pleasant, especially for a quick cuppa while shopping on nearby Lincoln Road. However, lingering over coffee and cake earns you scowls around lunchtime, when hungry shoppers queue for the Med-style cuisine from a surprisingly ambitious daily changing menu. Don't forget to save room for dessert; the restaurant's Chocolate Delight was named one of the 'best cakes in America' by Oprah Winfrey.

## Jerry's Famous Deli
*1450 Collins Avenue, at Española Way (1-305 534 3244, www.jerrysfamousdeli.com). Bus C, H, K, W, South Beach Local.* **Open** 24hrs daily. **Main courses** $8-$25. **Credit** AmEx, MC, V. **Map** p280 D3 ⑱ **Deli**
At the top of the broadsheet-style menu (allow a good 45 minutes to read it) is a quote: 'Some is good. More is better. Too much is just right.' That about sums up Jerry's ethos – feed 'em until they burst. Expect the usuals: dogs, burgers, melts, reubens, platters and breakfasts, all served around the clock. The setting is a former cafeteria-turned-ballroom, with enough seating for Latvia and decor that pulls out all the stops – mirror tiles, swags and swirls. Add a disco soundtrack, full bar and prices that would make any Jewish grandmother plotz.

## Joe's Stone Crab
*11 Washington Avenue, at 1st Street (1-305 673 0365, www.joesstonecrab.com). Bus H, W.* **Open** 6-10pm Mon-Thur, Sun; 6-11pm Fri, Sat (hours can vary seasonally; call ahead). **Main courses** $15-$60. **Credit** AmEx, DC, MC, V. **Map** p280 F3 ⑲ **American**
South Florida's most famous restaurant, Joe's (which turns 100 in 2013) is as much a Miami must-see as Ocean Drive. It attracts locals, tourists and celebs,

serving seasonal stone crabs (October-May) with a 'secret' sauce, garlic creamed spinach, fried sweet potatoes, coleslaw and hash browns. If you don't like seafood, try the fried chicken, or the liver and onions. Joe's doesn't take reservations, so be prepared for a horrendously long wait, first to register your name, then for a table. Alternatively, if you can't face that, just go with takeaway from the adjacent shop.

## Juvia
*1111 Lincoln Road, at Lenox Avenue (1-305 763 8272, www.juviamiami.com). Bus C, G, H, K, L, M, South Beach Local.* **Open** noon-3pm, 6pm-midnight Mon-Wed, Sun; noon-3pm, 6pm-1am Thur-Sat. **Main courses** $16-$79. **Credit** AmEx, MC, V. **Map** p280 C2 ⑳ **Fusion**
Make sure you're sitting down when the bill comes – the total could make you a little woozy. So could the cocktails. Or the phenomenal view, which diners take in from the penthouse level of the famed Herzog & de Meuron-designed Lincoln Road parking garage. Just remember you're paying for the views as well as the talent, which is prodigious. In the kitchen is Laurent Cantineaux, a protégé of Daniel Boulud; former Nobu chef Sunny Oh, and pastry chef Gregory Gourreau, who honed his sweet tooth under the tutelage of Alain Ducasse and François Payard. Together, the trio create a wonderfully eclectic menu of East-meets-West-meets-Paris dishes. For special occasions and/or absurdly wealthy diners only.

## Katsuya
*SLS South Beach, 1701 Collins Avenue, at 17th Street (1-305 455 2995, www.sbe.com/katsuya/south-beach). Bus C, G, H, L, M, South Beach Local.* **Open** 6pm-midnight Mon-Wed, Sun; 6pm-1am Thur-Sat. **Main courses** $14-$30. **Credit** AmEx, MC, V. **Map** p280 C3 ㉑ **Japanese**

Katsuya.

CONSUME

Macchialina.

Katsuya is what happens when haute cuisine meets high style. Located within the SLS hotel (*see p140*), this sleek and sexy Japanese eaterie is a feast for the senses, with sushi dishes courtesy of master chef Katsuya Uechi (whose signature plates include crispy rice with spicy tuna and yellowtail sashimi with jalapeño) and the eye-catching design by the legendary Philippe Starck.

### Lantao Kitchen
*Surfcomber, 1717 Collins Avenue, at 17th Street (1-305 604 1800, www.lantaorestaurant.com). Bus C, G, H, L, M, South Beach Local.* **Open** 7-11am, 5-10pm Mon, Tue, Sun; 7-11am, 5-11pm Wed-Sat. **Main courses** $12-$26. **Credit** MC, V. **Map** p280 C3 ㉒ **South-east Asian**
This ode to South-east Asian street food has a small but tasty menu of breakfast and dinner entrées that range from the traditional to the experimental. Early risers can partake in Hong Kong-style chicken and waffles or puffed rice-crusted French toast, while evening diners will find a range of snacks (blue crab spring rolls are a standout), salads, noodle dishes and entrées, served in a comfortable, oceanfront setting. There's an impressive menu of innovative libations, designed to complement the fare. The Tongue Tango – green pepper-infused tequila with lime juice, cilantro and simple syrup – is appropriately named.

### Lime Fresh Mexican Grill
*1439 Alton Road, at 14th Court (1-305 532 5463, www.limefreshmexicangrill.com). Bus H, M, W, South Beach Local.* **Open** 11am-11pm daily. **Main courses** $6-$12. **Credit** AmEx, DC, MC, V. **Map** p280 D2 ㉓ **Mexican**

Though far from the beach, this Mexican fast-food joint still attracts queues. Expect the usual array of tacos and quesadillas, though the food is a cut above most chain fare: guacamole and salsa are homemade; fresh seasonal fish – mahi mahi, yellowtail – fills the tacos. And you don't get fresh margaritas at Taco Bell. Healthy options abound, too – the South Beach burrito (low carb, low fat) or, for Atkins devotees, the Nudie burrito (no tortilla, all fillings). Diners sit on a patio and eat to a rock'n'roll beat.

### ★ Macchialina
*820 Alton Road, at 8th Street (1-305 534 2124, www.macchialina.com). Bus 113, 119, 123.* **Open** 6pm-midnight Tue-Thur, Sun; 6pm-1am Fri, Sat. **Main courses** $12-$47. **Credit** MC, V. **Map** p280 E2 ㉔ **Italian**
Rustic and homey, this off-the-beaten-path Italian (from the same folks behind the Pubbelly family of restaurants) is full of locals looking to escape the madness of South Beach. Luckily, they've found a place to do it where the laid-back vibe is totally authentic and the food is damn good, too. Antipasti includes a creamy *burrata* cheese (locally made) served with pickled aubergine. A small pasta menu ticks all the right flavour notes (the short rib lasagna is a customer favorite). Pizza, too, is dependably delicious and well thought out, with fried eggs, meatballs and mushroom fricassée as toppings.

### La Marea
*King & Grove Tides, 1220 Ocean Drive, at 12th Street (1-305 604 5070, www.thetidessouthbeach. com). Bus C, H, K, W, South Beach Local.* **Open** 7am-11pm Mon-Thur, Sun; 7am-midnight Fri,

CONSUME

Sat. **Main courses** $30-$45. **Credit** AmEx,
DC, MC, V. **Map** p280 D3 ㉕ **Seafood**
The sea is the motif at La Marea. Designer Kelly
Wearstler has fashioned an ethereal homage to the
beach at sunset. The soothing aesthetic – peach,
beige, ivory and pink hues – is a classy respite from
tawdry Ocean Drive. A wall of faux-tortoise shells
lends a natural vibe, as do shells, driftwood and
stones. Sheer silk drapes add sensuality. Too bad
the cuisine – ambitious but average nouveau Italian
seafood – pales next to the decor.

### ★ Meat Market
*915 Lincoln Road, at Jefferson Avenue (1-305
532 0088, www.meatmarketmiami.com). Bus C,
G, H, K, L, M, South Beach Local.* **Open** 5pm-
midnight Mon-Thur, Sun; 5pm-1am Fri-Sat.
**Main courses** $22-$95. **Credit** AmEx, MC, V.
**Map** p280 C2 ㉖ **Steakhouse**
No, it's not a pick-up joint. Cited as one of the city's
'buzziest restaurants' by *Condé Nast Traveler*, Meat
Market is one of the classier spots to set up shop on
Lincoln Road. It's enormous, too (4,400sq ft, with a
cute outdoor café for al fresco dining). The 'Meat' in
the title refers to the high-quality slabs of beef that
are trucked in from local farms and flown in from
New York and Australia. Signature steaks – like a
prime filet mignon – can be ordered as full or half-
cuts. Vegetarians, meanwhile, can indulge in a menu
of specially crafted cocktails, which are as beautiful
to look at as they are fun to guzzle.

### Monty's
*300 Alton Road, at 3rd Street (1-305 672
1148, www.montyssobe.com). Bus 113, 123.*
**Open** 11.30am-10pm Mon-Thur, Sun; 11.30am-

**My Ceviche.**

midnight Fri; 11.30am-11pm Sat. **Main courses**
$15-$40. **Credit** AmEx, DC, MC, V. **Map** p280 F2
㉗ **Seafood**
The Disney World of waterfront dining, Monty's
offers the chance to eat shrimp or stone crabs before
renting a boat and heading out to sea. Though the
indoor dining room overlooking the water is scenic,
it's stuffy and overpriced. The outside tiki hut area
is more popular with the happy-hour set for its
relaxed vibe and casual bar menu.

### My Ceviche
*235 Washington Avenue, at 2nd Street (1-305
397 8710, www.myceviche.com). Bus H, M, W.*
**Open** 11.30am-10pm Mon-Thur, Sun; 11.30am-
11pm Fri, Sat **Main courses** $10-$15. **Credit**
AmEx, Disc, MC, V. **Map** p280 F3 ㉘ **Seafood**
With a name like My Ceviche and a tagline that reads
'Go Fish, Go Fresh', it doesn't take the most imaginative of diners to get what the theme is here. yes,
it's fresh fish. Fusing elements of mostly Mexican
cuisine with Asian, Caribbean and Latin American
elements too, this tiny storefront is really little more
than a takeaway stand. But if offers some of the most
flavourful bites on the beach, making it a great spot
for a quick and cheap-o lunch while you're doing the
beach thing. You pick the size and the protein (fish,
shrimp, octopus or all three) for your ceviche, which
comes in six varieties and is served with sweet
potato, yellow corn and spicy popcorn.
**Other locations** 1250 S Miami Avenue,
at SW 12th Street (1-305 960 7825)

### News Café
*800 Ocean Drive, at 8th Street (1-305 538 6397,
www.newscafe.com). Bus C, H, K, W, South Beach
Local.* **Open** 24hrs daily. **Main courses** $10-$20.
**Credit** AmEx, DC, MC, V. **Map** p280 E3 ㉙ **Café**
This place practically invented the sport of South
Beach people-watching, and it remains the café king
of Ocean Drive. Wait for an outside table to fully
appreciate the experience. Service is as slow as ever,
but the menu has some good bites and the portions

**Meat Market.**

**CONSUME**

# Manhattan Comes to Miami

*NYC's finest on Lincoln Road.*

If it weren't for the wall-to-wall sunshine and palm trees, you could walk along South Beach's Lincoln Road Mall and swear you were in Manhattan. And not just because of the crushing parade of tourists lumbering their way along the pavement, half-forgetting that some people actually live in Miami and have places to be. From the ocean to Biscayne Bay, more and more of New York City's most famous restaurants are heading south to set up shop along this pedestrian paradise. For burgers and beer, there's **Five Napkin Burger** (455 Lincoln Road, at Drexel Avenue, 1-305 538 2277, www.5napkinburger.com/south-beach-miami) or **Shake Shack** (1111 Lincoln Road, at Lenox Avenue, 1-305 434 7787, www.shakeshack.com/location/south-beach). For more exotic flavours, there's **SushiSamba Dromo** (*see p89*), perhaps the world's only Japanese/Brazilian/Peruvian fusion restaurant, or upscale south-of-the-border eats at **Rosa Mexicano** (1111 Lincoln Road, at Alton Road, 1-305 695 1005, www.rosamexicano.com). And if you've still got room for something sweet, order up a Frrrozen Hot Chocolate from legendary dessert café **Serendipity 3** (1102 Lincoln Road, at Lenox Avenue, 1-305 403 2210, www.serendipity3.com).

SushiSamba Dromo.

are huge. International newspapers and magazines from the in-house shop might fill the time until the food arrives. The café also has a separate bar, also open 24 hours daily.

## Nobu

*Shore Club, 1901 Collins Avenue, at 20th Street (1-305 695 3232, www.noburestaurants.com). Bus C, G, H, L, M, S.* **Open** 7pm-midnight Mon-Thur; 7pm-1am Fri, Sat; 7-11pm Sun. **Main courses** $10-$48. **Credit** AmEx, MC, V. **Map** p280 C3 ㉙ **Japanese**

Nobu Matsuhisa is regarded as the world's greatest sushi chef, but that's not why this place is booked up weeks in advance. No, this outpost of the global raw fish superpower is lodged at the Shore Club (*see p140*) and it's the combination of hotelier-with-the-Midas-touch Ian Schrager and Nobu backer Robert De Niro that makes it celeb central. The likes of Madonna and J-Lo might only drop by once in a blue moon, but it's the people hoping to spot them who pack Nobu every night.

## Ola

*Sanctuary, 1745 James Avenue, at 17th Street (1-305 695 9125, www.olamiami.com). Bus M, W, South Beach Local.* **Open** 6-11pm Mon-Thur; 6pm-midnight Fri, Sat; 6-10pm Sun. **Main courses** $18-$42. **Credit** AmEx, MC, V. **Map** p280 C3 ㉛ **Latin American**

Back in the 1980s, chef Douglas Rodriguez started the nouveau Cuban craze in Miami and then moved to New York, where he became a huge star. After returning to Miami, he opened Ola. The trendy minimalist decor feels dated, but the food is sophisticated and imaginative. Ceviche is a forte: the wahoo with watermelon jalapeño juice and cucumber sorbet is sublime. Dishes such as braised pork with black bean broth and steamed yucca remind smug foodies that Miami, not Manhattan, was first in the *nuevo Latino* scene. And the deconstructed key lime pie (served with meringue, vanilla bean ice-cream and toasted cinnamon walnut tuile) puts the original in the shade. Be warned: you'll need to knock back a few mojitos to digest the Manhattan-style bill.

## Osteria del Teatro

*1443 Washington Avenue, at Española Way (1-305 538 7850, www.osteriadelteatromiami. com). Bus C, H, K, W, South Beach Local.* **Open** 6-11pm Mon-Thur; 6pm-midnight Fri, Sat. **Main courses** $17-$31. **Credit** AmEx, DC, MC, V. **Map** p280 D3 ㉜ **Italian**

This is the long-standing holder of the title of 'the Beach's best Italian' – although fans of Casa Tua and Escopazzo would beg to differ. The prices draw a lot of flak, although the northern Italian specialities are tremendous and the service is exceptional. We love the view out of the big picture windows of the parade of partygoers arriving at nearby nightclub Cameo.

## Parrilla Liberty

*609 Washington Avenue, at 6th Street (1-305 532 7599, www.laparrillaliberty.com). Bus C, H, K, W, South Beach Local.* **Open** noon-11.30pm daily. **Main courses** $8-$25. **Credit** AmEx, DC, MC, V. **Map** p280 E3 ❸ **Steakhouse**

Where's the beef? At this mom-and-pop Argentinian steakhouse. The menu is a carnivore's dream – skirt, flat and New York steaks. The mixed grill (blood sausage, causage, sweetbreads, short rib and flat meat) will satisfy gluttons and harden arteries Sides include South American specialities (Russian salad, hearts of palm with prosciutto).

## ★ Pasha's

*900 Lincoln Road, at Jefferson Avenue (1-305 673 3919, www.pashas.com). Bus C, G, H, K, L, M, S, W, South Beach Local.* **Open** 11am-midnight Mon-Thur, Sun; 11am-1am Fri, Sat. **Main courses** $5-$13. **Credit** AmEx, DC, MC, V. **Map** p280 C2 ❸ **Middle Eastern**

If all fast-food restaurants were as healthy as Pasha's, *Super Size Me* would never have been made – no wonder it has been endorsed by South Beach Diet guru Arthur Agatston. The Middle Eastern fare incorporates meze (houmous, baba ghanoush, falafel, tabbouleh), grilled kebab platters, fresh salads, soups and assorted wraps, plus omelettes at breakfast. The sleek and minimalist interior is more stylish than most fast food joints, as is the beverage menu: fresh-squeezed fruit juices, smoothies – and champagne.

**Other locations** 3801 Biscayne Boulevard, Design District (1-305 573 0201); 1414 Brickell Avenue, Downtown (1-305 416 5116); Four Seasons, 1441 Brickell Avenue, Downtown (1-305 381 3938); Aventura Mall, 19501 Biscayne Boulevard, Aventura (1-305 917 4007).

## Pizza Rustica

*863 Washington Avenue, at 9th Street (1-305 674 8244, www.pizza-rustica.com). Bus C, H, K, W, South Beach Local.* **Open** 11am-6am daily, **Pizza slice** $3-$5. **Credit** AmEx, Disc, MC, V. **Map** p280 E3 ❸ **Pizza**

South Beach's refuelling pit stop par excellence, Rustica is a tiny, standing-room-only space that's packed in the early hours with clubbers who come to boost their carbs and sponge up the booze. But the Tuscan-style pizza is good enough to eat sober, with excellent toppings including meatball with sweet red onions, rosemary potato and goat's cheese, and the classic four cheeses. One slice is a meal.

**Other locations** 1447 Washington Avenue, at 14th Street (1-305 538 6009); 667 Lincoln Road, at Euclid Avenue (1-305 672 2334); 500 Brickell Avenue, at SE 5th Street (1-786 787 8422).

## Prime 112

*112 Ocean Drive, at 1st Street (1-305 532 8112, www.mylesrestaurantgroup.com). Bus M, W, South Beach Local.* **Open** noon-3pm, 5.30pm-midnight Mon-Thur; noon-3pm, 5.30pm-1am Fri, Sat; 5.30pm-midnight Sun. **Main courses** $19-$88. **Credit** AmEx, DC, MC, V. **Map** p280 F3 ❸ **Steakhouse**

Who in their right mind would ever pay $25 for a hot dog – OK, a Kobe beef hot dog? Diners at this posh steakhouse, that's who. Command central for carnivores and those who devour a good, star-studded scene, Prime 112 ('Prime One Twelve') is perennially packed. The aged beef is delish, as are the soy-marinated sea bass and the massive salads and side dishes, but the real dish here is the crowd, a silicone- and Botox-enhanced mass of glamazons and wannabes on the hunt for a man – or woman – who can afford to pay $25 for a wiener without batting a surgically improved eyelash.

## Pubbelly

*1418 20th Street, at Purdy Avenue (1-305 532 7555, www.pubbelly.com). Bus 117, 123.* **Open** 6pm-midnight Tue-Thur, Sun; 6pm-1am Fri, Sat. **Main courses** $10-$35. **Credit** AmEx, MC, V. **Map** p280 C2 ❸ **Asian**

Andreas Schreiner, Jose Mendin and Sergio Navarro – the trio behind Pubbelly – have got quite a growing business on their hands. In addition to this original outpost, the city's first Asian-inspired gastropub, they've grown their family of restaurants to include Pubbelly Sushi right next door, which – yep, you guessed it – is more than just Asian-inspired. And now there's Pubbelly Steak. Rustic Italian eaterie Macchialina (*see p84*) and tapas-focused Barceloneta (*see p80*) are all part of the family too. Could Pubbelly Vegan be next?

**Other locations** Pubbelly Sushi, 1424 20th Street, at Purdy Avenue, South Beach (1-305 531 9282, www.pubbellysushi.com); Pubbelly Steak 1787 Purdy Avenue, at 18th Street, South Beach (1-305 695 9550, www.pbsteak.com).

## Puerto Sagua

*700 Collins Avenue, at 7th Street (1-305 673 1115). Bus C, H, K, W, South Beach Local.* **Open** 7am-2am daily. **Main courses** $7-$30. **Credit** AmEx, MC, V. **Map** p280 E3 ❸ **Cuban**

The best place for breakfast on Collins is this trad (as in authentically old, rather than retro) Cuban diner. Choose from a long list of set combinations, many of which give change from six bucks. Later in the day, an entertaining mix of old-time Cubanos, hip hop kids and beach bums drop by for paella-style chicken and rice, ham croquettes and fried pork chops.

## Quattro

*1014 Lincoln Road, at Michigan Avenue (1-305 531 4833, www.quattromiami.com). Bus C, G, H, K, L, M, S, W, South Beach Local.* **Open** noon-3pm, 7pm-midnight daily. **Main courses** $18-$48. **Credit** AmEx, MC, V. **Map** p280 C2 ❸ **Italian**

Chic and sleek, Quattro's swanky Euro interior – terrazzo floors, green glass, mirrors and chandeliers

**CONSUME**

– entices A-listers, and the northern Italian cuisine pulls in the foodies. Antipasti include the usual heirloom tomatoes and buffalo mozzarella, eggplant parmigiana and cured Italian meats. For mains, an 8oz beef filet satisfies the expense-account crowd – this is a power lunch hotspot – while squid ink tagliolini makes for a decadent dinner, accompanied by a choice of 300 Italian wines. A good place to soak up South Beach glam, even if the ambience occasionally overshadows the food.

### La Sandwicherie
*229 14th Street, at Washington Avenue (1-305 532 8934, www.lasandwicherie.com). Bus C, H, K, W, South Beach Local.* **Open** 10am-5am Mon-Thur, Sun; 8am-6am Fri, Sat. **Main courses** $6-$12. **Credit** AmEx, MC, V. **Map** p280 D3 ⓴ **Sandwiches**
Second only to Pizza Rustica (*see p87*) for late-night bingeing, South Beach's original gourmet sandwich bar caters to a fabulous mix of clubbers, drinkers, limo drivers and tattoo artists, along with anyone else who appreciates a well-made prosciutto and mozzarella, ham and turkey, or veggie sandwich on a fresh baguette.
**Other location** 34 SW 8th Street, Brickell (1-305 374 9852).

### Sardinia
*1801 Purdy Avenue, at 18th Street (1-305 531 2228, www.sardinia-ristorante.com). Bus A, W.* **Open** noon-midnight daily. **Main courses** $16-$43. **Credit** AmEx, DC, MC, V. **Map** p280 C2 ⓴ Italian

Local foodies have embraced this stylish bayfront spot, characterised by hearty Sardinian cooking and a boisterous evening crowd. The decor is glossy rustic, with dark wood, brick and a wood-burning oven. Unusual pastas and earthy, decadent ingredients are trademarks: *orecchiette* with wild boar sausage, say, or Sardinian teardrop pasta with braised Colorado baby lamb. Dishes such as *coniglio*, braised rabbit with leeks and sautéed spinach, ooze authenticity, but the preparation is not always perfect. And the acoustics are lousy: quiet conversation is hard, even if scenesters like the buzz.

### Segafredo
*1040 Lincoln Road, at Lenox Avenue (1-305 673 0047, www.sze-originale.com). Bus C, G, H, K, L, M, S, W, South Beach Local.* **Open** 11am-1am Mon-Thur, Sun; 11am-2am Fri, Sat. **Main courses** $6-$15. **Credit** AmEx, DC, Disc, MC, V. **Map** p280 C2 ⓴ Italian
Dear 'Fredo started out as an unassuming espresso joint, but has since spiralled into the South Beach hangout that it is today. It's permanently mobbed with hipsters artfully draped over the oversized upholstered chairs, looking like they're the cats that got all the cream. The menu includes sandwiches, salads, carpaccios and desserts. Cool lounge music until the wee hours and a full bar add to the appeal.

### Smith & Wollensky
*1 Washington Avenue, at South Pointe Park (1-305 673 2800, www.smithandwollensky.com). Bus H, M, W.* **Open** noon-11pm Mon-Thur;

Sosta Pizzeria.

STK.

noon-midnight Fri; 11am-midnight Sat; 11am-11pm Sun. **Main courses** $21-$53. **Credit** AmEx, DC, MC, V. **Map** p280 F3 ⑱ **Steakhouse**
Nestled at the southern tip of the Beach, overlooking Government Cut, this cavernous, 550-seat chain steakhouse, which was founded in New York in 1977, offers one of the best views in the city. And pretty good steaks, too, with choice cuts of prime-grade, dry-aged beef. The waterfront location makes it a fave for Friday happy hours, Sunday brunches or for toasting passing cruise ships.

### ★ Sosta Pizzeria

*1025 Lincoln Road, at Lenox Avenue (1-305 722 5454, www.sostapizzeria.com). Bus C, G, H, K, L, M, South Beach Local.* **Open** noon-midnight daily. **Main courses** $9-$15. **Credit** AmEx, MC, V. **Map** p280 C2 ⑯ **Pizza**
There are plenty of places to grab a bite along Lincoln Road – not all of them deserving of your hard-earned cash. But Sosta is. Identical twin chefs Nicola and Fabbrizio Corro (of Quattro; see p87) are at the helm of this pizzeria, where thin crust rules and fresh toppings are a foregone conclusion. The standard margherita is above-average – particularly for the area – but the burrata is even better. Antipasti, salads and fresh pastas are all well made and served in generous portions (particularly considering the price). Weekday happy hours attract gourmet early birds, who can't argue with $3 Peroni drafts and $7 pizzas. The wine list is large and impressive, with 75 varieties available by the bottle.

### STK

*Perry South Beach, 2377 Collins Avenue, at 23rd Street (1-305 604 6988, www.togrp.com). Bus 103, 112, 113, 119, 120, 150.* **Open** 6pm-1am Mon, Fri, Sat; 6-11pm Tue, Wed, Sun; 6pm-midnight Thur. **Main courses** $28-$95. **Credit** AmEx, MC, V. **Map** p280 B3 ⑱ **Steakhouse**
Steak gets sexy at STK Miami, the bi-level steak-house-cum-nightclub located in the chic Perry South Beach (*see p144*). Executive chef Aaron Taylor sets the gastronomic tone with naturally raised cuts of beef, which can be customised with all sorts of unique toppings – foie gras, truffle butter or peppercorn crust anyone? Signature bites include shrimp rice krispies, parmesan truffle fries, Lil' BRGs (aka sliders) and sweet corn pudding. A revolving round up of international DJs keeps the party going past dessert.

### SushiSamba Dromo

*600 Lincoln Road, at Pennsylvania Avenue (1-305 673 5337, www.sushisamba.com). Bus C, G, H, K, L, M, S, W, South Beach Local.* **Open** noon-midnight Mon; noon-1am Tue-Thur; 11.30am-2am Sat; 11.30am-1am Sun. **Main courses** $12-$40. **Credit** AmEx, MC, V. **Map** p280 C3 ⑰ **Fusion/sushi**
This hip Japanese/Brazilian/Peruvian sushi parlour has a look straight out of the pages of *Wallpaper** – we adore the mother-of-pearl-speckled bar. The likes of king crab roll and yellowtail ceviche are as much accessories as food to the Prada-toting PYTs who convene here.

### Umi Sushi & Sake Bar

*Delano Hotel, 1685 Collins Avenue, at 17th Street (1-305 674 5752, www.delano-hotel.com). Bus C, G, H, L, M, S.* **Open** 7pm-midnight Mon-Thur, Sun; 7pm-1am Fri, Sat. **Main courses** $9-$26. **Credit** AmEx, DC, MC, V. **Map** p280 C3 ⑰ **Sushi**
South Beach just can't get enough sushi, which explains why the trendier-than-thou Delano (*see p135*) turned its Starck-designed, eat-in lobby kitchen into a sushi bar serving cucumber cocktails and $15 spicy tuna rolls for hipsters who don't mind sharing a communal table and paying through the nose.

**CONSUME**

### Tap Tap

*819 5th Street, at Meridian Avenue (1-305 672 2898). Bus C, K, M, S, South Beach Local.* **Open** 1-11pm Mon-Fri; noon-11pm Sat, Sun. **Main courses** $11-$20. **Credit** AmEx, MC, V. **Map** p280 E3 ⑱ **Haitian**

It looks like a shack from the outside, but that's all part of the package at this funky, arty restaurant, which pays homage to Haitian culture and cuisine. Inside, colourful murals spice up the place, and music, art exhibitions and poetry readings complement a basic menu of fish, lamb and goat, plus vegetable stews. It's like a trip to Little Haiti but with a much improved chance of finding your car where you left it at the end of the night.

### Tapas Y Tintos

*448 Española Way, at Drexel Avenue (1-305 538 8272, www.tapasytintos.com). Bus C, G, H, K, L, M, S, W, South Beach Local.* **Open** 5pm-3am Mon, Tue; noon-3am Wed; noon-4am Thur; noon-4.30am Fri, Sat; noon-2am Sun. **Main courses** $8-$55. **Credit** AmEx, MC, V. **Map** p280 D3 ⑲ **Tapas**

Known more for its live music, flamenco and tango lessons than for its culinary fireworks, this small outdoor café and wine bar is never short on atmosphere. Situated on Española Way, a quaint backstreet, it feels more Madrid than Miami, with a traditional tapas menu.

### Villa Azur

*309 23rd Street, at Liberty Avenue (1-305 763 8688, www.villaazurmiami.com). Bus 103, 112, 113, 119, 123.* **Open** 6.30pm-3am daily. **Main courses** $21-$55. **Credit** AmEx, MC, V. **Map** p280 B3 ⑳ **French**

In the heart of nightclub central, Villa Azur is a welcome reminder that the art of fine dining is not always lost on the party-'til-the-sun-rises crowd. This French newcomer – co-owned by actor Olivier Martinez (who, at press time, was set to become Mr Halle Berry) – channels a bit of the French Riviera and an inspired France-meets-Italy menu (Mediterranean bouillabaisse casserole and risotto with fresh lobster and purple artichoke hearts are two standout dishes). You'll be transported the moment you walk inside the door into a lobby that Marie Antoinette would have loved – crystal chandeliers, antique wood fixtures and sleek chairs and couches lead the way to the dining room. But the courtyard is where the action happens. All the usual accoutrements – like a $600 helping of Kaluga caviar and more celebrities than you can shake a stick at – are here. But the end result is surprisingly down to earth.

### ★ Yardbird

*1600 Lenox Avenue, at 16th Street (1-305 538 5220, www.runchickenrun.com). Bus C, G, H, K, L, M, South Beach Local.* **Open** 11.30am-11pm

1500° at Eden Roc.

Mon-Thur; 11.30pm-midnight Fri; 10am-midnight Sat; 10am-11pm Sun. **Main courses** $10-$15. **Credit** MC, V. **Map** p280 C2 ㉒ **American**

Flashy though it may be, Miami is still a part of the American South: the region that spawned fried chicken, fried green tomatoes, pretty much fried anything. One need only venture a few steps off Lincoln Road to try these comfort food staples, all of them made from scratch and most of it sourced locally. The buzz surrounding Yardbird has been deafening since its birth in 2011 (plans to expand the concept to New York City and Las Vegas are currently in the works). At the centre of this publicity maelstrom? Yardbird's now-famous fried chicken – a recipe that takes 27 hours to prepare and can be ordered up as a slider (Mama's Chicken Biscuits) or on a plate (Llewellyn's Fine Fried Chicken). Wash it down with a whiskey-based house cocktail (Blackberry Lemonade – made with lemon juice, organic blackberries, cardamom and sparkling wine – is a customer favourite).

## MID BEACH

### ★ 1500° at Eden Roc

*Eden Roc Renaissance Miami Beach, 4525 Collins Avenue, at 45th Street (1-305 674 5594, www.1500degreesmiami.com). Bus G, H, L, S.* **Open** 6-10pm Mon-Thur, Sun; 6-11pm Fri, Sat.

Main courses $26-$33. **Credit** AmEx, MC, V.
**Map** p281 F4 **㉜ Modern European**
Gordon Ramsay couldn't break chef Paula DaSilva.
The former *Hell's Kitchen* finalist rose to the front of
the kitchen line at the Eden Roc's signature restaurant
back in 2011, the same year *Esquire* magazine named
it one of the best new restaurants in America. DaSilva
takes an innovative approach to her farm-to-table cuisine, with a regularly changing menu of small and big
plates, steaks and a raw bar. While 'locally sourced'
means you'll find a lot of fish on the menu, the chef is
serious about her steaks. So much so that they have
their own menu of sauces (from cabernet to horserad-
ish crème fraîche) and butters (the likes of black garlic
truffle and smoked sweet onion).

## Cecconi's

*Soho Beach House, 4385 Collins Avenue, at 44th
Street (1-786 507 7902, www.cecconismiamibeach.
com).* Bus G, H, L, S. **Open** 7am-11pm Mon-Thur,
Sun; 7am-midnight Fri, Sat. **Main courses** $14-$44.
**Credit** AmEx, MC, V. **Map** p281 F4 **㉝ Italian**
If you're hoping for a star sighting, your chances will
be greatly improved by taking in a meal – and the
gorgeous decor – at Cecconi's, the open-to-the-public
Italian restaurant on the ground floor of the mem-
bers-only Soho Beach House. Open for breakfast,
lunch and dinner, the Miami outpost of the Venetian
original serves up the same inspired dishes, from
braised lamb ravioli with peas and pecorino to veal
saltimbocca with sautéed spinach.

## Forge

*432 41st Street, at Royal Palm Avenue (1-305
538 8533, www.theforge.com).* Bus C, J, K, M, T.
**Open** 6-11pm Mon-Thur, Sun; 6pm-1am Fri, Sat.
**Main courses** $20-$55. **Credit** AmEx, Disc, MC,
V. **Map** p281 F3 **㉞ Steakhouse**
Local legend has it that Al Capone is alive and well
and living in this steakhouse's acclaimed wine cellar.
The place itself is a rococo-lover's fantasy: multi-cham-
bered, ornately decorated (and priced) and completely
OTT. Although it stands as a monument to decadent
wines, steak and fish, there are plenty of options for
calorie-conscious diners. You can tour and dine in the
300,000-bottle wine cellar if you wish. *Photo p92.*

## Hakkasan

*Fontainebleau, 4441 Collins Avenue, at 44th
Street (1-786 276-1388, www.fontainebleau.com/
hakkasan).* Bus G, H, L, S. **Open** 6-11pm Mon-
Thur, Sun; noon-2.45pm, 6pm-midnight Fri, Sat.
**Main courses** $18-$78. **Credit** AmEx, MC, V.
**Map** p281 F4 **㉟ Chinese**
As if dining at the Fontainebleau weren't already a
first-class outing, in 2009 the legendary hotel welcomed the first American edition of the even more
legendary London eaterie (and the only Michelin-
rated Chinese restaurant in the UK). Dining here is
for high rollers only, as even a handful of appetisers
comes with a $100-plus price tag. Still, reservations
are tough to get hold of. But if you can afford the
splurge, you won't regret it. Behind the scenes, chef
de cuisine Jian Heng Loo utilises the restaurant's $1
million kitchen (yes, really) to perfection, churning
out perfectly executed Cantonese classics, including
crispy duck salad and jasmine tea-smoked ribs.
Weekends bring a traditional dim sum lunch, with
dumplings ranging from steamed squid ink *har gau*
with caviar to wok-fried soft shell crabs.

**CONSUME**

Cecconi's.

Forge. *See p91.*

# NORTH BEACH

## Café Prima Pasta
*414 71st Street, at Harding Avenue (1-305 867 0106, www.primapasta.com). Bus G, L, K, R.* **Open** noon-midnight Mon-Thur; noon-1am Fri; 1pm-1am Sat; 5pm-midnight Sun. **Main courses** $15-$30. **Credit** MC, V. **Map** p281 B4 ⑤⑥ **Pasta**
A bright spot on a dingy street, Prima Pasta offers home-made pastas that pack 'em in, with crowds of eager carb-cravers queueing up on the pavement. Rich scents of garlic and oil waft outside, making the inevitable wait almost too much to bear. But it's worth it.

## Las Vacas Gordas
*933 Normandy Drive, at 71st Street (1-305 867 1717, www.lasvacasgordas.com). Bus L.* **Open** 6-11.30pm Mon-Fri; 1-11.30pm Sat, Sun. **Main courses** $12-$24. **Credit** AmEx, DC, MC, V. **Map** p281 B3 ⑤⑦ **Steakhouse**
The Argentinians are coming – and opening steakhouses all over town. This lively North Beach spot is not for the faint of heart or stomach. Inside, the music is deafening and the abrupt wait staff have yet to master the art of ingratiating American customer service. Vegetarians would be horrified by the mixed grill – sweetbreads, sausages, blood sausages, entrails and grilled meats galore – but carnivores will rejoice in the whopping big short ribs and flat steaks. Outside, the sidewalk seating feels more civilised: sip on Argentinian wine and pretend you're in Buenos Aires.

## Shuckers Bar & Grill
*1819 79th Street Causeway, off E Treasure Drive (1-305 866 1570, www.shuckersbarandgrill.com). Bus K, R.* **Open** 11am-2am daily. **Main courses** $8-$15. **Credit** AmEx, DC, MC, V. **Seafood**
On the waterfront, Shuckers has a perfect view and a breezy vibe. The open-air space draws a boisterous, beer-and-wings crowd who shoot pool or down bloody marys to a classic rock soundtrack. This is not a foodie destination, but the fresh seafood – conch fritters, shrimps, snapper sandwiches with fries – goes well with pitchers of lager, as do the burgers. There are salads galore, but the Key lime pie is sickly sweet. A great spot to watch the sunset. And possibly spot a dolphin.

# SURFSIDE TO GOLDEN BEACH

## Café Ragazzi
*9500 Harding Avenue, at 95th Street (1-305 866 4495, www.caferagazzi.com). Bus H, R, S, T.* **Open** 11.30am-11.30pm Mon-Thur, Sun; 11.30am-midnight Fri, Sat. **Main courses** $16-$33. **Credit** MC, V. **Map** p281 inset ⑤⑧ **Italian**
Size definitely doesn't matter at this tiny neighbourhood Italian spot, where people willingly wait out on the street for a table. The stellar cuisine includes garlicky, home-made rigatoni with eggplant, seared salmon steak and veal parmigiana.

## Josh's Delicatessen
*9517 Harding Avenue, at 96th Street, (1-305 397 8494). Bus X, Y, Z.* **Open** 8.30am-5pm daily. **Main courses** $5-$14. **Credit** AmEx, Disc, MC, V. **Map** p281 inset ⑤⑨ **Deli**
This traditional, New York-style deli is a refreshing alternative to the usual Miami Beach fare, with offerings such as corned beef on rye, house-cured tongue, matzo ball soup, cold cuts, plus a slew of other Jewish favourites. The house Jewban piles pastrami, roast pork, pickles and swiss cheese on Cuban bread.

## Il Mulino New York
*Acqualina, 17875 Collins Avenue, Sunny Isles Beach (1-305 466 9191, www.ilmulino.com). Bus K, S.* **Open** 5.30-11pm daily. **Main courses** $45-$75. **Credit** AmEx, MC, V. **Italian**
An idyllic match for the elegant and Italian-inspired oceanfront resort of Acqualina (*see p153*), acclaimed Italian restaurant Il Mulino New York brings with it a reputation of tremendous success. It's renowned for its bustling atmosphere, market-fresh daily specials, extensive selection of fine Italian wines and impeccably polished wait staff. Sure, it comes at a price, but it's cheaper than two weeks in Tuscany.

## ★ Palm
*9650 East Bay Harbor Drive, at 96th Street, Bay Harbor Islands (1-305 868 7256, www.thepalm.com/miami). Bus 107.* **Open** 5-11pm

Palm.

CONSUME

daily. **Main courses** $30-$50. **Credit** AmEx, MC, V. **Map** p281 inset ⑩ Steakhouse

There's no shortage of options in Miami when it comes to steakhouses. But when you're looking for a true, old-school American steakhouse, the Palm has little competition. Founded in New York City in 1926, the cavernous Miami edition of Palm – located in the Bay Harbor Islands – is full of wood (on the walls, floors, banquettes, chairs, tables and even the ceilings) and oozes good-old-boy charm. Steaks are, of course, the speciality, but family recipes for Italian dishes like veal marsala and linguine and clams have been on the menu since the mid 1920s. There's a good reason why there are now 30 locations of this upmarket chain worldwide, from Miami to London.

### Timo

*17624 Collins Avenue, off NE 175th Terrace, Sunny Isles Beach (1-305 936 1008, www.timo restaurant.com). Bus K, S.* **Open** 11.30am-2pm, 6-10pm Mon-Thur; 11.30am-2pm, 6-11pm Fri; 6-11pm Sat; 6-10pm Sun. **Main courses** $12-$42. **Credit** AmEx, DC, MC, V. **Italian**

Chef Tim Andriola made his culinary mark with Timo. It's a fine Italian restaurant that's been the subject of much talk among the snowbirds (that's wintering Yankees and Canadians) since its opening in early 2003. The rustic chic atmosphere is abuzz with noise, thanks to happy eaters enjoying a top-notch menu of dishes such as burrata ravioli with fresh tomato, and any one of Andriola's wood-oven pizzas. It seats 120 but, even so, good luck getting a reservation.

## DOWNTOWN

### Area 31

*EPIC Hotel, 16th Floor, 270 Biscayne Boulevard Way, at SE 4th Street (1-305 424 5234, www. area31restaurant.com). Bus 3, 93, 119.* **Open** 11.30am-3pm, 6-10pm Mon-Thur, Sun; 11.30am-3pm, 6-11pm Fri, Sat. **Main courses** $19-$38. **Credit** AmEx, MC, V. **Map** p282 E3 ⑤ Seafood

Even if it didn't boast one of the city's most spectacular views – the Miami skyline is laid out in front of you from the 16th floor of the EPIC Hotel – chef E Michael Reidt's innovative seafood, much of it sourced from the waters you can gaze out upon, would surely be packing in the patrons. Reidt was recently named one of *Ocean Drive Magazine*'s 'hot new chefs', and fresh ingredients are his culinary weapon of choice – he's got his very own patio garden to prove it. The menu changes regularly, but expect fresh ceviche and tartares. Reidt gets experimental with a section of the menu labelled Chefie Things; on a recent visit it yielded crispy fish collar, smoked shrimp guacamole and pork cheek with a chilli graham cracker crumble. *Photo p94.*

### Azul

*500 Brickell Key Drive (1-305 913 8358, www.mandarinoriental.com/miami).* **Open** 7am-11pm Tue-Sat. **Main courses** $33-$65. **Credit** AmEx, DC, MC, V. **Map** p282 F4 ⑫ **International**

If you're dining on an expense account, if someone else is paying or if you're just plain rich, Azul is *the* place to splurge. The priceless water views of the city set the stage for chef Jacob Anaya. The result is a tour de force of international cuisine, inspired by Caribbean, French, Argentine, Asian and American flavours. Among the standouts: Moroccan-inspired lamb cassoulet, king salmon and beluga lentils and lobster pot pie – the culinary equivalent of an Ivy League education once you see the bill. Diners range from stuffy to celebratory: power suits, socialites and special-occasion crowds.

### Capital Grille

*444 Brickell Avenue, at SE 4th Street (1-305 374 4500, www.thecapitalgrille.com). Metromover Knight Center.* **Open** 11.30am-3pm, 5-10pm Mon-Thur; 11.30am-3pm, 5-11pm Fri; 6-11pm Sat; 5-10pm Sun. **Main courses** $28-$49. **Credit** AmEx, DC, MC, V. **Map** p282 E3 ❸ **Steakhouse**
Located on the Capitol Hill of Miami's business movers and shakers, this is the quintessential spot for a power lunch. Like the conversation, the food here is quite heavy: think dry-aged beef sirloin, filet mignon and prime rib. Although there is a serious wine list, we recommend a trip to the clubby bar for one of the very fine pineapple-saturated Stolis.

### Il Gabbiano

*335 S Biscayne Boulevard, at NE 3rd Street (1-305 373 0063, www.ilgabbianomiami.com).* **Open** noon-3pm, 5-11.30pm Mon-Fri; 5-11.30pm Sat. **Credit** AmEx, DC, MC, V. **Map** p282 E4 ❻ **Italian**
One of the few restaurants in Miami with an actual view of the water, this pricey pasta joint is ideal for fans of garlic, truffles and home-made pasta that's a far cry from Ragu. Spaghetti alla carbonara will set you back $27, while risotto with porcini mushrooms is a divine culinary creation with an ungodly price tag of $37. If you really want to splurge, there's a filet of beef with sautéed foie gras for $55. Service is old school, verging on stuffy, but what you're paying for here is the view. Considering Miami's volatile real estate market, it makes sense.

### Gordon Biersch Brewery Restaurant

*1201 Brickell Avenue, at SE 12th Street (1-786 425 1130, www.gordonbiersch.com). Bus 24, 48, B/Metromover Financial District.* **Open** 11.30am-midnight Mon-Thur, Sun; 11.30am-1am Fri, Sat. **Main courses** $10-$29. **Credit** AmEx, DC, MC, V. **International**
The ideal chaser to the city's martini madness, this hangout is a vast homage to beer. But there's also an impressive gourmet menu that includes lobster bisque and cashew chicken stir-fry, as well as pizza, burgers and salads. It gets packed with young professionals during happy hour (4-7.30pm Mon-Fri).

### Hoxton

*1111 SW 1st Avenue, at SW 11th Street (1-305 677 8466, www.hoxtonmiami.com). Bus 6, 8, 48, 102.* **Open** 5pm-midnight

**Area 31**. *See p93.*

Mon-Thur, Sun; 5pm-3am Fri, Sat. **Main courses** $8-$12. **Credit** AmEx, MC, V. **Seafood**
The Hoxton is what happens when Miami and New England collide. Everything about the resto-lounge – from the beachy decor to the seafood-focused menu – is like a hyper-stylised version of Cape Cod. The menu is basically comprised of two things: fresh seafood (grilled oysters, steamed mussels, chilled Florida shrimp) and deep-fried pub fare (fish and chips, buttermilk fried chicken, crispy crab cakes). And all of it's well priced. The cocktail menu, too, makes use of fresh ingredients; try the signature Hoxton Lemonade, freshly squeezed with basil, strawberry and vodka, then topped with ginger beer.

### Oceanaire Seafood Room

*900 S Miami Avenue, at SW 9th Street (1-305 372 8862, www.theoceanaire.com).* **Open** noon-10pm Mon-Thur, noon-11pm Fri; 5-11pm Sat; 5-10pm Sun. **Main courses** $23-$40. **Credit** AmEx, DC, MC, V. **Map** p282 F2 ❻❺ **Seafood**
A cross between a glam ocean liner and a swish 1930s nightclub, Oceanaire is certainly visually appetising. As befits the elaborate nautical setting, the seafood menu is exhaustive – and expensive. But the seafood – from Ecuadorian mahi mahi to Palm Beach cobia, Peruvian ceviche to Costa Rican wahoo – is top notch. Appetisers and side dishes are old school: jumbo shrimp cocktail, New England clam chowder, creamed corn and sour cream mashed potatoes. Desserts – baked Alaska, root beer float, ice-cream and cookies – are similarly comforting. Be warned: the portions are huge, and the effusive service borders on parody.

### Perricone's Marketplace & Café

*15 SE 10th Street, at S Miami Avenue (1-305 374 9449, www.perricones.com). Metrorail Brickell.* **Open** *Market* 7am-11pm Mon-Thur,

Sun; 7am-11.30pm Sat. *Restaurant* 11am-11pm
Mon-Thur; 8am-11.30pm Sat; 9am-11pm Sun.
**Main courses** $10-$37. **Credit** AmEx, MC, V.
**Map** p282 F2 ❻❻ **Italian**
This charming Italian restaurant has a woody, rustic
setting – the building is actually an 18th-century barn
relocated from Vermont to Downtown Miami.
Attractions include excellent wines, pastas and sal-
ads, and a sumptuous Sunday brunch. For gourmet
grub on the go, there's a fantastic Italian marketplace.

### Los Ranchos

*401 Biscayne Boulevard, at NE 4th Street (1-305
375 8188, www.beststeakmiami.com). Metromover
College or Bayside.* **Open** 11.30am-10.30pm Mon-
Thur, Sun; noon-11pm Fri, Sat. **Main courses** $9-
$29. **Credit** AmEx, DC, MC, V. **Map** p282 C4 ❻❼
**Latin American**
This Nicaraguan chain is a great place to sink your
teeth into some carcass, the menu is stacked with
steak, steak and more steak. The must-try is the
*churrasco* – grilled flank steak with chilli salsa.
**Other locations** 8888 SW 136th Street, the Falls,
at US 1 (1-305 238 6867); 125 SW 107th Avenue,
at W Flagler Street, Sweetwater (1-305 552 6767).

### ★ Garcia's Seafood Grille & Fish

*398 NW North River Drive, at NW 4th Street
(1 305 375 0765, www.garciasseafoodgrill.com).*
**Open** 11am-9.30pm daily. **Main courses** $12-
$25. **Credit** AmEx, MC, V. **Seafood**
Down by the river, tucked behind a maze of downtown freeways and bridges, this seafood shack is a
hidden gem. From the nautical interior and rustic
waterfront deck to the fishing boats that chug by,
this place oozes character. Conch fritters, gorgeous
ceviche and Florida stone crab are warm-ups for the

entrées: juicy grilled jumbo shrimp, say, or grilled
yellowtail, grouper or lobster, served alongside but-
tery parsley potatoes, green plantains, caesar salads
or fries. The Key lime pie is one of the best in town.
Tricky to find, but worth the effort.

### River Oyster Bar

*650 S Miami Avenue, at SE 6th Street (1-305
530 1915, www.therivermiami.com). Metromover
5th Street.* **Open** noon-10.30pm Mon-Thur; noon-
midnight Fri; 4.30pm-midnight Sat; 4.30-9.30pm
Sun. **Main courses** $12-$34. **Credit** AmEx, DC,
Disc, MC, V. **Map** p282 F2 ❻❽ **Seafood**
Take a sleek, minimalist interior, a fantastic raw bar
(oysters, ceviches, clams and seafood cocktails, plus
glorious sauces) and daily fresh catches, and you
have a winner. The local business crowd loves it,
and fans say these are the freshest oysters in town.

### Taverna Opa

*900 S Miami Avenue, at SE 8th Street (1-305 673
6730, www.tavernaopa.com). Bus 6, 8, 95, 102.*
**Open** 11am-1am daily. **Main courses** $6-$33.
**Credit** AmEx, MC, V. **Map** p282 F2 ❻❾ **Greek**
Top of the list for good-time dining, Opa is a big
spartan barn of a place that quickly fills most nights
with rafter-raising raucousness. The inspiration is
festive Greek, the eats are meze, meat and grilled
seafood; the plates are for smashing; and the tables
are for dancing on. Order a Zorbatini – vodka, blue
curacao, pineapple juice and banana liqueur – and
let it be known: Greece is the word.

### Toro Toro

*InterContinental Miami, 100 Chopin Plaza
(1-305 372 4710, www.torotoromiami.com).
Bus 3, 11, 77, 93, 95, 119.* **Open** 11.30am-3pm

Hoxton.

CONSUME

CONSUME

daily; 6pm-midnight Mon-Wed, Sun; 6pm-1am Thur-Sat. **Main courses** $22-$65. **Credit** MC, V. **Map** p282 E4 ⑦ **Steakhouse**

The traditional American steakhouse gets a very Miami (read: pan-Latin) twist at this acclaimed restaurant, which arrived all the way from Dubai in late 2012. The decor is sophisticated and masculine, with dark wood furnishings, leather seating and wrought-iron details. Opt for the Rodizio Experience for the most memorable meal; priced at $65 per person, this tableside service offers unlimited consumption of *picanha* steak, Omaha ribeye, lamb chop, chorizo sausage and *achiote* chicken, with classic sides, from rice and black beans to creamed spinach.

## CORAL GABLES

### El Chalan

*7971 Bird Road, at SW 79th Avenue (1-305 266 0212).* **Open** 11am-10pm Mon-Thur; 11am-11pm Fri, Sat; 9am-10pm Sun. **Main courses** $6-$19. **Credit** AmEx, Disc, MC, V. **Peruvian**

Miami's best food is often found in strip malls, and this budget Peruvian caff is a case in point. The aesthetics are cheap: bright, unflattering lights, laminated menus and photographs of the food. But the home cooking is top notch. The ceviche is fresh and tangy, the *lomo saltado* is present and correct, and the medley of traditional Peruvian cuisine is simple and comforting (*aji de gallina*, boneless chicken in a creamy sauce; tripe stew in yellow mint sauce). If you can't afford the elegant Francesco's (*see below*), this is a great intro to Peruvian cuisine.

**Other locations** 1580 Washington Avenue, at 16th Street, South Beach (1-305 532 8880).

### Christy's

*3101 Ponce de León Boulevard, at Malaga Avenue (1-305 446 1400, www.christysrestaurant.com). Bus 24, 52, 72, Coral Gables Circulator.* **Open** 5-10pm Mon-Thur; noon-10.30pm Fri; 5-10.30pm Sat. **Main courses** $28-$50. **Credit** AmEx, Disc, MC, V. **Map** p284 C4 ⑦ **Steakhouse**

You can almost taste the power surging through this traditional, clubby steakhouse, where the excellent food and service attract an impressive clientele. Expect superlative lamb chops, steaks and prime rib, a decent caesar salad and classic desserts like baked Alaska for two. Live jazz begins every Friday night at 7pm.

### ★ Francesco

*325 Alcazar Avenue, at Salzedo Street (1-305 446 1600). Bus 72.* **Open** noon-3pm, 6-10pm

Toro Toro. *See p95.*

## THE BEST CHEAP EATS

For fresh fish on the beach
**My Ceviche.** See p85.

For when only a hot dog will do
**Dogma Grill.** See p99.

For healthy fast food with a kick
**Lime Fresh Mexican Grill.** See p84.

For a taste of old New York
**Josh's Delicatessen.** See p92.

For a slice any time
**Pizza Rustica.** See p87.

Mon-Thur; noon-3pm, 6-10.30pm Fri; 6-10.30pm Sat. **Main courses** $27-$48. **Credit** AmEx, DC, MC. **Map** p284 B4 ⑫ Peruvian
Located discreetly down a Coral Gables backstreet, Francesco is a class act. The upmarket decor may be a bit bland – white tablecloths, earth tones – but the gorgeous Peruvian cuisine has a kick. For starters, try the moreish potato dishes: Peruvian yellow potatoes, say, topped with aji Amarillo and white cheese. The Peruvian bouillabaisse, and the squid ink risotto with shrimp, hit the spot. And you can't go wrong with the ceviche. The loyal crowd of Latin American regulars says it all.

### Miss Saigon Bistro
*148 Giralda Avenue, at Ponce de León Boulevard (1-305 446 8006, www.misssaigonbistro.com). Bus 24, 42, 72, Coral Gables Circulator.* **Open** 11.30am-3pm, 5.30-10pm Mon-Thur; 11.30am-3pm, 5.30-11pm Fri; 5.30-10pm Sat; 5.30-9.30pm Sun. **Main courses** $8-$21. **Credit** MC, V. **Map** p284 B4 ⑬ Vietnamese
Get over the fact that this family-run Vietnamese bistro has been named after the cheesy musical (the soundtrack plays as nauseum). It is a knockout. Servers recommend dishes and even tailor them to your taste. They often suggest you order a few starters (the summer rolls are sublime), a noodle dish and a main course such as grilled salmon with mango.

### Ortanique on the Mile
*278 Miracle Mile (SW 24th Street), at Ponce de León Boulevard (1-305 446 7710, www. ortaniquerestaurants.com). Bus 24, 42, 72, Coral Gables Circulator.* **Open** 11.30am-2.30pm Mon-Fri; 5-10pm Mon, Tue; 5-11pm Wed-Sat; 5-9.30pm Sun. **Main courses** $22-$55. **Credit** AmEx, DC, MC, V. **Map** p284 C4 ⑭ Caribbean
Named after a rare tropical fruit (an ortanique is a hybrid orange native to Jamaica – apparently), this restaurant serves creative Caribbean cooking. The focus here is on cuisine, not scene, and the food, by

top chef Cindy Hutson, is outstanding. Dishes such as jerked double pork chop with guava rum sauce and tropical fruit flambé are a blissful orgy of flavour.

## COCONUT GROVE

### Le Bouchon du Grove
*3430 Main Highway, at Grand Avenue (1-305 448 6060, www.lebouchondugrove.com). Bus 37, 42, Coconut Grove Circulator.* **Open** 10.30am-3pm, 6-11pm Mon; 9.30am-3pm, 6-11pm Tue-Thur; 9.30am-3pm, 6pm-midnight Fri; 8.30am-3pm, 6pm-midnight Sat; 8.30am-3pm, 6-11pm Sun. **Main courses** $20-$30. **Credit** AmEx, Disc, MC, V. **Map** p285 B3 ⑮ French
Everything about this bistro screams 'France' – except for the warm service. The cosy room, the closely packed tables and the convivial buzz are all *très* Parce. The home-made foie gras terrine and the onion soup are especially good.

### Gibraltar
*Grove Isle Hotel & Spa, Grove Isle Drive, off S Bayshore Drive (1-305 857 5007, www.grove isle.com). Bus 48.* **Open** 7am-3pm, 6.30-10pm Mon-Thur, Sun; 7am-3pm, 6.30-11pm Fri, Sat. **Main courses** $18-$45. **Credit** AmEx, DC, Disc, MC, V. Seafood
Gibraltar is different from most of Miami's all-style, no-substance waterfront eateries: it provides priceless views of Biscayne Bay and pricey nouveau seafood that is actually worth every cent. Located on an island just off Coconut Grove, the restaurant boasts a glass-walled indoor space and a classical waterside courtyard. The menu is fish and shellfish, and the preparation and execution are top class.

### GreenStreet Cafe
*3468 Main Highway, at Commodore Plaza (1-305 444 0244, www.greenstreetcafe.net). Bus 42, 48, Coconut Grove Circulator.* **Open** 7.30am-1am Mon, Tue, Sun; 7.30am-3am Wed-Sat. **Main courses** $12-$25. **Credit** AmEx, DC, MC, V. **Map** p285 B2 ⑯ Café
This is the Grove's command central for the socio-anthropological sport of people-watching, thanks to the GreenStreet's strategic placement on a bustling corner. To accompany this activity, management thoughtfully provides excellent salads, flatbreads, pastas and burgers.

### ★ Peacock Garden Cafe
*2889 McFarlane Road, at Grand Avenue (1-305 774 3332, www.peacockspot.com). Bus X, Y, Z.* **Open** 8am-10pm Mon-Thur, Sun; 8am-11pm Fri, Sat. **Main courses** $13-$32. **Credit** MC, V. **Map** p285 B3 ⑰ Café
It doesn't get much more quaint than this dainty little café, which celebrates the south Florida lifestyle with its cute nautical theme, verdant garden setting and regional breakfast, lunch and dinner fare. The

CONSUME

restaurant pays tribute to the history of Coconut Grove with a number of historical artefacts (photos, paintings, furnishings and even an old typewriter in tribute to the neighbourhood's arty culture), all curated by historian Arva Moore Parks.

## LITTLE HAVANA

### La Carreta
*3632 Calle Ocho (SW 8th Street), at SW 36th Avenue (1-305 444 7501, www.lacarretta.com). Bus 8, 37.* **Open** 8am-midnight Mon-Thur, Sun; 8am-2am Fri; 8am-3am Sat. **Main courses** $6-$23. **Credit** AmEx, DC, MC, V. **Cuban**
This Cuban chain offers large doses of the usual local nostalgia for Batista-era Cuba. You can't miss the massive sugar-cane plants growing on the front lawn. Expect large portions on the plates and a back-room café for strong Cuban coffee, sweet pastries and strange sugar-cane juice.
**Other locations** throughout the city.

### ★ Hy Vong
*3458 Calle Ocho (SW 8th Street), at SW 34th Avenue (1-305 446 3674). Bus 6, 8, 37.* **Open** 6-11pm Wed-Sun. **Main courses** $12-$17. **Credit** AmEx, Disc, MC, V. **Vietnamese**
A neighbourhood mainstay for more than 25 years, this tiny Vietnamese restaurant has only 35 seats, all constantly occupied by locals. Fill up on expertly prepared Asian specials such as kingfish with yellow curry sauce, cooked on a six-burner stove. If you arrive after 7pm, the wait for a free table can be brutal – up to two hours on occasions – and the service can be slow too. But fans swear the food is worth it.

### Versailles
*3555 Calle Ocho (SW 8th Street), at SW 35th Avenue (1-305 444 0240, www.versailles restaurant.com). Bus 8, 37, 42.* **Open** 8am-1am Mon-Thur; 8am-2.30am Fri; 8am-3.30am Sat; 9am-1am Sun. **Main courses** $6-$26. **Credit** AmEx, MC, V. **Cuban**
Almost as famous locally as its palatial namesake is in France, Versailles is a kitschy Cuban diner with wall-to-wall mirrors, a constant buzz and an unabridged menu featuring every dish going. Not to everybody's taste, but a local legend and definitely worth a visit.

## THE DESIGN DISTRICT, WYNWOOD, LITTLE HAITI & AROUND

### Andiamo
*5600 Biscayne Boulevard, at 56th Street (1-305 762 5751, www.andiamopizzamiami.com). Bus 3.* **Open** 11am-11pm Mon-Thur, Sun; 11am-midnight Fri, Sat. **Main courses** $9-$18. **Credit** MC, V. **Pizza**
Pizza fans make the out-of-the-way trek to this Upper East Side gem to chow down on gourmet pizza in a former garage (complete with functioning carwash). Brick oven delicacies take their cue from

---

## ¡Buen Provecho!
*Chow down Cuban-style.*

Cuban cuisine is a mix of Caribbean, Spanish and African flavours, and its trademark dishes are mostly calorific (they love to fry) but wonderfully savoury. The Cuban menu is carb-heavy, revolving around beans and rice. It's also laden with sauces, with an emphasis on plantains and meat, mostly pork and beef, and often laced with garlic, cumin, onion, oregano and bay leaves. Don't even think about asking for anything low-fat or low-calorie – there's no such thing in Cuban cuisine. The following is a list of the most popular Cuban delicacies. So stop counting the calories and tuck in.

**arroz con pollo** roast chicken with saffron-seasoned yellow rice and diced vegetables.
**boniato** similar to a sweet potato.
**café cubano** strong black coffee, served in thimble-sized cups with lots of sugar.
**camarones** shrimp.

**ceviche** raw fish seasoned with spice and marinated in vinegar and citrus.
**churros** elongated, doughnut-like pastry.
**croquetas** golden-fried croquettes of ham, chicken or fish.
**mojo** marinade consisting of hot olive oil, lemon juice, sliced raw onion, garlic and a touch of pepper.
**moros y cristianos** ubiquitous Cuban side dish of black beans and white rice.
**palomilla** thinly sliced beef, similar to American minute steak.
**pan cubano** long, white crusty Cuban bread.
**picadillo** rich stew of ground meat, brown gravy, peas, pimientos, raisins and olives.
**plátano macho** deep-fried plantain.
**pollo asado** roasted chicken with onions.
**ropa vieja** shredded beef stew. The name literally means 'old clothes'.
**sofrito** sauce made of onion, green pepper, oregano and ground pepper in olive oil.

CONSUME

Cafeina.

every corner of the country: New England clam, Trenton tomato, South Philly cheese and Hawaiian pineapple are just some of the options.

## Cafeina

*297 NW 23rd Street, at NW 3rd Avenue (1-305 438 0792, www.cafeinamiami.com). Bus 2.* **Open** 11.30am-3pm Wed; 11.30am-3pm, 5pm-3am Thur, Fri; 11.30am-3pm, 9pm-3am Sat; 11.30am-4pm Sun. **Main courses** $9-$13. **Credit** MC, V. **Map** p285 F2 ⓲ **Tapas**

Part restaurant, part lounge, part garden, part art gallery, Wynwood's Cafeina is many things to many people – especially the steady stream of hipsters who count this comfortable, living room-like spot among their regular hangouts. The tapas dishes here are solid and wide-ranging. The cocktails are inventive too; it doesn't take more than a single café con leche martini to keep you buzzing all night. The on-site gallery features a roster of artists, many of them local but plenty of international talent too.

## Dogma Grill

*7030 Biscayne Boulevard, at 70th Street (1-305 759 3433, www.dogmagrill.com). Bus 3.* **Open** 10am-10pm daily. **Main courses** $5-$7. **Credit** MC, V. **Hot dogs**

This hip little hot dog stand (motto: 'a frank philosophy') on the corner of what used to be known as Crack and Crank Boulevards attracts the chic elite who have no qualms about sucking down a classic Chicago-style dog on the fringe of the ghetto.

## Federal Drink & Provisions

*5132 Biscayne Boulevard, at NE 52nd Street (1-305 758 9559, www.thefederalmiami.com). Bus 3, 16, 62.* **Open** 6-10pm Tue-Thur; 6-11pm Fri, Sat; 11.30am-4pm, 6-10pm Sun. **Main courses** $12-$32. **Credit** AmEx, MC, V. **Gastropub**

Go on, play with your food. The folks at the Federal won't mind. Experimentation is encouraged at this bustling gastropub, located in a not-so-bustling strip mall on the upper part of Biscayne Boulevard. Co-

owners Cesar Zapata and Aniece Meinhold treat this gem as if it were their very own nightly dinner party, and in a way it is. Which is why you'll see the same faces here several nights a week, chowing down on newfangled editions of classic American dishes. Starters include a Jar-o-Duck (a Mason jar full of duck, layered with charred fluff and candied sweet potato) and buffalo-style pig wings. Popular mains include the daily-changing Not Your Granny's Pot Pie, and a lamb burger served with grilled pickled onions on a pretzel bun.

## Jimmy's Eastside Diner

*7201 Biscayne Boulevard, at NE 72nd Street (1-305 754 3692). Bus 3, 16.* **Open** 6.30am-9pm daily. **Main courses** $5-$10. **No credit cards.** **American**

The sign outside declares that Jimmy's is 'Your Friendly Neighbourhood Eatery', and it's one of the few places left in the city where you can spend $5 on breakfast and have some silver left over. It's not in the most fashionable area and you'll need a car to get there. But this greasy spoon knows how to pack in the patrons.

## ★ Joey's

*2500 NW 2nd Avenue, at NW 25th Street (1-305 438 0488, www.joeyswynwood.com). Bus 2, 6.* **Open** 11.30am-3.30pm, 6-11pm Mon-Thur; 11.30am-3.30pm, 6pm-midnight Fri; noon-midnight Sat; noon-10pm Sun. **Main courses** $9-$24. **Credit** MC, V. **Map** p285 F2 ⓲ **Italian**

A pioneer of the Wynwood Arts District culinary scene, Joey's boasts a vast menu of classic (and affordable) Italian dishes. But it's the thin-crust pizza that keeps diners coming back – it was named as one of the country's best by *Food & Wine Magazine*. The inventive menu includes the Dolce e Piccante (fig, gorgonzola, honey and hot peppers) and the signature Joey (tuna in olive oil with spicy salami, gorgonzola, capers and spinach). There's live music to accompany your gorging every Thursday evening and happy hour specials on Fridays. *Photo p100.*

**CONSUME**

Joey's. See p99.

## Jumbo's

*7501 NW 7th Avenue, at NW 75th Street,*
*Little Haiti (1-305 751 1127).* **Open** 24hrs
daily. **Main courses** $5-$17. **Credit** AmEx,
DC, MC, V. **American**
A Miami tradition for more than 60 years, this
family-run place is known for its world-famous fried
shrimp, fried chicken, catfish fingers and collard
greens. Sure, it's located in what locals call the
'ghetto', but it's open 24/7 and worth slumming it.
And there's history here too: Jumbo's was the first
restaurant in Miami to integrate in 1966 and the first
to hire African American employees in 1967.

## Lost & Found Saloon

*185 NW 36th Street, at NW 2nd Avenue*
*(1-305 576 1008, www.thelostandfoundsaloon-*
*miami.com).* **Open** 11am-3am daily. **Main**
**courses** $5-$19. **Credit** AmEx, DC, MC, V.
**Map** p285 D2 ⑩ **Café**
This funky café brings the Wild West to the Design
District, with tongue firmly in cheek. There are
wagon wheel chandeliers, a Grand Canyon mural
and posters of John Wayne. Drinks are served in
Mason jars. The menu is vaguely Southwestern:
think burritos and black bean soup, with lots of veg-
etarian fare (meatless chilli, omelettes). Microbrews
on tap hit the spot with local hipsters.

## ★ Michael's Genuine Food & Drink

*130 NE 40th Street, at NE 1st Avenue (1-305 573*
*5550, www.michaelsgenuine.com).* **Open** 11.30am-
3pm, 5.30-11pm Mon-Thur; 11.30am-3pm, 5.30pm-
midnight Fri, Sat; 11am-2.30pm, 5.30-10pm Sun.
**Main courses** $12-$47. **Credit** AmEx, DC,
MC, V. **Map** p285 D3 ⑪ **American**

This buzzy restaurant is a true star. Decor and menu
are classy yet casual, and the service also strikes just
the right note. The interior mixes industrial chic – concrete floors, exposed ducts – with warmth (red lamps,
flickering candles, modern art and a brick oven glow-
ing from the open kitchen). With an emphasis on local
ingredients, the high-end comfort food ticks all the
right boxes. Mains change daily but might include a
selection of wood-fired pizzas; a whole 'poulet rouge'
chicken with plumped raisins, toasted pine nuts and
rocket; and duck confit with tangerine marmalade and
spiced pumpkin seeds. Hedy Goldsmith's innovative
desserts – including bread pudding and weekend pop
tarts – are indeed a grand finale.

## Michy's

*6927 Biscayne Boulevard, at NE 69th Street*
*(1-305 759 2001, www.michysmiami.com).*
*Bus 3.* **Open** 6-10.30pm Tue-Thur, Sun; 5.30-
11pm Fri, Sat. **Main courses** $8-$25. **Credit**
AmEx, DC, MC, V. **Fusion**
Brazenly located in the gritty Upper East Side, bold
and beautiful Michy's has helped slowly to gentrify
the neighbourhood. The flamboyant decor is pure
1970s retro glam, complete with kitsch florals and
shell chandeliers. Celebrity chef Michelle Bernstein
has fashioned a similarly playful menu, a brave mix
of Latin, Southern, French and comfort food, all
available in half portions. The white gazpacho is
moreish, and the creamy polenta is chock full of truffles. Peruvian-style ceviche is a classic starter, while
foie gras is done with a twist: seared and served with
a crêpe and blood orange marmalade. The sinful fettuccine carbonara combines serrano ham, poached
egg and saint-andré cheese, and fans drive across
town for the bread pudding.

## Oak Tavern

*35 NE 40th Street, at N Miami Avenue (1-786 391 1818, www.oaktavernmiami.com). Bus 36, 110, 202.* **Open** noon-10.30pm Mon-Thur; noon-midnight Fri; 6pm-midnight Sat; 10.30am-2.30pm, 4.30-9.30pm Sun. **Main courses** $10-$15. **Credit** AmEx, Disc, MC, V. **Map** p285 D3 🖲️ **Modern European**

The inside of this Design District newcomer is as warm and woody as the name indicates, with banquettes and communal tables made from reclaimed wood (though the moniker comes from the gigantic oak tree in the restaurant's patio area). The menu is comfort food with an upscale twist; devilled eggs are topped with paddlefish caviar, and crispy pig's ears are served with kale, pimento and fried egg. Being a sister restaurant to River Oyster Bar (*see p95*) means there's plenty of seafood on offer as well. *Photo p102.*

## ★ S&S Diner

*1757 NE 2nd Avenue, at NE 18th Street (1-305 373 4291).* **Open** 7.30am-6pm Tue-Fri; 7.30am-5pm Sat; 7.30am-3pm Sun. **Main courses** $2-$8. **No credit cards. American**

A vintage slice of classic Americana, Miami's oldest diner is cool without even having to try. The retro decor is deeply fabulous, from the red Formica counter and bar stools to the ancient gumball machine and old Western Union clock - it's all pure film noir. To complete the picture, there's even a wisecracking, seen-it-all-before waitress pouring coffee to the motley crew of customers: hookers and truckers, doctors and lawyers, club kids. The food is cheap and comforting classic diner fare: chilli con carne, meatloaf with gravy, split pea soup, and – of course – the inevitable cheeseburger with fries. God bless America.

# Interview Michael Schwartz

*Heating up the Design District.*

The food scene in Miami's Design District can be divided into two distinct eras: pre-Michael Schwartz and post-Michael Schwartz. The city's hungriest denizens are thankful for the latter epoch, which began in 2007 when the Philadelphia native opened **Michael's Genuine Food & Drink** (*see p100*). Conceived as a neighbourhood bistro in an area that had been previously bypassed by the city's culinary movers and shakers, the philosophy behind this 100-seat coterie was simple: create a comfortable space for diners to savour an array of locally sourced ingredients assembled in dishes at once both familiar and experimental. Schwartz was clearly on to something.

Schwartz added 'James Beard Award Winner' to his business card when the prestigious organisation named him Best Chef: South in 2010, the same year he debuted a second Genuine outpost in sunny Grand Cayman. In 2011, he opened a second restaurant in the Design District, Harry's Pizzeria, followed by the Cypress Room in March 2013.

**As a chef, what was it that spoke to you most about Miami?**
Diversity. There are a lot of cultures here and while I think there was some

time [where] that might have inhibited chefs, it has also helped Miami sort of grow up and define itself.

**How has the food scene changed most since you first arrived here in 1994?**
Everything has changed here. Miami was all about South Beach and the scene, and less about the food and the people. It has evolved, just as the community has, and become more comfortable with itself – less flashy, much more ingredient driven.

**In terms of location, you were a pioneer with Michael's Genuine, as it was the Design District's first 'real' restaurant. What made the neighbourhood feel ripe for a great restaurant?**
It was historically a place that attracted people who knew about good taste and [were] seeking it out. To me, that's what it was all about – doing something simple and pure that people could keep coming back to.

**Your food philosophy is a fairly straightforward one: fresh and local reign supreme. What are the three local ingredients you couldn't live without?**
Heirloom tomatoes, fish off the boat and citrus.

CONSUME

**CONSUME**

### Soyka

*5556 Biscayne Boulevard, at NE 55th Street (1-305 759 3117, www.soykarestaurant.com). Bus 3, 16, 62.* **Open** 11am-11pm Mon-Thur, Sun; 11am-midnight Fri, Sat. **Main courses** $12-$34. **Credit** AmEx, DC, MC, V. **Modern European**

Mark Soyka is a man who can spot a trend. He's the guy behind South Beach's News Café (*see p85*), and he was one of the first to stake a claim on Biscayne with this enormous, semi-industrial eaterie. The aesthetic is urban, but the restaurant is comfortable – if noisy. It draws mainly local professionals with unfussy dishes such as lobster ravioli and grilled skirt steak. Potent martinis are served at the bar.

### Wynwood Kitchen & Bar

*2550 NW 2nd Avenue, at NW 25th Street (1-305 722 8959, www.wynwoodkitchenandbar.com). Bus 2, 6.* **Open** 11.30am-3.30pm, 5.30-11pm Mon-Thur; 11.30am-3.30pm, 5.30pm-midnight Fri, Sat. **Main courses** $9-$16. **Credit** AmEx, Disc, MC, V. **Map** p285 F3 ⓾ **Latin American**

Opened during Art Basel 2010, this neighbourhood tavern fits in perfectly with its arty surroundings. Executive chef Miguel Aguilar has assembled a series of small plates that are straightforward but elegant; a collection of food on a stick includes skewered chicken with spring onion and chipotle aioli, and baby octopus with oregano purée. Mains have a pan-Latin flair, sauced and sided with piquillo pepper purée and corn salsa. Art is around every corner, too; sip on a Shepard Fairey – pisco with St Germain, simple syrup, pineapple juice and fresh mint – while gazing at the famed graffiti artist's floor-to-ceiling mural, which features in the bar and lounge area.

## NORTH MIAMI & BEYOND

### Chéen-Huaye

*15400 Biscayne Boulevard, at NE 154th Street (1-305 956 2808, www.cheenhuaye.com). Bus 3.* **Open** 11.30am-10.30pm Mon-Thur; 11.30am-11pm Fri, Sat; 11.30am-10pm Sun. **Main courses** $9-$22. **Credit** AmEx, DC, MC, V. **Mexican**

Another strip mall find, Chéen-Huaye brings soulful Yucatan cuisine to the suburbs. Apart from pictures of Mayan ruins and the obligatory sombrero, the decor resists Mexican kitsch. Instead, the flavours do the talking: house-made guacamole or fragrant *sopa de lima* to start. Mains include the usual medley of tacos, but with authentic seasonings such as chipotle aioli, sour orange and mole sauce.

### Gourmet Diner

*13951 Biscayne Boulevard, at NE 139th Street (305 947 2255). Bus 3, 28.* **Open** 11am-10pm Mon-Thur; 11am-10.30pm Fri; 9am-10.30pm Sat; 9am-10pm Sun. **Main courses** $12-$24. **Credit** AmEx, MC, V. **Modern European**

As the only 'diner' in town where you can order escargots, this is not your average greasy spoon. Creations such as rocket and endive salad with goat's cheese lend weight to the 'gourmet' claims. Happily, though, prices aren't prohibitive.

### ★ Hiro's Yakko-san

*3881 NE 163rd Street, at Eastern Shores Boulevard (1-305 947 0064, www.yakko-san.com). Bus 105, 108.* **Open** noon-3am daily. **Main courses** $7-$15. **Credit** AmEx, Disc, MC, V. **Japanese**

This unpretentious Japanese restaurant has chowhounds abuzz and is adored by the city's chefs,

Oak Tavern. *See p101.*

who hang out here until the wee hours. The food is authentic and exotic, though not exactly for the squeamish. The blackboard menu includes the likes of fried chicken livers, black pork belly, crispy-fried gizzard and beef-tongue steak. That said, there are some Japanese staples, including superb sashimi (tuna, salmon, hamachi), but even the tempura is unusual (it's made with chrysanthemums). By contrast, the prices are down to earth. No reservations are taken, so get here early.

### Michael Mina: Bourbon Steak
*Turnberry Isle, 19999 W Country Club Drive, at Spoke Road, Aventura (1-786 279 6600, www.michaelmina.net). Bus E, S, V, Biscayne Max.* **Open** 6-10pm Mon-Thur, Sun; 6-11pm Fri, Sat. **Main courses** $26-$80. **Credit** AmEx, DC, Disc, MC, V. **Steakhouse**
Yet another steakhouse, this time in the chi-chi Turnberry Isle resort. But this one pulls out all the stops. It's the latest venture by Michael Mina, the Michelin-starred chef who, paired with tennis star Andre Agassi, has opened glitzy restaurants in San Francisco, Las Vegas and Arizona. The setting is big, bold and glossy. The all-natural steak is poached in butter before being grilled in a wood-burning oven. Options range from Florida grass-fed filet mignon ($52) to Angus dry-aged bone-in ribeye ($75). Signature sides include truffled mac and cheese, and salt-baked loaded potato.

## SOUTH MIAMI & BEYOND

### Kon Chau
*8376 SW 40th Street, at SW 83rd Avenue (1-305 553 7799). Bus 40, 87.* **Open** 11am-9.30pm Mon-Sat; 10am-9.30pm Sun. **Main courses** $5-$19. **Credit** MC, V. **Chinese**
It's not much of a looker, but how can you go wrong with wonderful dim sum at under $15? Try shrimp dumplings, lotus buns and the like by the dozen.

### Shorty's BBQ
*9200 S Dixie Highway, at Dadeland Boulevard (1-305 670 7732, www.shortys.com). Metrorail Dadeland South.* **Open** 11am-10pm Mon-Thur, Sun; 11am-11pm Fri, Sat. **Main courses** $5-$18. **Credit** MC, V. **American BBQ**
This friendly barbecue pit is a last vestige of pre-developed, pre-trendy Miami. Barbecued chicken and ribs are served in a casual atmosphere at long picnic tables. Prissy folk need not apply – eating with your hands is de rigueur.
**Other locations** 1575 SW 40th Street, at SW 57th Avenue (1-305 227 3196); 2255 NW 87th Avenue, at NW 23rd Street (1-305 471 5554).

### Tropical Chinese
*7991 SW 40th Street, at SW 79th Avenue (1-305 262 1552, www.tropicalchinesemiami.com). Bus 40.* **Open** 11.30am-10.30pm Mon-Thur; 11.30am-11pm

**Wynwood Kitchen & Bar.**

Fri; 11am-11pm Sat; 10.30am-10pm Sun. **Main courses** $9-$24. **Credit** AmEx, DC, MC, V. **Chinese**
It's hard to find decent Chinese food in this city, but follow local Chinese-American families south and you'll discover some in a nondescript strip mall. This is the place for Hong Kong style Chinese food, and the best dim sum in the area.

### Two Chefs
*8287 S Dixie Highway, at Snapper Creek Expressway (1-305 663 2100, www.twochefs restaurant.com). Metrorail Dadeland South.* **Open** 11.30am-2.30pm, 6-9pm Mon; 11.30am-2.30pm, 6-10pm Tue-Fri; 6-10pm Sat. **Main courses** $12-$37. **Credit** AmEx, DC, MC, V. **Bistro**
Originally a cooking school, Two Chefs is now also a casual bistro beloved of foodies. The vibe is glossy, beige and suburban. Signature dishes include coq au vin with bacon and mushrooms, and meat loaf with black beans, mashed potatoes and asparagus. For dessert, choose from an assortment of soufflés.

**CONSUME**

# Bars & Pubs

*Sugar and spice and Miami's favourite vice.*

Don't be fooled by the never-ending display of oversized margarita glasses being sipped along Ocean Drive, each filled with a frozen beverage of a colour not found in nature. Miami's cocktail scene is seriously sophisticated, you just need to know where to look (starting with steering clear of the tourist traps, no matter how bling they may look). If cocktailing isn't your thing, don't despair – there are still plenty of opportunities to belly up to the bar for an ice-cold brewski. While true pubs in this city are as rare as buxom blondes with unenhanced upper bodies, there's a bar in virtually every hotel and restaurant. Whatever your tipple, you certainly won't go thirsty.

## MIAMI BEACH
### South Beach

#### Abbey Brewing Company
*1115 16th Street, at Alton Road (1-305 538 8110, www.abbeybrewingingcompany.com). Bus M, S, W.* **Open** 1pm-5am daily. **Credit** AmEx, MC, V. **Map** p280 C2 **❶**

Sick of candy-coloured martinis? Seek salvation in this hole-in-the-wall-turned-microbrewery, which offers rare European imports plus several own-made beers. Luckily, it didn't lose its classic dive-bar soul in the conversion process – or the dartboard. It's a fine place to meet the locals, and even better when preceded by a meal at Southern food star Yardbird right next door (*see p165*).

#### Abraxas Lounge
*407 Meridian Avenue, at 5th Street (1-305 534 9005). Bus C, K, M, S, South Beach Local.* **Open** 9pm-2am Mon, Sun; 7.30pm-5am Tue-Sat. **Credit** AmEx, MC, V. **Map** p280 E3 **❷**

From the outside, Abraxas looks like a small white house tucked away on a quiet backstreet. Inside, it's a fantastic little lounge bar with a great selection of wines and beers (around 120 bottles), comfy sofas, cool tunes and live music. A friendly crowd of locals smokes contentedly off the beaten tourist path.

> **❶** Green numbers given in this chapter correspond to the location of each bar/pub on the street maps. *See pp280-285.*

#### Automatic Slims
*1216 Washington Avenue, at 12th Street (1-305 672 2220, www.automatic-slims.com). Bus C, H, K, W, South Beach Local.* **Open** 10pm-5am Tue-Sat. **Credit** AmEx, DC, Disc, MC, V. **Map** p280 D3 **❸**

How can anyone resist a place whose motto is 'Where the beautiful people come to get ugly'? We couldn't have put it better when describing this wannabe dive bar. Its inspiration was *Coyote Ugly*, in which sassy shot girls stand atop the bar pouring unknown libations down guys' throats. It makes for a testosterone-charged environment with major fist-pumping and slack-jawed ogling. But for the antithesis of South Beach pretentiousness, this is the place. Ladies, beware the grim toilets.

#### Blues Bar
*National Hotel, 1677 Collins Avenue, at 17th Street (1-305 423 7211, www.nationalhotel.com/blues). Bus C, H, K, W, South Beach Local.* **Open** 4pm-1am daily. **Credit** AmEx, Disc, MC, V. **Map** p280 C3 **❹**

It's considered one of Miami's best cocktail bars, as much for its retro style (in an elegant, *Mad Men* way) as for its impressive drinks list. Try the signature National, a savoury take on the traditional margarita with Grand Marnier, Cointreau, agave syrup and sea salt. It's so SoBe.

#### ★ Buck 15
*437 Lincoln Lane, at Drexel Avenue (1-305 534 5488). Bus C, H, K, W, South Beach Local.* **Open** 10pm-5am Fri, Sat. **Credit** AmEx, Disc, MC, V. **Map** p280 C3 **❺**

Imagine your best friend's basement circa 1979, throw in some Japanese anime, move it up to the second floor, and you've got this oasis of kitsch complete with green and orange crushed velvet couches, concert posters and toys in glass cases. DJs spin everything from hip hop to bar mitzvah faves. Best of all, the place is hard to find, so you won't see any white-sock-and-black-shoe tourists, unless they dressed like that for the funk factor and know exactly where they are.

### Catalina Hotel & Beach Club

*1756 Collins Avenue, at 17th Street (1-305 674 1160, www.catalinahotel.com). Bus C, G, H, L, M, S.* **Open** 7am-5am daily. **Credit** AmEx, MC, V. **Map** p280 C3 ⑥

This constantly expanding hipster hangout features not one but three bars in three different buildings. In the main lobby bar there's a shagadelic, shabby-chic vibe thanks to the red shag carpeting and Austin Powers-style mod furniture, not to mention the requisite lobby lounge music. Across the street from the chi-chi Delano and the Shore Club, it occasionally lures their glamourpuss guests for a low-key drink. The rooftop bar has priceless views and pricey cocktails.

### Clarke's

*840 1st Street, at Jefferson Avenue (1-305 538 9885, www.clarkesmiamibeach.com). Bus H, M, W, South Beach Local.* **Open** 5pm-midnight Mon; noon-midnight Tue-Sat; 11am-11pm Sun. **Credit** AmEx, MC, V. **Map** p280 F2 ⑦

The Irish owner's last name may be Cullen, but she named this pubby South of Fifth hotspot after what

Buck 15

is allegedly the most common surname in Ireland. Take that, the Guinness on tap, some bangers and mash and shepherd's pie and add to it a motley crew of police chiefs, high-profile athletes, moguls and barflies. Result? A scene that's not quite South Beach and not exactly Dublin, but somewhere in between. Whatever it is, it's a whole lot of fun. *Photos p106.*

### ★ Clevelander

*1020 Ocean Drive, at 10th Street (1-877 532 4006, www.clevelander.com). Bus C, H, K, W, South Beach Local.* **Open** 11am-5am daily. **Credit** AmEx, DC, MC, V. **Map** p280 D3 ⑧

The archetypal Miami Beach bar, the Clevelander offers a high concentration of tiki stylings, pink neon and booze – it claims to sell more Bud than any other bar in the nation – all served under open skies and illuminated palms. Like many of the models who participate in the body painting and other cheesy contests here, it has recently undergone some costly cosmetic enhancements. But all the best bits remain, including the nightly bands on the back stage that crank up the volume to the max. This is the stuff that spring breaks are made of: expect at least one drunken goon to fall into the shallow pool that fronts the stage (and a few free-spirited ladies to willingly follow suit). *Photo p107.*

### FDR at Delano

*Delano, 1685 Collins Avenue, at 17th Street (1-305 674 6152, www.delano-hotel.com). Bus C, G, H, L, M, S, South Beach Local.* **Open** 8pm-4am Mon, Wed-Sat; 8pm-2am Tue, Sun. **Credit** AmEx, MC, V. **Map** p280 C3 ⑨

The Delano's subterranean speakeasy is the very antithesis of its trendy parent hotel. The dimly lit den of chandeliers mixes old-school Florida decor with the aesthetic of a swanky cruise-ship lounge. Though it only has a capacity of 200, it attracts a diverse crowd: everyone from young hipsters and chic sophisticates to Golden Girls clones on a fancy night out on the town. *Photo p108.*

**CONSUME**

## Finnegan's Road

*942 Lincoln Road, at Michigan Avenue (1-305 538 7997). Bus C, G, H, K, L, M, S, W, South Beach Local.* **Open** noon-4am Mon-Thur; noon-5am Fri, Sat. **Credit** AmEx, DC, Disc, MC, V. **Map** p280 C2 🔟

Finnegan's is about as divey as you're going to get on Lincoln Road. The drinks are well priced – particularly for this stretch of eateries – and daily specials (such as two-for-one happy hours) make it a real bargain. Grab a seat outside for some seriously great people-watching; inside, it's dark and brash, with a long bar counter but little in the way of seating. TVs are tuned to sport, but commentary is drowned out by the din of the drinkers and the whooping and hollering by the pool tables. Perhaps its oddest accoutrements are the bathroom attendants, who don't do much besides sit there and wait for you to tip them.

## Foxhole Bar

*1218 14th Court, at Alton Road (1-305 534 3511, www.foxholebar.com). Bus M, S, W.* **Open** 5pm-5am daily. **Credit** AmEx, Disc, MC, V. **Map** p280 D2 ⓫

On the bay side of South Beach – far removed from the main tourist and nightclub drag – Foxhole Bar means it when it refers to itself as an 'upscale locals' joint'. This late-night hotspot is still jumping as the sun starts to rise, with Miamians jockeying for position among the plush banquettes or playing darts and pool. At the beginning of the night, early birds can take advantage of the weekday happy hour (5-8pm) offering $3 beers and $5 cocktails.

## Gemma Lounge

*529 Lincoln Road, at Pennsylvania Avenue (1-305 534 3662, www.gemmalounge.com). Bus A, C, G, K, L, M, S, W, South Beach Local.* **Open** 9pm-midnight Wed-Sat. **Credit** AmEx, MC, V. **Map** p280 C3 ⓬

Perched one storey above Lincoln Road, this hard-to-find spot is worth seeking out if you're in the mood for a chilled, hassle-free drink. Unfortunately, Gemma hasn't made its mark on South Beach yet, and the place can feel a little too empty at times. But with its comfy leather couches, the sprawling lounge is an inviting spot for a pre- or post-dinner drink. Don't be put off by the velvet ropes out front; they're just for show. Indeed, if you want high drama, you'll need to head elsewhere.

## HaVen Lounge

*1237 Lincoln Road, at Alton Road (1-305 987 8885, www.havenlounge.com). Bus C, G, H, K, L, M, S, W, South Beach Local.* **Open** 6pm-5am daily. **Credit** AmEx, Disc, MC, V. **Map** p280 C2 ⓭

Located at the western end of Lincoln Road, HaVen isn't a gastropub but a gastro-lounge. Which means that it takes an anything-goes attitude towards its libations. So, don't be too surprised to find a few leaves of arugula in your cocktail glass or a spicy apple foam top. *Photo p110.*

## Highbar

*Dream South Beach, 1111 Collins Avenue, at 11th Street (1-305 534 8455, www.dreamsouthbeach. com). Bus C, H, K, W, South Beach Local.* **Open** 9am-11pm Mon-Wed, Sun; 9am-2am Thur-Sat. **Credit** AmEx, Disc, MC, V. **Map** p280 D3 ⓮

By day, it's the pool bar for the hip Dream South Beach hotel (which is open to non-guests, you just need to order up a cocktail). At night, this all-white, retro-styled rooftop lounge offers perfect views of the Atlantic and a chilled alfresco atmosphere where you can actually hear what your partner's saying.

**Clarke's**. *See p105.*

Clevelander. *See p105.*

An entertainingly diverse cocktail menu includes Face Down in the Pool, a mix of rum and candied pineapple. *See also p141.*

### Hofbräu München Beer Hall
*943 Lincoln Road, at Jefferson Avenue (1-305 538 8066, www.hofbraumiami.com). Bus C, G, H, K, L, M, S, W, South Beach Local.* **Open** 11am-11pm Mon-Thur; 11am-midnight Fri; 9.30am-12.30am Sat; 10.30am-11.30pm Sun. **Credit** AmEx, MC, V. **Map** p280 C2 ⑮
Don't be fooled by the name: this is not a beerhall. But this Lincoln Road café offers signature German brews in lager, wheat and dark, imported from Munich and served in massive *steins* that can only be lifted by South Beach muscle boys and girls. The outdoor tables are ideal for people-watching, but footie fans prefer to remain inside where they can watch the match on TV. The wurst is recommended, as are the piping hot soft pretzels. The restaurant recently added a small wine list to its repertoire.

### ★ Living Room
*W South Beach, 2201 Collins Avenue, at 23rd Street (1-305 938-3000, www.wsouthbeach.com/ living-room-bar). Bus C, G, H, L, M, S.* **Open** 11am-midnight Mon-Thur; 11am-2am Fri-Sun. **Credit** AmEx, MC, C. **Map** p280 B4 ⑯
The lobby bar at W South Beach probably doesn't look anything like your living room. Unless your living room happens to be decked out with the sleekest velvet and faux fur furniture, and looks out on to one of the most beautiful pool areas in South Beach. It's oceanfront, too, though you wouldn't know it from the ground floor – a wall of perfectly landscaped hedges blocks your view of the beach, but also keeps the boardwalk gawkers at bay. In late 2012, the venue had a major mixology makeover, enlisting the assistance of famed cocktail connoisseur Scott Beattie (who literally wrote the book on *Artisanal Cocktails*) to devise drinks that look and taste like art in a glass. *Photo p111.*

### Love Hate Lounge
*423 Washington Avenue, at 5th Street (1-305 695 8616, www.lovehatemiami.com). Bus C, H, K, W, South Beach Local.* **Open** 9pm-5am daily. **Credit** AmEx, MC, V. **Map** p280 F3 ⑰
The stars of *Miami Ink*, Bravo's reality television show about a tattoo parlour, opened their own bar at the height of the show's popularity. But though Ami James and Chris Nunez have tried to create a gritty biker hangout, it attracts a more stylish crowd with its hip hop happy soundtrack and assorted flavoured vodkas.

### Mac's Club Deuce
*222 14th Street, at Collins Avenue (1-305 531 6200). Bus C, H, K, W, South Beach Local.* **Open** 8am-5am daily. **No credit cards**. **Map** p280 D3 ⑱
It's surprising the Deuce has even got a phone. The place is charmingly out of character for the area – a mere block from the ocean – and 'eclectic' doesn't begin to describe the mix of South Beach denizens who gather here nightly. From transsexual hookers and down-and-out locals to nightclub glitterati and slumming celebs, the Deuce attracts the mothiest, coolest, scariest crowd of any bar in Miami. (Celebrity chef Anthony Bourdain has often touted

CONSUME

---

### INSIDE TRACK TIPPING POINT

OK, so technically any gratuity is optional. But as with restaurants in South Beach – most notably on and around Ocean Drive and Collins Avenue – even bar tabs come with an automatic gratuity added, typically 18 per cent. With the average cocktail already retailing for about $15 to $20, don't forget to include this outrageous additional cost when debating whether or not to say 'yes' to another round.

**FDR at Delano**. *See p105.*

his love of this place.) We've been beaten here at pool by a go-go-ing blonde, shared cigarettes with a real-life cowboy and traded shots of JD with a writer of erotic fiction. For anyone who ever fancied a bit part in a Charles Bukowski story, this dive bar would be the right place to audition. *Photo p113.*

### Playwright Irish Pub & Restaurant

*1265 Washington Avenue, at 13th Street (1-305 534 0667, www.playwrightirishpub.com). Bus C, H, K, W, South Beach Local.* **Open** 11am-5am daily. **Credit** AmEx, DC, MC, V. **Map** p280 D3 ⑲

A heart-warmingly inauthentic ye olde Miami pubbe, providing a home from home for the Beach's expat Brits and Irish (there are more of them than you'd think). Hand pumps deliver proper draught beer, served in pints; Premiership footie is shown on the telly. There are a couple of pool tables, live music evenings and a kitchen that rustles up decent English-style pub food.

### Purdy Lounge

*1811 Purdy Avenue, at 18th Street (1-305 531 4622, www.purdylounge.com). Bus A, W.* **Open** 3pm-5am Mon-Fri; 6pm-5am Sat, Sun. **Credit** AmEx, MC, V. **Map** p280 C2 ⑳

On the far west side of the Beach, near the foot of the Venetian Causeway, the location of the Purdy Lounge has influenced its character. During the week, it's an unassuming and comfortable respite for locals who want to escape the tourists (Monday reggae nights are very popular). But on the weekend, it draws a bridge-and-tunnel crowd (or, as they're known here, the Causeway Crowd), whose main goal is dancing and scoring. The dim lighting, dark red walls and lava lamps – not to mention a 5am closing time – add a bit of decadence.

### ★ Regent Cocktail Club

*Gale South Beach, 1690 Collins Avenue, at 17th Street (1-305 673 0199, www.galehotel.com/ nightlife). Bus C, G, H, L, M, S, South Beach Local.* **Open** 7pm-2am daily. **Credit** AmEx, MC, V. **Map** p280 C3 ㉑

The newest addition to the Collins Avenue cocktail crawl is already gaining plenty of accolades, as cordial mixologists – waistcoats and all – pour deliciously inventive drinks in a space that feels worlds away from the hustle of South Beach, yet is in the heart of it all. The Club's retro stylings, complete with leather banquettes, live lounge music and a side patio for cigar smoking, make it feel as if the Rat Pack could walk through the door at any moment.

### Rok Bar

*1905 Collins Avenue, at 19th Street (1-305 397 8804, www.rokbarmiami.com). Bus C, G, H, L, M, S.* **Open** 11pm-5am Tue-Sat. **Admission** $20. **Credit** AmEx, MC, V. **Map** p280 C3 ㉒

Former Mötley Crüe rocker Tommy Lee is co-owner of this down 'n' dirty-meets-swank South Beach bar and lounge, best known for its high-priced drinks, scantily clad cocktail waitresses and a, uh, motley soundtrack of Lynyrd Skynyrd, Michael Jackson and Lee's arch nemesis, Kid Rock. Despite being a rock bar, the door policy is as snooty as ever.

### Room

*100 Collins Avenue, at 1st Street (1-305 531 6061, www.theroommiamibeach.com). Bus H, M, W.* **Open** 7pm-5am daily. **Credit** AmEx, Disc, MC, V. **Map** p280 F3 ㉓

Off the beaten track in the ritzy South of Fifth (SoFi) area, the Room is something of a haven: a small, candlelit beer- and wine-only bar where it's quiet enough

# Hip with Your Kip

*Check into Miami's coolest hotel bars.*

Miami's hotels aren't just for sleeping – they're also at the heart of the city's bar scene. But what constitutes a hip hotel? Steady bookings from overseas are always good, but the right buzz among locals is key. Get the Beach scenesters on board, and the fashionistas and celebs will follow. Then, before you know it, *Condé Nast* wants to do a shoot and Michael Bay is wondering if he can stage a drowning in the pool for his next blockbuster. Good restaurants help, too – hot bars are often attached to high-profile eateries.

Working from south to north, kick off at the Royal at the **Royal Hotel** (bar entrance 758 Washington Avenue; *see p147*), which is a mixed bag: the front half is cool with crushed velvet furniture and cigar cabinets, but the rear resembles a faded cinema foyer. The vibe is a bit seedy, but in a film noir sort of way.

Next, walk towards the beach: the lobby bar at the **Hotel** (801 Collins Avenue; *see p142*) is tiny, but a drink here is a must to sample the cool martinis served with neon ice cubes ('non-toxic, FDA-approved', natch).

Back on Washington, the dark and swanky bar at the newly renovated **Hotel Astor** (no.956; *see p142*) is romantic, especially on the serene little garden terrace. Next, make your way up and over to Ocean Drive's **Betsy** (1440 Ocean Drive; *see p135*) for innovative cocktails that feature seasonal local ingredients (plus a few concoctions that make use of savoury staples such as jalapeño peppers and white balsamic vinegar).

Collins Avenue, between Lincoln Road and 20th Streets, offers a heavenly cocktail crawl. If you must have a mojito (bartenders in these parts call them PITS – as in Pain in the Ass), do so at the resplendent oceanfront DiLido Beach Club at the **Ritz Carlton-South Beach** (1 Lincoln Road; *see p138*). Next door is the **Sagamore** (1671 Collins Avenue; *see p138*), the so-called art museum where you can look at a bona fide Damien Hirst while sipping a lychee martini. Mango martinis are cocktail *du jour* at Rose Bar at the **Delano** (1685 Collins Avenue; *see p135*). Boasting upholstered pink walls and Venetian chandeliers, it's a glitzy spot for Tinseltown types. Even better is the back bar, by the palm-fringed pool.

Gorgeous as the Rose Bar is, the drinks are better at the dim and cosy Martini Bar at the **Raleigh** (1775 Collins Avenue; *see p137*). Be warned that the Raleigh observes the first rule of Miami barkeeping: namely, the cost of drinks is proportional to the stylishness of the venue. And this place is very, very stylish.

The **Shore Club** (1901 Collins Avenue; *see p140*) is home to a once-popular nightspot, the Skybar, whose velvet rope policy got so out of hand that people refused to go. Now anyone willing to pay the absurd prices is welcomed. It's worth a look, if not the money.

Next, try the BONDST lounge at the **Townhouse** (150 20th Street; *see p147*), a snug, Zen-like basement eatery and bar with flattering lighting and Oriental-inspired cocktails that, in tandem, make everyone look great. The same is true at the stunning **Setai** (2001 Collins Avenue; *see p138*), which boasts an interior bar and courtyard plus an oceanfront beach bar. The chilli passion cocktail – comprising rum, passion fruit, chilli seeds and ginger – tastes as divine as the setting: the hotel's luxe lobby is adorned with mother of pearl. But when you get the bill – at $20 per drink – you may want to crawl into a shell of your own.

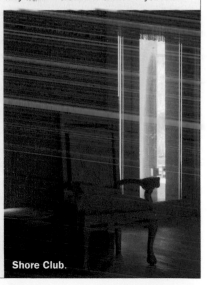

**Shore Club.**

CONSUME

to have an audible conversation (although the later it gets, the more incoherent the crowd becomes). The soundtrack beats to a decidedly different drum, fusing indie, retro and offbeat.

### Segafredo L'Originale

*1040 Lincoln Road, at Lenox Avenue (1-305 673 0047, www.sze-originale.com). Bus C, G, H, K, L, M, S, W, South Beach Local.* **Open** 11am-1am Mon-Thur; 11am-2am Fri, Sat; 11am-1am Sun. **Credit** AmEx, DC, Disc, MC, V. **Map** p280 C2 ㉔
Don't be fooled by the espresso signs here; although you can technically order a latté, Segafredo is best known for its boozy brand of European café society. Mobbed with a colourful crowd, the mostly outdoor café lures elegant slummers with its hefty cocktail menu. There's also wine and beer, and snacks to go with it, but most 'Fredo devotees are on a liquid diet. A Downtown branch (1421 S Miami Avenue, at SE 14th Street, Downtown, 1-305 577 9811), in the Brickell Avenue business district, features a sprawling indoor/outdoor seating area and nightclub, Spazio Nero, so you can get your groove on.

### Skybar at the Shore Club

*1901 Collins Avenue, at 19th Street (1-305 695 3100, www.shoreclub.com). Bus C, G, H, L, M, S.* **Open** *Redroom* 7pm-2am Mon-Wed, Sun; 10pm-3am Thur-Sat. *Garden* 4pm-2am Mon-Wed, Sun; 4pm-3am Thur-Sat. *Rumbar* 7pm-2.30am Thur-Sat. **Credit** AmEx, Disc, MC, V. **Map** p280 C3 ㉕
Sure, it's got great views of the sky, but the reason this outdoor oasis of inequity is so popular is because of its elitist ways. Staff may not serve minors under 21 here, but if you're not Beyoncé, Posh or Becks, you may not get served either: the velvet rope reigns supreme. Consider it a favour if they don't admit you as cocktails are stratospherically priced. *Photo p114.*

### ★ Sunset Lounge

*Mondrian South Beach, 1100 West Avenue, at 11th Street (1-305 514 1941, www.mondrian-miami.com). Bus M, S, W.* **Open** 5pm-midnight Mon-Wed, Sun; 5pm-2am Thur-Sat. **Credit** AmEx, MC, V. **Map** p280 D2 ㉖
Yet another hotel lounge, this one is on South Beach's Bayside. The name says it all: there's simply no better place to watch the sun go down than from the playful rooftop of the Mondrian South Beach. Tuck into one of the private cabanas with a signature caipirinha and let the night envelop you. *Photo p115.*

### Ted's Hideaway

*124 2nd Street, at Ocean Drive (1-305 532 9869). Bus H, M, W.* **Open** noon-5am daily. **Credit** MC, V. **Map** p280 F3 ㉗
If Kim Kardashian is your role model or you never leave home without Armani, take note: Ted's doesn't want you. Ted's people are normal people (with the exception of Bono, who frequented the dive when the U2 tour hit town), the kind who drink Bud, take their bar snacks with a side of cheese fries and cheer for the Marlins on TV. When it comes to sociability versus social standing, the former always wins at Ted's.

### Waxy O'Connor's

*1248 Washington Avenue, at 13th Street (1-305 534 7824, www.waxys.com). Bus C, H, K, W, South Beach Local.* **Open** 10am-5am daily. **Credit** AmEx, Disc, MC, V. **Map** p280 D3 ㉘

HaVen Lounge. *See p106.*

Straight out of a James Joyce novel, Waxy's has a bar imported from Ireland and authentic millwork decor. It caused a stir in South Beach when it opened across from Irish mainstay Playwright (*see p108*); the Edge, if you will, to Waxy's more polished Bono. The pub grub is complemented by a pool table and eight plasma TVs showing football and rugby. Regular two-for-one happy hours and $9 PBR pitchers keep the locals interested.

## WD 555

*555 Jefferson Avenue, at 6th Street (1-305 672 6161, www.wd555usa.com). Bus C, K, M, S, South Beach Local.* **Open** 11am-3pm, 6-11pm Mon-Fri; 11am-11pm Sun. **Credit** MC, V. **Map** p280 E2 ㉙

It looks like a retail wine shop – and it is. But walk past the shelves of vino, all the way to the back of this store in the South of Fifth neighbourhood, and you'll find an outdoor patio offering an extensive wine list alongside an impressive bistro menu (think escargot and monkfish ceviche).

## Mid & North Beach

### Broken Shaker

*Freehand Miami, 2727 Indian Creek Drive, at 28th Street (1-305 531 2727, www.thefreehand. com). Bus C, G, H, L, M, S.* **Open** 6pm-2am daily. **Credit** AmEx, Disc, MC, V. **Map** p280 B4 ㉚

Elad Zvi and Gabriel Orta are the forward-thinking mixologists behind the Broken Shaker, a popular pop-up bar that established a permanent home at the Freehand, an innovative hostel concept (*see p150*). As the name indicates, cocktails are the thing here, and the menu changes almost daily, as drinks are all handcrafted with fresh-pressed ingredients and infusions made from a variety of herbs and spices, picked by the bartenders themselves.

### Happy's Stork Lounge

*1872 79th Street Causeway, North Bay Village (1-305 865 0621) Bus L.* **Open** 11am-5am daily. **Credit** MC, V.

While Miami Beach revels in tropical glory, Happy's is determined to defy its name. It's small, dark and just a little bit seedy. Pull up a stool at the bar counter (there's no other seating) and eavesdrop on dialogue straight out of an Elmore Leonard novel. Despite the talk of handguns, fast cars and some other things that lawyers would advise us against repeating, we've always found the folks friendly enough, although you do wonder about a sign on the gents that reads: 'No more than two at a time'.

### La Côte

*Fontainebleau, 4441 Collins Avenue, at 44th Street (1-305 674 4710, www.fontainebleau.com/ lacote). Bus G, H, L, S.* **Open** 11am-6pm Mon-Wed, Sun; 11am-9pm Thur-Sat. **Credit** AmEx, Disc, MC, V. **Map** p281 F4 ㉛

**Living Room**. *See p107.*

Inspired by the Côte d'Azur, the Fontainebleau's (*see p150*) bi-level beach club is not your late-night party destination. But it is the perfect place to sit back and take in the picturesque ocean views around you (while breathing in some of that salty sweet air). That's not to say that La Côte doesn't know how to have fun, though – a regular slate of DJs keep the beats rocking throughout the day. In addition to its innovative cocktail menu, there's also an extensive wine list, featuring half a dozen seaside-appropriate varietals of bubbly and rosé by the glass.

### ★ Lou's Beer Garden

*7337 Harding Avenue, at 73rd Street (1-305 704 7879, www.lousbeergarden.com). Bus 112, 117, 119, 120.* **Open** 5pm-2am Mon-Wed; 2pm-2am Thur, Fri, 11am-2am Sat, Sun. **Credit** AmEx, MC, V. **Map** p281 A4 ㉜

For the gourmet grub you'd find in South Beach's best restaurants – minus the hassle and attitude – head north to this happening neighbourhood gastropub, where the beer menu boasts more than two dozen options (bottles and draught), with a focus on American microbrews.

### Norman's American Bar & Grill

*6700 Collins Avenue, at 67th Street (1-305 868 9248, www.normans.biz). Bus 112, 117, 119, 120.* **Open** noon-5am daily. **Credit** AmEx, Disc, MC, V. **Map** p281 B4 ㉝

Locals have been coming to Norman's since 1970 for its cosy pub feel, no-frills attitude, killer happy hours and decent bar food.

### Shuckers Bar & Grill

*1819 79th Street Causeway, North Bay Village (1-305 866 1570, www.shuckersbarandgrill.com). Bus L.* **Open** 11am-2am daily. **Credit** AmEx, DC, MC, V.

CONSUME

The restaurant of a Best Western hotel might not be the first place you'd think of for a night out, but with its cheap beer and seafood, classic rock soundtrack and enormous waterfront deck (we've witnessed dolphins swimming), you may actually need to wait for a seat at this popular hangout.

## DOWNTOWN

### ★ Bahía

*Four Seasons Hotel Miami, 1435 Brickell Avenue, at SW 15th Street (1-305 358 3535, www.four seasons.com/miami). Bus 24, 48, B/Metromover Financial District.* **Open** 11am-6pm daily. **Credit** AmEx, DC, MC, V.

Day drinkers only need apply at Bahía, as it closes at 6pm. Of course, it takes something pretty special to get the Beach crowd to venture west over the MacArthur Causeway. But since its opening, Bahía has had them them flocking in. It's the open-air bar on the seventh-floor terrace of the swanky Four Seasons, and it's gorgeous. Tables, love seats and day beds are set amid manicured topiary. Off to one side is a cool expanse of blue pool, on the other is a cinema screen-sized water feature. Drinks are Latino cocktails (caipirinhas, margaritas, mojitos and piscos), complemented by premium South American beers.

### Blackbird Ordinary

*729 SW 1st Avenue, at SW 8th Street (1-305 671 3307, www.blackbirdordinary.com). Metromover 5th Street.* **Open** 3pm-5am Mon-Fri; 5pm-5am Sat, Sun. **Credit** MC, V. **Map** p282 F2 ㉞

If drinking tequila and/or whisky into the wee hours is your idea of a great night out, welcome home. Truth be told, there's nothing ordinary about Blackbird; in a town full of blink-and-you'll-miss-'em bars, this one's got a distinct personality. And staying power too. Take your libations straight up or in a handcrafted cocktail. The signature Blackbird – a mix of sweet tea vodka, fresh lemonade and blackberries served on the rocks – is the perfect antidote to the sizzling south Florida sun.

### Corner

*1035 N Miami Avenue, at NE 10th Street (1-305 961 7887, www.thecornermiami.com). Bus 103, 119.* **Open** 4pm-5am Mon-Thur, Sun; 4pm-8am Fri, Sat. **Credit** AmEx, Disc, MC, V. **Map** p282 B2 ㉟

Occupying an unassuming space in a not yet thriving area of Downtown, the Corner is a surprisingly upscale throwback to the cocktail bars of old, complete with a vintage wooden bar. Yes, there's beer. And live music too. But the extensive cocktail list –

**CONSUME**

# Miami Vine

*Wine bars are popping up all over town.*

Distilleries spend a fortune trying to convince this city that flavoured vodkas and rums are the drink of choice. But a city just isn't a city without a selection of swanky wine bars – and Miami has finally embraced the trend. You can get your first taste immediately upon arrival, in Terminal D of MIA, where **Beaudevin** (1-305 869 1961, www.hmshost.com, 6am-11pm daily) gets travellers buzzing at its 42-seat wine and cheese bar. To stay or not to stay, that is the question at **WD 555** (*see p111*), which is as much wine shop as wine bar. But walk all the way to the back and you'll find a fauna-filled outdoor patio, complemented by stylish Starck-designed chairs, perfect for sampling the wares. And if you like what you're sipping, you can pick up a bottle to go.

As its vast beer menu numbers more than 75 varietals, the **Room** (100 Collins Avenue;

Room.

*see p108*) isn't a wine bar in the strictest sense. But its impressive wine list and romantic, candlelit vibe make it the perfect place to relax.

In North Beach, newly renovated fortysomething hotspot the **Forge** (432 41st Street) offers farm-to-table fare in an elegant steakhouse setting, plus 80 wines by the glass, courtesy of an Enomatic system that allows customers to decide between a one-, three- or five-ounce pour.

Recently given a 'best wine selection' nod by *New Times*, **Cibo Wine Bar** (*see p113*) encourages diners to savour the grape (it offers more than 200 varietals) the way it was intended – while noshing on a plate of rustic Italian eats. Don't miss the daily happy hour (4-7pm), featuring half-price drinks. Cibo's formula has proven so popular, it's opening a second location, in SoBe, in autumn 2013.

which boasts more than a dozen signature drinks, divided into 'Classique' and 'Nouveau' categories – is the best reason to venture here. For a true Miami experience, try the Floridita daiquiri, the Corner's take on a Hemingway daiquiri (made with rum, grapefruit juice, rum, lime, rum, maraschino liqueur, and more rum).

### Fadó Irish Pub

*900 S Miami Avenue, at SW 9th Street (1-786 924 0972, www.fadoirishpub.com). Bus 119, 120.* **Open** 11.30am-2am Mon-Thur, Sun; 11.30am-4am Fri, Sat. **Credit** AmEx, Disc, MC, V. **Map** p282 F2 ㊱

For a perfectly poured Guinness, you'd be hard pressed to do better than Fadó, a family-friendly tavern in Mary Brickell Village. For those sitting on the outdoor deck, it's Fido-friendly too. Everything about this casual eaterie screams 'Erin Go Bragh!' from the all-day Irish breakfast and Gaelic steak boxty (a brandy-soaked slab of meat topped with onion, mushroom and green peppercorn sauce) to the live Irish music, which ranges from traditional to pop. Don't be surprised to find Fadó's doors open earlier than officially posted either; if there's soccer or rugby on TV, they're going to screen it.

### Finnegan's River

*401 SW 3rd Avenue, at SW 5th Street (1-305 285 3030, www.finnegansriver.com). Metromover 5th Street.* **Open** 11am-4am daily. **Credit** AmEx, Disc, MC, V. **Map** p282 E1 ㊲

A sprawling complex of bars, plasma televisions, more bars, a pool and marina, Finnegan's River is Downtown's best sports bar – if not for the rowdy sports fans who go there, then for the best views of the Miami skyline.

### M-Bar at the Mandarin Oriental

*Mandarin Oriental Miami, 500 Brickell Key Drive, at Brickell Avenue (1-305 913 8358, www.mandarinoriental.com/miami). No public transport.* **Open** 5pm-midnight Mon-Thur, Sun; 5pm-1am Fri, Sat. **Credit** AmEx, DC, Disc, MC, V. **Map** p282 F4 ㊳

Tucked away in the corner of the lobby of one of Miami's poshest hotels (*see p155*) – in one of its most exclusive neighbourhoods – the M-Bar is not an Ian Schrager-esque haute spot but, rather, a popular place for after-work types looking to impress their co-workers and clients, and well-heeled hotel guests. The long martini list earns the M its place in the little black book of any lush, and its stunning views of Biscayne Bay are the reason you're visiting Miami in the first place.

### ★ Tobacco Road

*626 S Miami Avenue, at SW 7th Street (1-305 374 1198, www.tobacco-road.com). Bus 6, 8.* **Open** 11.30am-5am daily. **Credit** AmEx, DC, MC, V. **Map** p282 F2 ㊴

**Mac's Club Deuce.** *See p107.*

Al Capone once drank and gambled at the 101-year-old Road, which holds the oldest liquor licence in Miami-Dade County. These days it's renowned as a live music venue – blues legends such as John Lee Hooker and Buddy Guy have played here. But even when the stages are silent, the former speakeasy still qualifies as one of the finest – and grittiest – drinking establishments around. The food's good, too: stop by on Tuesday for the $13 lobster special. Patrons are advised to heed the management's advice and drink responsibly… using both hands.

## CORAL GABLES

### Cibo Wine Bar

*45 Miracle Mile, off Merrick Way (1-305 442 4925, www.cibowinebar.com). Bus 24, 42, 72, Coral Gables Circulator.* **Open** 11.30am-midnight Mon-Wed, Sun; 11.30am-2am Thur-Sat. **Credit** AmEx, MC, V. **Map** p284 B4 ㊵

A wine list numbering more than 200 varietals combines with an extensive menu of rustic Italian fare to create one amazing culinary experience. A daily happy hour (4-7pm) features half-price drinks. While the quality of the menu makes it worth the trek to Coral Gables, a second location – opening in South Beach in autumn 2013 – will make things easier.

### Duffy's Tavern

*2108 SW 57th Avenue (Red Road), at SW 21st Street (1-305 264 6580). Bus 24.* **Open** 10am-1am daily. **No credit cards. Map** p284 B1 ㊶

On the far west side of the Gables, this humble pub is a favourite hangout with University of Miami football players past and present (the place prides itself on its jock-friendliness). UM supporters – some of the most powerful city fathers – are also known to be frequent habitués. The result is a mix of old Anglo

**CONSUME**

**Skybar at the Shore Club**. *See p110.*

establishment types and the newer Latin versions. When they're not knocking back brewskis, patrons are munching burgers and beer-battered chips.

### John Martin's Irish Pub

*253 Miracle Mile (SW 24th Street), at Ponce de León Boulevard (1-305 445 3777, www. johnmartins.com). Bus 24, 42, Coral Gables Circulator.* **Open** 11.30am-midnight Mon, Tue, Sun; 11.30am-2am Wed-Sat. **Credit** AmEx, MC, V. **Map** p284 B4 ⑫

Do a little jig: this landmark pub is the Irish heart of Miami, with plenty of boozing and bonhomie. There's Irish cabaret on Saturday nights and a Celtic-tinged open-mic night on Sunday. A happy hour with a free buffet draws in the Gables prissies hoping to score a rough Irish lad. Instead, they usually find the male version of themselves.

## COCONUT GROVE

### Flanigan's Laughing Loggerhead

*2721 Bird Avenue (SW 40th Street), at SW 27th Avenue (1-305 446 1114). Bus 22, 27, 42.* **Open** 11.30am-5am daily. **Credit** AmEx, MC, V.

A Grove institution, the Loggerhead stocks 200 brands of bottled beer and serves decent grub, including some splendid ribs and juicy burgers. A fishing motif prevails, with Hemingway-esque photos of anglers and their catches. Kitsch? Yep. But you can drink here until 5am.

### Monty's Raw Bar

*2550 S Bayshore Drive, at Aviation Avenue, Coconut Grove (1-305 856 3992). Bus 48, Coconut Grove Circulator.* **Open** 11.30am-10.30pm Mon-Thur; 11.30am-2am Fri; 1.30pm-2am Sat, Sun. **Credit** AmEx, MC, V. **Map** p285 A4 ⑬

Located next to a marina, this popular Grove hangout is a good place for drinks and seafood. Thatch-roofed, open-walled miniature tiki huts surround a stage from which reggae and calypso bands do their damnedest to persuade the diners and drinkers to dance. Those who believe young kids and alcohol don't mix should avoid it in the early evenings. But sensible parents keep the children home on Friday, when Monty's has its happening happy hour.

## WYNWOOD & LITTLE HAITI

### Churchill's Pub

*5501 NE 2nd Avenue, at NE 55th Street, Little Haiti (1-305 757 1807, www.churchillspub.com). Bus 9, 10.* **Open** 11am-3am daily. **Admission** $5. **Credit** AmEx, MC, V.

This is Miami's most famous dive bar, in the heart of smash-and-grab-central Little Haiti. It's had the shit kicked out of it so many times it wears its bruises with pride. The beer's cheap, as is the food (good booze-soaking fare such as scotch eggs and curry). There are a couple of pool tables, Space Invaders video games and a jukebox stuffed with skatepunk. Bands of varying quality play nightly in the back.

### ★ Wood Tavern

*2531 NW 2nd Avenue, at NW 26th Street (1-305 748-2828, www.woodtavernmiami.com). Bus 3, 9, 10, 16, J.* **Open** 5pm-3am Tue-Sat; 3-9pm Sun. **Credit** AmEx, Disc, MC, V. **Map** p285 F3 ⑭

Art galleries run rampant in Wynwood, but honest-to-goodness pubs? Not so much. Which makes Wood Tavern a particularly welcome addition to the neighbourhood (and a great pit stop before or after a movie at the arty O Cinema Wynwood). The backyard patio features communal picnic table seating, making it easy to strike up conversation with a local

Sunset Lounge. See p110.

CONSUME

# Shops & Services

*Where to buy everything under the sun.*

When it rains in Magic City, it pours shoppers – and now they have more choice than ever before. In recent years, Miami's retail scene has stepped up to rival New York and Los Angeles in the fashion big league: Hermès, Prada, Louis Vuitton, Cartier, Céline… the list of newcomers reads like the September issue of *Vogue*. Finally, the city has the high-end couture to counteract all those schlocky T-shirt shops. But bargain hunters don't have to travel far to find excellent discount outlets. The major retail areas (read: malls) are easy to access by bus, train or shuttle. But if you plan on buying big, it's far easier to have your own transport – and, of course, an extra suitcase.

## Where to Shop

*Plot your spree around the city.*

### SOUTH BEACH
South Beach, especially Lincoln Road and along Collins Avenue between 5th and 8th Streets, is the area for boutiques and vintage clothing shops, plus plenty of chain stores.

### BAL HARBOUR
Brimming with chi-chi Euro designers, Bal Harbour Shops (*see p118*) is haute couture heaven.

### CORAL GABLES
Coral Gables is good for posh homewares and designer furniture. Village of Merrick Park mall (*see p119*) keeps the rich and famous in high-priced labels.

### THE DESIGN DISTRICT
The Design District is 'one square mile of style' with a fantastic array of ritzy interiors showrooms.

### NORTH & SOUTH MIAMI
For one-stop shopping out of town, the Aventura Mall (*see p117*) and Dadeland Mall (*see p118*) are sprawling fashion meccas, with chains galore.

## General

### DEPARTMENT STORES

#### Bloomingdale's
*The Falls, 8778 SW 136th Street, at S Dixie Highway (US 1), South Miami (1-305 252 6300, www.bloomingdales.com). Bus 1, 52, 65.* **Open** 10am-9pm Mon-Sat; noon-7pm Sun. **Credit** AmEx, MC, V. **Map** p279.
'Bloomies' features classy cuts from top labels such as Donna Karan, Calvin Klein, Chanel and Fendi, plus trendier pieces such as 7 For All Mankind jeans and Diane von Furstenberg wrap dresses. Homewares, gifts, accessories and shoes also feature.
**Other locations** Aventura Mall, 19555 Biscayne Boulevard, Aventura (1-305 792 1000); Dolphin Mall, 11401 NW 12th Street (1-305 597 2080).

#### Macy's
*Aventura Mall, 19535 Biscayne Boulevard, at NE 196th Street, Aventura (1-305 682 3300, www. macys.com). Bus 3, 9, E, S.* **Open** 10am-10pm Mon, Thur-Sat; 9am-10pm Tue; 9am-11pm Wed; 11am-8pm Sun. **Credit** AmEx, MC, V. **Map** p278.
The quintessential all-American department store, Macy's offers upscale and mid-range clothing labels, homewares, fashion accessories and cosmetics.
**Other locations** The Falls, 9100 SW 136th Street, South Miami (1-305 278 3300); Dadeland Mall, 7303 SW 88th Street, South Miami (1-305 662 3400); 1675 Meridian Avenue, Miami Beach (1-305 674 6300); 22 E Flagler Street, Downtown (1-305 577 1500).

CONSUME

### Neiman Marcus
*Bal Harbour Shops, 9700 Collins Avenue, off
Park Drive, Bal Harbour (1-888 884 6136, 1-305
865 6161, www.neimanmarcus.com). Bus H, K,
S, T.* **Open** 10am-9pm Mon-Sat; noon-7pm Sun.
**Credit** AmEx, MC, V. **Map** p281 inset.
Offering upmarket merchandise, Neiman Marcus is
a favourite of the smart set. But be warned: it earned
the nickname 'Needless Markups' for a reason.
**Other locations** Village of Merrick Park, 390 San
Lorenzo Avenue, Coral Gables (1-786 999 1000).

### Nordstrom
*Village of Merrick Park, 4310 Ponce de León
Boulevard, at San Lorenzo Avenue, Coral Gables
(1-786 999 1313, www.nordstrom.com). Metrorail
Douglas Road.* **Open** 10am-9.30pm Mon-Sat;
noon-8pm Sun. **Credit** AmEx, DC, Disc, MC, V.
**Map** p284 E4.
Priding itself on top customer service and superb
selection, this outpost of the 112-year-old Seattle-
based chain carries something for everyone, from
designer togs to affordable middle-of-the-road fare.
**Other locations** Aventura Mall, 19507 Biscayne
Boulevard, Aventura (1-305 356 6900); Dadeland
Mall, 7239 North Kendall Drive, off S Dixie
Highway, South Miami (1-786 709 4100).

### Saks Fifth Avenue
*Bal Harbour Shops, 9700 Collins Avenue,
off Park Drive, Bal Harbour (1-305 865 1100,
www.saksfifthavenue.com). Bus H, K, S, T.*
**Open** 10am-9pm Mon-Sat; noon-7pm Sun.
**Credit** AmEx, MC, V. **Map** p281 inset.
One of the country's best-known upscale chains,
Saks Fifth Avenue boasts an impressive range of
designer labels: Gucci, Chanel, Prada, Armani,
Donna Karan, Dolce & Gabbana and Versace all fea-
ture. As the old saying goes, if you have to ask how
much it costs…
**Other locations** Dadeland Mall, 7687 N Kendall
Drive, South Miami (1-305 662 8655).

## MALLS

### ★ Aventura Mall
*19501 Biscayne Boulevard, off Abigail Road,
Aventura (1-305 935 1110, www.aventuramall.
com). Bus 3, 9, E, S.* **Open** 10am-9.30pm
Mon-Sat; noon-8pm Sun. **Map** p278.
Miami's best all-rounder, Aventura Mall boasts all
the biggies: Bloomingdale's, Macy's and Nordstrom.
It also has boutique locations for 7 For All Mankind,
Burberry, Calvin Klein, Pucci and Ted Baker. In
addition, there's a 24-screen cineplex (*see p166*) and
popular restaurants such as the Cheesecake Factory
and Johnny Rockets. It's easy to get to from South
Beach, as several buses terminate here – it's just a
hell of a long ride. And as a taxi can cost as much
as $50 each way, it's worth the price of a one-day
car rental to stock up.

Bal Harbour Shops. *See p118.*

CONSUME

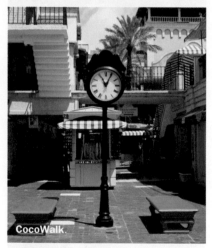

CocoWalk

## Bayside Marketplace

*401 Biscayne Boulevard, at NE 4th Street,*
*Downtown (1-305 577 3344, www.bayside*
*marketplace.com). Metromover College/Bayside.*
**Open** 10am-10pm Mon-Thur; 10am-11pm Fri,
Sat; 11am-9pm Sun. **Map** p282 C4.

Come to this bland Anytown, USA waterside development to get your fill of touristy sightseeing tours,
gambling cruises and Hard Rock Cafe T-shirts. The
usual suspects line up for a chance at your wallet,
including Bath & Body Works, Victoria's Secret,
Gap, Express and Sunglass Hut.

## CocoWalk

*3015 Grand Avenue, at Virginia Street, Coconut*
*Grove (1-305 444 0777, www.cocowalk.net). Bus*
*42, 48, Coconut Grove Circulator.* **Open** 10am-
10pm Mon-Thur, Sun; 10am-11pm Fri, Sat (bars
stay open until 3am). **Map** p285 B3.

Residents of this one-time boho ghetto howled at
the arrival of corporate America in the form of
this multi-storey, semi-outdoor mall. It's everything
you'd expect from a block whose residents include
Gap, Victoria's Secret and Starbucks. There's also a
13-screen Paragon movie theatre (*see p167*).

## Dadeland Mall

*7535 N Kendall Drive, at SW 74th Court, South*
*Miami (1-305 665 6226, www.simon.com/mall/*
*dadeland-mall). Metrorail Dadeland North or*
*Dadeland South.* **Open** 10am-9.30pm Mon-Sat;
noon-7pm Sun. **Map** p279.

This supermall fronts Florida's largest Macy's (*see*
*p116*). Among the other 200-odd stores are Saks Fifth
Avenue (*see p117*) and a two-storey Louis Vuitton.
Dadeland is also one of the only malls easily accessible on Miami's Metrorail system.

## Falls

*8888 SW 136th Street, off S Dixie Highway*
*(US 1), South Miami (1-305 255 4570, www.*
*simon.com/mall/the-falls). Bus 1, 52, 65.* **Open**
10am-9pm Mon-Sat; noon-7pm Sun. **Map** p279.

Cashing in on the outdoor mall trend, the Falls aims
to calm with lush foliage, wooden plank walkways,
waterfalls and reflecting ponds. Anchors include a
United Artists megaplex, Macy's (*see p116*) and
Bloomingdale's (*see p116*), though you'll also find
Abercrombie & Fitch, Gap and Brooks Brothers for
fashion, plus beauty products from Origins and the
latest gadgets at the Apple Store (*see p121*). There's
no tacky food court; try upscale eateries such as Brio
Tuscan Grille and BJ's Restaurant Brewhouse.

## Mayfair in the Grove

*2911 Grand Avenue, at Virginia Street, Coconut*
*Grove (1-305 448 1700, www.mayfairinthegrove.*
*com). Bus 42, 48, Coconut Grove Circulator.*
**Open** hours vary. **Map** p285 B3.

Staying true to the pedestrian feel of the Grove, this
mall offers wide pavements, balconies, outdoor cafés

## Bal Harbour Shops

*9700 Collins Avenue, off Park Drive, Bal Harbour*
*(1-305 866 0311, www.balharbourshops.com).*
*Bus H, K, S, T.* **Open** 9am-10pm Mon-Sat (some
department stores close earlier; phone ahead);
noon-6pm Sun. **Map** p281 inset.

Where the ladies who lunch go with their lap dogs,
and where the PYTs go with their GWMs (guys with
money), the oh-so-exclusive Bal Harbour Shops has
long been pinned as Miami's Rodeo Drive. In this
two-storey, modernist Bali Hai, you'll find big-bucks
labels, including Prada, Gucci, Tiffany & Co, Chanel,
Versace, Bulgari, Oscar de la Renta and Chloé, rub-
bing padded shoulders with upscale department
stores Neiman Marcus and Saks Fifth Avenue (for
both, *see p117*). *Photos p117*.

and a broad promenade. Yes, it's got many of the expected mall retailers, but there's also a great boutique feel to the storefronts that occupy this space, with plenty of speciality food shops, art galleries and even an improv comedy club in residence.

### Shops at Midtown Miami
*3401 N Miami Avenue, at NW 36th Street, Design District (1-305 573 3371, www.shop midtownmiami.com). Bus 9, 10, J.* **Open** 10am-9pm Mon-Sat; noon-6pm Sun.
This sprawling big box complex of stores is not exactly in keeping with the Design District's chichi feel. Shops include bargain retailers Target, Marshalls, Loehmann's and HomeGoods. The discount fashion will appeal to tourists, but mainly this is a draw for locals who can go to Target and buy toilet paper in bulk. Additionally, there's a West Elm for home design fanatics and Ross Dress for Less for those really on a budget.

### Shops at Sunset Place
*5701 Sunset Drive (SW 72nd Street), at US 1 & Red Road, South Miami (1-305 663 0873, www.simon.com/mall/the-shops-at-sunset-place). Metrorail South Miami.* **Open** 11am-10pm Mon-Thur; 11am-11pm Fri, Sat; 11am-9pm Sun. **Map** p279.
With its over-the-top architecture, giant man made banyan trees and waterfalls, this is the Disney World of malls. Stores include Armani Exchange, Banana Republic, Gap, Urban Outfitters and Victoria's Secret. A GameTime arcade, 24-screen multiplex (*see p166*) and luxury bowling alley make this a hotspot for teens with time to kill. *Photos p120.*

### Village of Merrick Park
*358 San Lorenzo Avenue, at Ponce de León Boulevard, Coral Gables (1-305 529 0200, www. villageofmerrickpark.com). Metrorail Douglas Road.* **Open** 10am-9pm Mon-Sat; noon-6pm Sun. **Map** p284 E4.
South Florida's newest upscale mall is anchored by department stores Neiman Marcus and Nordstrom. Three open-air storeys boast 115 shops and boutiques, including the likes of Burberry, Gucci, Etro, Adolfo Domínguez, Jimmy Choo, Diane von Furstenberg and Agent Provocateur. Jewellery brands include Tiffany and Tourneau. *Photo p121.*

## DISCOUNT MALLS

### Sawgrass Mills
*12801 W Sunrise Boulevard, Sunrise (1-954 846 2305, www.simon.com/mall/sawgrass-mills). Daily shuttle buses run from Miami Beach hotels; ask concierge to arrange or see www. sawgrassexpress.com.* **Open** 10am-9.30pm Mon-Sat, 11am 8pm Sun.
The venerable Sawgrass Mills is in Broward, the next county north of Miami-Dade. It's a trek, but worth the effort. There are more than 350 designer stores enclosed in a two-mile-long structure designed by noted postmodernists Arquitectonica. Names include Barneys, Calvin Klein, Levi's, Nordstrom Rack, Off Saks Fifth Avenue and Tory Burch. Stores at a newer upscale enclave, the Colonnade Outlets at Sawgrass, include Burberry, Valentino and Ferragamo – and there's valet parking. When shopping fatigue sets in, try the GameRoom video-game parlour or the 23-screen cinema.

Louis Vuitton.

CONSUME

**Dolphin Mall**
*11401 NW 12th Street, at NW 111th Avenue,*
*Sweetwater (1-305 365 7446, www.shopdolphin*
*mall.com). Bus 11, 71.* **Open** 10am-9.30pm Mon-
Sat; 11am-8pm Sun. **Map** p279.
Set off the beaten path, the Dolphin Mall lacked pres-
tige when it opened in 2001. But its reputation has
grown: the current line-up includes Brooks Brothers,
Neiman Marcus, Off Saks Fifth Avenue and Ralph
Lauren. There's also a cinema and bowling alley.

# Specialist

## BOOKS & MAGAZINES

Though chain bookstores are quickly
disappearing in the US, **Barnes & Noble** still
has about half a dozen stores in the Miami area,
usually in malls, including the Shops at Sunset
Place in South Miami. There's also a well-
stocked location in Coral Gables (152 Miracle
Mile, 1-305 446 4152, open 9am-11pm daily),
which stays open late and hosts a regular
roster of speakers and other literary events.
Visit www.bn.com for more information.

## General

### ★ Books & Books
*265 Aragon Avenue, at Ponce de León Boulevard,*
*Coral Gables (1-305 442 4408, www.booksand*
*books.com). Bus 24, 42, 72, Coral Gables*
*Circulator.* **Open** 9am-11pm Mon-Thur, Sun;
9am-midnight Fri, Sat. **Credit** AmEx, MC, V.
**Map** p284 B4.
Heaven for book-lovers, Books & Books is a superb
independent, well stocked with bestsellers but also
lots of small publishers. Its wooden-floored rooms
include one devoted to antiquarian rarities and
another to kids' books. There's a café, as well as regular discussion groups and author readings.
**Other locations** 927 Lincoln Road, South Beach
(1-305 532 3222); Bal Harbour Shops, 9700 Collins
Avenue, Bal Harbour (1-305 864 4241); Miami
International Airport, Concourse D, Gate D25
(1-305 876 0468).

### Bookstore in the Grove
*3390 Mary Street, at Grand Avenue (1-305 443*
*2855, www.thebookstoreinthegrove.dreamhosters.*
*com). Bus 48, Grove Circulator.* **Open** 7am-
10pm Mon-Sat; 8am-10pm Sun. **Credit** MC, V.
**Map** p285 B3.
In leafy Coconut Grove, this indie bookstore offers
a smart selection and cool, café-style ambience.
It also does a great job of creating a community
space, hosting regular Local Author Nights and less
literary events such as beer tastings.

### TASCHEN
*1111 Lincoln Road, at Alton Road, South Beach*
*(1-305 538 6185, www.taschen.com). Bus C, G,*
*H, K, L, M, S, W.* **Open** 11am-9pm Mon-Thur;
11am-10pm Fri, Sat; noon-9pm Sun. **Credit**
AmEx, MC, V. **Map** p280 C2.

**Shops at Sunset Place.** *See p119.*

Village of Merrick Park. *See p119.*

CONSUME

Yes, it's a bookstore. But don't be surprised to stumble across a must-have hardcover with a price tag of $3,000 or more. Many of this 33-year-old art publisher's titles are extremely limited editions and made of the highest-quality materials (hence the hefty price tag). But even some of the priciest books – which focus on the worlds of art, photography, design, fashion and cinema – have discounted, paperback counterparts. *Photo p122.*

## CHILDREN
### Fashion & toys

#### Children's Exchange
*1415 Sunset Drive, at SW 54th Avenue, Coral Gables (1-305 666 6235, www.thechildren exchange.com). Metrorail South Miami.* **Open** 10am-6pm Mon-Thur; 10am-8pm Fri, Sat. **Credit** AmEx, DC, MC, V.
The Saks Fifth Avenue of gently worn children's clothing has Polo, Juicy Couture and True Religion, plus toys, small baby gear, name-brand shoes and even ski clothes for kids.

#### ★ Genius Jones
*2800 NE 2nd Avenue, at NE 29th Street, Wynwood (1-305 571 2000, www.genius jones.com). Bus 3, 9, 10, 16, 93, 95.* **Open** 10am-7pm Mon-Sat; noon-6pm Sun. **Credit** AmEx, DC, Disc, MC, V. **Map** p285 E3.
Design snobs shop for their children here. Find bold wooden children's furniture by Agatha Ruiz de la Prada and David Netto, plus toys designed to inspire without lighting up or blinking.

#### ★ LoudGirl Exchange
*6621 Biscayne Boulevard, at 67th Street, Upper East Side (1-305 458 5783, www.loudgirl exchange.com). Bus 3, 16.* **Open** 10am-6pm Mon-Wed, Sat; 10am-6.30pm Thur, Fri. **Credit** MC, V.
For one of the city's most interesting selections of new, gently used and locally sourced designer kids' clothes and art pieces, have a look at LoudGirl Exchange. Particularly worth a gander is the store's eclectic selection of designer and vintage toys, which recently included an old-school Radio Flyer wagon for a bargain $29.

## ELECTRONICS & PHOTOGRAPHY

Some of the discount electronics stores in Downtown and on Lincoln Road in South Beach have a reputation for selling goods that have fallen off the back of a truck, so to speak. Get a guarantee, and never leave without a receipt and the name of the member of staff who served you. For mobile phone rental, *see p.268.*

#### Apple Store
*738 Lincoln Road, at Meridian Avenue, South Beach (1-305 421-0400, www.apple.com/retail/ lincolnroad). Bus C, G, H, K, L, M, S, W, South Beach Local.* **Open** 10am-11pm Mon-Sat; 10am-10pm Sun. **Credit** AmEx, Disc, MC, V. **Map** p280 C3.
There never seems to be a quiet moment to visit the Lincoln Road outpost of this popular showroom for Apple's latest gadgets.

**Other locations** The Falls, 8888 SW 136th Street (1-305 234 4565); 7509 N Kendall Drive, Kendall (1-305 341 9812); Aventura Mall, 19501 Biscayne Boulevard, Aventura (1-305 914 9826).

### Best Buy

*1131 5th Street, at Alton Road, South Beach (1-305 535 8539, www.bestbuy.com). Bus 103, 113, 120.* **Open** 10am-9pm Mon-Sat; 11am-7pm Sun. **Credit** AmEx, Disc, V, MC. **Map** p280 E2.
The first name in big box electronics stores, Best Buy offers customers the guaranteed best price on pretty much anything you have to plug in to make work (televisions, game systems, iPods, mobile phones, computers, printers, appliances). The store also has a resident 'Geek Squad' to help with any malfunctions with the aforementioned devices.

## FASHION

### Beachwear

### Beach Bunny

*750 Collins Avenue, at 8th Street, South Beach (1-305 673 2319, www.beachbunnyswimwear. com). Bus 23, 103, South Beach Local.* **Open** 10am-9pm daily. **Credit** AmEx, MC, V. **Map** p280 E3.
You've got to be pretty fit to pull off one of these bikinis, designed by company founder Angela Chittenden, who also happens to be a former swimsuit model. Using lingerie as its inspiration, the range has bagged more pages of the *Sports Illustrated Swimsuit* edition than any other.

### Orchid Boutique

*224 8th Street, at Collins Avenue, South Beach (1-305 397 8994, www.theorchidboutique.com). Bus 23, 103, South Beach Local.* **Open** 11am-9pm Mon-Sat; noon-8pm Sun. **Credit** AmEx, MC, V. **Map** p280 E3.
In addition to internationally known designers such as Badgley Mischka, Betsey Johnson, True Religion and Nanette Lepore, this well-organised boutique also carries its own Orchid Label, which is well priced with plenty of sub-$100 options. A fun selection of jewellery and handbags can easily take you from poolside to nightclub.

### ★ Ritchie Swimwear

*160 8th Street, at Collins Avenue, South Beach (1-305 538 0201, www.ritchieswimwear.com). Bus C, H, K, W, South Beach Local.* **Open** 10am-9pm Mon-Fri; 10am-10pm Sat; 10am-8pm Sun. **Credit** AmEx, MC, V. **Map** p280 E3.
Welcome to wild bikinidom: bright tanks, strings and one-pieces fit for a *Baywatch* babe, all made in sunny Miami. Mix-and-match tops and bottoms start at $30. You can even choose your fabric by resort name, from Santorini to Capri, via Beverly Hills and Saint Tropez.

TASCHEN. *See p120.*

### Designer

### Alchemist

*1111 Lincoln Road, at Alton Road, South Beach (1-305 531 4815, www.shopalchemist.com). Bus C, G, H, K, L, M, S, W.* **Open** 10am-9pm daily. **Credit** AmEx, MC, V. **Map** p280 C2.
Browse through the latest items from the likes of Givenchy, Rick Owens and Dior Homme while taking in a sky-high view of Lincoln Road below you at this big name-only, two-storey fashionista paradise. The store is located in one of the city's stunning architect-designed garages (*see p38* **Parking Fine**).

### Atrium

*1931 Collins Avenue, at 19th Street, South Beach (1-305 695 0757, www.atriumnyc.com). Bus C, G, H, M, L, S.* **Open** 10am-10pm Mon-Sat; 11am-9pm Sun. **Credit** AmEx, MC, V. **Map** p280 C3.
A South Beach unisex shopping hotspot, Atrium is also a great place to stalk celebrities if you don't feel like breaking the bank on a $2,300 Alexander McQueen clutch. With designer brands at designer prices, don't be surprised if you see the same $200 white T-shirt on a Kardashian in the latest issue of your favourite tabloid.

CONSUME

## Barneys New York Co-op

*832 Collins Avenue, at 8th Street, South Beach (1-305 421 2010, www.barneys.com). Bus C, H, K, W, South Beach Local.* **Open** 11am-9pm Mon-Thur; 11am-10pm Fri, Sat; noon-8pm Sun. **Credit** AmEx, MC, V. **Map** p280 E3.

The Miami outpost of the Big Apple department store features designer fashions by 7 For All Mankind jeans, Daryl K, Marc by Marc Jacobs, Diane von Furstenberg and more. Barneys 'Co-Ops' are not discount outlets, but more of a curated collection of emerging and indie designers, meaning a T-shirt might cost $150 instead of $300. *Photos p125.*

## ★ BASE USA

*939 Lincoln Road, at Jefferson Avenue, South Beach (1-305 531 4982, www.baseworld.com). Bus C, G, H, K, L, M, S, W, South Beach Local.* **Open** 11am-10pm Mon-Thur, Sun; 11am-11pm Fri, Sat. **Credit** AmEx, MC, V. **Map** p280 C2.

In addition to fancy, monochromatic threads, BASE is also known for its funky soundtrack (its CD collection is for sale, of course), coffee table books, candles and even Japanese anime. Just how cool is the stuff? Consider this: the store has a small location at the Delano hotel (*see p135*) plus a 24/7 vending machine of goodies at the Mondrian South Beach (*see p137*).

## Intermix

*634 Collins Avenue, at 6th Street, South Beach (1-305 531 5950, www.intermixonline.com). Bus C, H, K, W, South Beach Local.* **Open** 10am-9pm Mon-Sat; 11am-9pm Sun. **Credit** AmEx, DC, MC, V. **Map** p280 E3.

Oh so-trendy Intermix gathers the choicest styles by top designers such as Derek Lam, Stella McCartney, Current/Elliott, Givenchy and Helmut Lang. **Other locations** Bal Harbour Shops, 9700 Collins Avenue, off Park Drive, Bal Harbour (1-305 993 1232).

## Scoop

*Shore Club, 1901 Collins Avenue, at 19th Street, South Beach (1-305 532 5929, www.scoopnyc. com). Bus C, G, H, L, M, S.* **Open** 10am-8pm Mon-Thur; 10am-10pm Fri, Sat; 11am-7pm Sun. **Credit** AmEx, DC, Disc, MC, V. **Map** p280 C3.

The only outpost of this starlet store beyond the north-east carries chic clothes and accessories, including own-label wares and designer pieces by the likes of Marc Jacobs and Paul Smith.

## Webster

*1220 Collins Avenue, at 12th Street, South Beach (1-305 673 5548, www.thewebstermiami.com). Bus C, H, K, W, South Beach Local.* **Open** 11am-8pm Mon-Sat; noon-6pm Sun. **Credit** AmEx, MC, V. **Map** p280 D3.

This emporium features 20,000sq ft of labels, labels and more labels. Straight-off-the-runway pieces include exclusives for both sexes from Tom Ford,

Balenciaga and Miu Miu. Steer clear if you haven't got a platinum card. Even window-shopping will feel painfully pricey.

# Discount

## ★ Loehmann's

*19915 Biscayne Boulevard, at Aventura Boulevard, Aventura (1-305 792 9240, www. loehmanns.com). Bus 3, 93, 105, 183.* **Open** 9.30am-9pm Mon-Sat; 11am-7pm Sun.

Comb the racks carefully for great bargains on top designers at the Aventura outlet of this nationwide bargain department store chain. If you plan on doing some serious damage to your credit card here (or spending more than $250), it might be worth paying the $25 fee to become a Gold Insider, which gets you a fancy card and an additional 10-20% off your entire purchase.

**Other locations** The Shops at Midtown, 3201 Miami Avenue, at NW 33rd Street, Wynwood (1-305 571 9500); 8525 Mills Drive, Suite 305, off SW 88th Street, Kendall (1-305 270 3387).

## Marshalls

*16800 Collins Avenue, off NE 163rd Street, Sunny Isles Beach (1-305 944 0223, www. marshallsonline.com). Bus K, S.* **Open** 9.30am-9.30pm Mon-Sat; 11am-8pm Sun. **Credit** AmEx, MC, V.

Marshalls is Miami's most popular discount shop, offering a vast selection of designer and brand-name fashions for men, women and children – as well as homewares and gifts – all at 20-60% below department store prices.

**Other locations** throughout the city.

## Target

*3401 N Miami Avenue, at NE 36th Street, Wynwood (1-786 437 0164, www.target.com). Metrorail Dadeland North.* **Open** 8am-10pm Mon-Sat; 8am-9pm Sun. **Credit** AmEx, MC, V.

America's coolest budget chain, Target boasts a signature line of homewares and gifts by celebrated architect Michael Graves, limited edition collections of goods and clothing by Zac Posen, Missoni and Isaac Mizrahi, and great prices on everything including toiletries, entertainment, electronics and toys.

**Other locations** throughout the city.

## TJ Maxx

*1149 5th Street, at Alton Road, South Beach (1-305 538 3310, www.tjmaxx.com). Bus 103, 113, 120.* **Open** 9.30am-9.30pm Mon-Fri, Sun; 9am-10.30pm Sat. **Credit** AmEx, Disc, MC, V. **Map** p280 E2.

There are ten branches of this discount designer clothing store across the city, but none quite like the South Beach outpost. Boasting speciality 'Runway' sections for both genders, you'll find the most exclusive designer names from the US, Europe and

**CONSUME**

beyond (both clothing and shoes), with as much as 60% off retail prices. Sure, you may end up spending $150 on a pair of shoes. But for a brand-new pair of Prada sandals, that's a steal.

**Other locations** throughout the city.

## General

### ★ Rebel

*6669 Biscayne Boulevard, at NE 67th Street, Upper East Side (1-305 758 2369, www.rebel miami.com). Bus 3/Metrorail Omni.* **Open** 10am-7pm Mon-Sat; noon-5pm Sun. **Credit** AmEx, Disc, MC, V.

Long Island transplants flock to Rebel to purchase top-of-the-line T-shirts with grand embellishments and price tags to match. Find a selection of jeans of the moment and other items from the likes of Juicy Couture, Vince and Sass & Bide. It's worth going just for the sale room.

### Urban Outfitters

*653 Collins Avenue, at 7th Street, South Beach (1-305 535 9726, www.urbanoutfitters.com). Bus C, H, K, W, South Beach Local.* **Open** 10am-10pm Mon-Thur; 10am-11pm Fri, Sat; noon-9pm Sun. **Credit** AmEx, MC, V. **Map** p280 E3.

Clothing and accessories for men and women come in UO's own labels, alongside brand names such as Diesel, Mook, Paul Frank, Camper and Stüssy. The two-storey industrial space also has homewares perfect for studio-dwellers and assorted campy giftage. **Other locations** Shops at Sunset Place, 5701 Sunset Drive, South Miami (1-305 663 1536); Aventura Mall, 19575 Biscayne Boulevard, Aventura (1-305 936 8358).

## Used & vintage

### ★ C Madeleine's

*13702 Biscayne Boulevard, at 137th Street, North Miami (1-305 945 7770, www.cmadeleines.com).*

## THE BEST FASHION STORES

For sun goddesses
**Beach Bunny**. *See p122.*

For vintage hounds
**C Madeleine's**. *See above.*

For shoe fetishists
**Tuccia di Capri**. *See p128.*

For bargain hunters
**Loehmann's**. *See p123.*

For mini fashionistas
**Genius Jones**. *See p121.*

*Bus 3.* **Open** 11am-6pm Mon-Sat; noon-5pm Sun. **Credit** AmEx, MC, V.

Do you need a drop-waist dress from the 1920s? Can't manage without a Pucci print skirt from the '70s? You'll find both here, along with high-necked linen and lace dresses, funky neckties, costume jewels, shoes, furs and postcards. Brands include Gucci, Balenciaga, Chanel, Vuitton and even hard-to-find Zandra Rhodes.

### Miami Twice

*6562 SW 40th Street (Bird Road), at SW 65th Avenue, South Miami (1-305 666 0127, www. miamitwice.com). Bus 40, 73.* **Open** 10am-7pm Mon-Sat. **Credit** AmEx, MC, V.

Open since the mid 1980s, Miami Twice is a retro department store with an extensive Bakelite jewellery and accessories collection. It also stocks a brilliant range of homewares – 1950s dinettes, Fiestaware, lunchboxes – and clothes spanning the decades from flapper dresses to old leather jackets. MT supplies films and is said to be a favourite haunt of Cameron Diaz.

### Rabbit Hole

*17032 W Dixie Highway, at NE 170th Street, North Miami (1-305 705 2343, www.shoprabbit hole.com). Bus 3, 93.* **Open** noon-8pm Tue-Sat; 2-6pm Sun. **Credit** AmEx, Disc, MC, V.

At the base of the Rabbit Hole's thriving online business is this small North Miami shop, which the *New Times* has declared one of the city's best. Among the curated selection of vintage clothing is a great range of party dresses from the 1970s and '80s, offering one-of-a-kind looks for $50 to $100 a pop. Modern threads – dresses, skirts, tops and accessories – can be had for half that price.

### Red White & Blue Thrift Store

*12640 NE 6th Avenue, at 126th Street, North Miami (1-305 893 1104, www.redwhiteandblue thriftstore.com). Bus 10, 16, J.* **Open** 9am-6pm Mon-Sat. **Credit** AmEx, MC, V.

Located in a Hialeah strip mall, Red, White and Blue isn't glamorous. But if you don't mind combing through racks of other people's junk, you may discover homeware and clothing treasures – a $500 Dana Buchman jacket for $7.99; an original Persian miniature painting for $3.99; and embroidered curtains at $19.99 a pair.

## FASHION ACCESSORIES & SERVICES

### Jewellery

### Turchin Jewelry

*130 NE 40th Street, at NE 2nd Avenue, Design District (1-305 573 7117, www.turchinjewelry. com). Bus 9, 10, J.* **Open** 10am-6pm Mon-Fri. **Credit** AmEx, MC, V.

**Barneys New York Co-op**. *See p123.*

Though designed by local Teresa Turchin in her shop studio, these pricey, vaguely New Age baubles are crafted using materials from around the world, including Tibet, Nepal, India and Africa. Each piece is blessed by a Buddhist monk.

### Morays

*50 NE 2nd Avenue, at E Flagler Street, Downtown (1-305 374 0739, www.morays jewelers.com). Metromover 1st Street.* **Open** 10.30am-5pm Mon-Fri. **Credit** AmEx, DC, MC, V. **Map** p282 D3.

The oldest jewellers in Downtown, fiftysomething Morays stocks every conceivable watch brand. It's in Miami's so-called Little Switzerland (oh, please), near the Seybold Building arcade, which houses ten floors of jewellers, engravers and watchmakers. Speaking Spanish can help you get a better deal.

## Lingerie & underwear

### La Perla

*Village of Merrick Park, 320 San Lorenzo Avenue, at Ponce de León Boulevard, Coral Gables (1-305 448 8805, www.laperla.com). Bus H, K, S, T.* **Open** 10am-9pm Mon-Sat; noon-6pm Sun. **Credit** AmEx, MC, V. **Map** p284 E4.

Impeccably made Italian silk and lace fancies, plus stunning swimwear and accessories, all of which cost a pretty penny.

**Other locations** Bal Harbour Shops, 9700 Collins Avenue (1-305 864 3173).

### Sexy Secrets Lingerie Boutique

*6572 SW 40th Street (Bird Road), at SW 67th Avenue, South Miami (1-305 662 5518, www. sexysecretsmiami.com). Bus 40, 73.* **Open** 11am-7pm Mon-Sat. **Credit** MC, V.

The light pink walls give this shop, which bills itself as a 'playground for your imagination', a cool vintage feel. But the affordable boudoir get-ups are utterly contemporary. For those looking for some sexy swagger to go with their purchase, Sexy Secrets offers pole- and belly dancing classes.

## Luggage

### Bodymindtravel

*111 Lincoln Road, at Collins Avenue, South Beach (1-305 538 2307, www.bodymindtravel.com). Bus 103, 120, 123, 150, South Beach Local.* **Open** 10am-8pm Mon-Sat. **Credit** AmEx, Disc, MC, V. **Map** p280 C3.

The thoughtful proprietors behind Bodymindtravel know that even the most relaxing trip has an element of stress. So they've curated a wide selection of items that no journey(wo)man should be without: there's brand-name luggage from Tumi, Victorinox and Brics, plus a wide range of accessories – everything from aromatherapy candles and bamboo-fibre clothing to books, music and games – all aimed at making

**CONSUME**

**CONSUME**

# Gallery Guide

*Hit these essential spaces in the city's arty enclaves.*

Once, the closest thing you'd find to art in Miami were postcard-sized club flyers promoting ladies' nights and amateur striptease. But since the arrival of Art Basel (*see p24*) in 2001, the local scene has gone global, as the annual culture-fest brings international dealers, curators and collectors together to do business by the beach. Ironically, the gentrification of South Beach in the early 1990s and its new ability to attract such prestigious events boosted rental prices, driving out the very artists who spearheaded its renewal. The bulk of the art scene has been forced into the Design District and Wynwood neighbourhoods, which are now home to the cutting-edge galleries that showcase young local talent.

## SOUTH BEACH

The South Beach gallery scene has all but vanished, and former studios now house high-rent operations such as Starbucks. Some art is still sold at the Lincoln Road Antiques Market, which is held on Sundays from October to May, and a couple of stalwarts remain.

### ArtCenter South Florida
*800 Lincoln Road, at Meridian Avenue (1-305 538 7887, www.artcentersf.org). Bus C, G, H, K, L, R, S, W, South Beach Local.* **Open** noon-9pm Mon-Thur; 11am-10pm Fri, Sat; 11am-9pm Sun. **Credit** AmEx, MC, V. **Map** p280 C2.
A mixture of artists' studios and rotating gallery space occupy the three separate structures that make up this alternative, non-profit art centre. Exhibitions reflect Miami's diverse communities and prices are affordable.

### Britto Central
*818 Lincoln Road, at Meridian Avenue, South Beach (1-305 531 8821, www. britto.com). Bus 101, 115, 123.* **Open** 10am-11pm Mon-Thur, Sun; 10am-midnight Fri, Sat. **Map** p280 C2.
For all things Romero Britto – Miami's most iconic neo-pop artist – this dedicated gallery is the place. It didn't take long for the Brazilian-born artist to make a splash when he moved to Magic City in 1989. His bright, bold patterns quickly caught the eye of Michel Roux, the brainchild behind Absolut Vodka, who hired him to bring his creative genius to its vodka bottles. He has since worked with a variety of other major corporations and his public commissions can be seen in urban spaces from São Paulo to New York City. From original works and reproductions to brightly decorated luggage, if Britto paints it, Britto Central sells it.

## THE DESIGN DISTRICT & WYNWOOD

Once semi-derelict areas of showrooms and warehouses from the 1920s and '30s, the Design District and neighbouring Wynwood are now visual art meccas. Espresso-fuelled designers manoeuvre their portfolios past the crack kids to visit new installations and blue-chip interiors stores. For more information visit www.miamidesigndistrict.net and www.wynwoodartdistrict.com.

### Center for Visual Communication
*541 NW 27th Street, at NW 5th Avenue (1-305 571 1415, www.visual.org). Bus 3, 9, 10, 16, J.* **Open** 9.30am-5.30pm Mon-Sat. **No credit cards**. **Map** p285 F2.
Don't be put off by the earnest name: rotating exhibitions at this respected gallery feature prints and photographs from seminal US artists such as Jasper Johns, Barnett Newman and Robert Rauschenberg.

### David Castillo Gallery
*2234 NW 2nd Avenue, at NW 22nd Street (1-305 573 8110, www.david castillogallery.com). Bus 3, 9, 10, 16, J.* **Open** 10am-5pm Tue-Sat or by appointment. **Credit** AmEx, MC, V. **Map** p285 F2.
Formerly a private dealer, David Castillo has made a splash in Wynwood with a beautifully renovated building that exhibits high-calibre contemporary work by emerging and mid-career artists, in various media.

### Diana Lowenstein Gallery
*2043 N Miami Avenue, at NE20th Street (1-305 576 1804, www.dlfinearts.com). Bus 3, 9, 10, 16, J.* **Open** 10am-5pm Tue-Fri; 10am-3pm Sat. **Credit** AmEx, MC, V. **Map** p285 F3.

Founded in Buenos Aires, Diana Lowenstein Gallery moved to Miami in 2000. The sleek and influential gallery represents some 40 contemporary artists from around the world, with a focus on Latin America and Miami.

### Emerson Dorsch
*151 NW 24th Street, at N Miami Avenue (1-305 576 1278, www.dorschgallery. com). Bus 3, 9, 10, 16, J.* **Open** *noon-5pm Tue-Sat or by appointment.* **Credit** *AmEx, MC, V.* **Map** *p285 F3.*
Emerson Dorsch (formerly known as the Dorsch Gallery) is as well known for hosting great parties as organising exhibitions. His expansive gallery hosts regular celebrations with live music and performances, and eclectic shows by local artists.

### Fredric Snitzer Gallery
*2247 NW 1st Place, at N Miami Avenue (1-305 448 8976, www.snitzer.com). Bus 3, 9, 10, 16, J.* **Open** *11am-5pm Tue-Sat.* **Credit** *AmEx, MC, V.* **Map** *p285 F2.*
Fredric Snitzer is more than a dealer: he's long been a mentor to Miami-based artists. His warehouse is the focus of the Wynwood scene, and his roster includes members of Cuba's famed '80s Generation (notably José Bedia), recent graduates of Miami's New World School of the Arts and local stars such as Hernan Bas.

### Gary Nader Fine Art
*62 NE 27th Street, at N Miami Avenue (1-305 576 0256, www.garynader.com). Bus 3, 9, 10, 16, J.* **Open** *10am-6pm Mon-Sat.* **Credit** *AmEx, DC, MC, V.* **Map** *p285 F3.*
Gary Nader is a major player on the Latin American market, organising an annual auction in December and dealing in the resale of work by masters such as Wifredo Lam, Fernando Botero and Roberto Matta. There are also monthly exhibitions of new artists held at the gallery.

### Harold Golen Gallery
*2294 NW 2nd Avenue, at NW 23rd Street (1-305-989-3359, www.harold golengallery.com). Bus 3, 9, 10, 16, J.* **Open** *1-5pm Sat or by appointment (suggested).* **Credit** *AmEx, MC, V.* **Map** *p285 E1.*

Harold Golen specialises in lowbrow and pop surrealist works, in a space that the *Miami New Times* referred to as 'funky retro-futuristic'. In addition to monthly openings, the gallery hosts parties and experimental music gigs.

### Locust Projects
*3852 N Miami Avenue, at NW 39th Street (1-305 576 8570, www.locustprojects.org). Bus 36, 110, 202.* **Open** *noon-5pm Thur-Sat.* **No credit cards.** **Map** *p285 D3.*
Locust Projects is a non-profit art centre that focuses on multimedia installations and experimental work by emerging artists. Locust's fundraising auctions (including an annual one during the spring) and sales provide a great opportunity to buy art at accessible prices.

## CORAL GABLES

I like the neighbourhood they inhabit, Coral Gables' galleries are upscale and conservative. Openings are held during the Coral Gables Gallery Walk, held on the first Friday of each month.

### Americas Collection
*4213 Ponce de León Boulevard, at San Lorenzo Avenue (1-305 446 5578, www.americascollection.com). Bus 24, 42, Coral Gables Circulator.* **Open** *10.30am-5.30pm Mon-Fri; noon-5pm Sat.* **Credit** *AmEx, MC, V.* **Map** *p284 C4.*
Contemporary paintings, especially landscapes and portraits, are typical offerings at this long-running Coral Gables gallery. It also features works by well-known Latin American artists.

### ArtSpace Virginia Miller Galleries
*169 Madeira Avenue, at Ponce de León Boulevard (1-305 444 4493, www.virginia miller.com). Bus 24, 42, Coral Gables Circulator.* **Open** *11am-6pm Mon-Fri; Sat, Sun by appointment.* **Credit** *AmEx, MC, V.* **Map** *p284 B4.*
Since opening her gallery in 1974, Virginia Miller has reflected the trends and showed daring installation work, photography and murals. These days the gallery showcases figurative and abstract painters from the US and Latin America. Miller also brokers masterworks from international markets.

**CONSUME**

**CONSUME**

Kartell. *See p130.*

customers' adventures more enjoyable. The store also offers luggage repair, for when that pesky wheel won't stay on its track.

### Luggage Gallery

*1622 Washington Avenue, at Lincoln Road, South Beach (1-305 532 1289, www.luggagegallery.com). Bus 103, 120, 123, 150, South Beach Local.* **Open** 9am-9pm Mon-Sat; 10am-8pm Sun. **Credit** AmEx, Disc, MC, V. **Map** p280 C3.
As the name suggests, there's a broad range of bags on display at this 35-year-old luggage megastore, where you'll find everything from backpacks to briefcases. Expect reasonable prices on popular names like Tumi, Samsonite, Hartmann and Kipling.

## Shoes

### Capretto Shoes

*5822 Sunset Drive, at 58th Avenue, South Miami (1-305 661 7767). Metrorail South Miami.* **Open** 10am-6pm Mon-Sat. **Credit** AmEx, MC, V.
Designer belts, handbags, jewellery, plus a discerning selection of women's sandals, pumps, mules, boots and loafers from the likes of Gucci and Prada.

### Koko & Palenki Shoes

*Aventura Mall, 19501 Biscayne Boulevard, at NE 196th Street, Aventura (1-305 792 9299, http://koko-palenki.com). Bus 3, 9, E, S.* **Open** 10am-9.30pm Mon-Sat; noon-8pm Sun. **Credit** AmEx, DC, MC, V. **Map** p278.
Elegant and exotic styles from D&G, Charles Jourdan, Guess, Casadei, Anne Klein and more, along with matching purses and men's shoes and belts.

**Other locations** Dadeland Mall, 7535 SW 88th Street, South Miami (1-305 668 2233); CocoWalk, 3015 Grand Avenue, Coconut Grove (1-305 444 1772).

### ★ Tuccia di Capri

*1630 Pennsylvania Avenue, at Lincoln Road, South Beach (1-305 534 5865, www.tucciadi capri.com). Bus C, G, H, K, L, M, S, W.* **Open** 11am-7pm daily. **Credit** AmEx, MC, V. **Map** p280 C2.
Cobbling isn't exactly an art form on South Beach, which is what makes Tuccia di Capri stand out. A shoe fetishist's dream, this design-your-own-shoe boutique lets you pick everything from heel to toe. Prices are around $200 to $300.

## FOOD & DRINK

### General

### ★ Epicure Market

*1656 Alton Road, at 16th Street, South Beach (1-305 672 1861, www.epicuremarket.com). Bus M, R, W.* **Open** 9am-9pm daily. **Credit** AmEx, MC, V. **Map** p280 C2.
This gourmet market is pricey, but worth it, especially the kosher deli. There's also a fine butcher and an excellent bakery.

### Whole Foods Market

*1020 Alton Road, at 10th Street, South Beach (1-305 938 2800, www.wholefoodsmarket.com). Bus 113, 119.* **Open** 8am-11pm daily. **Credit** AmEx, MC, V. **Map** p280 D2.

Organic superstore with a right-on selection of natural foods: fine meats, prepared dishes, baked goods, plus vitamins, toiletries and superior wines. **Other locations** 6701 Red Road, Coral Gables (1-305 421 9421); 11701 South Dixie Highway, at SW 117th Street, Pinecrest (1-305 969 5800); 21105 Biscayne Boulevard, off NE 210th Street, Aventura (1-305 682 4400).

## Specialist

### ★ Dylan's Candy Bar

*801 Lincoln Road, at Meridian Avenue, South Beach (1-305 531 1988, www.dylanscandybar. com). Bus 101, 115, 119, 123.* **Open** 11am-midnight Mon-Fri; 11am-1am Sat; 11am-11pm Sun. **Credit** AmEx, Disc, MC, V. **Map** p280 C2.
Fashion legend Ralph Lauren's daughter Dylan is like a modern-day Willy Wonka, offering more than 5,000 kinds of candy from around the world – not to mention ice-cream, macaroons and a sidewalk café serving up candy-inspired cocktails such as the Pop Rock Explosion – at this fun-for-all-ages emporium.

### Fresh Market

*1800 West Avenue, at 18th Street, South Beach (1-305 532 0377, www.thefreshmarket.com). Bus 113, 119.* **Open** 8am-10pm daily. **Credit** AmEx, Disc, MC, V. **Map** p280 C2.
All the organic produce you could possibly desire, including fresh fish and seafood, plus a café.
**Other locations** throughout the city.

### La Estancia Argentina

*17870 Biscayne Boulevard, at 178th Street, Aventura (1-305 932 8477, www.laestanciaweb.com). Bus 3, 9, E, S.* **Open** 8am-10pm daily. **Credit** AmEx, Disc, MC, V.
Opened by Buenos Aires expats, this gourmet store offers Latin American items, from chorizos and chimichurris to outstanding malbecs.

## Gifts & souvenirs

### HistoryMiami Gift Shop

*101 W Flagler Street, at NW 1st Avenue, Downtown (1-305 375 1492, www.history miami.org). Metromover Government Center.* **Open** 10am-5pm Tue-Fri; noon-5pm Sat, Sun. **Credit** AmEx, MC, V. **Map** p282 D1.
Pure Floridiana. Here's where you buy those souvenirs for the folks back home: Southern cracker cookbooks, Seminole Indian arts and crafts, plus a wide range of local books and arts.

### Wolfsonian-FIU Gift Shop

*1001 Washington Avenue, at 10th Street, South Beach (1-305 531 1001, www.wolfsonian.org). Bus C, H, K, W, South Beach Local.* **Open** noon-6pm Mon, Tue, Thur-Sun; noon-9pm Fri. **Credit** AmEx, MC, V. **Map** p280 D3.

A shop devoted to beautiful design. Pieces include a colander by Starck, rare designer pens and reproductions of classic clocks by George Nelson.

## HEALTH & BEAUTY
### Hairdressers

### Julien Farel Salon & Spa

*200 S Biscayne Boulevard, at NE 2nd Street, Downtown (1-305 372 1278, www.julienfarel miami.com). Bus 3, 24, 93, 113.* **Open** 10am-8pm Mon-Sat. **Credit** AmEx, MC, V. **Map** p282 D3.
Hairstylist to the stars Julien Farel (who counts Gywneth Paltrow, Kate Moss and Salma Hayek among his clients) chose Downtown Miami for his first freestanding venture outside NYC, offering a full menu of cutting, colouring and spa services.

### Salon Vaso

*1500 Alton Road, 2nd Floor, at 15th Street, South Beach (1-305 674 7470, www.salonvaso.com). Bus 113, 119, 123.* **Open** 10am-7pm Tue-Sat. **Credit** AmEx, MC, V. **Map** p280 D2.
In addition to reasonably priced cuts, colour and extensions, this friendly salon offers regular specials such as a $25 shampoo and blow-dry from Tuesday to Thursday. The eclectic space is decked out with vintage barber-shop chairs shipped from New York.

### Van Michael Salon

*1667 Michigan Avenue, at Lincoln Road, South Beach (1-305 534 6789, www.vanmichael.com). Bus C, G, H, K, L, M, S, W, South Beach Local.* **Open** noon-5pm Mon; 9am-9pm Tue; 9am-9.30pm Wed-Sat; noon-7pm Sun. **Credit** AmEx, MC, V. **Map** p280 C2.
Naturally chic, this is the ultimate showcase for Aveda's plant-based haircare, beauty treatments, make-up and lifestyle products.

### Opticians

### Optica

*Bal Harbour Shops, 9700 Collins Avenue, at 96th Street, Bal Harbour (1-305 866 2020). Bus H, K, S, T.* **Open** 10am-9pm Mon-Sat; noon-6pm Sun. **Credit** AmEx, MC, V. **Map** p281 inset.
Stylish specs for those who care as much about being seen as they do about seeing. Among the posh brands are Chanel, Cartier, Dior and Gucci.

### SEE

*921 Lincoln Road, at Jefferson Avenue, South Beach (1-305 672 6622, www.seeeyewear.com). Bus C, G, H, K, L, M, S, W, South Beach Local.* **Open** noon-9pm Mon-Thur, Sun; 11am-11pm Fri, Sat. **Credit** AmEx, MC, V. **Map** p280 C2.
For those with champagne tastes on a shandy budget, SEE offers edgy styles made by the designers' manufacturers, only at discounted prices.

**CONSUME**

Other locations 5826 Sunset Drive, at SW 58th Avenue, South Miami (1-305 663 7939).

## Shops

### Brownes Merchants & Trading Company
*1688 Jefferson Avenue, at 17th Street, South Beach (1-305 276-9637, www.brownesbeauty. com). Bus C, G, H, K, L, M, S, W, South Beach Local.* **Open** 10am-8pm Mon-Sat; 10am-7pm Sun. **Credit** AmEx, MC, V. **Map** p280 C2.
Hard-to-get cosmetics from the likes of Trish McEvoy, Kiehl's, Aveda, Philosophy, Dr Hauschka and Geo Trumper. Get a haircut, citrus pedicure, facial or other spa treatments at Some Like it Hot, its full-service salon.
**Other locations** 87 NE 40th Street, at NE 1st Avenue, Design District (1-888 276 9637).

### MAC
*673 Collins Avenue, at 7th Street, South Beach (1-305 604 9040, www.maccosmetics.com). Bus C, H, K, W, South Beach Local.* **Open** 11am-9pm Mon-Wed; 10am-10pm Thur-Sat; noon-7pm Sun. **Credit** AmEx, MC, V. **Map** p280 C2.
RuPaul, Lil' Kim and Nicki Minaj have all been spokesfolk for this innovative line of cosmetics. Marvellous makeovers from pros on the premises come by appointment.
**Other locations** 19501 Biscayne Boulevard, at 195th Street, Aventura (1-305 682-0460); 1107 Lincoln Road, at Alton Road (1-305 538 1088).

## Spas & salons

*See also p129* **Julien Farel Salon & Spa** and **Van Michael Salon**.

### Club Essentia
*Delano Hotel, 1685 Collins Avenue, at 17th Street, South Beach (1-305 674 6100, www.club essentia.com). Bus C, G, H, L, M, S.* **Open** 9am-7pm daily for women; 7.30-11pm daily (by appointment) for men. **Credit** AmEx, MC, V. **Map** p280 C3.
This is where the celebs spa, although the Standard (*see below*) is becoming the place to be seen (and scrubbed). Minimalist decor and a rooftop solarium make for a Zen experience. Expect shiatsu and deep-tissue massages, luxury treatments and facials.

### ★ Standard Spa
*40 Island Avenue, at the Venetian Causeway, Miami Beach (1-305 673 1717, www.standard hotels.com). Bus A.* **Open** times vary. **Credit** AmEx, DC, Disc, MC, V. **Map** p280 C1.
The coolest spa in town, the Standard is notable for its soothing waterfront location and old-school health and beauty regimes, from Chinese medicine baths and hydrotherapy to a big Turkish hammam.

# HOUSE & HOME
For the interior design stores in the Design District, *see p131* **Shopping by Design**.

## Antiques & vintage

### Architectural Antiques
*2520 SW 28th Lane, at 27th Avenue, Coconut Grove (1-305 285 1330, www.miamiantique.com). Metrorail Coconut Grove.* **Open** 10am-6pm daily. **Credit** MC, V.
This warehouse is filled to the gills with large-scale goodies (wooden doors that came from a cathedral, for example), although you'll also find smaller pieces such as lights and artworks. Bring a truck, though, just in case something big appeals.

### Stone Age Antiques
*3236 NW S River Drive, at NW 32nd Street, North Miami (1-305 633 5114, www.stoneage-antiques.com). Bus 32, 36, J.* **Open** 9am-4.45pm Mon-Sat. **No credit cards**.
A favourite of movie prop scouts for nearly 50 years, Stone Age also sells old posters, military memorabilia, cowboy gear, primitive tribal masks and stuffed animals. You know, all the stuff you really need.

## General

### Fendi Casa
*90 NE 39th Street, at NE 2nd Avenue, Design District (1-305 438 1660, www.fendi.com). Bus 9, 10.* **Open** 10am-6pm Mon-Fri; 11am-4pm Sat. **Credit** AmEx, Disc, MC, V. **Map** p285 D2.
*See p131* **Shopping by Design**.

### Glottman
*219 NW 26th Street, at NE 2nd Avenue (1-305 438 3711, www.glottman.com). Bus 2, 6.* **Open** 9.30am-6.30pm Mon-Fri; by appointment only Sat, Sun. **Credit** AmEx, Disc, MC, V. **Map** p285 F3.
Hipsters say that Glottman resembles the set of the *Cabinet of Dr Caligari* – it's a funky, trippy showroom with witty furniture and playful accessories such as glass sugar dispensers shaped like snowmen.

### ★ Kartell
*170 NE 40th Street, at NE 2nd Avenue, Design District (1-305 573 4010, www.kartell.com). Bus 9, 10.* **Open** 10am-6pm Mon-Fri; noon-5pm Sat. **Credit** AmEx, MC, V. **Map** p285 D2.
A fantastic plastic paradise featuring a wide variety of pricey products created by internationally known designers, including gnome tables by Philippe Starck, modular bookshelves by Giulio Polvara and storage units by Anna Castelli Ferrieri. *Photos p128*.

### Luminaire
*2331 Ponce de León Boulevard, at Aragon Avenue, Coral Gables (1-305 448 7367,*

# Shopping by Design

*Add some couture to your couch.*

Not everyone comes to Miami looking for a plastic flamingo and an art deco fridge magnet – many tourists are after designer furniture. And they head straight for the Design District (www.miamidesigndistrict. net), which boasts 60 interiors shops, including global names whose only US branch is in Miami. Even if your budget is more IKEA, it's still fun to window-shop.

**Fendi Casa** (*see p130*) is more sleek than swanky. The furniture arm of the Italian couture house is beloved of fashionistas, who can buy furniture that resembles a Fendi handbag; a butter leather couch complete with couture imprint, say, for tens of thousands of dollars. The lean sofas and coffee tables are enriched by crystal lamps, damask fabrics and fur cushions.

**Luminaire** (*see p130*) is practically a Design District poster child. It features a greatest hits medley of modern designers, with pieces by Ron Arad, Arne Jacobsen, Philippe Starck, Zaha Hadid et al.

Imagine Willy Wonka was diabetic and had to channel his love for sweets instead into a technicolour world of glass, furniture, lighting and accessories. The result would be **NiBa Home** (*see p133*), a funky store offering cool furniture and flamboyant accessories, both new and vintage.

**Poliform Miami** (*see p133*) takes industrial chic to new heights. The style is pristine verging on the clinical: the cutting-edge kitchens almost look too clean to eat in. But these are the coolest wardrobes, wall units and furnishings this side of Milan.

Another Italian import, **Poltrona Frau** (*see p133*) is famous for its streamlined leather sofas – which are upholstered by hand – and minimalist tables. But it's also good for star spotting. The brand is favoured by the likes of Janet Jackson and Beyoncé, who have been known to meander round the showroom.

More details on the Design District can be found in **Explore** (*see pp64-65*).

**CONSUME**

Luminaire.

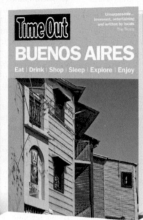
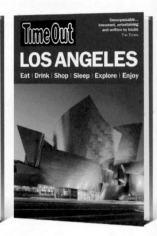

*www.luminaire.com). Bus 24, 42, 72, Coral Gables Circulator.* **Open** 10am-6pm Mon-Sat. **Credit** AmEx, MC, V. **Map** p284 B4.

This glass box showroom is a beacon for buyers of classic modern furniture by the likes of Le Corbusier, Arne Jacobsen and Jasper Morrison. For the Design District location, *see p131* **Shopping by Design.** **Other locations** 3901 NE 2nd Ave, at NE 40th Street, Design District (1-305 576 5788).

### ★ NiBa Home
*39 NE 39th Street, at N Miami Avenue, Design District (1-305 573 1939, www.nibahome.com). Bus 9, 10.* **Open** 10am-6pm Mon-Fri; noon-5pm Sat. **Credit** AmEx, MC, DC, V. **Map** p285 D3. *See p131* **Shopping by Design.**

### Poliform Miami
*180 NE 39th Street, at NE 2nd Avenue, Design District (1-305 573 9950, www.poliformusa.com). Bus 9, 10.* **Open** 9am-6pm Mon-Fri; 10am-4pm Sat. **Credit** AmEx, Disc, MC, V. **Map** p285 D2. *See p131* **Shopping by Design.**

### Poltrona Frau
*3800 NE Miami Court, between NE 38th & 39th Streets, Design District (1-305 576 3636, www.poltronafraumiami.net). Bus 9, 10.* **Open** 10am-6pm Mon-Fri; 11am-5pm Sat. **Credit** AmEx, MC, V. **Map** p285 D3. *See p131* **Shopping by Design.**

## Specialist

### La Cuisine & Clark Appliance
*50 Aragon Avenue, at Galiano Street, Coral Gables (1-305 442 9006, www.lacuisine professional.com). Bus 24, 42, 72.* **Open** 10am-6pm Mon-Fri; 10am-5pm Sat; noon-5pm Sun. **Credit** AmEx, Disc, MC, V. **Map** p284 B4.

Whether you're a star chef or merely faking it, the products stocked here can elevate your kitchen to a professional level, with glass-door industrial fridges and top-of-the-line appliances.

## MUSIC & ENTERTAINMENT
### CDs & records

### Sweat Records
*5505 NE 2nd Avenue, at NE 55th Street, Little Haiti (1-786 693 9309, www.sweatrecordsmiami. com). Bus 9, 10.* **Open** noon-10pm Tue-Sat; noon-5pm Sun. **Credit** MC, V.

A local indie fave, Sweat is located near divey music hangout Churchill's Pub and its stock is similarly edgy. Expect assorted indie, electronic, underground and undiscovered kitsch, available in CD, LP or DVD. The shop also hosts listening parties and book clubs, and features a high-end DJ set-up where anyone can come and spin.

### Uncle Sam's Musicafe
*1141 Washington Avenue, at 12th Street, South Beach (1-305 532 0973, www.unclesamsmusic. com). Bus C, H, K, W, South Beach Local.* **Open** 10am-midnight Mon-Sat; 11am-midnight Sun. **Credit** AmEx, DC, MC, V. **Map** p280 D3.

Dirty street kids and slick ravers mix at this store, which offers the latest in new and used dance, trip hop, trance, house and so on. This is also the spot to go for rave gear, hair dye, incense and stickers.

### Yesterday & Today Records
*9274 SW 40th Street (Bird Road), at 92nd Avenue, South Miami (1-305 554 1020, www. vintagerecords.com). Bus 40.* **Open** noon-7pm Tue-Thur; noon-8pm Fri; 11am-8pm Sat; noon-4.30pm Sun. **Credit** AmEx, MC, V.

This packed second-floor store features vintage vinyl. The stock covers everyone from the Beatles to Benny Goodman via Barbra Streisand.

## SPORT & FITNESS
### Adidas Originals
*226 8th Street, at Collins Avenue, South Beach (1-305 673 8317, www.adidas.com). Bus C, H, K, W, South Beach Local.* **Open** 11am-8pm Mon-Thur; 11am-9pm Fri, Sat; 11am-7pm Sun. **Credit** AmEx, MC, V. **Map** p280 E3.

Everyone can have their Adidas in this popular brand's SoBe outpost, filled with classic yet-trendy sports clothing, as well as gym bags, hats and, of course, sneakers, all bearing the trio of stripes.

### South Beach Dive & Surf
*850 Washington Avenue, at 8th Street, South Beach (1-305 531 6110, www.southbeachdivers. com). Bus C, H, K, W, South Beach Local.* **Open** 9am-7pm Mon-Sat; 10am-6pm Sun. **Credit** AmEx, MC, V. **Map** p280 E3.

Surf jams, thongs, shades (Arnettes, Dragons, Black Fly, Oakleys), surfboards, boogie boards, wakeboards and skateboards. There are no surfboard rentals, though the store does have a cheap styrofoam version (looks unimpressive, but works).

## TICKETS
The main booking agency for concerts, shows and sports events is **Ticketmaster** (1-800 745 3000, www.ticketmaster.com).

## TRAVELLERS' NEEDS
Got carried away in the shops? **XS Baggage** (1-866 656 6977, www.xsbaggage.com) will ship a single suitcase or multiple boxes to almost anywhere in the world, by air or sea. **Bodymindtravel** (*see p125*) sells all manner of travel aids and accessories. For mobile phone hire, *see p268*.

# Hotels

*Find your dream room in a retro motel or posh pleasure palace.*

Hotels literally put Miami on the map when Henry Flagler built the opulent Royal Palm in 1897 and transformed the sleepy backwater into hot property. And, a century later, another hotel put Miami back on the tourist map after years in the wilderness. In 1995, when Ian Schrager and Philippe Starck revamped the Delano (*see p135*), it marked Miami's return to glory. Out went the dowdy apartments and drug dealers, in came a slew of designer hotels. And today, the superstar openings keep on coming. Leading the pack is SLS Hotels, the five-star Beverly Hills-born group that mixes cutting-edge style with old-world glamour. After making a splash with the oceanfront SLS South Beach (*see p140*) in late 2012, the company is planning a second location in Brickell, scheduled to open in 2015. And the trend for revitalising historic properties continues – the James Royal Palm (*see p136*) and Gale South Beach (*see p142*) are just two of the deco gems to have undergone recent overhauls and garnered rave reviews.

## WHERE TO STAY

With its art deco architecture and trendy hotels, South Beach is a hotspot for Miami's style-conscious visitors. Ocean Drive and Collins Avenue are the main drags, between 5th and 23rd Streets. If you go north of 23rd, particularly up in Mid Beach or North Beach, you'll need a car. Whatever your bed preference, Miami isn't lacking in options. If you want a modicum of style in South Beach, but can't afford the Delano, there are party hotels such as the **Catalina** (*see p145*); small hidden gems such as the **Cadet** (*see p148*); and characterful 1930s apartments such as the **Villa Paradiso** (*see p150*). Retro-loving hipsters are drawn to Miami's collection of vintage motels – there's even a so-called boutique motel on Biscayne Boulevard (*see p152* **Paradise Motels**). Mid Beach, the **Freehand** (*see p150*) has put an upscale twist on the typically rowdy hostel concept, offering both shared dorms and private rooms in a decidedly hip setting.

The big drawback of South Beach is the dearth of parking. If valet parking is available at your hotel, use it and swallow the obscene cost (usually $20-$30). Just be sure that this fee allows you in-and-out privileges (so that you can actually make use of the car you're paying to keep at the ready). If you can't afford it, ask your concierge if they sell Miami Beach Parking Cards. But it might be easier to do away with the car entirely. A cab ride from Miami International Airport to South Beach costs a flat rate of $33 (plus tip); once you get there, a pair of comfy flipflops should get you around just fine.

If you are in the city for Art Basel, business or don't care about the beach, consider staying on the mainland in Downtown, Coral Gables or Coconut Grove.

## PRICES AND INFORMATION

Rates for rooms in Miami hotels vary wildly. Peak season, from November to the end of April, is the most expensive. Prices are often hiked up for events such as Art Basel, the Winter Music Conference or the Boat Show. You can pay considerably less in the summer.

Hotels within this chapter are organised by area and price. The rates given, based on the

❶ Red numbers given in this chapter correspond to the location of each hotel on the street maps. *See pp280-285.*

cost of a double room from the cheapest in the low season to the most expensive in the high season, were correct at the time of going to press, but hotels can change them at any time. Bear in mind that the rates quoted do not include sales tax, which adds another 13 per cent to the bill. Some hotels also charge a daily 'resort fee', typically $15-$20 per day, which covers such 'free' amenities as breakfast and internet access. Call the hotel or visit its website beforehand to get the lowdown on all fees so that you can budget accordingly.

# The Beaches

## SOUTH BEACH
Deluxe

### Angler's Boutique Resort
660 Washington Avenue, at 6th Street (reservations 1-866 729 8800, front desk 1-305 534 9600, www.theanglersresort.com). Bus C, H, K, W, South Beach Local. **Rates** $210-$700 double. **Rooms** 45. **Credit** AmEx, DC, MC, V. **Map** p280 E3 **❶**
Small and chic, this chi chi boutique hotel is helping to gentrify tawdry Washington Avenue. Comprising a Mediterranean Revival-style building and a few MiMo knockoffs, the architecture makes a refreshing change from deco. The lobby doubles as the trendy, Nuevo Latin-influenced 660 at the Angler's restaurant and much of the clientele is European. Perhaps they appreciate the tasteful bedrooms, designed by J Wallace Tutt, who did the interiors of Versace's mansion. Bamboo floors and sisal matting complement the colour scheme: think cream, beige, gold and mahogany. King-size beds add a decadent touch and lush floral photographs by Miami artist Sheila DeLemos inject cultural cred. The pool is tiny, but the beach is just two blocks away. Some of the pricier rooms come equipped with their own private patios and jacuzzis.
*Bar. Concierge. Disabled-adapted rooms. Gym. Internet (wireless, free). No-smoking rooms. Parking ($32/day). Pool (1, outdoor). Restaurant. Room service. TV: DVD/pay movies.*

### ★ Betsy
*1440 Ocean Drive, at 14th Street (reservations 1-866 792 3879, front desk 1-305 531 6100, www.thebetsyhotel.com). Bus C, H, K, W, South Beach Local.* **Rates** $185-$685. **Rooms** 61. **Credit** AmEx, Disc, MC, V. **Map** p280 D3 **❷**
The Betsy stands out among its South Beach neighbours, and not just because its colonial-style building à la *Gone with the Wind* is an anomaly in a sea of art deco. Situated on the northernmost end of Ocean Drive (read: the quieter part), the hotel boasts one of the best locations on the beach, with

a generous helping of Southern hospitality. You won't find bathtubs full of mineral water and rose petals here, but you will find charming little touches, such as poems left on your pillow, a pitcher of iced water with lemon by the pool and Malin+Goetz goodies in the bathrooms. The 61 rooms and suites are well appointed and comfortable, if occasionally a little on the small side and – in the case of the pool-facing rooms – missing out on that ocean view. If it's vistas you're after, head to the decked roof terrace, which is perfect for a day of baking in the sun or a romantic cocktail as the sun sets. The on-site restaurant, BLT Steak (*see p81*), is a New York City transplant that serves up some of the city's best slabs of beef.
*Bar. Concierge. Disabled-adapted rooms. Gym. Internet (wireless, free). No-smoking rooms. Parking ($37/day). Pool. Restaurant. Room service. Spa. TV.*

### Delano
*1685 Collins Avenue, at 17th Street (reservations 1-800 606 6090, front desk 1-305 672 2000, www.delano-hotel.com). Bus C, G, H, L, M,*

CONSUME

*South Beach Local.* **Rates** $330-$615 double.
**Rooms** 194. **Credit** AmEx, DC, Disc, MC, V.
**Map** p280 C3 **❸**

A few newer hotels may have stolen some of its cutting-edge cachet, but the Delano – the designer hotel that put Miami back on the A-list in 1995 – is still a South Beach icon. The trendy lobby remains foolishly appealing, even if it does feel dated: think textbook Starck minimalism, complete with billowing white curtains, Venetian chandeliers, and surreal art and furniture. The stark white bedrooms have been spruced up with splashes of texture and colour, floating flatscreen TVs and lush white Carrera marble bathrooms. The swimming pool – sorry 'water salon' – is ethereal, with its waterfall, palms and celestial bodies, but the posing can be a bit much. The substance matches the style, however, at the fabulous Bianca (*see p80*) restaurant on the patio. The tiny Rose Bar also packs in the beautiful people, as does the hip FDR at Delano (*see p105*), a subterranean lounge that mixes old-school glamour with sexy, modern twists. If you've come to Miami for South Beach glitz, the Delano still ticks all the right boxes.

*Bars (2). Business centre. Concierge. Disabled-adapted rooms. Gym. Internet (wireless, free). No-smoking floors. Parking ($37/day). Pool (1, outdoor). Restaurants (2). Room service. Spa. TV: pay movies.*

### ★ James Royal Palm

*1545 Collins Avenue, at 16th Street (reservations 1-888 526 3778, front desk 1-305 604 5700, www.jameshotels.com/miami). Bus C, G, H, L, M, South Beach Local.* **Rates** $245-$540.
**Rooms** 390. **Credit** AmEx, Disc, MC, V.
**Map** p280 C3 **❹**

The newly opened James Royal Palm aims to distinguish itself among the sea of hotels that line Collins Avenue by offering unparalleled service. Public spaces and guest rooms are elegant without being ostentatious; taking a cue from its oceanfront setting, the colour palette leans towards pale greens, creamy whites and warm wooden furnishings. Rooms – which range in size from 275 to 560sq ft – include 42-inch plasma televisions, complimentary WiFi for all, small work/dining alcoves, bathrobes and slippers, and a nightly turndown service. Some rooms even feature floor-to-ceiling windows or balconies overlooking the ocean. In-house dining options include two of the city's most popular new eateries: the regional Florida Cookery (*see p82*) and global seafood house CATCH, from *Top Chef* winner Hung Huynh. South Shore – an intimate, guests-only rum bar – serves up a menu of small plates and has table football, should the competitive spirit strike you.

*Bars (5). Concierge. Disabled-adapted rooms. Gym. Internet (wireless, free). No-smoking rooms. Parking ($35/day). Pool. Restaurant. Room service. Spa. TV.*

James Royal Palm.

### ★ King & Grove Tides South Beach

*1220 Ocean Drive, at 12th Street (reservations 1-800 439 4095, front desk 1-305 604 5070, www.tidessouthbeach.com). Bus C, H, K, W, South Beach Local.* **Rates** $450-$695 double. **Rooms** 45.
**Credit** AmEx, DC, MC, V. **Map** p280 D3 **❺**

Possibly the loveliest hotel on South Beach, the King & Grove Tides is a thing of beauty inside and out. A masterpiece of art deco by L Murray Dixon, it boasts porthole windows, abundant stainless steel and ocean liner curves. The interior was beautified by designer *du jour* Kelly Wearstler, who swapped the old minimalist decor for sensuousness and beachy romance. The stark whites have been replaced by coral, peach and creamy beige; the clean lines have been softened by lovely textures: shag rugs, woven rope chairs, hemp wallpaper and petrified woods. Trumpet shell lamps and vintage brass palm trees add to the ocean theme. La Marea, the Italian seafood restaurant, is adorned with faux tortoiseshells; sip martinis in the outdoor lounge and watch the world go by.

*Bars (2). Concierge. Disabled-adapted rooms. Gym. Internet (wireless, $10/day). No-smoking floor. Parking ($35/day). Pool (1, outdoor). Restaurant. TV: DVD.*

## Loews Miami Beach

*1601 Collins Avenue, at 16th Street (reservations 1-800 235 6397, front desk 1-305 604 1601, www.loewshotels.com). Bus C, H, K, W, South Beach Local.* **Rates** $319-$599 double. **Rooms** 790. **Credit** AmEx, DC, MC, V. **Map** p280 C3 ⑥
This massive convention hotel is peppered with name-tagged conventioneers, but if you like big, it's got your name on it, too; 790 rooms, including 57 suites, some with sea views. Signature restaurant Preston's offers one of South Beach's only truly oceanfront views. There's a gigantic fitness centre and spa, an oceanfront swimming pool and 20 butler-serviced cabanas.
*Bars (3). Business centre. Concierge. Disabled-adapted rooms. Gym. Internet (high speed, $14.95/day). No-smoking rooms. Parking ($39/day). Pool (1, outdoor). Restaurants (3). Room service. Spa. TV: pay movies.*

## ★ Mondrian South Beach

*1100 West Avenue, at 11th Street (1-305 672 2662, www.mondriansouthbeach.com). Bus 113, 119, 123.* **Rates** $249-$629. **Rooms** 330. **Credit** AmEx, Disc, MC, V. **Map** p280 D2 ⑦
Sister property to the Delano (*see p135*) and Shore Club (*see p140*), the Mondrian distinguishes itself from its siblings most notably by its location, which is bayfront, not beachside. Located in a mostly residential neighbourhood (with plenty of restaurants nearby and Lincoln Road Mall within walking distance), this supremely stylish hotel is a great choice for travellers who want first-class amenities without the first-class craziness of South Beach's main tourist drag. Marcel Wanders designed the hotel to look like Sleeping Beauty's castle, which in this case means over-the-top and whimsical. There's lush foliage throughout the hotel, giving it an indoor/outdoor living feel – some of it resembles topiary straight out of *Edward Scissorhands*. But Mondrian's most impressive feature just may be its rooftop pool and Sunset Lounge (*see p110*), which is the place to be when the sun sets over Miami. Have your camera ready – you'll want to snap pics of this.
*Bar. Concierge. Disabled-adapted rooms. Gym. Internet (wireless, $15/day). No-smoking rooms. Parking ($32/day). Pool. Restaurant. Room service. Spa. TV.*

## National Hotel

*1677 Collins Avenue, at 17th Street (reservations 1-800 327 8370, front desk 1-305 532 2311, www.nationalhotel.com). Bus C, H, K, W.* **Rates** $279-$799 double. **Rooms** 151. **Credit** AmEx, DC, MC, V. **Map** p280 C3 ⑧
Its big-name neighbours – the Raleigh, Delano, SLS – are fab and flashy. The National, by contrast, is quietly elegant. Instead of bling, it sticks to its art deco roots and meticulously re-creates the ambience of a 1930s hotel. Inside, there are terrazzo floors, shiny chrome lights, angular mirrors, walnut furni-

ture and geometric railings. The glamour extends to the grounds: the sleek infinity pool is framed by rows of palms; the pinstriped sunbeds add to the fashionable feel. In early 2013, the hotel completed a multi-million-dollar renovation; guest rooms got a glamour upgrade and better soundproofing.
*Bars (2). Business centre. Concierge. Disabled-adapted rooms. Gym. Internet (wireless, free). No-smoking rooms. Parking ($35). Pools (2, outdoor). Restaurant. Room service. TV: pay movies.*

## Raleigh

*1775 Collins Avenue, at 18th Street (reservations 1-866 539 0036, www.raleighhotel.com). Bus C, G, H, L, M, S.* **Rates** $325-$750 double. **Rooms** 104. **Credit** AmEx, DC, Disc, MC, V. **Map** p280 C3 ⑨
Following a recent renovation, the historic Raleigh is once again having its day in the sun. This 1940 L Murray Dixon-designed structure boasts all the mod cons, down to bedside buttons controlling everything from lights to room temperature. Sleek furniture matches the clientele – primarily fashion-industry types – and staff (many of whom are models). The hotel's biggest asset, though, is its voluptuous swimming pool. Calling to mind a Busby Berkeley musical, it was indeed the setting for many an Esther Williams film during the 1940s. Even non-guests can get a look at this storied hole in the ground by sidling up to the pool bar.
*Bars (2). Business centre. Concierge. Disabled-adapted rooms. Internet (wireless, free). No-smoking rooms. Parking ($35/day). Pool (outdoor). Restaurants (2). Room service. TV: DVD.*

**CONSUME**

**National Hotel.**

Ritz-Carlton South Beach.

## Ritz-Carlton South Beach

*1 Lincoln Road, at Collins Avenue (1-786 276 4000, www.ritzcarlton.com). Bus C, G, H, L, M, S.* **Rates** $399-$599. **Rooms** 375. **Credit** AmEx, DC, Disc, MC, V. **Map** p280 C3 ⑩

This is not your grandfather's Ritz. The former deco landmark is a deluxe addition to South Beach and for a chain hotel it feels young – heck, even vibrant. A whopping $200 million was thrown into the restoration of this MiMo classic, designed in 1953 by Morris Lapidus and Melvin Grossman. The revamped version is a beauty, featuring custom-designed contemporary Venetian glass and stainless-steel light fixtures, a curved wall of polished cherry wood, and original black terrazzo floors. All the big pluses that you expect from the Ritz are here: exceptional service, comfortable yet elegant rooms and amenities galore, with the bonus of the beach on your doorstep.

If South Beach is too manic for your tastes and you prefer a more Caribbean-style escape, the Ritz-Carlton Key Biscayne (455 Grand Bay Drive, 1-305 365 4500) is a beachfront haven for the likes of Brad Pitt, John Travolta and other stars who want to escape the South Beach paparazzi. Even if you don't stay there, its open-air beachfront restaurants – including the breezy Mexican eaterie Cantina Beach – offer an idyllic setting for a meal.

With only 88 rooms, the Ritz-Carlton Coconut Grove (3300 SW 27th Avenue, 1-305 644 4680) is the most intimate of the three properties. The beach is

a bit of a hike from here, but the bayfront setting, with two acres of tropical gardens, makes up for it, and it's handy for doing business Downtown and chilling out in trendy Coconut Grove.
*Bars (2). Business centre. Concierge. Disabled-adapted rooms. Gym. Internet (wireless, $9.95/day). No-smoking rooms. Parking ($36/day). Pool (1, outdoor). Restaurants (2). Room service. Spa. TV: DVD.*

## Sagamore

*1671 Collins Avenue, at 17th Street (1-305 535 8088, www.sagamorehotel.com). Bus C, G, H, L, M, S.* **Rates** $249-$875 double. **Rooms** 93. **Credit** AmEx, DC, Disc, MC, V. **Map** p280 C3 ⑪

The lobby of the Sagamore doubles as a brilliant art gallery (with a rotating collection of edgy works by the likes of Cindy Sherman, Gerhard Richter and Olafur Eliasson), and provocative pieces hang throughout the hotel (*see p139* **Rooms with a Viewing**). It's no surprise, then, that the Sagamore houses a quietly hip crowd, and one that couldn't care less about the action next door at the Delano's pool. The generous, apartment-sized rooms are also a plus; for maximum luxury, there are whirlpool bath/showers in every room. The oceanfront infinity pool is another work of art. *Photo p140.*
*Bars (2). Business centre. Concierge. Disabled-adapted rooms. Gym. Internet (wireless, $11.95/day). No-smoking rooms. Parking ($37/day). Pool (1, outdoor). Restaurant. Room service. Spa. TV: DVD.*

## Setai

*2001 Collins Avenue, at 20th Street (1-305 520 6000, www.thesetaihotel.com). Bus C, G, H, L, M, S.* **Rates** $650-$1,700 double. **Rooms** 130. **Credit** AmEx, DC, Disc, MC, V. **Map** p280 C3 ⑫

When it comes to opulent digs, the Setai boasts a four-bedroom penthouse with a $30,000 rack rate and the starriest clientele in town (Madonna has been known to hole up in said suite, and Beyoncé and Jay-Z have stayed there so often they were reportedly contemplating buying it at one point). But despite its celeb credentials, the Setai's brand of bling is understated; it avoids flash in favour of pristine Asian decor. The lobby's dark floor is made from Shanghai brick; jade pieces from Japan banish the bad spirits; and a Zen garden keeps the A-list clientele calm. Teak floors, furniture and blinds lend warmth to the minimalist bedrooms, as do the floral sculptures. Bathrooms come stocked with granite tubs, rainshower heads and Laura Tonatto toiletries. Three side-by-side infinity pools ensure there are no crowds when you swim. Decadence rules in the restaurant, where the lavish menu includes black angus filet mignon and Kumamoto oysters. Sadly, there are no early-bird specials. Even if you can't afford to sleep here, it's worth the (pricey) cost of a drink to sit at the oceanfront pool bar and enjoy the scenery. *Photos p141.*

# Rooms with a Viewing

*You won't find naff nautical paintings in Miami's hotel-cum-galleries.*

Art-gazing is more than just an occasional pastime in Miami, home to the US offshoot of Art Basel and a growing number of world class museums and galleries, particularly in the Wynwood Art District. But you may not even need to leave your hotel to get a glimpse of a bona fide masterpiece. On South Beach, the **Sagamore** (*see p138*) has dubbed itself the 'Art Hotel' and delivers in spades. Purchased by renowned art collectors Cricket and Marty Taplin in 2001, the creative hoteliers saw the Sagamore as the perfect opportunity to share their love of art – and some of the key pieces they've collected over the past three decades. From rotating photography exhibitions to sundeck sculptures, art is everywhere you look both inside and outside this boutique property.

Not to be outdone, next-door neighbour the **Delano** (*see p135*) has its own impressive art collection on show. Assembled by designer Philippe Starck, it includes paintings, furniture and various other objets d'art from an international slate of masters including Dalí, Man Ray, Mark Newson and Gaudí.

On Ocean Drive, the **Betsy** (*see p135*) fulfils a dual role as luxury hotel and cultural centre. The hotel partners with a range of local and international art groups to offer a year-round calendar of cultural programming, which could be anything from a poetry reading to a jazz concert. Most impressive, however, are its regularly rotating art exhibits, which fill the hotel's lobby, hallways, restaurant and other public spaces with exciting photography. In conjunction with Art Basel's 2012 edition, the hotel displayed more than 200 rarely seen photographs of the Beatles and Rolling Stones taken by former tour manager Bob Bonis.

The art assault at the **InterContinental Miami** (100 Chopin Plaza, Downtown, 1-305 577-1000www.icmiamihotel.com) begins in the lobby, where each year more than 500,000 people stop to look at *The Spindle*, a 70-ton marble sculpture created by Henry Moore (the hotel commissioned the work and had the lobby built around it).

Betsy.

**Sagamore**. *See p138.*

Bars (2). Business centre. Concierge. Disabled-adapted rooms. Gym. Internet (wireless, free). No-smoking rooms. Parking ($40/day). Restaurants (2). Spa. Pools (3, outdoor). Room service (24hrs). TV.

### Shore Club

*1901 Collins Avenue, at 19th Street (reservations 1-800 606 6090, front desk 1-305 695 3100, www.shoreclub.com). Bus C, G, H, L, M, S.* **Rates** $310-$615 double. **Rooms** 405. **Credit** AmEx, DC, Disc, MC, V. **Map** p280 C3 ⓭

The scene at the pool of the Shore Club sometimes resembles a rap video: scantily clad women; chiselled guys with lots of bling; and a hip hop soundtrack to facilitate the booty shaking. Hell, there was even a shooting here, way back in 2005, when rap mogul Suge Knight took a bullet in the leg at a party for Kanye West. The incident didn't scare guests away; on the contrary, the Shore Club now has more street cred. But it's not all about gangsta glam. The rooms have been given a fashionably minimalist but colourful makeover by Brit architect David Chipperfield. The filthy rich hole up in the Beach House, a private oceanside bungalow with pool. Added swoon factor comes courtesy of the restaurants – which include Robert De Niro's Nobu (*see p86*) – and the Skybar (*see p110*), a sprawling Moroccan-chic affair that is packed out with everyone from demi celebs to cigarette girls selling lollies.

*Bars (3). Business centre. Concierge. Disabled-adapted rooms. Gym. Internet (wireless, free).*

*No-smoking rooms. Parking ($42/day). Pools (2, outdoor). Restaurants (2). Room service. Spa. TV.*

### SLS South Beach

*1701 Collins Avenue, at 17th Street (1-305 674 1701, www.slshotels.com/southbeach). Bus C, G, H, L, M, South Beach Local.* **Rates** $285-$795. **Rooms** 15. **Credit** AmEx, Disc, MC, V. **Map** p280 C3 ⓮

Opened in late 2012, SLS brings together the visions of developer/entrepreneur Sam Nazarian, legendarily whimsical designer Philippe Starck and master chef José Andrés to create a painfully popular boutique hotel. All you need to bring is your swimsuit, a chic change of clothes and your credit card (you're really going to need that latter item) and let SLS take care of the rest. The high-tech hotel features WiFi throughout, plus MP3 connectivity and an iPad in each room. The decor is elegant but playful, thanks to Starck's reimagining of this 1939 L Murray Dixon-designed building, as evidenced by the 700lb silver 'rubber' ducky sculpture that hangs out by the pool. Renowned chef José Andrés sets the culinary bar high with his on-site restaurant, Bazaar by José Andrés (*see p80*), and an on-site salon and spa will ensure you're relaxed and looking your best. You can also take advantage of the hotel's chauffeur-driven BMW.

*Bar. Concierge. Disabled-adapted rooms. Gym. Internet (wireless, free). No-smoking rooms. Parking ($44/day). Pool. Restaurant. Room service. Spa. TV.*

## Expensive

### Albion Hotel

*1650 James Avenue, at 17th Street (reservations 1-877 782 3557, front desk 1-305 913 1000, www.rubellhotels.com). Bus A, M, R, S.* **Rates** $199-$399 double. **Rooms** 100. **Credit** AmEx, DC, MC, V. **Map** p280 C3 ⓯

The Albion has a couple of claims to fame: it's owned by the Rubell clan (as in the Rubell Family Collection, *see p65*) and the streamlined nautical building was designed by art deco master Igor Polevitzky in 1939. This incarnation of the hotel was opened in 1997 and it feels slightly dated. But it still possesses a certain South Beach panache, with slick interiors by Ecuadorian designer Carlos Zapata and a stylish bar. The stark white lobby is enlivened by splashes of colour; glass walls overlook a courtyard and pool. Rooms wear the design mag uniform: crisp white bedding and Barcelona chairs. It's next to Lincoln Road shopping and the beach is not far. For hipsters, it's an affordable alternative to the Delano. *Bar. Business centre. Concierge. Disabled-adapted rooms. Gym. Internet (wireless, free). No-smoking rooms. Parking ($35/day). Pool (1, outdoor). Restaurant. Room service. TV.*

### Clevelander

*1020 Ocean Drive, at 10th Street (reservations 1 800 815 6829, front desk 1-305 531 3485, www.clevelander.com). Bus C, H, K, W, South Beach Local.* **Rates** $250-$350 double. **Rooms** 60. **Credit** AmEx, DC, MC, V. **Map** p280 D3 ⓰

This party institution sometimes has a whiff of the frat house about it, as evidenced by its oceanfront bar, which features three bars, a swimming pool and a constantly buzzing stage where female dance contests and body painting are known to regularly break out. But it's all good fun. There's also a funky lounge bar, roof deck and slick sports bar to go with the minimalist rooms. But don't be fooled by the boutique rebranding: the website remains chock-a-block with bikini babes. The art deco Essex Hotel (1001 Collins Avenue, at 10th Street; 1-305 534 2700, www.essexhotel.com) around the corner is owned by the same group, but with less of a party atmosphere. *Bars (5). Concierge. No-smoking rooms. Pool (1, outdoor). Restaurant. TV.*

### ★ Dream South Beach

*1111 Collins Avenue, at 11th Street (reservations 1-877 753 7326, front desk 1-305 673 4747, www.dreamhotels.com). Bus C, H, K, W, South Beach Local.* **Rates** $175-$375. **Rooms** 108. **Credit** AmEx, Disc, MC, V. **Map** p280 D3 ⓱

Art deco glamour meets French Moroccan style, courtesy of designer Michael Czysz, with a result that somehow looks a bit space age. Opened in 2011, Dream lives up to its name by creating the kind of guest room that makes you reluctant to get out of

Setai. *See p138.*

**CONSUME**

bed. Quarters boast flatscreen TVs, free WiFi and generously stocked minibars. Upstairs is Highbar (*see p106*), a 1970s-inspired rooftop pool and lounge, with comfy white seating and a couple of private cabanas (for those who require yet another flatscreen TV to go with their lounge chairs). On weekends, DJs spin throughout the day and after dark, when the pool turns into a popular nightspot. Downstairs, an outpost of popular New York City Italian restaurant Serafina occupies much of the ground floor (try the white pizza). And all this just one block from the beach.

*Bar. Concierge. Disabled-adapted rooms. Gym. Internet (wireless, free). No-smoking rooms. Parking ($34/day). Pools (1, outdoor). Restaurant. Room service. Spa. TV.*

### ★ Gale South Beach

*1690 Collins Avenue, at 17th Street (1-305 673 0199, www.galehotel.com). Bus C, G, H, L, M, South Beach Local.* **Rates** $259-$395. **Rooms** 87. **Credit** AmEx, Disc, MC, V. **Map** p280 C3 ⑬

This 1941 L Murray Dixon-designed tropical deco stalwart received a $35 million top-to-bottom makeover courtesy of Menin Hotels (the folks behind Sanctuary, *see p144*), before its grand reopening in late 2012. Guest rooms recall the 1940s, with streamlined dark wood furniture, silver silk curtains and simple white and blue colour schemes; gadgets include iPod docking stations and 55-inch flatscreen TVs. Dining and drinking options keep an old-school flavour; the Regent Cocktail Club (*see p108*) mixes up classic concoctions, while the Rec Room evokes a hint of 1970s-style basement playroom. On the roof, there's a 5,000sq ft sun deck complete with infinity pool, loungers and 360-degree views.

*Bars (3). Concierge. Disabled-adapted rooms. Internet (wireless, free). No-smoking rooms. Parking ($35/day). Pool. Restaurant. Room service. TV.*

### ★ Hotel

*801 Collins Avenue, at 8th Street (1-305 531 2222, www.thehotelofsouthbeach.com). Bus C, H, K, W.* **Rates** $229-$425 double. **Rooms** 73. **Credit** AmEx, DC, MC, V. **Map** p280 E3 ⑲

The Hotel has all the right style mag credentials: it was designed in 1939 by architect L Murray Dixon, and redecorated by clothing designer Todd Oldham in 1998. Formerly known as the Tiffany, it was forced to change its name by the jewellery giant. But it's still one of the coolest (albeit lesser known) joints on South Beach. The mosaic-tiled bathrooms and tie-dye robes lend a whimsical feel to the small but avant-garde rooms. The cosy lobby shows off with polished terrazzo floors and couches upholstered in emerald, gold and ruby velvet. The rooftop pool is one of the city's hidden gems (it's open to guests only); it's small but offers spectacular beach views. Though its official address is on Collins Avenue, just one block from the beach, oceanfront rooms are available in the hotel's extended location, in the floors above the always-buzzing News Café (*see p85*).

*Bars (3). Business centre. Concierge. Disabled-adapted rooms. Gym. Internet (wireless, free). No-smoking rooms. Parking ($25/day). Pool (1, outdoor). Restaurant. Room service. TV.*

### Hotel Astor

*956 Washington Avenue, at 10th Street (1-877 894 0857, front desk 1-305 531 8081,*

Hotel Victor.

---

## THE BEST CHEAP DIGS

For a designer dorm
**Freehand**. *See p150.*

Where Fido can crash
**Aqua**. *See p148.*

Good enough for Clark Gable
**Cadet**. *See p148.*

Out of a film noir
**Villa Paradiso**. *See p150.*

---

*www.hotelastor.com). Bus C, H, K, W, South Beach Local.* **Rates** $179-$489. **Rooms** 42. **Credit** AmEx, DC, MC, V. **Map** p280 D3 ⑳
A suave 1936 streamline hotel buffed up and polished for 21st-century consumption. The intimate lobby is softly illuminated and decorated in sandy hues, while the elegant bedrooms boast European king-size beds, imported cotton sheets and fleecy robes in the marble bathrooms. All the rooms are double-insulated against the hustle of Washington Avenue. Dei Frescobaldi, the dreamy new restaurant and wine bar created by leading Tuscan wine producer Marchesi de' Frescobaldi, looks promising.
*Bar. Business centre. Concierge. Disabled-adapted rooms. Internet (wireless, free). No-smoking rooms. Parking ($30/day). Restaurant. Room service. TV.*

### Hotel Victor
*1144 Ocean Drive, at 11th Street (1-305 779 8787, www.hotelvictorsouthbeach.com). Bus K, W.* **Rates** $229-$499 double. **Rooms** 88. **Credit** AmEx, Disc, MC, V. **Map** p280 D3 ㉑
Adjacent to the Versace Mansion, the Victor – a Thompson Hotel – is every bit as rich and opulent as the designer label itself. Another designer, however, Jacques Garcia (the man behind Paris's Hôtel Costes), is responsible for beautifully adapting the 1930s into the Victor's modern structure. He based the interiors on warm beige tones and distinctly accented the lobby with bold onyx, mauve and emerald furnishings. The mosaic-tiled pool – while small – is similarly striking, as are the spa (with hammam) and Bice Ristorante. Luxurious guest rooms have a touch of boudoir about them, plus infinity bathtubs and huge walk-in showers.
*Bars (3). Business centre. Concierge. Disabled-adapted rooms. Gym. Internet (wireless, free). No-smoking rooms. Parking ($32/day). Pool (1, outdoor). Restaurants (2). Room service. Spa. TV: DVD.*

### Metropole
*635 Collins Avenue, at 6th Street (reservations 1-877 762 3477, front desk 1-305 672 0009, www.metropolesouthbeach.com). Bus C, H,*

*K, W, South Beach Local.* **Rates** $149-$499 double. **Rooms** 40. **Credit** AmEx, DC, MC, V. **Map** p280 E3 ㉒
If the goal of your vacation is to walk in the footsteps of the *Jersey Shore* castmates, this is your place: the Metropole was their home during the (thankfully) now-cancelled show's second season. Part of the South Beach Group's boutique stable, the Metropole is a cut above its rowdy cousins. Wild parties and candy colours have been replaced by a hushed ambience and smart flats with kitchens. There is no bar – a good thing if you want peace. And the courtyard entrance is fashionable: bamboo plants, smart brown sunbeds and oriental wood furniture. The lobby is stylishly discreet – it's off an interior courtyard – but too cramped for suitcases. The apartments are dark and sleek: grey walls, white leather furniture, chrome accents, pinstriped drapes. There are some design flaws – not enough lights, no telephones beside the bed in some rooms – but the kitchens are well equipped and a budget-saving alternative to eating out three times a day. Its hidden location, near the low key SoFi neighbourhood, is a plus. See also the Catalina (*p145*), Chelsea (*p146*) and Whitelaw (*p150*).
*Concierge. Internet (wireless, free). No-smoking rooms. Parking ($32). TV.*

### ★ Palms Hotel & Spa
*3025 Collins Avenue, at 30th Street (reservations 1-800 550 0505, front desk 1-305 534 0505, www.thepalmshotel.com). Bus C, G, H, L, M, S.* **Rates** $179-$489 double. **Rooms** 251. **Credit** AmEx, DC, Disc, MC, V. **Map** p280 A4 ㉓
Combining old-school Havana, Deep South sultriness and a touch of glam, this boutique hotel is a romantic alternative to the South Beach brigade. The airy lobby feels colonial, with its Bombay-style ceiling fans, wood floors, rattan furniture and lush greenery. On the veranda, you half expect to see a Southern belle sipping a mint julep or a colonial officer with a G&T. Dotted with palms, parrots and hammocks, the gardens are a luscious setting for the pool. The recently renovated guest rooms feature custom wood furnishings and spa-inspired rainshower heads in the bathroom. A spa, stocked with Aveda products, puts you in an unwinding kind of mood. South Beach is a bit of a trek (on foot, at least), but the boardwalk is a lovely way to get there.
*Bars (2). Business centre. Concierge. Disabled-adapted rooms. Gym. Internet (wireless, free). No-smoking rooms. Parking ($29). Pool (1, outdoor). Restaurant. Room service (6.30am-11pm). Spa. TV.*

### Park Central
*640 Ocean Drive, at 6th Street (1-305 538 1611, www.theparkcentral.com). Bus C, H, K, W, South Beach Local.* **Rates** $149-$399 double. **Rooms** 127. **Credit** AmEx, DC, MC, V. **Map** p280 E3 ㉔

**CONSUME**

The late Tony Goldman, the man largely responsible for the South Beach renaissance in the late 1980s (he passed away in 2012), renovated this 1937 Henry Hohauser hotel by taking its old deco glory and infusing it with sleek, modern touches such as octagonal, etched-glass windows. Ceiling fans, tropical-print carpets, plump beds and period furnishings fill the 127 rooms. The rooftop sun deck provides patrons with an alternative to sand between the toes. The lobby bar is no longer as hip as it once was, but still attracts a decent crowd.
*Bar. Business centre. Concierge. Disabled-adapted rooms. Gym. Internet (wireless, free). No-smoking rooms. Parking ($28/day). Pool (1, outdoor). Restaurant. Room service. TV.*

### Perry South Beach

*2377 Collins Avenue, at 23rd Street (reservations 1-855 737 7972, front desk 1-305 604 1000, www.perrysouthbeachhotel.com). Bus C, G, H, L, M, S.* **Rates** $259-$419. **Rooms** 340. **Credit** AmEx, DC, MC, V. **Map** p280 B4 ㉕
The Perry is a $500 million playground that's helping to liven up a sleepy stretch of Collins with its jaw-dropping extravagance and high style. The showpiece is a $1 million fish tank in the lobby, and a massive rooftop pool that doubles as a bar in the evenings. STK, its trendy steakhouse, lures foodies. The bedrooms are large and plush but restrained: a tasteful mix of grey and white hues, with raspberry and turquoise accents. The lower part of South Beach is a bit of a schlep from here, but you may not want to leave the hotel.
*Bars (2). Concierge. Disabled-adapted rooms. Internet (high-speed, free). No-smoking rooms. Parking ($38/night). Pools (2, outdoor). Restaurant. Room service. Spa. TV: pay movies.*

### Sanctuary

*1745 James Avenue, at 18th Street (1-305 673 5455, www.sanctuarysobe.com). Bus A, M, R, S.* **Rates** $225-$555 double. **Rooms** 30. **Credit** AmEx, DC, Disc, MC, V. **Map** p280 C3 ㉖
Though it's located right in the heart of Miami Beach, this sleepy little all-suite hotel feels worlds away – at least during the daytime. This is due in large part to the serene bamboo garden courtyard, spa and relaxing rooftop pool. But after sunset, it's a different story: the rooftop trades in its Zen-like oasis for parties, and the 'Floribbean' restaurant, Ola, is buzzing.
*Bar. Concierge. Internet (wireless, free). No-smoking rooms. Parking ($30/day). Pool (1, outdoor). Restaurant. Room service. Spa. TV: DVD.*

### ★ Sense Beach House

*400 Ocean Drive, at 4th Street (1-305 538 5529, www.sensebeachhouse.com). Bus South Beach Local.* **Rates** $229-$599. **Rooms** 18. **Credit** AmEx, Disc, MC, V. **Map** p280 E3 ㉗

**Park Central.** *See p143.*

With just 18 rooms, the secluded Sense Beach House is the next best thing to having your own South Beach spread. Located in the quiet South of Fifth neighbourhood, the hotel is far enough removed from the bustle of South Beach to make it feel like you're in your own private paradise, but within easy walking distance to some of the city's hottest restaurants, clubs and boutiques. World-famous Joe's Stone Crab (*see p83*) is just a few doors down, as is the brand-new Story nightclub. The hotel's interiors aim to relax and rejuvenate, with a palette of pale blues and soft browns. Rooms feature 46-inch flatscreen televisions, free WiFi and Molton Brown toiletries. Treat yourself by opting for an ocean-view room with balcony. Though the beach is just steps away, the hotel has a lush rooftop pool and terrace, with perfect 360-degree views of South Beach.
*Bar. Concierge. Disabled-adapted rooms. Internet (wireless, free). No-smoking rooms. Parking ($29/day). Pool. Restaurant. Room service. TV.*

## Moderate

### Avalon Hotel

*700 Ocean Drive, at 7th Street (reservations 1-800 933 3306, front desk 1-305 538 0133, www.avalonhotel.com). Bus C, H, K, W, South Beach Local.* **Rates** $129-$499 double. **Rooms** 72. **Credit** AmEx, DC, MC, V. **Map** p280 E3 ㉓
The streamlined architecture of this classic deco hotel is more interesting than the rooms themselves, which are small but tidy. But that doesn't hurt its

popularity: it's a friendly and functional place to stay in a prime location. Although not all of the rooms have ocean views, A Fish Called Avalon, the hotel's fun and casual restaurant, sits right on Ocean Drive among the babble and glitz.

*Bar. Concierge. Disabled-adapted rooms. Internet (wireless, free). No-smoking rooms. Parking ($27/day). Restaurant. TV.*

## Cardozo

*1300 Ocean Drive, at 13th Street (reservations 1-800 782 6500, front desk 1-305 535 6500, www.cardozohotel.com). Bus C, H, K, W, South Beach Local.* **Rates** *$199-$379 double.* **Rooms** *43.* **Credit** AmEx, MC, V. **Map** p280 D3 ㉙

The Cardozo is a bit of a movie star. The hotel debuted in the 1959 Frank Sinatra film *A Hole in the Head* and has since featured in Joel Schumacher's *8MM* and the Farrelly brothers' *There's Something About Mary*. It's got some pop credentials, too: it's owned by Gloria Estefan. Built in 1939 by Henry Hohauser, whose architectural firm was responsible for more than 300 buildings in Miami, the keystone building is a classic of streamline design. Inside it's Dalí meets deco, with a whimsical modern feel, wrought-iron furniture and glossy cherry-wood floors. The four apartment-sized suites feature breakfast nooks, king-size beds and delicious whirlpool baths.

*Bar. Concierge. Disabled-adapted rooms. Internet (wireless, free). No-smoking rooms. Parking ($35-$50/day). Pool (1, outdoor). Restaurant. Room service. TV.*

## Catalina Hotel & Beach Club

*1732 Collins Avenue, at 17th Street (1-305 674 1160, www.catalinahotel.com). Bus C, G, H, L, M, S.* **Rates** *$129-$319 double.* **Rooms** *190.* **Credit** AmEx, DC, MC, V. **Map** p280 C3 ㉚

The flagship boutique of the South Beach Group, the Catalina is fun, trendy and affordable, if a bit rough around the edges. Set in three deco-style buildings on Collins, it's a sprawling party palace for those who can't afford the Delano. The Catalina wing boasts a funky white lobby bar with retro touches: shag rug, Eero Aarnio globe chairs and vintage film posters – a playful setting for happy hour (where guests are fed free cocktails from 7pm to 8pm nightly). Bedrooms here are small, minimalist affairs. But next door, in the Dorset wing, the aesthetic is more chic. Bedrooms are dark and slick with brown cushions, damask wallpaper, wall sconces and wood floors. On the roof, there's a swimming pool. Downstairs, Kung Fu Sushi, Maxine's 24-hour bistro and Red Bar buzz on weekends. Ask for a quiet room if you don't like a party (though expect funny looks). See also the Chelsea (*p146*), Metropole (*p143*) and Whitelaw (*p150*).

*Bars (3). Concierge. Disabled-adapted rooms. Internet (wireless, $15/day). No-smoking rooms. Parking ($35/day). Pools (2, outdoor). Restaurants (2). Room service. TV.*

## Clinton Hotel

*825 Washington Avenue, at 8th Street (1-305 938 4040, www.clintonsouthbeach.com). Bus C, H, K, W, South Beach Local.* **Rates** *$149-$379*

**Sense Beach House.**

double. **Rooms** 89. **Credit** AmEx, Disc, DC, MC, V. **Map** p280 E3 ㉛
The grot of Washington Avenue is forgotten when you step into the Clinton's lobby. Designed by French architect Eric Raffi, it's a swell combination of cool and warmth, with rich dark-wood accents and rainbow-blue hues. In fact, it's downright sexy. This theme carries through to the bedrooms – naturally – which, complete with flatscreen TVs, down-filled duvets and pillows and designer bath products – are cocoons of chic. A select few also have whirlpool baths and terraces. Lounge by the pool or slump on overstuffed cushions at low tables for breakfast and light lunch served by the respectable house restaurant, the Goods.
*Bar. Business centre. Internet (high speed, free). Parking ($25/day). Pool (1, outdoor). Restaurant. Room service. Spa.*

### Hotel Chelsea
*944 Washington Avenue, at 9th Street (reservations 1-877 762 3477, front desk 1-305 534 4069, www.thehotelchelsea.com). Bus C, H, K, W, South Beach Local.* **Rates** $129-$451 double. **Rooms** 42. **Credit** AmEx, DC, MC, V. **Map** p280 E3 ㉜
This 42-room boutique hotel has mastered the art of feng shui without forcing it on guests. The bamboo floors and amber lighting relax and refresh, while serene rooms with low, Japanese-style beds are designed simply for a good night's sleep. The hospitality, too, is reserved yet attentive. Lightly publicised but heavily consumed, the free cocktail hour fills the lobby with guests every night. See also the Catalina Beach Club (*p145*), Metropole (*p143*) and Whitelaw (*p150*).
*Bar. Concierge. Disabled-adapted rooms. Internet (wireless, free). No-smoking rooms. Parking ($32/day). Room service. TV.*

### Impala Hotel
*1228 Collins Avenue, at 12th Street (1-305 673 2021, www.impala-miami.com). Bus C, H, K, W, South Beach Local.* **Rates** $150-$305 double. **Rooms** 17. **Credit** AmEx, DC, Disc, MC, V. **Map** p280 D3 ㉝
Synonymous with Mediterranean villa charm, the Impala Hotel offers a Euro-style respite from the art deco barrage, right down to the Greco-Roman frescoes and perfumed garden. The bedrooms are the definition of comfort, with upholstered Florentine-style headboards, hypoallergenic linens, wrought-iron fixtures and rich fruit-wood furniture. The slick bathrooms are done out in coral rock and stainless steel. Surprisingly private, the Impala has been a hideaway for numerous celebrity guests whose identities the management, of course, would never divulge.
*Concierge. Disabled-adapted room. Internet (wireless, free). No-smoking rooms. Parking ($25/day). Restaurant. Room service. TV.*

**INSIDE TRACK BEACH CHAIRS**

A 'beach chair' may not seem like a particularly exciting amenity. But the first time you hit the beach and are asked for $25 (per person) in cold, hard cash in exchange for the pleasure of sitting on something other than a towel, you'll understand why you should be excited. If your hotel doesn't have its own beach club, free beach chairs (which you sign for down on the beach itself, no carrying required) are the next best thing.

### ★ Lords South Beach
*1120 Collins Avenue, at 11th Street (reservations 1-877 448 4754, front desk 1-305 674 7800, www.lordssouthbeach.com). Bus C, H, K, W, South Beach Local.* **Rates** $179-$239. **Rooms** 54. **Credit** AmEx, Disc, MC, V. **Map** p280 D3 ㉞
Calling itself 'a quantum leap in gay travel', Lords is geared toward LGBT travellers. That said, any visitor would find a lot to love about this boutique hotel, which brings a bit of fun to the South Beach hotel scene. Located just one block from the beach, Lords is as bright as the Florida sunshine, from the eye-catching awning outside to the golden-walled rooms inside. *See also p172* **Yellow Fever**.
*Bars (2). Concierge. Disabled-adapted rooms. Gym. Internet (wireless, free). No-smoking rooms. Parking ($27/day). Pools (3). Restaurant. Room service. TV.*

### Nassau Suite Hotel
*1414 Collins Avenue, at 14th Street (reservations 1-866 859 4177, front desk 1-305 532 0043, www.nassausuite.com).* **Rates** $159-$229 double. **Rooms** 22. **Credit** AmEx, DC, MC, V. **Map** p280 D3 ㉟
Not the hippest hotel on the block, but it offers tremendous value. The 1936 art deco building and the Collins location score points. And the designers have gamely tried to keep up with the in crowd, even if it's not *Architectural Digest*. The spacious grey bedrooms boast polished wood floors, pristine white bedlinens and bowl-style washbasins, plus granite counters and chrome fridges. They come with kitchens, sofas, flatscreen TVs and huge closets. In the basement, there's a gym, computer room with free internet, and a small theatre room complete with velvet curtain. There's no swimming pool, but the beach is just one block east.
*Business centre. Concierge. Disabled-adapted rooms. Gym. Internet (wireless, free). No-smoking rooms. Parking ($20/day). TV.*

### Pelican
*826 Ocean Drive, at 8th Street (reservations 1-800 773 5422, front desk 1-305 673 3373,*

*www.pelicanhotel.com). Bus C, H, K, W, South Beach Local.* **Rates** $175-$330. **Rooms** 30. **Credit** AmEx, DC, MC, V. **Map** p280 E3 **36**
What do you get when you mix the Diesel fashion label with an art deco hotel? The most whimsical place to stay in Miami. Swedish designer Magnus Erhland was given total freedom to design the rooms here – and he went wild. Rooms include the 'Viva Las Vegas' (complete with bikini-babe bed headboard), 'Best Whorehouse' (red walls, heart backed love chairs) and 'Me Tarzan, You Vain' (African sculptures, jungle fittings). The staff select rooms to fit a guest's profile, or you can make requests – rooms are visible on the website.
*Bar. Business centre. Concierge. Internet (wireless, free). No-smoking rooms. Parking ($25/day). Restaurant. Room service. TV.*

### Royal Hotel South Beach
*763 Pennsylvania Avenue, at 8th Street (reservations 1-888 394 6835, front desk 1-305 673 9009, www.royalsouthbeach.com). Bus C, H, K, W, South Beach Local.* **Rates** $99-$279 double. **Rooms** 42. **Credit** AmEx, DC, MC, V. **Map** p280 E3 **37**
The Royal is a treat. Designer Jordan Mozer transformed its hyper-hued guest rooms into futuristic sleeping quarters. The curvy white plastic beds boast headboards with dual use: they're also bars,

**Standard.**

complete with stools. Shades of lilac, powder blue, mint and tangerine accent the stark white. High-tech chaises longues have computer and TV connections; small pets are allowed too.
*Bar. Concierge. Disabled-adapted room. Internet (high speed, $5/day). No-smoking rooms. Parking ($27/day). Restaurant. TV.*

### ★ Standard
*40 Island Avenue, at the Venetian Causeway (1-305 673 1717, www.standardhotels.com). Bus A.* **Rates** $195-$250. **Credit** AmEx, DC, Disc, MC, V. **Map** p280 C1 **38**
One of the coolest hotels on Miami Beach isn't on the beach at all. But the Standard, a Florida offshoot of André Balasz's fashionable LA and NYC lodgings, is on the waterfront: it boasts dreamy views of Biscayne Bay from its ethereal saltwater infinity pool. In some ways, the location beats the beach: you still get the sea breeze but without the crowds, and at night the twinkling lights of Miami's skyline add romance. Nirvana is reached via the outdoor mud bath, massage table or waterfall jacuzzi (there's a hammam inside the hotel). A Zen-like calm also permeates the meditation garden, complete with fire pit, swings and daybeds. The rooms are chilled too. Combining blond wood walls and white linens, the cabin-like spaces are simple and classy, some with outdoor clawfoot tubs. The lobby, by contrast, is a funky bohemian showpiece, with retro wall hangings, beanbag coffee tables, a driftwood check-in desk and 1960s orange sofas. On the first Sunday of each month, scenesters gather for bingo night. Hip but not haughty.
*Bars (2). Concierge. Disabled-adapted rooms. Gym. Internet (wireless, free). No-smoking rooms. Parking ($37). Pool (1, outdoor). Restaurants (2). Room service. Spa. TV. DVD.*

### Townhouse
*150 20th Street, at Collins Avenue (1 305 534 3800, www.townhousehotel.com). Bus C, G, H, L, M, S.* **Rates** $150-$299 double. **Rooms** 69. **Credit** AmEx, DC, Disc, MC, V. **Map** p280 C3 **39**
This small boutique hotel is a first-rate knock-off. It was opened in 2000 by Jonathan Morr, and the Starck-Schrager influence is obvious. Stylish, minimalist decor (from designer India Mahdavi)? Check. Eye-candy staff? Check. A trendsetting bar serving sushi? Check. DJs spinning slick tunes on the rooftop? Check. The difference is in the price. A room at the Townhouse costs a fraction of what you'd drop at the neighbouring Shore Club or Delano. Space doesn't allow for a pool, but the rooftop terrace does offer relaxing loungers, playful waterbeds and shade umbrellas to keep guests cool. Although, if they're staying here, their coolness is not in doubt.
*Bar. Concierge. Disabled-adapted rooms. Gym. Internet (wireless, free). No-smoking floors. Parking ($25/day). Restaurant. Room service. TV.*

**CONSUME**

Freehand. *See p150.*

## Budget

### Aqua

*1530 Collins Avenue, at 15th Street (1-305 538 4361, www.aquamiami.com). Bus C, H, K, W, South Beach Local.* **Rates** $119-$234 double. **Rooms** 45. **Credit** AmEx, DC, MC, V. **Map** p280 D3 ⑩

This place has an attitude that's friendly verging on frisky (its tagline is 'sleep with me…'). Aqua advertises itself as '*Jetsons* meet *Jaws*', a description that's not far off the mark in terms of the funky decor. The rooms are basic but big, and the ambience reeks of budget cool. Unusually for boutique hotels, the hospitality extends to guests' pets.
*Concierge. No-smoking rooms. Internet (wireless, free). Parking ($20/day). Restaurant. TV.*

### Beachcomber Hotel

*1340 Collins Avenue, at 14th Street (reservations 1-888 305 4683, front desk 1-305 531 3755, www.beachcombermiami.com). Bus C, H, K, W, South Beach Local.* **Rates** $149-$189 double. **Rooms** 29. **Credit** AmEx, DC, MC, V. **Map** p280 D3 ⑪

The immaculate white exterior houses an inviting porch and a sunny lobby, where breakfast is served. There are few luxuries here, but the beach is a block away, bars can be found in every direction and there's a 24-hour launderette just around the corner. Rooms are small, functional and well scrubbed, and staff are friendly.
*Concierge. No-smoking rooms. Internet (wireless, free). Parking ($20/day). TV.*

### Cadet Hotel

*1701 James Avenue, at 17th Street (reservations 1-800 432 2338, front desk 1-305 672 6688, www.cadethotel.com). Bus A, M, R, S.* **Rates** $170-$199 double. **Rooms** 34. **Credit** AmEx, DC, MC, V. **Map** p280 C3 ⑫

Set on a sleepy backstreet, this low-rise 1930s hotel is an undiscovered gem. Its claim to fame is that Clark Gable stayed here (in Room 225) during World War II, when he was stationed in Miami with the Army Air Corps (the hotel is named after the cadets who resided here). But guests care more about the modest prices and tasteful art deco decor. Floors are a classy mix of terrazzo, dark wood, bamboo and sisal matting. Walls are pastel shades. In some rooms, there are Chinese-style four-poster beds and antique wood furniture. Flatscreen TVs and watering can showers are further perks; breakfast is served in a lush garden. In the small lobby bar, you can swoon at Gable's photograph. The Cadet isn't perfect. But frankly, at these prices, we don't give a damn.
*Bar. Concierge. Disabled-adapted rooms. Internet (wireless, free). No-smoking rooms. Restaurant. TV.*

### Clay Hotel

*1438 Washington Avenue, at Española Way (reservations 1-800 379 2529, front desk 1-305 534 2988, www.clayhotel.com). Bus C, H, K, W, South Beach Local.* **Rates** $86-$252. **Rooms** 120. **Credit** MC, V. **Map** p280 D3 ⑬

The Clay's location – on the corner of Washington and the café-lined, Euro-style Española Way – is excellent: nightlife is nearby, as are Lincoln Road

Mall and the beach. The Mediterranean-style building was once the headquarters of Al Capone's gambling syndicate and, later, a set for *Miami Vice*. These days it attracts adventurous nomads. Cut-rate lodgings are basic but clean.
*Shared kitchen. Internet (free). Parking ($19/day). TV.*

### Crest Hotel

*1670 James Avenue, at 17th Street (reservations 1-877 531 3880, front desk 1-305 531 0321, www.crestgrouphotels.com).* **Rates** $125-$215 double. **Rooms** 66. **Credit** AmEx, DC, MC, V. **Map** p280 C3 ④
Hidden on a backstreet near Lincoln Road, this low-key, boutique-style hotel boasts affordable prices and moderate charm. In a 1939 deco building, it still has period touches such as terrazzo floors, chrome lampshand wrought iron railings, mixed with quirky modern pieces. Rooms are soft in feel with willow green walls, blond wood accents and earth-toned carpets. Suites come with kitchens; a café by the small pool serves breakfast and lunch.
*Concierge. Disabled-adapted rooms. Internet (wireless, free). No-smoking rooms. Parking ($30/day). Pool (1, outdoor). Restaurant. TV.*

### Kent

*1131 Collins Avenue, at 11th Street (reservations 1-866 826 5268, front desk 1-305 604 5068, www.thekenthotel.com). Bus C, H, K, W, South Beach Local.* **Rates** $99-$250 double. **Rooms** 59. **Credit** AmEx, DC, MC, V. **Map** p280 D3 ④

The Kent certainly didn't skimp on decor or personality during its recent renovation. The lobby is like a metallic candy box, with orange, pink and purple accents splashed all over steel fixtures. The rooms retain their original wood features, but now have lilac and steel to throw the Kent into the future. Not to be missed is the *Barbarella*-esque suite, with its Lucite fittings. There's no pool, but the beach is nearby. It's a cheap and funky choice, and an on-site restaurant is in the works.
*Business centre. Internet (wireless, free). No-smoking rooms. Parking ($20/day). TV.*

### Loft Hotel

*952 Collins Avenue, at 10th Street (front desk 1-305 534 2244, www.thelofthotel.com). Bus C, H, K, W.* **Rates** $99-$199 double. **Rooms** 21. **Credit** AmEx, DC, MC, V. **Map** p280 E3 ④
Sister to Villa Paradiso, an atmospheric budget apartment hotel (*see p150*), the Loft has a similar setup but a more polished feel. The long low-rise building is flanked by a narrow courtyard filled with tropical foliage, the outdoor corridors overlook the greenery. Spacious and airy, the cool white studios are gussied up with wrought-iron beds, beige bedspreads, animal-print chaises longues, and wooden or tiled floors. Sheer drapes separate the bed from the living area. All of the rooms come equipped with kitchens.
*Concierge. Disabled-adapted rooms. Internet (wireless, free). No-smoking rooms. TV: DVD.*

---

### INSIDE TRACK
### POOL CRASHING

South Beach's pool scene can be as wild as the nightclub scene. But most hotels won't allow non-guests to occupy a sun lounger, and even those that do may change the rules on occasion (ie, it's OK during the week, but a no-no on the weekends). If you want to hang out at the small-but-sexy rooftop pool at **Dream South Beach** (*see p141*), you must be a paying customer. So order up a cocktail and soak in the sun. The **Standard** (*see p147*) sometimes offers pool passes for $20 per day and the **Raleigh** (*see p137*) does the same for $25, but it depends on the day of the week, the season and possibly even the staff member. If you have money to burn, you can rent a cabana at the **Fontainebleau** (*see p150*), but chairs start at $250 per day. Then there are the **Delano** (*see p135*) and **Loews** (*see p137*), widely considered the two toughest pools to crack. Your best bet? Come armed with a smile, ask before sitting and make sure you order something.

CONSUME

**CONSUME**

### Villa Paradiso

*1415 Collins Avenue, at 14th Street (front desk 1-305 532 0616, www.villaparadisohotel.com). Bus C, H, K, W.* **Rates** $120-$320 double. **Rooms** 17. **Credit** AmEx, DC, MC, V. **Map** p280 D3 ④⑦

Tucked amid the designer hotels and South Beach party palaces, this 1930s apartment house is an old-fashioned anomaly – and a bargain. Oozing faded charm, the yellow deco low-rise resembles the set of an old film noir. The courtyard is shaded by a lush overgrown garden. The bedrooms look like your grandmother's old apartment – right down to the vintage TVs, dial phones, junk shop lamps and 1960s-era bathrooms – but are strangely comforting (just don't expect a jacuzzi bath or designer toiletries). All rooms have kitchens, but no high-tech appliances. The creaky wooden floors, French doors and fans add to the cinematic vibe. The dated charm draws production companies and fashion crews, along with families and middle-aged couples. *Concierge. Disabled-adapted rooms. Internet (wireless, free). No-smoking rooms. TV.*

### Whitelaw Hotel

*808 Collins Avenue, at 8th Street (reservations 1-877 762 3477, front desk 1-305 398 7000, www.whitelawhotel.com). Bus C, H, K, W, South Beach Local.* **Rates** $100-$365 double. **Rooms** 49. **Credit** AmEx, DC, MC, V. **Map** p280 E3 ④⑧

The glamour girl of the South Beach Group stable, the Whitelaw is the epitome of cheap chic. The gaudy lobby bar sets the playful tone: a black Venetian chandelier, hot pink drapes, shag rug and glitzy Versailles-style furniture. The paisley ceiling ups the decorative volume further. It's a riotous setting for the raucous happy hour, when the party crowd quaffs complimentary cocktails. The bedrooms are similarly loud: expect chandeliers and fuchsia walls,

along with ostentatious white leather headboards and big flatscreen TVs; stark white sheets inject a touch of minimalism. Service is iffy, but staff are friendly and plugged into the scene (guests get free access to certain clubs). There are also free transfers to the airport. See also the Catalina Beach Club (*p145*), Chelsea Hotel (*p146*) and Metropole (*p143*). *Bar. Concierge. Disabled-adapted rooms. Internet (wireless, free). No-smoking rooms. Parking ($32/day). Restaurant. Room service. TV.*

## Hostels

### ★ Freehand

*2727 Indian Creek Drive, at 28th Street (1-800 491 2772, front desk 1-305 531 2727, www.thefreehand.com). Bus C, G, H, L, M, S.* **Rates** $29-$35 shared dorm; $185-$300 private room. **Rooms** 61. **Credit** AmEx, DC, MC, V. **Map** p280 B4 ④⑨

Small, intimate and quirky, the Freehand has more character than many of its South Beach competitors. The interior is a whimsical pueblo-deco blend, dotted with vintage pieces from flea markets. Pleasant rooms – choose from shared rooms for four or eight or private rooms for two – offer tasteful touches such as writing desks; indeed, the whole place has a homely feel. Not so retro is the Broken Shaker, the hotel's bar – which is as popular with locals as it is with guests – where handcrafted cocktails are the drinks *du jour*. The House, a new restaurant, bar and common area, was under construction at press time and due to open in mid 2013. *Photos p148. Bar. Concierge. Disabled-adapted rooms. Internet (wireless, free). No-smoking rooms. Parking ($10.70/day). Pool. TV.*

### Miami Beach International Travellers Hostel

*236 9th Street, at Washington Avenue (1-305 534 0268, www.hostelmiamibeach.com). Bus C, H, K, W, South Beach Local.* **Rates** $27-$35 dorm; $35-$99 private room. **Credit** MC, V. **Map** p280 E3 ⑤⓪

Utility at its finest. This is the place to stay if you've got a lot of cash to spend on drinks and none to spend on living quarters. Lodgings range from dorms for four to private rooms. Bathrooms are all en suite. What's more, the location is phenomenal. What more do you really need? *Internet (wireless, free). TV.*

## MID BEACH
### Deluxe

### Fontainebleau Miami Beach

*4441 Collins Avenue, at 44th Street (reservations 1-800 548 8886, front desk 1-305 538 2000, www.fontainebleau.com). Bus G, H, L, S.* **Rates** $359-$629 double. **Rooms** 1,504. **Credit** AmEx, DC, MC, V. **Map** p281 F4 ⑤①

Built in 1954 by modernist god Morris Lapidus, whose dictum was 'less is a bore', the Fontainebleau's undulating curves and flashy style stood apart from the crowd. Back in the day, it was the pinnacle of excess: the lobby was a sea of chandeliers; a 'staircase to nowhere' was built solely so that women could deposit their coats in the cloakroom at the top and make a grand entrance back down to the lobby; and air-conditioning was cranked up to protect all the mink coats. The Rat Pack, Elvis and Marilyn were regulars. After its fortunes began to fade, a consortium of architects joined forces to recapture its former glory, and gave the most famous hotel in Miami Beach a billion-dollar facelift. Reflecting the Las Vegas-ification of Miami, the 'new' resort boasts 1,500 rooms; the first US branch of Hakkasan, London's glam Chinese restaurant; and a sister steakhouse to New York's Michelin-starred Gotham Bar and Grill.

*Bars (4). Beauty salon. Business centre. Concierge. Disabled-adapted rooms. Gym. Internet (wireless, free). No-smoking floors. Parking ($38-$52/day). Pools (4 outdoor). Spa. Restaurants (5). Room service. TV.*

## Moderate

### Circa 39

*3900 Collins Avenue, 39th Street (reservations 1-877 824 7223, front desk 1-305 538 4900, www.circa39.com). Bus C, G, H, L, M, S.* **Rates** $149-$319. **Rooms** 100. **Credit** AmEx, DC, MC, V. **Map** p281 F4 ⑫

This wannabe boutique hotel brings the South Beach party north to Mid Beach. The airy lobby ticks the trendy boxes: white walls, Starck-style furniture and airy light fixtures. During one stay, Brazilian models colonised the place for a fashion shoot. Purple corridors and a red elevator liven up the minimalism. There's a bar off the lobby where guests congregate at happy hour. The small pool hosts the odd party and the courtyard has curtained beds for canoodling. The stark white bedrooms range from tiny to sprawling, and are a bit rough around the edges (the fluorescent bathroom lights are especially unflattering). But the vibe is lively and the staff are friendly.

*Bar. Concierge. Disabled-adapted rooms. Internet (wireless, free). Parking ($24/day). Pool (1, outdoor). Restaurant. Room service. TV: pay movies.*

### ★ Deauville Beach Resort

*6701 Collins Avenue, at 67th Street (reservations 1-800 327 6656, front desk 1-305 865 8511, www.deauvillebeachresort.com). Bus C, H, L, S.* **Rates** $125-$415 double. **Rooms** 484. **Credit** AmEx, DC, MC, V. **Map** p281 R4 ⑬

This icon is famous for two reasons: it's a prime example of Jetsonian-esque MiMo architecture (it was built in 1957 by Melvin Grossman, a protégé of Morris Lapidus); it was also the site of Beatlemania in 1964 (see p246 **Beatles on the Beach**). Today, it oozes faded grandeur and retro cool (there's more character in its flamboyant lobby than in many a whole boutique hotel). True, parts of it look distinctly dowdy (chipped paint, dull corridors) and the bedrooms are a bit chainy. But it still bustles and the rooms cost a fraction of designer hotels. And it retains an old Miami feel: the silver-haired Jewish grannies, long banished from South Beach, are still in evidence. The rooms become marginally more stylish the higher you go (the 15th and 16th floors are best; below ten and things are more budget). The

Canyon Ranch Hotel & Spa. *See p153.*

**CONSUME**

# Paradise Motels

*Discover the joys of kitsch.*

Back in the 1950s, Sunny Isles Beach was motel central, a theme park of cheesy fun in the sun. Its strip was lined with exotically named resort motels: the Castaways, the Sahara, the Tangiers, the Oasis, the Waikiki and the Driftwood. They were fronted by flashy neon signs and decorative statues: mermaids, camels, tiki masks – even a sphinx. A postwar fantasy for America's new car-owning middle classes, the strip offered affordable glitz and was immortalised in the 1959 Frank Sinatra film, *A Hole in the Head*.

These days, a sea of condos has washed away Sunny Isles' motels, but two glorious gems remain – and you should get there before the wrecking ball does. Designed by Norman Giller, the **Days Inn Thunderbird Beach Resort** (*see p154*) is spectacularly tacky, complete with vintage T-bird car, a statue of Marilyn Monroe, stained-glass windows and a giant aquarium. There's a diner, tiki bar and huts, and a courtyard swimming pool. The bedrooms are clean and generic – almost identical to **Travelodge Monaco** (*see p154*) just down the strip. Built in 1954, the latter boasts an iconic neon sign and a chintzy tropical lobby swimming in rattan furniture. It, too, boasts a tiki bar and courtyard swimming pool, where ageing housewives bake on old-school sun loungers. There's a whiff of faded glory in the air, but it hasn't descended into seediness.

Less kitsch but more spiffy, the **Best Western Oceanfront Resort** (*see p153*) is a cheerful low-rise in swanky Bal Harbour. Its three 1952 buildings sport lemon walls adorned with stuffed swordfish, tropical shrubbery, two pools and apartment-style suites. The **Silver Sands** (*see p154*), Key Biscayne's nostalgia fest, is a budget Shangri-La, set amid lush palms and overgrown greenery.

On the mainland, one brave business is trying to capitalise on the slow gentrification of Biscayne Boulevard, a once great motel strip that descended into squalour a few decades back. The revamped **Motel Blu** (*see p157*) has christened itself the strip's first boutique motel. That may be a bit of a stretch, but the lobby has been smartened up and Red Light, the old diner and a one-time haunt of Sinatra, has been jazzed up. Rooms are ordinary, rather than ornate, but some open on to the river, where you can see herons, pelicans and manatees. The pool has a bronze nude water feature, perhaps a nod to the strip club across the way. With its proximity to the Design District and the Wynwood art scene, the motel is luring edgier tourists and may yet spruce up the strip. But all of the motels should take a leaf out of **Casa Morada's** book (*see p224*). Set in the Keys, this luxurious oasis is one motel that's worth the drive.

Best Western Oceanfront Resort.

seafront balcony rooms offer stellar views: the hotel is near the water and the sands are silky smooth. The Deauville Lounge features live music, a nod to the hotel's swinging heyday.

*Bars (3). Business centre. Concierge. Disabled-adapted rooms. Gym. Internet (wireless, free). No-smoking rooms. Parking ($30). Pool (1, outdoor). Restaurants (2). Room service. Spa. TV.*

# NORTH BEACH
## Deluxe

### ★ Canyon Ranch Hotel & Spa

*6801 Collins Avenue, at 68th Street (reservations 1-800 742 9000, front desk 1-305 514-7000, www.canyonranch.com/miamibeach).* Bus 112, 115, 117, 119, 120. **Rates** $365-$640. **Rooms** 120. **Credit** AmEx, Disc, MC, V. **Map** p281 B4 ⑤⑷

Long considered one of America's top spa hotels, Canyon Ranch's Miami location is worlds away from South Beach, both in terms of pace and location (it's about a 15-minute drive by car). The North Beach location makes sense when you consider the hotel's goal: a vacation for body, mind and soul. This holistic holiday is achieved with a variety of amenities, including all-suite accommodation, 750 ft of pristine beachfront, a top-rated wellness spa, on-site dining that makes health food taste good (even the cocktails are organic), and a shuttle service to and from the nearby Bal Harbour Shops. For guests more inclined to keep active, there are yoga and Beach Boot Camp classes, plus golf, tennis and surfing all nearby. *Photos p151.*

*Bar. Concierge. Disabled-adapted rooms. Gym. Internet (wireless, free). No-smoking rooms. Parking ($35/day). Pools (4, outdoor). Restaurant. Room service. Spa. TV.*

## Budget

### Best Western on the Bay Inn & Marina

*1819 NE 79th Street Causeway, at Normandy Drive, North Bay Village (reservations 1-800 021 0062, front desk 1-305 866-7400, www.bestwesternonthebay.com).* Bus L. **Rates** $119-$179 double. **Rooms** 125. **Credit** AmEx, DC, MC, V.

At first glance, this is a typical outpost of the Best Western chain, located in sedate North Bay Village near North Beach. But one thing sets this place apart from its sister hotels: the fabled sunset view from Shuckers (*see p92*) restaurant and bar downstairs. Relaxed locals even arrive by boat at this popular joint, home of beach volleyball, fresh seafood, beer and, at times, live reggae. Some rooms have kitchenettes; the hotel also offers free transfers to the airport and sea port.

*Bar. Disabled-adapted rooms. Internet (wireless, free). No-smoking rooms. Parking (free). Pool (1, outdoor). Restaurant (1). TV.*

# SURFSIDE TO GOLDEN BEACH
## Deluxe

### Acqualina Resort & Spa

*17875 Collins Avenue, at 178th Street, Sunny Isles Beach (reservations 1-877 312 9742, front desk 1-305 918 8100, www.acqualinaresort.com).* Bus E, K, S, V. **Rates** $425-$850 double. **Rooms** 98. **Credit** AmEx, DC, MC, V.

Modelled after a grand European piazza, this magnificent oceanfront property features stately architectural details: iron gates, sculpted archways, baroque fountains and a *porte-cochère* with a domed cupola. Inside, the 51-storey faux Mediterranean tower scales the heights of luxury: there are 97 swish rooms, done up in earthy tones and equipped with glossy bathrooms. Private terraces afford views of the Intracoastal Waterway or the Atlantic. Adults can drop their kids off at the (free) marine biology day camp, and then get pampered in the ESPA spa or swim in one of three oceanfront swimming pools. The extravagance continues at Il Mulino New York, sister of the well-known Big Apple restaurant.

*Bars (2). Business centre. Concierge. Disabled-adapted rooms. Gym. Internet (wireless, free). No-smoking rooms. Parking ($35/day). Pools (4, outdoor). Restaurants (4). Room service. Spa. TV.*

### Trump International Beach Resort

*18001 Collins Avenue, at 180th Street (1-305 692 5600, www.trumpmiami.com).* Bus E, K, S, V. **Rates** $289-$547 double. **Rooms** 390. **Credit** AmEx, DC, MC, V.

This polished hotel is less ostentatious than you might expect. There is a real international vibe, and the multilingual staff are impressive. Located up in Sunny Isles Beach, it's far from the hubbub. And, despite the sea of condos being constructed all around, it boasts a pristine section of beach, overlooked by a lavish grotto-style swimming pool with luxury cabanas. The unspoiled Haulover Beach Park, with its nudist section, is nearby, as are the shopping meccas of Bal Harbour and Aventura mall. Bedrooms are classy affairs: earthy tones and grand bathrooms, distinguished by dreamy pillowtop mattresses and balconies. At the Aquanox spa, you can have your body scrubbed with sugar cane and fruit enzymes.

*Bars (2). Business centre. Concierge. Disabled-adapted rooms. Gym. Internet (wireless, free). Parking ($30/day). Pools (3, outdoor). Restaurants (2). Room service. Spa. TV: pay movies.*

## Moderate

### Best Western Oceanfront Resort Bal Harbour

*9365 Collins Avenue, at 93rd Street (reservations 1-800 327 1412, front desk 1-305 864 2232, www.bestwestern.com).* Bus E, K, S, V. **Rates**

$189-$229 double. **Rooms** 93. **Credit** AmEx, DC, MC, V. **Map** p281 inset ⑮
*See p152* **Paradise Motels**.
*Disabled-adapted rooms. Internet (wireless, free). No-smoking rooms. Parking ($18/day). Pool. TV.*

### Sea View

*9909 Collins Avenue, at 99th Street, Bal Harbour (1-305 866 4441, www.seaview-hotel.com). Bus H, K, S, T.* **Rates** $215-$330 double. **Rooms** 220. **Credit** AmEx, DC, MC, V.
On the beach in sleepy, ritzy Bal Harbour, the Sea View attracts a conservative clientele and celebrities in temporary hermitage. The lobby is an understated mix of antique and contemporary furniture. Not so subtle, however, is the massive chandelier hanging in the entrance. The commodious and tasteful rooms face the ocean or Biscayne Bay. The swanky shops of Bal Harbour are out the front.
*Bars (2). Business centre. Concierge. Disabled-adapted rooms. Gym. Internet (wireless, free). No-smoking floors. Parking ($18/day). Pool (1, outdoor). Restaurant. Room service. TV.*

## Budget

### Days Inn Thunderbird Beach Resort

*18401 Collins Avenue, at 184th Street (reservations 1-800 225 3297, front desk 1-305 931 7700, www.resorthunderbirdbeach.com). Bus E, K, S, V.* **Rates** $90-$257 double. **Rooms** 180. **Credit** AmEx, DC, MC, V.
*See p152* **Paradise Motels**.
*Bar. Concierge. Disabled-adapted rooms. Gym. Internet (wireless, free). No-smoking rooms. Parking ($9-$11/day). Pool (1, outdoor). Restaurant. Room service. TV.*

### Travelodge Monaco Beach Resort

*17501 Collins Avenue, at 175th Street (reservations 1-800 227 9006, front desk 1-305*

---

### THE BEST LUXE RESORTS

For star-spotting
**Delano**. *See p135.*

To book a $30,000 penthouse
**Setai**. *See p138.*

For deco dazzle
**National**. *See p137.*

Off the beaten path
**Acqualina Resort & Spa**. *See p153.*

For playing 18 holes
**Biltmore**. *See p157.*

---

932 2100, www.resortmonacobeach.com).
*Bus E, K, S, V.* **Rates** $70-$250 double.
**Rooms** 110. **Credit** AmEx, DC, MC, V.
*See p152* **Paradise Motels**.
*Bar. Concierge. Disabled-adapted rooms. Gym. Internet (wireless, free, lobby only). No-smoking rooms. Parking ($11/day). Pool (1, outdoor). Restaurant. Room service. TV.*

## KEY BISCAYNE

Owing to strict zoning laws, there are only two hotels on Key Biscayne. Residents of this tropical paradise want to keep out the riffraff. That leaves the lavish **Ritz-Carlton** (*see p138*) and a lone motel (*see below*).

## Moderate

### Silver Sands Beach Resort

*301 Ocean Drive, Key Biscayne (1-305 361 5441, www.silversandsbeachresort.com). Bus B.* **Rates** $129-$309 double. **Rooms** 56. **Credit** AmEx, DC, MC, V.
Staying on fabulous Key Biscayne doesn't have to cost you an arm and a leg. Silver Sands, a sleepy 1950s motel, will just take the arm. The main rooms are dowdy time capsules of naff 1980s decor, but they are clean and some have kitchens. Many open on to the lush overgrown courtyard and swimming pool. The grounds are wonderfully romantic, as are the rustic pine cottages, which can accommodate families. Its waterfront Eagles Nest bar was blown away during Hurricane Andrew, leaving full-frontal views of the beach. A budget Shangri-La.
*Internet (wireless, free). Parking (free). Pool (1, outdoor). Restaurant. TV: DVD.*

# The Mainland

## DOWNTOWN

### Deluxe

### Four Seasons Hotel Miami

*1435 Brickell Avenue, at SE 14th Lane (reservations 1-800 819 5053, front desk 1-305 358 3535, www.fourseasons.com/miami). Bus 24, 48, B/Metromover Financial District.* **Rates** $309-$529 double. **Rooms** 221. **Credit** AmEx, DC, Disc, MC, V.
A high-flyer (70 storeys) in the Downtown financial district, the Four Seasons could be mistaken for an office building. But beyond the façade and utilitarian lower lobby, it's pure palatial chic. Marble-lined public areas double as gallery space for an impressive art collection, anchored by three massive Botero sculptures. The rooms boast views over Biscayne Bay, to be gazed at from padded window-ledge love seats. Amenities include a vast spa and sports club.

CONSUME

**Biltmore Hotel.** *See p157.*

Bars (2). Business centre. Concierge. Disabled-adapted rooms. Gym. Internet (wireless, $18.95/day). No-smoking rooms. Parking ($36/day). Pools (2, outdoor). Restaurant. Room service. Spa. TV: DVD.

### Mandarin Oriental Miami

*500 Brickell Key Drive (reservations 1-866 888 6780, front desk 1-305 913 8288, www.mandarinoriental.com/miami). No public transport.* **Rates** $219-$679 double. **Rooms** 326. **Credit** AmEx, DC, MC, V. **Map** p282 F4 ⑤⑥

Certain members of the bling dynasty – Will Smith and Mary J Blige, to name but two – apparently count the Mandarin as one of their favourite places to chill. It's far from low-key, however: $100 million was needed to construct the hotel on a small island adjacent to the city's financial district. Rich fabrics and modern furnishings decorate the rooms, many of which have balconies. Bathrooms are clad in Spanish marble, and some of the suites have their own kitchens. An expansive spa, state-of-the-art fitness centre and beach club contribute to the lavishness. There are two restaurants, Café Sambal and Azul (*see p93*), plus the lovely M-Bar (*see p113*). Bars (2). Business centre. Concierge. Disabled-adapted rooms. Gym. Internet (high speed, $15/day). No-smoking rooms. Parking ($34/day). Pool (1, outdoor). Restaurants (2). Room service. Spa. TV.

## Expensive

### Conrad Miami

*1395 Brickell Avenue, at NE 14th Street (reservations 1-800 266 7237, front desk 1-305 503 6500, www.conradhotels.com). Bus 24, 48, B/Metromover Financial District.* **Rates** $179-$409 double. **Rooms** 306. **Credit** AmEx, DC, MC, V.

Downtown Miami is the next place to be, if you believe the hipsters. The Conrad, an iconic skyscraper, is certainly chic. The streamlined glass and steel architecture, by Bermello Ajamil, will please modernists. And the classy 25th-floor lobby offers a sweeping panorama of skyscrapers and Biscayne Bay. The bedrooms are simple and elegant, with luxurious materials (ostrich leather headboards, creamy marble bathrooms and 700 thread-count sheets). The rooftop pool and tennis court are cooled by a breeze, and you can munch on a Kobe burger while you sun yourself. The slick Atrio Restaurant and Wine Room, and the bar off the lobby, both have a romantic vista of twinkly lights. The downside? There's little to do around here.

Bar. Business centre. Concierge. Disabled-adapted rooms. Gym. Internet (high speed/wireless, $14.95). No-smoking rooms. Parking ($28/day). Pool (1, outdoor). Restaurant. Room service. Spa. TV: DVD/pay movies.

### EPIC Hotel

*270 Biscayne Boulevard Way, at SE 2nd Avenue (reservations 1-866 760 3742, front desk 1-305 424 5226, www.epicmiami.com). Bus 24, 95.* **Rates** $229-$539. **Rooms** 411. **Credit** AmEx, Disc, MC, V. **Map** p282 E3 ⑤⑦

EPIC, a Kimpton Hotel, is further proof of the tourist scene blowing up Downtown. Located on the banks of the Miami River, in the midst of the city's banking district, the hotel is a popular choice for financial wheelers and dealers. Guest rooms – all of which have balconies, some with city views, others waterfront – are big, and keep things uncomplicated with neutral tones and natural wood furnishings. Unsurprisingly, the hotel's Area 31 restaurant (*see p93*) has become the go-to destination for power lunches. And even the most moneyed of travellers appreciate a good freebie: complimentary morning coffee and tea and an evening wine hour are included. Bar. Concierge. Disabled-adapted rooms. Gym. Internet (wireless, $10/day). No-smoking rooms. Parking ($37/day). Pools (2, outdoor). Restaurant. Room service. Spa. TV.

# Inspiration
# wherever you are

## LITTLE HAVANA
### Moderate

#### Miami River Inn
*118 SW South River Drive, at SW 4th Avenue
(reservations 1-800 468 3589, front desk 1-305
325 0045, www.miamiriverinn.com). Bus 8.*
**Rates** $109-$199 double. **Rooms** 38. **Credit**
AmEx, DC, Disc, MC, V. **Map** p283 C4 ⑱
This B&B is steeped in history. Actually a compound
made up of five restored clapboard buildings dating
from 1906, the Inn looks as if it was transported from
New England. Rooms are furnished in traditional
style with plank floors, brass beds, flowered wallpaper, wicker chairs and wood panelling. The Inn is
now listed on the National Register of Historic Places.
*Disabled-adapted rooms. Internet (wireless, free). No-
smoking rooms. Parking (free). Pool (outdoor). TV.*

## CORAL GABLES
### Deluxe

#### ★ Biltmore Hotel
*1200 Anastasia Avenue, at Granada Boulevard,
(reservations 1-855 311 6903, front desk 1-305
445 1926, www.biltmorehotel.com). Bus 72.* **Rates**
$209-$479 double. **Rooms** 275. **Credit** AmEx,
DC, MC, V. **Map** p284 D2 ⑲
A majestic monument to the Gables of the Florida
boom years, the Biltmore boasts a 300ft bell tower
modelled after the Giralda in Seville, as well as the
largest pool in the US. It's worth checking in for the
history alone. The lobby has a hand-painted vaulted
ceiling, and French and Spanish furniture, along with
large wooden aviaries containing songbirds. Marble
floors, oriental rugs and soaring columns add to the
grandeur. Upstairs, Egyptian cotton duvets and
plump feather beds add comfort to the period drama.
To top it off, there's a world-class golf course, spa,
wine club and sumptuous Sunday brunches. The
only drawback is the lonely location. *Photo p155.*
*Bars (3). Business centre. Concierge. Disabled-
adapted rooms. Gym. Internet (wireless, free). No-
smoking floors. Parking ($25/day). Pool (1, outdoor).
Restaurants (3). Room service. Spa. TV: pay movies.*

### Expensive

#### Westin Colonnade Hotel
*180 Aragon Avenue, at Ponce de León Boulevard,
(reservations 1-866 837 4251, front desk 1-305
441 2600, www.westincoralgables.com). Bus 24,
40, 72, Coral Gables Circulator.* **Rates** $169-$279
double. **Rooms** 157. **Credit** AmEx, DC, MC, V.
**Map** p284 B4 ⑳
Coral Gables oozes history, and despite the Westin
sheen, the Colonnade Hotel is no different. Once the
offices of Gables' founder George Merrick, this
stately building later housed the Florida National
Bank. So it makes sense that the hotel now caters to
a business clientele. But there's still romance: the
immense entrance is a two-storey rotunda with
Corinthian columns, crystal chandeliers, marble
floors and a fountain. Rooms are equally plush.
*Bar. Business centre. Concierge. Disabled-adapted
rooms. Gym. Internet (wireless $12.95/day). No-
smoking floors. Parking ($26/day). Pool (1,
outdoor). Restaurant. Room service. TV.*

### Moderate

#### Hotel St Michel
*162 Alcazar Avenue, at Ponce de León Boulevard
(reservations 1-800 848 4683, front desk 1-305
444 1666, www.hotelstmichel.com). Bus 56, 73.*
**Rates** $115-$185 double. **Rooms** 28. **Credit**
AmEx, DC, MC, V. **Map** p284 B4 ㉛
This hotel, built in 1926 and refurbished in 1995, is
a tiny, European-style gem in the heart of Coral
Gables. Fresh flowers and fans adorn the cosy lobby.
The distinctive rooms have wood floors, dark pan-
elled walls, antique furniture and fruit baskets.
*Concierge. Disabled-adapted rooms. Internet
(wireless, free). No-smoking rooms. Parking
($14/day). TV.*

## COCONUT GROVE
### Expensive

#### Grove Isle Hotel & Spa
*4 Grove Isle Drive, off S Bayshore Drive
(reservations 1-800 884 7683, front desk 1-305
858 8300, www.groveisle.com). No public
transport.* **Rates** $299-$449 double. **Rooms** 50.
**Credit** AmEx, DC, Disc, MC, V.
Set in lush tropical landscaped gardens, Grove Isle
also boasts a peachy view over Biscayne Bay.
Rooms are pleasant with terracotta floors; some have
canopy beds shrouded in butterfly netting. Although
secluded, the hotel has its fair share of Miami eccen-
tricity – garish palm-tree columns, paintings of monkeys and fixtures made of pineapples. Gibraltar, the
resident restaurant, is one of the Grove's best.
*Bar. Concierge. Disabled-adapted rooms. Gym.
Internet (wireless, free). Parking ($24/day). Pool.
Restaurant. Room service. Spa. TV.*

## UPPER EAST SIDE
### Budget

#### Motel Blu
*7700 Biscayne Boulevard, at 77th Street (1-305
757 8451, www.motelblu.com). Bus A, M, R, S.*
**Rates** $65-$300 double. **Rooms** 65. **Credit**
AmEx, DC, MC, V.
*See p152* **Paradise Motels***.*
*Concierge. Internet (wireless, free). No-smoking rooms.
Parking (free). Pool (1, outdoor). Restaurant. TV.*

CONSUME

# Arts & Entertainment

# Children

*Fun in – and out of – the sun.*

Miami's main attraction for visitors of all ages is undoubtedly the beach, but kids are big business in this family-friendly destination so you won't be stuck for things to do when the sun gets too intense or some storm clouds roll in. Attractions range from animal haven Jungle Island to the state-of-the-art Miami Children's Museum across the causeway, and Magic City also has acres of green space; among the city's 100-plus public parks are the world-famous Everglades and Amelia Earhart Park, which has its own petting zoo. The hitch? Most attractions aren't accessible by public transport, so hiring a car is essential if you're exploring *en famille*.

**ARTS & ENTERTAINMENT**

## SIGHTSEEING
### Attractions & museums

Greater Miami has a glut of attractions ideal for keeping children amused, many of which are described and listed in other chapters in this guide. Chief among these is the delightful **Venetian Pool** (*see p55*) in Coral Gables, with its waterfalls, grotto and underwater cave, although kids under three are not admitted. **Zoo Miami** (*see p75*) in South Dade is a big hit with kids: in addition to the animals, the zoo has interactive exhibits and special animal-related education programmes. **Bill Baggs Cape Florida State Park** (*see p47*) on Key Biscayne is a winner for older children, with plenty of aquatic activities to wear them out, and it can be combined with a visit to the **Miami Seaquarium** (*see p45*) to check out all the usual sealife, including dolphins, seals and whales. Miami's wet and wild attraction, **Grapeland Water Park** (1550 NW 37 Avenue, 1-305 960 2950, www.miamigov. com/parks/pages/grapeland.asp, admission $7-$15), is open in the spring and summer only.

Many museums offer regular events aimed specifically at a younger audience. At **HistoryMiami** (*see p49*) kids can clamber on to boats, pile into trolley cars and play with old-fashioned toys. Every second Saturday of the month there are free family fun days, with special activities. The **Lowe Art Museum** (*see p55*) holds biannual Family Days, which use music, dance, storytelling and crafts to encourage an interest in art from a young age. The museum's more in-depth Beaux Arts programme (www.beauxartsmiami.org/art_camp) offers year-round art instruction in drawing, painting, ceramics and beyond.

On the second Saturday of each month at the **Miami Art Museum** (*see p49*), staff lead kids in an afternoon of creative projects inspired by the museum's exhibits, while the **Museum of Contemporary Art of North Miami**'s (*see p69*) monthly Creative Arts for Kids programme teaches youngsters how to paint, draw and sculpt in the style of the masters.

---

**INSIDE TRACK BEACH SAFETY**

Miami beaches are clean and protected by lifeguards, but you'll still need to take some basic precautions. Don't underestimate the strength of the sun, even on overcast days – buy the highest SPF sunblock you can find and cover your kids from ears to toes; repeat this process frequently, even if the cream is waterproof. Make sure they wear a hat and play under beach umbrellas or covered areas whenever possible. Heed lifeguard warnings regarding riptides and warn kids about the dangers of Portuguese men-of-war, jellyfish-like creatures that look like purplish-blue balloons but have a vicious sting (for advice on what to do if you're stung, *see pp34-35* **Life's a Beach**).

Also check out the website of the **Miami Science Museum** (*see p59*) for its regular lineup of special events, including First Fridays, an evening full of lasers, star-gazing and hands-on activities for kids.

### Jungle Island

*1111 Parrot Jungle Trail, MacArthur Causeway, Watson Island (1-305 400 7000, www.jungle island.com). Bus C, K, M, S.* **Open** 10am-5pm Mon-Fri; 10am-6pm Sat, Sun. **Admission** $34.95; $26.95-$32.95 reductions; free under-3s. **Credit** AmEx, MC, V.

In 2001, this long-running attraction moved from its suburban South Miami location to Watson Island, giving families much easier access to the same popular parrot and wildlife shows and petting zoo. Bring loads of change to buy seeds so that the kids can feed the parrots – but remind them that these birds do indeed bite.

### ★ Miami Children's Museum

*980 MacArthur Causeway, Watson Island (1-305 373 5437, www.miamichildrensmuseum.org). Bus C, K, M, S.* **Open** 10am-6pm daily. **Admission** $16; $12 Florida residents; free under-1s. **Credit** AmEx, MC, V.

Situated across the causeway from Jungle Island, the Miami Children's Museum turns as many heads as the parrots, with its futuristic design by stellar architecture firm Arquitectonica. Inside, it's a highly interactive kids' playground. The fun includes a colourful mosaic-tiled, two-storey sandcastle, a sea room designed specially for under-fives, the world's most cultural teddy-bear exhibition and a television studio. But what kids seem to like best of all are the exhibits celebrating the mundane: the bank with teller stations and fake cheques, the supermarket with checkout lanes, and the police motorcycle and fire truck. *Photo p162.*

## Parks & nature

Special programmes and events at many parks and other natural attractions can turn a ho-hum visit into a genuine learning experience. Places such as South Miami's **Fairchild Tropical Garden** (*see p73*) produce special activity booklets for kids to use while exploring. At the two national parks located in the county, the **Everglades** (*see pp214-218*) and **Biscayne National Underwater Park** (*see p72*), a Junior Ranger Program lets kids earn a badge for completing activities. Elsewhere, Miami-Dade County Parks runs **EcoAdventure** (1 305 365 3018, www.miamidade.gov/ecoadventures), introducing young visitors to parks with canoe trips, bike trips, kayaking, marine wading tours, wildlife encounters and bird walks. For more animal-centric attractions, *see p160* **Attractions & museums**.

Jungle Island.

ARTS & ENTERTAINMENT

**ARTS & ENTERTAINMENT**

**Miami Children's Museum.** *See p161.*

### Amelia Earhart Park
*401 E 65th Street, at NW 42nd Avenue/Le Jeune Road, Hialeah, North Miami (1-305 685 8389, www.miamidade.gov/parks/parks/amelia_earhart.asp). Bus 28, 42.* **Open** 9am-5pm daily. **Admission** free Mon-Fri; $5/car Sat, Sun. **No credit cards. Map** p278.
It's way up north in Hialeah, but this park has lots of distractions for children that make it well worth the trip, including several lakes, a farm village with petting zoo, pony rides, a skate park, a re-created pioneer homestead, an enormous playground and a 'bark park' for dogs. On weekends, you can rent bikes to traverse the park's mountain-bike trails.

### Bill Sadowski Park
*17555 SW 79th Avenue, at SW 175th Street, Palmetto Bay (1-305 255 4767, www.miami dade.gov/parks/parks/bill_sadowski.asp). No public transport.* **Open** 9am-5pm Wed-Sun. **Admission** free.
This 30-acre park and nature centre, located half a mile west of Old Cutler Road, has nature trails and organises birdwatching tours. It's also an observatory site for the Southern Cross Astronomical Society, which holds star-gazing sessions from 8pm to 10pm every Saturday night (weather permitting); call 1-305 661 1375 or visit www.scas.org for information.

### ★ Crandon Park
*6747 Crandon Boulevard, Key Biscayne (1-305 361 5421, www.miamidade.gov/parks/parks/crandon_beach.asp). Bus B.* **Open** sunrise-sunset daily. **Admission** $5/car weekdays; $6/car weekends. **No credit cards. Map** p279.

Aside from being home to one of the best (and safest) beaches in the county, Crandon Park boasts a family amusement centre complete with a restored vintage carousel, a roller rink (bring your own skates) and a nature centre with programmes that explore the seagrass and the fossilised mangrove reef. Best of all are the resident iguanas and unusual reptiles. For $20 an hour, you can rent a family-sized bike built for two pedallers and two strapped-in seats up front for the little ones. For more details, *see pp34-35* **Life's a Beach**.

### Matheson Hammock Park
*9610 Old Cutler Road, South Miami (1-305 665 5475, www.miamidade.gov/parks/parks/matheson_beach.asp). Bus 65.* **Open** sunrise-sunset daily. **Admission** $5/car weekdays; $6/car weekends. **No credit cards. Map** p279.
This picturesque park has an artificial atoll pool that's good for safe, quiet bathing. For lunching, the Red Fish Grill (1-305 668 8788, www.redfishgrill. net) is housed in a charming coral-rock building – and the food's not bad either. For more details, *see pp34-35* **Life's a Beach**.

### Pelican Harbor Seabird Station
*1279 NE 79th Street Causeway, North Bay Village (1-305 751 9840, www.pelicanharbor. org). Bus L.* **Open** 9am-noon, 2-5pm daily. **Admission** free (donations appreciated).
Not strictly an attraction but more of a working halfway house for seabirds rescued after being injured by fish hooks or nets. Guided tours are available with advance reservations, while feeding takes place at 4.15pm daily.

## Sea Turtle Awareness Program

*Haulover Beach Park, 10800 Collins Avenue, Miami Beach (1-305 947 3525, www.miami dade.gov/parks/parks/haulover_park.asp); Crandon Park Visitors & Nature Center, 6767 Crandon Boulevard, Key Biscayne (1-305 361 6767, www. miamidade.gov/ecoadventures/nature_crandon.asp).*

From March to October, south Florida beaches host the largest gathering of nesting sea turtles in the United States. Their numbers have diminished over the years because of the demand for meat, eggs and leather, and due to the loss of their habitat. Since 1980, thousands of endangered sea turtles have been hatched and released through this programme, which is typically open for public participation from July to September. The release takes place in the evenings; call for specific times and details.

# ARTS & ENTERTAINMENT

As well as theatre, dance and storytelling (the latter is a regular feature at the Miami-Dade and Miami Beach libraries; *see p264*), kiddie culture often extends to sports grounds. Happily, kids' tickets for the Miami Marlins and Miami Heat sports teams' pro games (*see pp196-197*) are reasonably priced – it's peanuts and parking you'll spend a fortune on.

## Concerts for Kids

*New World Center, 500 17th Street, at Washington Avenue, South Beach (1-305 673 3330, www.nws.org). Bus C, G, H, K, L, M, S, W, South Beach Local.* **Open** Box office 10am-5pm Mon-Fri; noon-5pm Sat on performance days. **Admission** varies. **Credit** AmEx, DC, MC, V. **Map** p280 C3.

A teaching orchestra, the New World Symphony has an impressive range of events, including occasional Concerts for Kids on Sunday afternoons. Phone or visit the website for schedule.

## Miami Children's Theater

*11155 SW 112th Avenue, at SW 112th Street, Kendall (1-305 274 3595, www.miamichildrens theater.com). Bus 71.* **Open** Box office 11am-6pm Mon-Fri. **Tickets** prices vary. **Credit** Disc, MC, V.

Performances here are produced, acted and choreographed by children. The audience is also underage, but watch out for the occasional PG rating. The theatre has additional locations in Coral Gables and Miami Beach. *Photos p164.*

## MTCplayground

*9806 NE 2nd Avenue, at W Dixie Highway, Miami Shores (1-305 751 9550, www.mtc miami.org/playground).* **Open** Box office 10am-4pm Mon-Fri. **Admission** $20. **Credit** AmEx, MC, V.

It may be housed in an art deco building and stage children's classics such as *The Steadfast Tin Soldier* and *Alice in Wonderland*, but Miami Theater Center's kids' programme isn't just pure nostalgia. It also presents contemporary productions and runs day camps and workshops.

---

# Big Tickets for Tykes

*Venues that lend a stage to spectacular touring shows.*

Major national productions for children always make sure they stop down in Miami. And you can expect shows that are so dazzling, with such vibrant costumes and elaborately realised effects, that adults are every bit as entertained as their offspring (even if they don't always admit it). Most shows sell tickets at the box office or via Ticketmaster (www.ticketmaster.com).

## AmericanAirlines Arena

*For listings, see p182.*
The AmericanAirlines Arena plays host to Disney on Ice, a larger-than-life version of the movies your kids have learnt by rote, among them *Toy Story*. The Wiggles also perform here to mobs of screaming toddlers, while children of all ages happily queue up each year to secure tickets to the Ringling Bros and Barnum & Bailey circuses.

## BankUnited Center

*1245 Dauer Avenue, at William E Walsh Avenue, Coral Gables (1-305 284 8686, www.bankunitedcenter.com). Bus 52, 56/Metrorail University.* **Open** Box office 10am-6pm Mon-Fri; 10am-4pm Sat. **Credit** AmEx, MC, V.
*Sesame Street Live* – featuring Muppets singing and dancing against amazing backdrops – has been held at this venue, along with stage versions of other major US television shows, such as *Clifford the Big Red Dog* and *Dragon Tales*.

## Fillmore Miami Beach at the Jackie Gleason Theater

*For listings, see p182.*
This theatre plays host to a wide variety of shows, from traditional ballets such as *The Nutcracker* to cartoon heroes along the lines of *Dora the Explorer*.

---

**Miami Children's Theater**.
*See p163*.

## Musical Theatre for Young Audiences

*Actors' Playhouse at the Miracle Theatre, 280 Miracle Mile (SW 24th Street), at Ponce de León Boulevard, Coral Gables (1-305 444 9293, www.actorsplayhouse.org). Bus 24, 72, Coral Gables Circulator.* **Open** *Box office* 10am-6pm Mon-Sat. **Tickets** $19.50. **Credit** AmEx, MC, V. **Map** p284 C4.

The Actors' Playhouse hosts acclaimed Musical Theatre shows each Saturday at 2pm, presenting everything from fairytales to modern classics.

## RESTAURANTS & CAFÉS

Miami is full of kid-friendly restaurants. Cuban spots such as **Puerto Sagua** (*see p87*) or any of several places in Little Havana (*see p98*) are a good bet, with reasonable prices and grub such as rice, beans and fried sweet plantains that should suit even the fussiest eaters. Eateries at retail complexes such as CocoWalk, Bayside Marketplace, Dadeland Mall and the Shops at Sunset Place (for all, *see pp118-119*) target families and can handle requests for high-chairs and booster seats. Chains such as Chili's, Denny's and TGI Friday's bring kids free crayons, colouring books and children's menus as soon as you arrive; check the phone book for your nearest branch. Alternatively, alfresco dining somewhere like Lincoln Road Mall on South Beach or along Main Highway in Coconut Grove can provide an ideal solution for noisy, restless kids. In addition to the eateries listed

below, **Taverna Opa** (*see p95*) and **Shorty's BBQ** (*see p103*) are both very good choices if you've got kids in tow.

### Big Pink

*157 Collins Avenue, at 2nd Street, South Beach (1-305 532 4700, www.bigpinkrestaurant.com). Bus H, M, W, South Beach Local.* **Open** 8am-midnight Mon-Wed; 8am-2am Thur; 8am-5.30am Fri-Sun. **Main courses** $10-$24. **Credit** AmEx, MC, V. **Map** p280 F3.

The comfort food menu is vast, the environment is fun, the portions are huge and there's outdoor seating. For the pickiest little eaters, the kids' menu includes macaroni cheese and chicken fingers.

### Daily Creative Food Co

*2001 Biscayne Boulevard, at NE 20th Terrace, Downtown (1-305 573 4535, www.thedaily creativefoodco.com). Bus 3.* **Open** 6am-9pm Mon-Sat; 8am-4pm Sun. **Main courses** $6.75-$12.95. **Credit** AmEx, Disc, MC, V. **Map** p285 F3.

Counter service for custom-made salads and sandwiches, home-made soups and blended coffee drinks.

### Fuddrucker's

*14875 S Dixie Highway, Palmetto Bay (1-305 238 5680, www.fuddruckers.com). Bus 38.* **Open** 11am-10pm Mon-Thur, Sun; 11am-11pm Fri, Sat. **Main courses** $8-$12. **Credit** AmEx, DC, Disc, MC, V. **Map** p285 C2.

Honest burgers, lots of neon and noise – you can't go wrong. Kids like the Oreo shakes and rootbeer floats, not to mention the sundaes and fudge brownies.

ARTS & ENTERTAINMENT

## Monty's Raw Bar

*2550 S Bayshore Drive, at Aviation Avenue,*
*Coconut Grove (1-305 856 3992). Bus 48,*
*Coconut Grove Circulator.* **Open** 11.30am-10pm
Mon-Thur; 11.30am-2am Fri; 11.30am-1am Sat,
Sun. **Main courses** $11-$24. **Credit** AmEx,
MC, V. **Map** p285 A4.

Skip the pricey stone crab restaurant upstairs (*see*
*p85*) and head directly to the casual bayside seafood
house downstairs. On weekends, order a bucket of
fried seafood and a pitcher of beer for yourself, and
send the kids off to dance to the live music.

## Perricone's Marketplace & Café

*15 SE 10th Street, at S Miami Avenue, Downtown*
*(1-305 374 9449, www.perricones.com). Metrorail*
*Brickell.* **Open** times vary. **Main courses** $11-
$33. **Credit** AmEx, MC, V. **Map** p282 F2.

Tucked away in Downtown Miami, Perricone's
Marketplace is popular among the area's working
professionals, but it's also a favourite for families.
In addition to a sprawling outdoor patio that can
more or less handle the occasional scream, there
are bibs and high-chairs. Check out the excellent
Sunday brunch buffet ($19.95 per person, $11.95
children). *See also p94.*

## ★ Yardbird

*1600 Lenox Avenue, at 16th Street, South Beach*
*(1-305 538 5220, www.runchickenrun.com).*
*South Beach Local.* **Open** 11.30am-11pm Mon-
Thur; 11.30am-midnight Fri; 10am-midnight
Sat; 10am-11pm Sun. **Main courses** $17-$43.
**Credit** AmEx, Disc, MC, V. **Map** p280 C2.

Parents with sophisticated palates will appreciate
the upscale twist on down home Southern cooking
at this popular, farmhouse-style eaterie (the walls
are constructed from an old North Carolina barn that
was torn down then reassembled in the restaurant)
while kids will like all the fun finger foods (read: fried
chicken). Dishes are designed to be shared.

# RESOURCES

Miami.com posts new listings for major
children's activities on Monday mornings, and
the free weekly *New Times* has comprehensive
listings on local happenings. The free monthly
*South Florida Parenting* and *Miami Family*
magazines, available from more than 2,400
family-focused businesses, including libraries,
bookshops, museums and toyshops, are always
chock-full of kids' stuff.

## Activity programmes

Many resort hotels offer special programmes
for kids, which are typically free for hotel
guests and accessible to non-guests for a fee.
Ritz Kids at the **Ritz-Carlton Key Biscayne**
(*see p138*) entertains kids island-style at the
beachfront Ritz Kids Pavilion, with beach
treasure hunts, shell expeditions, storytelling
and a posh children's menu (the Ritz-Carlton
South Beach offers a similar programme right
on Miami Beach). At **Loews Miami Beach**
(*see p137*), the kids' programme includes lending
game libraries, special menus, tours and welcome
gifts. In Coral Gables, the **Biltmore** (*see p157*)
has a 'family values' package with free kids'
passes to area attractions, a free in-room movie,
and cookies and milk delivered to the room.
The lavish **Fontainebleau Miami Beach**
(*see p150*) boasts a programme of family treats
including free toys, games and souvenirs. Up in
Sunny Isles, the **Acqualina** (*see p153*) hosts a
marine biology day camp for kids.

## Babysitting

Your hotel concierge will probably be able
to recommend babysitters. Otherwise, hire
a babysitter or nanny through an agency.
Babysitters will come to your hotel (you may be
charged a transport and/or parking fee) and will
require a four-hour minimum fee and five to 24
hours' notice. Rates vary with the number of
children and the time of day. Overnight and
long-term care are also available, and some
agencies also handle special-needs children.
**Nanny Poppinz**, listed below, is licensed.

## Nanny Poppinz

*1-305 767 2422, www.nannypoppinz.com.*
**Rates** vary, call for details. **Credit** MC, V.

**ARTS & ENTERTAINMENT**

# Film

*Location, location, location.*

On the surface of it, Miami's identikit multiplexes appear no different to those in any other big US city, but delve a little deeper and you'll find they're as likely to premiere an indie feature from Buenos Aires as the latest Hollywood blockbuster. South Florida's multicultural mix is also reflected in the vast number of films shot here. Not only has the area's lush landscape served as the setting for numerous big-budget movies, but the drop-dead gorgeous locals – comprising buff boys and cosmetically enhanced babes – have also made it a favourite location with reality TV producers.

ARTS & ENTERTAINMENT

## CINEMAS

The advent of multiplexes has resulted in an explosion in the number of movie screens in Miami and a simultaneous implosion in the average screen size. However, the diversity of film offerings in and around the city has greatly improved over the past few years, even if the places in which they're being screened are getting steadily more generic and uninspiring.

Both the daily *Miami Herald* and the weekly *New Times* publish film listings. The *Herald* covers every film that opens in Miami, but its reviews – most of which run on Friday –

are substantially shorter than those in *New Times*. You can also find reviews and film times online at sites such as www.miami.com.

### First-run cinemas

#### AMC Aventura 24
*Aventura Mall, 19501 Biscayne Boulevard, at NE 196th Street, Aventura (1-305 466 9880, www. amctheatres.com). Bus 3, 9, E, S.* **Screens** 24. **Tickets** $8-$11. **Credit** AmEx, MC, V. **Map** p278.
As part of the dismal mini-city that is the Aventura Mall (*see p117*), this place is always busy – yes, even with its staggering multiplicity of screens. All but one of its 24 screens will probably be devoted to mainstream Hollywood hits, with one token indie flick to soak up the oddballs.

#### AMC Sunset Place 24
*Shops at Sunset Place, 5701 Sunset Drive, at US 1 & Red Road, South Miami (1-305 740 8904, www.amctheatres.com). Metrorail South Miami.* **Screens** 24. **Tickets** $6-$10. **Credit** AmEx, MC, V. **Map** p279.
South Miami's multiplex caters to suburban families and University of Miami students with the latest Hollywood fare, concentrating on action films and child-friendly movies. Host mall Shops at Sunset Place (*see p119*) is reasonably attractive, with a decent mix of post-show restaurants and cafés.

#### CinéBistro
*Dolphin Mall, 11471 NW 12 Street (1-305 455 7373, www.cobbcinebistro.com/dolphin). Bus 7.* **Screens** 5. **Tickets** $12-$20. **Credit** AmEx, MC, V.

---

### INSIDE TRACK
### MOVIES BY MOONLIGHT

Miami makes the most of its near-perfect year-round weather with weekly outdoor movie screenings along the beachfront. From October to May, crowds gather on the lawn of the Frank Gehry-designed **New World Center** (500 17th Street, at Washington Avenue, South Beach, www. mbculture.com) for free weekly Wednesday night screenings of everything from hot new blockbusters to well-worn classics. Further up the beach, the **North Shore Park Band Shell** (7275 Collins Avenue, at 72nd Street, North Miami Beach, 1-305 861 3616, www.miamibeachfl.gov) screens a similar mix of free movies on Friday nights.

---

Paragon Grove 13.

CinéBistro is redefining the idea of 'dinner and a movie'. After 6pm, it's a 21-plus establishment, offering comfy seating, a full bar and a thoughtfully prepared American bistro menu. The movie menu offers something for everyone, too, with a nice mix of first-run Hollywood films and hard-to-find indies.

### Frank Theatres Intracoastal 8

*3701 NE 163rd Street (Sunny Isles Boulevard), Intracoastal Mall, North Miami Beach (1-305 775 1050, www.franktheatres.com). Bus E, H, V.* **Screens** 8. **Tickets** $6-$9. **Credit** AmEx, MC, V
Independent, foreign and classic films are revered here. In addition to the latest studio releases, the Intracoastal spotlights international film festival favourites not shown elsewhere in Miami. It also hosts regular midnight screenings and retro nights.

### Paragon Grove 13

*3015 Grand Avenue, at Virginia Street, Coconut Grove (1-305 446 6843, www.paragontheaters. com). Bus 42, 48, Coconut Grove Circulator.* **Screens** 13. **Tickets** $8-$11.50. **Credit** AmEx, MC, V. **Map** p285 B3.
This luxurious multiplex typically features blockbusters and up to three non-Hollywood films at a time. If you want to avoid being stuck between the many groups of teenagers who consider this a regular weekend hangout, opt for whatever's playing at one of the four Prestige Imports Premier screens, which boast overstuffed leather chairs and a gourmet menu for noshing while you watch.

### Regal South Beach Stadium 18

*1120 Lincoln Road, at Alton Road, South Beach (1-305 674 6766, www.regmovies.com/miami). Bus A, M, R, S, W, South Beach Local.* **Screens** 18. **Tickets** $8-$11. **Credit** AmEx, MC, V. **Map** p280 C2.

With its eye-catching art deco architecture and prime location, this big, glass-walled theatre is the hub of the South Beach cinema scene. Tragically, the majority of films are mindless Hollywood fare, but there are regularly screens to spare for independent and foreign films. On weekdays you can have the whole theatre to yourself, but weekend screenings of blockbusters and critically lauded flicks often sell out, so buy tickets early. The second-floor café offers real-food alternatives to the usual cinema junk.

## Arthouse and repertory

### ★ Bill Cosford Cinema

*University of Miami, Memorial Building, 2nd Floor, off Campo Sano Avenue & University Drive, Coral Gables (1-305 284 4861, www. cosfordcinema.com). Bus 48, 52, 56.* **Screens** 1. **Tickets** $7-$9. **Credit** AmEx, Disc, MC, V.
Named after the late *Miami Herald* film critic and completely renovated with funding from his family, this is a gem of an indie movie house. It's roomier and more plush than most first-run cinemas and offers an eclectic mix of Asian, European and arthouse fare. The downside is that it's difficult to get to via public transport. Thankfully, it's well worth the effort.

### Colony Theatre

*1040 Lincoln Road, at Lenox Avenue, South Beach (1-305 674 1040, www.colonytheatre miamibeach.com). Bus A, M, R, S, W, South Beach Local.* **Screens** 1. **Credit** AmEx, MC, V. **Map** p280 C2.
Film screenings are just one of the regular events you'll find at the historic Colony Theatre. And if there's one on the calendar, it's well worth the price of admission – if only to get a glimpse at the gorgeous art deco interior of this 1935 building, originally opened as part of Paramount Pictures' cinema chain.

ARTS & ENTERTAINMENT

## Miami Beach Cinematheque

*1130 Washington Avenue, at 11th Street, South
Beach (1-305 673 4567, www.mbcinema.com).
Bus C, H, K, W, South Beach Local.* **Screens** 1.
**Tickets** $8-$10. **No credit cards. Map** p280 D3.
The Carl Fisher-designed former City Hall hosts
Miami's only cinematheque. It's also the home of the
Miami Beach Film Society, which screens independ-
ent and experimental movies, along with film classics,
to an audience of just 50. Like every good alt arthouse,
the cinematheque is about more than movies. Art
exhibits hang on the walls, and there may be music,
a mini-festival or talks.

## ★ O Cinema Wynwood

*90 NW 29th Street, at North Miami Avenue,
Wynwood (1-305 571-9970, www.o-cinema.org).
Bus 3, 9, 10.* **Screens** 1. **Tickets** $9-$10.50.
**Credit** MC, V. **Map** p285 E2.
Wynwood's non-profit O Cinema proves that bigger
is not always better. Opened in 2011, this single-
screen gem offers an ever-changing line-up of the latest indie, arthouse, foreign and family titles, and is
one of the venues for the Miami International Film
Festival. As a tribute to its creative surroundings,
the cinema shows its support of local artists with an
in-house gallery, Art at O.

## Tower Theater

*1508 Calle Ocho (SW 8th Street), at SW 15th
Avenue, Little Havana (1-305 642 1264, www.
towertheatermiami.com). Bus 8, 17.* **Screens** 2.
**Tickets** $8-$10. **No credit cards. Map** p283 C2.
Miami Dade College has partnered with this historic
cinema in Little Havana to present new films from
Cuba and other Latin American countries, as well as
shorts and features by budding Miami cineastes.
Commercially released English-language films are
also shown with Spanish subtitles at discount prices.

## FESTIVALS

The **Miami International Film Festival**
(*see p21*) is famous for screening the latest
Latin American and Spanish cinema, as well
as showcasing international releases and new
US indie films. The festival runs for two weeks
during late February and early March, with
screenings held across town, and opens and
closes at the historic Gusman Center for the
Performing Arts. Special events include
Q&As with participating filmmakers plus
gala opening- and closing-night parties.

A variety of more niche film festivals are
held throughout the year. The **Brazilian Film
Festival** (www.brazilianfilmfestival.com),
held every summer at the Colony Theatre (*see
p167*), leads the pack of smaller, Latin-themed
festivals, often sponsored by embassies to
promote national film industries.

The **American Black Film Festival**
(www.abff.com), now in its 17th year, takes
place over five days in early summer. The
**Miami Gay & Lesbian Film Festival**
(1-305 751 6305, www.mglff.com) is held for a
week in late April at various locations around
town and features an impressive mix of
independent films. The **Miami Jewish Film
Festival** (1-305 573 7304, www.miamijewish
filmfestival.com), held in January, screens a
range of international films (many in Spanish)
with Jewish themes at the Colony Theatre
and Bill Cosford Cinema (for both, *see p167*).
Just north of Miami, the **Fort Lauderdale
International Film Festival** (1-954 760 9898,
www.fliff.com), held in October and November,
has a bias towards US independents and
Florida filmmakers. Several of its top offerings
also screen at the Regal South Beach (*see p167*).

Miami Beach Cinematheque.

# Essential Miami Films

*Celluloid city.*

Scarface.

### A HOLE IN THE HEAD
### FRANK CAPRA (1959)
Capra's penultimate movie lacks the resonance of his 1930s work and is a fairly wilful attempt to make our hearts heave. Frank Sinatra plays a widower struggling to save his Miami Beach hotel, which is about to be foreclosed on by the banks. Ol' Blue Eyes won an Oscar for the song 'High Hopes'.

### THE BELLBOY
### JERRY LEWIS (1960)
In his directing debut, Lewis ditched the saccharine plotlines of his previous work for a film of sketches based on the character of a bumbling bellboy at the luxurious Fontainebleau Hotel. The result boasts more hits than misses, including such superbly timed gags as the speedy assembling of chairs in a hall and the relapse of a hopeless diet-watcher.

### SCARFACE
### BRIAN DE PALMA (1983)
Today's Miami bears little resemblance to the city in this classic crime flick.

And that's a good thing. But there's no denying that *Scarface* is also a whole lot of fun, tracking homicidal Cuban homunculus Tony Montana (Al Pacino) from his first footsteps on US soil to his operatic demise in a cloud of AK-47 bullets and coke. In fact, cocaine-fuelled excess seems to power the whole movie, from Oliver Stone's overloaded, trashily self-aware script to Pacino's unpredictable, consonant-mangling mumble ('Manolo, choot dis piece a chit').

### MIAMI BLUES
### GEORGE ARMITAGE
### (1990)
Another Miami set crime-tinged flick, Armitage's adaptation of Charles Willeford's novel is a big-screen introduction to Hoke Moseley of the Miami Police Department, a middle-aged homicide sergeant harried by alimony and sporting a set of dentures made for him on the cheap by the technician who makes false teeth for the Miami Dolphins.

### THE BIRDCAGE
### MIKE NICHOLS (1996)
Robin Williams is unusually restrained while Gene Hackman reveals his under-used gift for comedy in this anodyne Hollywood remake of the 1978 gay farce *La Cage aux Folles*. It's worth seeing just for the opening sequence as the camera pans in from the sea to neon-lit Ocean Drive.

### THERE'S SOMETHING
### ABOUT MARY
### PETER AND BOBBY
### FARRELLY (1998)
Ben Stiller stars as geeky Ted, still hooked on his high-school dream girl ten years after their prom date ended in humiliation and hospitalisation. Prompted by a wandering romantic troubadour, Ted sets seedy private investigator Healy (Matt Dillon) on the case. He tracks down Mary (Cameron Diaz) in Miami, but falls for her himself and tries to throw Ted off the scent. You wouldn't expect subtlety from the makers of *Dumb & Dumber*, and you don't get it.

# Gay & Lesbian

*Strut your stuff on the Gay Riviera.*

Thanks to its rapidly expanding arts and culture scene, Miami has become very much a year-round destination for gay travellers these days. Miami Beach, of course, sits at the absolute heart of the action. The area is often referred to as the 'Gay Riviera': the rainbow flag flies proudly over its buzzing beaches and crystal clear waters, and gay pride is demonstrated not through political beliefs but through the right to have a good time. From parties and festivals to restaurants, bars and clubs, LGBT culture is alive and thriving in Magic City. Come join the fun.

## INFORMATION

For bars and clubs, check out *Hot Spots* and *Wire*, or *She* for events in the women's community. There's also *SFGN*, south Florida's gay newspaper. All are weekly, and available from drop boxes, gay venues and bookstores. 'Outlooks', a column on gay issues written by Steve Rothaus, runs in the *Miami Herald* every second and fourth Thursday of the month. He also has a comprehensive blog, www.gaysouth florida.blogspot.com, which has useful links to dozens of other local gay-related websites.

## GAY NEIGHBOURHOODS

During the day, you'll find the boys working up a sweat at the gym or baking in the sun at the gay **12th Street Beach** (look out for the high-flying rainbow flags), ready to hit the clubs tanned and toned that night. Other alfresco action can be had at **Flamingo Park**, where there's a pool and running track, plus basketball, handball and tennis – but be aware that it closes at 10pm. For nude swimming and sunbathing, head to the northern end of **Haulover Beach Park** (*see p34* **Life's a Beach**). For those in search of more highbrow stimulation, the **Wynwood Arts District** (*see p65*) is home to more than 50 galleries, studios and museums. Back on South Beach, every visitor's itinerary should include a stroll along Ocean Drive, shopping and cocktailing on Lincoln Road, and a trip to the **World Erotic Art Museum** (*see p39; photos p173*).

After dark, Miami's hotels, restaurants and clubs really come alive, filling with a mix of beautiful people, club kids, drag queens and international travellers all ready to party late. So, if you come here and never see the light of day, don't despair – there's always next year.

### INSIDE TRACK ONE-STOP SHOP

The Miami-Dade Gay & Lesbian Chamber of Commerce operates its own LGBT Visitor Center in the heart of South Beach. Located on the first floor of 1130 Washington Avenue, at 11th Street, this one-stop shop (open 9am-6pm Mon-Fri) keeps a calendar of gay-friendly events, stocks free LGBT publications and offers wireless internet access. Call 1-305 397 8914 or see www.gogaymiami.com for more information.

## THE QUEER CALENDAR

Miami hosts two of the US's largest events on the gay circuit – the **White Party** (*see p24*) and **Winter Party Week** (*see p21*). In April, the internationally acclaimed **Miami Gay and Lesbian Film Festival** (*see p168*) comes to town – it's a ten-day movie extravaganza showcasing more than 65 films from around the world. Since 2009, the city has also played host to the fast-growing **Miami Beach Gay Pride Festival** each April. This weekend-long celebration of the LGBT lifestyle attracted 60,000 people in 2012.

In May, thousands of women migrate south for **Aqua Girl** (1-305 576 2782, www.aquagirl. org), the largest charity women's weekend in the US, with 100 per cent of the proceeds benefitting the Aqua Foundation for Women, which promotes lesbian, bisexual and transgender rights. The three days of action include raucous comedy shows, pool parties, happy hours, and wine and cheese tastings.

For a regularly updated calendar of other women-only parties and events, visit www.icandeeproductions.

## WHERE TO STAY

Frankly, you'd be hard pressed to find a hotel in Miami that isn't welcoming to gay travellers, but the following places cater specifically to a gay clientele. For more recommendations, visit www.gogaymiami.com. Look out for the special Pink Flamingo designation, which indicates a Miami LGBT Visitor Center-approved business.

### European Guesthouse

*721 Michigan Avenue, at 7th Street, South Beach (1-305 673 6665, www.europeanguesthouse.com). Bus M, S, W, South Beach Local.* **Rates** $119-$219 double. **Credit** MC, V. **Map** p280 E2.
Promoted abroad in gay publications, the friendly European Guesthouse is a quaint little getaway decked out with Queen Anne-style furniture and plenty of chintz, plus a deck and jacuzzi.

### Island House

*1428 Collins Avenue, at 14th Street, South Beach (1-305 864 2422, www.islandhousesouth beach.com). Bus C, H, K, W, South Beach Local.* **Rates** $99-$259 double. **Credit** AmEx, DC, Disc, MC, V. **Map** p280 D3.
In the heart of SoBe, just steps from the 12th Street beach, Island House is gay central. The guesthouse mainly caters to men, although all open-minded adults are welcome to stay. Some of the rooms have a kitchen with a fridge, which can be a blessing for visitors on an extended stay.

### ★ Lords South Beach

*1120 Collins Avenue, at 11th Street, South Beach (1-877 448 4754, www.lordssouthbeach.com). Bus C, H, K, W, South Beach Local.* **Rates** $165-$325 double. **Credit** AmEx, DC, Disc, MC, V. **Map** p280 D3.
*See p172* **Yellow Fever**.

### SoBeYou Bed & Breakfast

*1018 Jefferson Avenue, at 10th Street, South Beach (1-305 534 5247, www.sobeyou.us). Bus C, H, K, W, South Beach Local.* **Rates** $125-$355 double. **Credit** AmEx, DC, MC, V. **Map** p280 D2.
Located on a low-key residential block, this pet-friendly B&B is one of the best gay and lesbian guesthouses in Miami. It features a sun deck, spa pool, wine and cheese parties, and breakfast by the pool. You'll feel like you're visiting old friends.

12th Street Beach.

**ARTS & ENTERTAINMENT**

## BARS & CLUBS

Miami's gay bar scene is pretty healthy, even if the number of venues has dwindled somewhat during the last few years. **Twist** is its undisputed landmark, while the aptly named **Score** has outdoor seating for alfresco cruising. The **Palace** (*see p174*) is also a major gay watering hole, the first and only one on Ocean Drive. For a guide to clubs and parties, visit www.jumponmarkslist or www.sobe socialclub.com or pick up a copy of *Hotspots* magazine (www.hotspotsmagazine.com), available at venues around town.

### Club Azúcar

*2301 SW 32nd Avenue, at SW 23rd Street, Coral Gables (1-305 443 7657, www.azucarmiami.com).* **Open** 10.30pm-4am Thur-Sun. **Admission** up to $10. **Credit** AmEx, MC, V.

A welcome change from sceney South Beach, Club Azúcar is a Latin stronghold where men dance together the old-fashioned way and Hispanic drag queens bitch and sing *en español*.

# Yellow Fever

*Live it up at luscious Lords South Beach.*

Since opening its yellow awning-covered doors in late 2010, **Lords South Beach** (*see p146*) has revolutionised the idea of gay-friendly accommodation in that it's specifically a gay hotel – and one full of first-class amenities at that. There are three plunge pools, a poolside cabana complete with full bar and the kind of old school-style front porch you'd expect to find in the American South, perfect for checking out the local eye candy. And we haven't even got to the rooms yet, which are the perfect mix of cheek and chic.

Options range from Pads and Pied-à-terres to Cabanas and expansive Penthouses complete with private terraces and space for four, but the dominant theme throughout is yellow: let's just say that if you have a problem with the colour, you'd be best advised to find digs elsewhere – even the south Florida sun rarely shines as brightly as the golden hues of the blinds and bedheads. There's plenty of substance to go with the style, with rooms decked out with flatscreen TVs, iPod docks, Frette linens and prints of Liz Taylor as Cleopatra.

Final mention must go to Lords' fabulously oversized artworks, including a nine-foot fibreglass polar bear in the lobby. South Beach has never had it so good.

## Discotekka

*950 NE 2nd Avenue, at NE 10th Street,
Downtown (1-305 371 3773, www.mekkamiami.
com).* **Open** 10pm-9am Sat. **Admission** $10-$30.
**Credit** AmEx, Disc, MC, V. **Map** p282 B3.
Opened in 2007 as part of after-hours club Mekka,
Discotekka has injected new life into the late-night
scene, even enticing clubbers to make the 30-minute
drive from Fort Lauderdale. Billed as a club for try-
sexuals, Discotekka attracts all types, most of them
young, but the vibe is definitely queer, with Latin
go go boys and drag queens getting down amid the
nonstop throbbing tunes and glittering disco balls.

## Eros Lounge

*8201 Biscayne Boulevard, at NE 82nd Street,
Upper East Side (1-305 754 3444, www.eros
loungemiami.net).* **Open** 5pm-3am Tue-Sat; 5pm-
1am Sun. **Admission** free. **Credit** AmEx, MC, V.
This relative newcomer keeps the week rolling along
with a rotating schedule of regular events, including
Boulevard Bingo – complete with cash prizes –
every Tuesday at 8pm; a Born to Drag show on
Fridays at 11pm; and a monthly Latin-themed event,
Meaneate, where the cuba libres flow for just $5 a
pop between 10pm and midnight.

## ★ Magnum Lounge

*709 NE 79th Street, at NE 9th Avenue, Little
Haiti (1-305 757 3368) Bus 3, 16.* **Open** 5pm-
2am Tue-Thur; 5pm-3am Sat, Sun. **Credit**
AmEx, DC, MC, V.
You remember the cliché about queens singing show
tunes around the piano? The cliché is alive and well
at Magnum. Every night, a group of gentlemen
gather at this cosy lounge to show off their pipes and
musical knowledge. 'My Funny Valentine',
'Bewitched, Bothered and Bewildered', 'Foggy Day,
London Town' and 'The Man that Got Away' – all
the chestnuts get an airing here, and with great
gusto. Far away from the muscles and techno of
South Beach, this bar is a time warp in the best
possible way. It's warm and elegant: under dim
lights, the crimson walls, red velvet drapes, oil paintings, gilt mirrors and wooden shutters create a
womb-like vibe. Lanterns, flickering candles and
snug booths add a romantic mood. Cocktails are gorgeous, as are the staff. Meals are served, too, and
they're good enough to attract a straight crowd. An
outdoor bar – the Shack – is open seven days a week
(unlike the main club, which is closed on Mondays).

## MOVA Lounge

*1625 Michigan Avenue, at Lincoln Lane South,
South Beach (1-305 534 8181, www.movalounge
miami.com). Bus C, G, H, K, L, M, S, W, South
Beach Local.* **Open** 3pm-3am daily. **Admission**
free. **Credit** AmEx, MC, V. **Map** p280 C2.
If you like your gay bars slick, posey and full of
pretty boys, your prayers have been answered.
MOVA – formerly known as Halo – embodies stark

**World Erotic Art Museum.** *See p170.*

WELCOME TO THE ꙍꙍꙮꙫ

South Beach minimalism with its white walls, shiny
black bar and red leather banquettes. Pink and blue
lighting notch up the glitz factor. Needless to say,
cocktails are more prevalent than brewskis (and
from 3pm to 9pm each night, they're half-price).

## Score

*727 Lincoln Road, at Meridian Avenue, South
Beach (1-305 535 1111, www.scorebar.net). Bus
C, G, H, K, L, M, S, W, South Beach Local.* **Open**
3pm-5am daily. **Admission** up to $10. **Credit**
AmEx, DC, MC, V. **Map** p280 C3.
The name says it all, really: with a prime site on busy
Lincoln Road, this video bar and dance club is
packed with men looking for Mr Right Now. It has
several bars, including one that overlooks the

**ARTS & ENTERTAINMENT**

**ARTS & ENTERTAINMENT**

crowded dancefloor. The cruising starts at the outdoor café, then continues into the night. International DJs take over the decks on Saturdays.

### Swinging Richards

*17450 Biscayne Boulevard, near Greynolds Park, North Miami Beach (1-954 357 2532, www.florida.swingingrichards.com).* **Open** 6pm-4am Tue-Thur; 6pm-6am Fri, Sat; 6pm-3am Sun. **Admission** $10. **Credit** AmEx, MC, V.
This place is a little bit of a hike north. Not for the faint-hearted, Swinging Richards is south Florida's only fully nude gay strip club. On Sundays, patrons get the chance to strut their stuff during Amateur Night (7pm-3am), with the winner walking away with $300 in cash and a free cruise to the Bahamas.

### ★ Twist

*1057 Washington Avenue, at 10th Street, South Beach (1-305 538 9478, www.twistsobe.com). Bus C, H, K, W, South Beach Local.* **Open** 1pm-5am daily. **Admission** free. **Credit** AmEx, MC, V. **Map** p280 D3.
Twist is South Beach's most well-established gay club. Two levels and seven bars make this a must-visit for every gay tourist, as you can bar-hop without ever having to step outside the premises (the two-for-one drink specials from 11pm to 3am on Thursday nights don't hurt either). Don't forget to stop at the back Bungalow Bar to check out the nightly dancers who boogie for dollars.

## RESTAURANTS & CAFES

Gay restaurants are often a contradiction in terms, but **Magnum** (*see p173*) serves excellent food. Our Restaurants & Cafés chapter (*see pp78-103*) includes more gay-friendly venues such as **Balans**, **News Café** and **Front Porch Café**.

### Palace

*1200 Ocean Drive, at 12th Street, South Beach (1-305 531 7234, www.palacesouthbeach.com). Bus C, H, K, W, South Beach Local.* **Open** 10am-midnight daily. **Main courses** $12-$22. **Credit** AmEx, MC, V. **Map** p280 D3.
Positioned across from the 12th Street gay beach, this place could serve sawdust and would still be packed. Thankfully, it doesn't: the salad and sandwich fare is basic but good. The Sunday T-Dance (4pm) spills over into the street; other draws include the Saturday drag shows (6pm) and burlesque Wednesdays (7pm). If a deranged drag queen doesn't give you the eye, some shirtless intoxicated muscle boy is bound to.

## SPORT & FITNESS

Gays tend to prefer cruising sports, and in-line skating along Ocean Drive is a must. Many South Beach skate shops offer classes, but the

beach is filled with buff boys to grab on to if you need to slow yourself down.

**Florida Great Outdoors** (www.florida greatoutdoors.org) puts together gay and lesbian camping trips, as well as clothing-optional sailing, and bike rides in the Everglades and local parks.

The **South Florida Amateur Athletic Foundation** has more than 20 softball teams – women's and mixed – that play each Sunday in the autumn. Check out www.sfaaa.net for further information.

The local gay swimming club, **Nadadores of South Florida** (www.nadadores.org), is Miami's master swim team, practising three times a week and holding an open swim on Sundays, to which everyone is welcome.

**Miami Frontrunners** organises group runs at 6.30pm on Wednesday evenings, with several four- to five-mile routes. They all start and finish in Flamingo Park on Miami Beach. For information, call 1-305 757 5581 or visit www.frontrunnersfortlauderdale.org/miami.

The **Miami Mavericks Tennis Club** (www.miamimavericks.com) welcomes new members of all levels to participate in ladders, team tennis, tournaments and social functions. The group's home court is Flamingo Park.

## Gyms

Miami queens are rampant gym bunnies. Below are some gay favourites, but also try **Crunch Fitness** and **David Barton Gym** (for both, *see p198*).

### Club Aqua

*2991 Coral Way, at SW 27th Avenue, Coral Gables (1-305 448 2214, www.clubaquamiami. com). Bus 6, 24, 37.* **Open** 24hrs daily. **Rates** $10 weekday; $12 weekend; $25 6mth membership. **Credit** MC, V.
This 'clothing optional' bath house and private men's club features free poolside buffets, safe sex shows and an occasional porn star doing what they do best, live and uncensored. There's a gym too, but that's not why anybody's here.

### Equinox Fitness Club

*520 Collins Avenue, at 5th Street, Miami Beach (1-305 673 1172, www.equinox.com). Bus 6, 24, 37.* **Open** 5.30am-11pm Mon-Fri; 8am-9pm Sat, Sun. **Rates** $138 1mth membership. **Credit** AmEx, MC, V.
A shiny gym with all the latest equipment and group classes from ballet to Atomic Yoga. General membership is mixed (*Burn Notice* star Jeffrey Donovan has been known to work out here), but it's also a gay fave; out-and-proud ex-boyband star Lance Bass was once spotted at the juice bar making time with some shirtless stud.

# Join the Party

*Head up to Fort Lauderdale for a slice of the action.*

Miami Beach may be more famous, but Fort Lauderdale has snatched its gay crown. Not only does it have its own gay beach and an orgy of gay-friendly hotels, but its booming nightlife puts Miami's in the shade. While the South Beach crowd is still waiting behind velvet ropes, Fort Lauderdale is ready for action, its clubs offering attitude-free cruising (with no VIP rooms). Parking is a whole lot easier too.

Whatever kind of action you're after, you'll find it here, about a 45-minute drive from Miami. Fort Lauderdale caters to all kinds of gay visitors – circuit boys, leather queens, drag queens and older souls. Some of the city's hottest spots include **Georgie's Alibi** (2266 Wilton Drive, 1-954 565 2526), where men and women watch sports or relax on the patio; and **Rosie's Bar and Grill** (2449 Wilton Drive, Wilton Manors, 1-954 567 1320, www.rosiesbar andgrill.com), a laid-back, indoor/outdoor bar and club.

The leather crowd can find a mate in uniform at **Ramrod** (1508 NE 4th Avenue, 1-954 763 8219); while bear hunters stalk their prey at **Cubby Hole** (823 N Federal Highway, 1-954 728 9001, www.thecubby hole.com); and country and western fans belly up to the bar, acting all butch and *Brokeback Mountain*, at **Scandals Saloon** (3073 NE 6th Avenue, Wilton Manors, 1-954 567 2432, www.scandalsfla.com). **Dudes** (3270 NE 33rd Street, 1-954 568 7777) features strippers, as well as a loungey gay piano bar; younger dancers congregate at **Johnny's** (1116 W Broward Boulevard, 1-954 522 5931, www.johnnys barfl.com) to dance for an older crowd. If you want to skip the strippers and get some action yourself, **Club** (110 NW 5th Avenue, 1-954 525 3344, www.the-clubs.com) is one of south Florida's most popular gay bath houses.

Fort Lauderdale is also south Florida's gay guesthouse capital. The formula goes something like this: clothing-optional pool and websites that promise naked Adonises (the reality is often more prosaic). **Elysium** (552 N Birch Road, 1-954 564 9601, www.elysiumresort, $109-$189 double) is the area's largest gay resort, but the most luxurious is arguably the **Royal Palms** (771 Breakers Avenue, 1-954 564 6444, www.royalpalms.com, $139-$229 double)

with lush gardens, tasteful rooms and a spa. The **Flamingo Resort** (2727 Terramar Street, 1-954 561 4658, www.theflamingo resort.com, $150-$370 double), a boutique-style hotel, possesses a certain euro flair, with statue-filled gardens, fountains and four-poster beds; the **Cabanas** (2209 NE 26th Street, 1-954 564 7764, www.the cabanasguesthouse.com, $109-$395 double) is similarly tasteful, distinguished by its canalside location.

**Coconut Cove** (3012 Granada Street, 1-954 523 3226, www.coconutcoveguest house.com, $99-$289 double), meanwhile, is the closest resort to the gay beach and features gingerbread architecture and a 28-man jacuzzi. **Schubert Resort** (855 NE 20th Avenue, 1-954 763 7434, www. schubertresort.com, $99-$169 double) serves up its raw flesh in a funky 1953 MiMo-style building; **Windamar Beach Resort** (543 Breakers Avenue, 1-954 561 0039, www.windamar.com, $95-$169 double) bills itself as 'clothing tolerated' rather than 'optional'; while **Alcazar** (555 N Birch Road, 1-954 567 2525, www.alcazarresort.com, $110-$185 double) has not one but two 'clothing-optional' pools.

Schubert Resort.

# Nightlife

*Duck under the velvet rope for a night in clubbing paradise.*

Nightlife is to Miami what cheese is to Wisconsin or wine is to Tuscany: a cottage industry. Whatever the time of year, it's a flashy, splashy scene, boosted by countless celebrity endorsements and appearances. And not all club kids are created equal: guest lists and velvet ropes are, sad to say, integral to the scene. But the club scene is expanding and becoming a bit more democratic, thanks to a new brand of nightlife in Downtown Miami – where 24-hour liquor licences are luring even die-hard South Beach loyalists. Whatever you do, don't get there early: it's a no-no to be seen at a club or lounge before 11pm.

Miami's music scene is sprawling, spontaneous and fickle. Hectic during the winter, it's lethargic in summer. Miami is not a big rock town, but over the years the city's recording studios have spawned great pop, and these days it's a hip hop mecca. If you're a fan of Latin tunes, you're in luck: there are tons of Spanish-language gigs.

## Clubs

South Beach clubs still sizzle, but some complain that they suffer from a Stepford-like sameness. On the other hand, a few slickly original bar-clubs maintain their individuality. The **Setai** (*see p109*), with $1,000-a-night rooms, a champagne and crustacean bar, and celebrity clientele, is the haughtiest. Some restaurants moonlight as lounges, among them **Prime 112** (*see p87*), the South Beach version of a steakhouse, where silicone-injected women look to land men with meaty bank accounts; **Bar Centro** at the Bazaar by José Andrés (*see p80*), where hipsters sip $26 glasses of champagne and munch on frozen blue cheese sandwiches; and **Nobu** (*see p86*), where sushi costs more than a day's wages for some people (but gawping is free in the sleek lounge).

### ESSENTIAL INFORMATION

You have to be 21 to drink alcohol in Florida. Take photo ID even if you're obviously older as clubs are paranoid. By law, clubs must stop serving alcohol at 5am. But at some places, if you're already in, you can party until 8am when they start selling again. Most establishments stay open until 4am, sometimes 5am. A growing after-hours scene is also developing

Downtown: the 24-hour liquor licence means you can party until the morning work commute begins (or, in some cases, the next afternoon).

Cover charges vary wildly: women often get in free, while men almost always have to cough up. Quite a few places don't charge any cover, a courtesy that allows you to club-hop while owners make their money on drinks. In most cases clubs run guest lists, although, contrary to popular belief, your name doesn't have to be Madonna or Kanye to get on. A club's website will often include information on how to get on the list (or at least an email address). Many concierges also have access to lists (especially if the club is located within the hotel, which is a common scenario on South Beach), so don't hesitate to ask to be put on one (or more).

Individuality is welcomed, but discretion is encouraged when hitting exclusive spots: some clubs turn away anyone not decked out in the latest couture. In general, casual dress is discouraged, but Dior gowns are too much. Generally, the freakier you're dressed (think Siouxie Sioux circa 1982), the better your chances. If all else fails, black is the universal safe bet. Some places don't allow jeans.

Drugs are forbidden. Having experienced a series of busts in the 1980s, many Miami clubs are strict about narcotics, and employ narcs and cops to grab the next offender. That said, the typical drugs of choice among club kids here are ecstasy, cocaine and rohypnol (the so-called 'date rape drug'). One other thing: never, ever leave your cocktail unattended in the clubs. You'll be risking the possibility of someone slipping a foreign substance into it.

Clubs in Miami appear and disappear with frequency and are often closed for private parties; call ahead or check listings in the *Miami New Times*.

## SOUTH BEACH

### Bamboo

*550 Washington Avenue, at 5th Street, South Beach (1-305 695 4771, www.bamboomiami beach.com). Bus C, H, K, W, South Beach Local.* **Open** 11pm-5am Tue, Thur-Sun. **Admission** $20-$2,500. **Credit** AmEx, DC, MC, V. **Map** p280 E3.

No, that admission price range is not a typo. Clubgoers who can shell out the dough are happy to pay as much as $2,500 for a reserved table at this South Beach hotspot, which took over the historic Paris Theater in early 2012. Melding many of the

27,000sq ft space's original art deco details with elements of over-the-top luxury (think crushed velvet drapes, marble tables, white crocodile banquettes and a two-ton Swarovski crystal chandelier) have made this one of the city's hottest after-dark tickets. The club's regular roster of A-list party hosts (such as Snoop Dogg and Flo Rida) bring in the club's highest-priced tickets. *Photo p178.*

### Cameo

*1445 Washington Avenue, at Española Way (1-786 235 5800, www.cameomiami.com). Bus C, H, K, W, South Beach Local.* **Open** 11pm-5am Fri, Sat. **Admission** $25-$30. **Credit** AmEx, DC, MC, V. **Map** p280 D3.

This renovated deco movie theatre is a premier venue for superstar DJs. In addition to the impressive aural assets, Cameo attracts a mod squad of glamazons and scensters. While the downstairs is dance central, the second-floor mezzanine is the VIP section, where suede and velvet banquettes accommodate the moneyed crowd, who get a bird's-eye view of all the happenings below. The door policy is brutal, not necessarily because they're choosy, but because this is one of the few bona fide dance clubs on the beach. Dress to be noticed and get there at the ungodly opening hour for the best chance of getting in.

---

# Doing Lines

*Access all areas.*

When it comes to getting in, Miami is famous for having some of the world's strictest door policies. In many cases, if you ain't a famous face – or at least a beautiful one – you can forget it. Instead, you're consigned to stand in line and patiently watch those more blessed (or surgically enhanced) waltz by. The hope is that perhaps the door staff might eventually relent and permit you a glimpse of club heaven. Yes, it sucks, but the velvet rope is now an ingrained part of Miami nightlife. Here are some tips on how to buck the system:

● Have patience. Looking annoyed will only increase your waiting time.
● Don't touch. Tugging on the velvet ropes or, even worse, on the person guarding the door is taboo. And whatever happens, don't snap your fingers at them. It's very rude.
● Dress to impress. The funkier the better, but don't overdo it. Nightlife is rarely a black-tie occasion: just a black one. When in doubt, go with the *noir*.
● Don't lie. If you claim to be a close pal of the club's owner, you'd better be telling

the truth. In any case, real friends of club owners don't use the owner's name at the door for access.
● Forget about being fashionably late. If you have any doubts about getting into a club, arrive early, when the doormen are bored. A good time is usually around 10.30pm or 11pm; in other words, when the clubs first open up.
● Tipping. Some doormen are offended if you shove money in their faces, unless you're prepared to part with a few hundred dollars. And trust us: no club is worth paying anyone $100 to get into. If you're planning on returning another night, though, a tip of at least $20 can help ensure you're remembered next time.
● Get guest-listed. Any concierge can help you do this, but you can also call the club yourself and add your name to the guest list, which often guarantees admittance. Most guest lists are open until around 8pm or 9pm.
● Attitude. Emit an air of confidence, not cockiness, and you'll get noticed.
● Move on. If none of the above is working, get over it and try again elsewhere.

**ARTS & ENTERTAINMENT**

**ARTS & ENTERTAINMENT**

## Dream

*1532 Washington Avenue, at 15th Street (1-305 674 8018, www.dreammia.com). Bus 103, 120, 123, 150, South Beach Local.* **Open** 11pm-5am Wed, Fri, Sat. **Admission** $20-$30. **Credit** AmEx, DC, MC, V. **Map** p280 D3.

Forget, if you can, that every member of the cast of *Jersey Shore* has partied here (or that the club promotes the fact on its website). Since 2007, Dream has hosted one of the city's most popular hip hop parties, Eye Candy Saturdays, which has been hosted by the likes of P Diddy.

## Hyde Beach

*SLS Hotel, 1701 Collins Avenue, at 17th Street, South Beach (1-305 674 1701, www.hydebeach. com). Bus C, G, H, L, M, South Beach Local.* **Open** 11am-sunset Mon-Wed, Sun; 11am-2am Thur-Sat. **Admission** prices vary. **Credit** AmEx, DC, MC, V. **Map** p280 C3.

Hollywood style found its way to South Beach in June 2012 when the SLS Hotel opened at the corner of Collins and 17th, and brought the ultra-exclusive Hyde nightclub with it. The indoor/outdoor space, which includes a popular pool area that overlooks the ocean just steps away, gets the party started early. DJs create a poolside party scene that is neither quiet nor subtle. From Thursday to Sunday, the action continues well past sunset, when scenesters hunker down within the whimsical, Philippe Starck-designed club.

## Lucky Strike Lanes

*1691 Michigan Avenue, at 17th Street, South Beach (1-305 532 0307, www.bowlluckystrike. com). Bus C, H, K, L, M, S, W, South Beach Local.* **Open** 11.30am-1am Mon-Thur; 11.30am-2am Fri; 11am-2am Sat; 11am-1am Sun. **Rates** $5-$10/game; $55-$75/hr. **Credit** AmEx, MC, V. **Map** p280 C2.

For those who want to have a ball – literally – check out Lucky Strike Lanes, a bowling alley where glow-in-the-dark pins, a full-service cocktail bar and loud tunes make for an entertaining night out. There are also two pool tables and 21 big-screen TVs for added distraction. Be aware that Miami's previously mentioned swanky dress code is enforced after 9pm; before that, you're likely to find families and denim short-wearing tourists. The killer happy hour makes it worth popping in while the sun's still shining.

## Mansion

*1235 Washington Avenue, at 12th Street (1-305 695 8411, www.mansionmiami.com). Bus C, H, K, W, South Beach Local.* **Open** 11pm-5am Tue-Sun. **Admission** $25-$30. **Credit** AmEx, DC, MC, V. **Map** p280 D3.

A longtime staple of Miami Beach's nightlife scene, Mansion has provided a home for top DJs such as David Guetta, deadmau5 and Skrillex, hosted parties for P Diddy and Jay-Z, and featured live performances by Prince and Velvet Revolver. The club maintains much of the glamour of its former life as a theatre, with the building's original 1936 chandelier still holding court in the grand lobby. The club hosts popular weekly events, including Excess Mondays and Cirque de Mansion Wednesdays.

## ★ Mokaï

*235 23rd Street, at Liberty Avenue (1-305 673 1409, www.mokaimiami.com). Bus M, S, C, H, G, L.* **Open** 11pm-5am Mon, Wed, Fri, Sat. **Credit** MC, V. **Map** p280 B3.

**Bamboo**. *See p177.*

Nikki Beach Club.

tiki bars, lounge chairs and torches. Decorated with beautiful people, it's like the Playboy mansion meets *Survivor*, where the fittest (as in toned, firm breasts and butts) don't merely survive, they flourish. Buxom beauties attract well-oiled, deep-pocketed sugar daddies, and the studs also get rewarded for their packaging. In addition to the restaurant and beach club, there's a club and lounge where the party gets started during daylight hours during Amazing Sundays: thongs and bikinis are de rigueur.

### Rec Room

*Gale Hotel, 1690 Collins Avenue, at 17th Street, South Beach (1-305 673 0199, www.galehotel. com/nightlife). Bus C, G, H, L, M, South Beach Local.* **Open** 11pm Tue, Thur-Sat. **Credit** AmEx, DC, MC, V. **Map** p280 C3.

The late-night subterranean lounge at the Gale Hotel brings everything you loved about hanging out in your childhood best friend's basement into the new millennium, including an extensive vinyl collection from which nightly DJs spin their sets. *Photo p181.*

### SET

*320 Lincoln Road, between Washington Avenue and Collins Avenue (1-305 531 2800, www.set miami.com). Bus C, G, H, M, L, S.* **Open** 11pm-5am Thur-Sun. **Admission** $20. **Credit** AmEx, MC, V. **Map** p280 C3.

A luxurious lounge with chandeliers and design magazine decor, SET attracts trendies, celebs and wannabes. Everyone aims to be upstairs, in the private VIP room, where Britney Spears was seen downing Purple Hooter shots shortly before she returned to Los Angeles and shaved her head in 2007. Despite these dubious credentials, SET is a classy joint.

### SL Miami

*James Royal Palm, 1545 Collins Avenue, at 15th Street, South Beach (1-305 604 5700, www. jameshotels.com/miami/eat-drink/sl-miami). Bus C, G, H, L, M, South Beach Local.* **Open** 11.30pm-4am Mon, Thur-Sat. **Credit** AmEx, DC, MC, V. **Map** p280 C3.

Opened in early 2013, SL Miami – an outpost of the NYC hotspot – is one of the latest 'intimate lounge' spots that are showing up all around South Beach. Located within the James Royal Palm hotel, this is the place to go if you're looking to avoid sticky door policies and the sort of thumping bassline that makes it impossible to carry on a conversation. Set over two levels, the club's horseshoe shape gives everyone a clear view of all the action happening around them.

### Story

*136 Collins Avenue, at 1st Street, South Beach (1-305 538 2424, www.storymiami.com). Bus H, M, W.* **Open** 11pm-5am Fri, Sat. **Admission** $25-$40. **Credit** AmEx, DC, MC, V. **Map** p280 F3.

Young Hollywood players have made a habit of Story since it opened in late 2012; Leonardo

Darling of the lounge scene, Mokaï is frequented by the city's so-called 'somebodies'. Be warned: even moguls have been snubbed by the brutal doorkeepers as they weren't on 'the list'. If you are on the list, lucky you: brick walls, dim lights and leather couches mean this tiny spot packs a powerful punch. Expect a mix of models, celebs and DJs who spin everything from house to kitsch. The Sexy Bitch party on Wednesdays is buzzing.

### Mynt Lounge

*1921 Collins Avenue, at 19th Street (1-305 532 0727, www.myntlounge.com). Bus C, G, H, L, M, S.* **Open** midnight-5am Wed-Sat. **Admission** $20. **Credit** AmEx, MC, V. **Map** p280 C3.

What was once a must for every clubber and celebrity (among them Britney, Christina and Justin) has become yet another back-up spot in case you can't get in elsewhere. That said, there are still some Mynt loyalists who insist this sleek lounge is the place to be, dancing to slinky house tunes and posing at the bar underneath the fancy lighting. See for yourself – the door policy isn't as ruthless as it used to be.

### ★ Nikki Beach Club

*1 Ocean Drive, at 1st Street (1 305 538 1111, www.nikkibeachmiami.com). Bus H, M, W.* **Open** 11am-6pm Mon, Tue; 11am-11pm Wed-Sat; 11am-5am Sun. **Admission** $10-$20. **Credit** AmEx, DC, MC, V. **Map** p280 F3.

The quintessential beach club, Nikki is an outdoor fantasyland sprawling over a stretch of sand with

ARTS & ENTERTAINMENT

DiCaprio, Bradley Cooper, Jonah Hill and Gerard Butler have all been spotted here. And it was in the VIP room of this very same space that Sofia Vergara and her fiancé allegedly got handsy (in a bad way) with each other. Whereas the latest clubs have strayed towards a smaller, more intimate feel, Story embraces the unique brand of lavish debauchery that put South Beach on the map in the first place.

## MID BEACH

### Arkadia
*Fontainebleau, 4441 Collins Avenue, at 44th Street, Miami Beach (1-305 674 4690, www. arkadiamiami.com). Bus G, H, L, S.* **Open** 11pm-5am Thur-Sat. **Admission** $25-$40. **Credit** AmEx, DC, MC, V. **Map** p281 F4.
Expect the unexpected at this house music-loving ultra-lounge in the Fontainebleau hotel. The ground floor space has hosted everything from fashion shows to pool parties. And it's at that very same swimming pool where the party starts early on Saturdays – 1pm to be exact – as DJs mix (and you lounge) by the water.

### LIV
*Fontainebleau, 4441 Collins Avenue, at 44th Street (1-305 674 4680, www.livnightclub.com). Bus G, H, L, S.* **Open** 11pm-5am Wed-Sun. **Admission** $30-$40. **Credit** AmEx, DC, MC, V. **Map** p281 F4.
LIV is Arkadia's bigger, flashier sister club, and it frequently tops the list of the world's most expensive nightclubs. It's rather exclusive, too, which means that it's one of the city's toughest doors to crack. If you do manage to bypass the velvet ropes, you'll find an over-the-top, Vegas-style lounge-cum-dance club where celebrities and mere mortals mix and mingle, shelling out as much as $2,000 for table service.

## DOWNTOWN

### Club Space
*34 NE 11th Street, at NE 1st Avenue (1-305 375 0001, www.clubspace.com). Bus 6, 9, 10, K, T/Metromover 11th Street.* **Open** 11pm Sat-2pm Sun. **Admission** $20. **Credit** AmEx, MC, V. **Map** p282 B2.
No, the hours above are not a mistake. Club Space, the venue of choice for superstar DJs such as Paul Oakenfold, Sasha and John Digweed, opens late

## Spin Doctors
*Show off your scratching skills.*

The aural equivalent of a gathering of world leaders, the **Winter Music Conference** (1-954 563 4444, www.wintermusic conference.com) is the most important event in many a DJ's life. For one week in March, everyone who's ever scratched the surface of vinyl, professionally or otherwise, descends on South Beach for a cacophonous confab that turns participants into musical zombies whose badges of honour – besides the free CDs and hang-tags – are dark circles under the eyes.

WMC is crucial in the throbbing world of dance: anyone who wants to move into the big league attends in the hope of being discovered. It's all about wheeling, dealing and spinning (music and PR). Representatives from over 70 countries flock here in the hopes of landing that elusive deal.

Perversely, many Miami DJs have fled these shores for bigger and better turntables. Victor Calderone, for instance, was discovered at now-defunct Liquid, where Madonna was so impressed she asked him to remix 'Frozen' in 1998. DJ Tracy Young also wowed Madge: not only was she invited to remix 'Music', but she was flown to Scotland to spin at Madonna's wedding to Guy Ritchie (too bad the union didn't last). Neither Young nor Calderone has forgotten their roots, however, and both appear at the WMC.

For those not in the biz – and, to be frank, for most of those who are – the WMC is all about the parties. Many are closed to the general public, but others are open to anyone with $20 or more to hear the next – or real – Paul Oakenfold or Markus Schulz. As well as the spinsters, a virtual who's who of dance divas perform at various venues on South Beach.

And if all this inspires you to quit your day job and be a DJ, **Wynwood's Scratch DJ Academy** (450 NW 28th Street, at NW 5th Street, 1-305 576 3868, www. scratch.com) is just the thing. Founded in 2002 by Run DMC'S Jam Master Jay, this is where local DJs teach courses in the basics, blending and mixing, and scratching. For the latter, take a lesson from Immortal. The Long Island-born jock has won more than 50 competitions, performed with Run DMC and Slick Rick, and opened for Kanye West and De La Soul. With teachers like this – and a few hundred bucks for six 100-minute lessons – you, too, could be a superstar DJ.

**Rec Room**. *See p179.*

Saturday night and stays open until Sunday afternoon. The Downtown diva had to close its doors at one point after officials cracked down in the search for drugs. But it reopened a few days later to the joy of the dedicated tranceheads and electronica freaks.

### Eve

*1306 N Miami Avenue, at NW 13th Street (1-786 444 8647, www.miamieve.com). Bus 3, 9, 10, 16, J.* **Open** 10pm-5am Thur Sat. **Admission** free-$20. **Credit** AmEx, Disc, MC, V. **Map** p282 A2.
Eve is made up of three massive rooms. There's a main lounge with a stage for live music, an open-air courtyard with private cabanas to assuage the nerves of the South Beach crowd (who break out in hives when they cross the bridge) and an intimate lounge. Music ranges from Britpop to indie rock, with the occasional event such as a fashion show thrown in for good measure.

### ★ Grand Central

*697 N Miami Avenue, at NE 7th Street, Downtown (1-305 377 2277, www.grandcentralmiami.com). Bus 2, 6, 7, 8.* **Open** 10pm-5am Fri, Sat. **Admission** $20-$75. **Credit** AmEx, MC, V. **Map** p282 C2.
This hipster enclave boasts an open, warehouse-like space in what was formerly a railroad station (it's actually still situated on the tracks). A state-of-the-art sound system and accompanying light show set the sensory tone for Grand Central's Friday and Saturday night parties, where you'll see everything from indie punk bands such as Suicidal Tendencies to progressive rockers UK. At Grand Central's club-within-a-club, the Garret (which has its own entrance on 7th Street), DJs prefer to keep it old school, spinning everything from early Michael Jackson to Usher.

### The Station

*62 NE 14th Street, at NE Miami Place, Downtown (1-305 215 3453). Bus 6, 9 113.* **Open** 10pm-10am Thur-Sat. **Credit** AmEx, DC, MC, V. **Map** p282 A2.

From its vintage gas station decor (in a past life it was indeed a gas station), one might mistake the Station for a diner. But its owners see it as the beginning of a new 'movement' in Miami nightlife: a hybrid lounge, restaurant and art space. Best of all, it's open late. Real late. So if you're not worn out from a night of dancing your way from one club to the next, you've still got about five hours left to call it a night here.

## SOUTH MIAMI & BEYOND

### La Covacha

*10730 NW 25th Street, at NW 107th Avenue (1-305 594 3717, www.lacovacha.com). No public transport.* **Open** 7am-7pm Mon-Wed; 7am-4am Thur-Sat; 10pm 4am Sun. **Admission** $10-$20. **No credit cards.**
Way out west near the Miami International Mall, this is still one of the city's best Latin clubs, even though it's gone trendy and introduced a Thursday sushi and disco night – which is about as un-Latin as it gets. For a less cheesy experience, try Noche Internacional on Fridays, with salsa, merengue and Spanish pop.

# Music

Tickets can usually be purchased via the venue's box office or website. Alternatively, try **Ticketmaster** (1-800 745 3000, www.ticketmaster.com).

## ROCK, POP, FUNK & ELECTRONICA

### AmericanAirlines Arena

*601 Biscayne Boulevard, at NE 6th Street, Downtown (1-786 777 1000, www.aaarena.com). Metromover Freedom Tower.* **Open** Box office 10am-5pm Mon-Fri & until 30mins after start of show. **Admission** prices vary. **Credit** AmEx, Disc, MC, V. **Map** p282 C3.

When it's not occupied by the Miami Heat basketball team or hosting mass motivational seminars, this 20,000-seat arena stages concerts from megastars such as Mariah Carey and Beyoncé.

### Bardot

*3456 N Miami Avenue, at NW 35th Street, Design District (1-305 576 5570, www.bardot miami.com). Bus 36, 110, 202.* **Open** 6pm-3am Mon-Fri; 9pm-3am Sat, Sun. **Admission** $25-$30. **Credit** AmEx, DC, MC, V. **Map** p285 E3.

With no neon sign outside and no valets to park your car, Bardot aims to keep a much lower profile than its brethren across the causeway. The venue has a soft spot for local musicians, and top-notch DJs often spin into the wee hours. The Thursday night Living Room Sessions feature well-known indie pop and hip hop artists such as Slick Rick and Junior Boy. Be sure to check out the erotic artwork on the walls.

### Churchill's Pub

*5501 NE 2nd Avenue, at NE 55th Street, Little Haiti (1-305 757 1807, www.churchillspub.com). Bus 9, 10.* **Open** 11am-3am daily. **Admission** free-$10. **Credit** AmEx, MC, V.

Often referred to as 'Miami's CBGB', Churchill's is a beloved hole-in-the-wall venue with music every night of the week: punk, rock, metal, rap or indie. Local bands participate in the 'Bored Shitless Fests'.

### Fillmore Miami Beach at the Jackie Gleason Theater

*1700 Washington Avenue, at 17th Street, South Beach (1-305 673 7300, www.fillmoremb.com). Bus A, C, G, K, L, M, S, W, South Beach Local.* **Open** *Box office* 11am-6pm Mon-Fri; from noon before show Sat, Sun. **Admission** $10-$85. **Credit** AmEx, MC, V. **Map** p280 C3.

Comedian Jackie Gleason put Miami in the spotlight in the 1960s when he taped his TV show here. Back then, Sinatra and his pack were in the audience. Today, the crowds are as eclectic as the programme. In 2013, performers included Il Volo, Alice in Chains and Sarah Silverman.

### Klipsch Amphitheater at Bayfront Park

*301 N Biscayne Boulevard, at NE 3rd Street, Downtown (1-305 358 7550, www.bayfrontpark miami.com). Metromover College/Bayside.* **Open** times vary. **Admission** $12-$100. **Credit** AmEx, Disc, MC, V. **Map** p282 D4.

This outdoor venue is surrounded by a hilly lawn, where food vendors set up stands. It's often booked at weekends for Latin, reggae, rap and rock festivals.

### Tobacco Road

*626 S Miami Avenue, at SW 7th Street, Downtown (1-305 374 1198, www.tobacco-road.com). Bus 6, 8.* **Open** 11.30am-5am daily. **Admission** $3-$5. **Credit** AmEx, DC, MC, V. **Map** p282 F2.

Tobacco Road is the one local bar that feels like part of the South, and blues stars such as BB King have performed here. Head out to the patio for acoustic blues, jazz, rock and folk.

## JAZZ & WORLD

### Coral Gables Congregational Church

*3010 DeSoto Boulevard, at Malaga Avenue, Coral Gables (1-305 448 7421, www.coralgables congregational.org). Douglas Road Metrorail then 72 bus.* **Open** *Office* 9am-5pm Tue-Fri; 8am-9pm Sun. **Tickets** $20-$30. **Credit** MC, V. **Map** p284 C2.

The Congregational Church makes a serene Mediterranean-style setting in which to enjoy superior jazz and world music gigs, and it also hosts a summer concert series that's renowned for its excellent schedule and accessible prices. Past performers have included pianist Ellis Marsalis, brother of Branford and Wynton.

### Gusman Concert Hall

*University of Miami, 1314 Miller Drive, at San Amaro Drive, Coral Gables (1-305 284 6477, www.music.miami.edu). Bus 52, 56/Metrorail University.* **Open** *Box office* 1hr before show. **Admission** free unless otherwise stated. **Credit** AmEx, Disc, MC, V. **Map** p284 F1.

The University of Miami holds its Festival Miami *(see p23)* here in the autumn, which attracts international jazz performers. The university's faculty orchestras and guest artists perform at other times.

### ★ Jazid

*1342 Washington Avenue, at 13th Street, South Beach (1-305 673 9372, www.jazid.net). Bus C, H, K, W, South Beach Local.* **Open** 10pm-5am daily. **Admission** $10 Fri, Sat. **Credit** AmEx, MC, V. **Map** p280 D3.

Smoky and sultry, illuminated by flickering candleabra, Jazid is a small club with a cool vibe. It's the kind of place where you might hear Sade's 'Smooth Operator' on constant rotation. Downstairs, local musicians perform modern jazz, soul and Latin, with tables close to the stage. Upstairs, there's a DJ spinning soul and funk. A simple formula of good music and no attitude has ensured Jazid has outlasted many a South Beach failure. Other clubs, please take note.

### ★ Olympia Theater at Gusman Center for the Performing Arts

*174 E Flagler Street, at NE 1st Avenue, Downtown (1-305 374 2444, www.gusmancenter.org). Metromover Miami Avenue.* **Open** *Box office* noon-2pm, 3-6pm Mon-Fri & 90mins before show. **Admission** $10-$100. **Credit** MC, V. **Map** p282 D3.

Once a 1926 silent movie palace, this is now an enchanting venue for the occasional jazz and Latin gig, complete with velvet seats, Shakespearean balconies and twinkling stars on the ceiling's painted night tableau.

# Essential Miami Albums

*Sounds of the city.*

### WWW.THUG.COM
### TRICK DADDY (1998)

The man formerly known as Maurice Young represents the new generation of Miami rap (not to mention his other skills as an actor and producer). This was his second album, following on from the breakthrough *Based on a True Story*. A quick word of warning: his music is not for the easily offended and it's all the better for it.

### LIVE AT MIAMI
### ARENA
### LOS VAN VAN (2003)

Police in riot gear were called in to protect concertgoers from the wrath of Cuban exile demonstrators at this 1999 performance of Cuba's most popular post-revolution band. As this two-CD set attests, art triumphed over politics on that night. It was nominated for a Latin Grammy.

### M.I.A.M.I.
### PITBULL (2004)

Rapper and producer Pitbull's debut album is actually an abbreviation for 'Money is a Major Issue', but don't try telling his hordes of hometown fans that. One of the album tracks, '305 Anthem', featuring Lil Jon, is indeed a hometown homage ('305' is a nickname for Miami, based on its telephone area code).

### DIAMOND PRINCESS
### TRINA (2002)

Eve, Missy Elliot and more hip hop luminaries join Miami's 'Baddest Bitch' for some dirty rhyming. The album – which went on to spawn three hit singles – reached no.5 on the *Billboard* R&B/Hip Hop Album charts, selling nearly 70,000 copies in its first week of release alone.

### REGALO DEL ALMA
### CELIA CRUZ (2003)

The patron saint of Miami's Cuban community – who passed away the same year as this album's release – left a gift for fans with her final, perfect album. It also ended up as her most decorated, reaching the top spot on the *Billboard* Top Latin Albums chart and earning a Grammy for Best Salsa/Merengue Album.

### FUACATA LIVE!
### SPAM ALLSTARS
### (2002)

*Fuacata live!* is excellent, but don't worry if you can't get it – any CD from Miami's most loved dance-funk band is worth a listen. The nine-piece group also regularly perform around the city, so you've got a good chance of catching them while you're here. Check out www.spam allstars.com for dates.

# Miami Sound Machine

*It's just your jive talkin'.*

Not only is Miami the background for holiday snaps, it has provided the soundtrack to our lives. On a drab backstreet in North Miami, behind the concrete walls of Criteria Studios, pop history has been made: 'I Feel Good' by James Brown; 'Young, Gifted and Black' by Aretha; 'Rumours' by Fleetwood Mac and 'Hotel California' by the Eagles were all recorded here. But Criteria's biggest claim to fame is as the birthplace of Bee Gees disco.

Back in 1958, when it opened, it was a small independent jazz studio. But in the mid-1960s, Atlantic Records mogul Ahmet Ertegün and his star producer, Jerry Wexler, fell in love with Miami. In 1967, Wexler moved to the city and brought soul producers Arif Mardin and Bob Dowd with him. After Aretha Franklin and Wilson Pickett recorded at Criteria, the great and the good followed. One of them was Eric Clapton, who made 'Layla' and 'I Shot the Sheriff' there. He recommended the studio to the Bee Gees, who badly needed a change.

In the late 1960s and early '70s, the band had racked up a string of hits with their acoustic ballads and Beatles-esque pop – 'To Love Somebody', 'Words' and 'How Can You Mend a Broken Heart' – but by 1974 their days were numbered. In 1975, they left England for Miami, a move that saved their careers. In the relaxed atmosphere of Criteria, the Bee Gees played basketball with Bob Seger and Crosby Stills and Nash, traded riffs with the Eagles – and let their creative juices flow.

Immersed in R&B, funk and soul, the Bee Gees found a new sound working with Mardin. One night, driving home from the studio, the brothers crossed a bridge and heard a 'tickety, tickety, tickety, tick'. 'I don't know where it came from, but I started singing "It's just your jive talkin" along to it,' remembered Barry Gibb. Thus 'Jive Talkin', their first disco single – and first number one in four years – was created. It came from the 1975 album *Main Course*, which yielded another disco-flavoured number one, 'Nights on Broadway'. While recording it, Mardin – fresh from a session with Aretha Franklin – encouraged Barry Gibb to try a falsetto, and the Bee Gees' trademark was born.

*Children of the World*, the band's next album, was also recorded at Criteria – and

it spawned another disco smash, 'You Should Be Dancing'. Though *Saturday Night Fever*'s famous sound was nurtured at Criteria, and indeed mixed there, most of the actual recording was done in France. But the Bee Gees made Miami their home (Barry Gibb still lives here in a mansion on North Bay Road). After the success of *Saturday Night Fever*, the Governor of Florida made the Brothers Gibb honorary citizens of the state. They returned to Criteria in 1979 to record their disco swansong, *Spirits Having Flown*. But in 1980, they opened their own Miami studio, Middle Ear, where they wrote a string of hits for other artists: Barbra Streisand's 'Guilty', Dionne Warwick's 'Heartbreaker', and 'Islands in the Stream' for Kenny Rogers and Dolly Parton.

Criteria Studios was taken over by New York's Hit Factory in 1999. These days, the trademark sound is hip hop. Renamed Hit Factory Criteria, it is used by super-producer Timbaland, who has twiddled knobs here for the likes of Missy Elliott and Justin Timberlake. It is also a hotbed of Latin pop; many of Gloria Estefan's chart-toppers were produced here.

But it is the Bee Gees who really put Miami on the musical map, and now they have changed the physical landscape as well. After the death of Maurice Gibb in 2003, the City of Miami Beach unveiled a memorial park in his name. Around the corner from the Bee Gees' old Middle Ear Studios (at 1801 Bay Road), it overlooks Biscayne Bay from the corner of Venetian Causeway and Purdy Avenue. Maurice used to take breaks from working in the studio in the park, where he would feed the seagulls and meditate. If you listen carefully, you just might hear his falsetto harmonies in the breeze.

## Van Dyke Café

*846 Lincoln Road, at Jefferson Avenue, South
Beach (1-305 534 3600, www.thevandyke.com).
Bus C, G, H, K, L, M, S, W, South Beach Local.*
**Open** 8am-2am daily. **Admission** $5 Mon-Thur,
Sun; $10 Fri, Sat. **Credit** AmEx, DC, MC, V.
**Map** p280 C2.

Van Dyke Café is a popular restaurant. But
upstairs it's also Miami's most serious jazz club.
Chatter during sets is not viewed kindly, but then
the nightly music here deserves attention. Expect
the best musos in Miami, plus well-known players
from out of town.

# LATIN

## Bongos Cuban Café

*American/Airlines Arena, 601 Biscayne Boulevard,
at NE 6th Street, Downtown (1-786 777 2100,
www.bongoscubancafe.com). Metromover Freedom
Tower.* **Open** *Restaurant* 5-10pm Tue-Fri;
10.30am-10pm Sat, Sun. *Club* from 10pm Sat, Sun.
**Admission** $20 cover. **Credit** AmEx, DC, Disc,
MC, V. **Map** p282 C3.

Gloria Estefan and hubbie Emilio are the brains
behind this Cuban club, which has the technicolour
feel of a Disney restaurant. Luckily, the house band
that performs on Saturday nights (from 11.30pm)
features some of Miami's most sought-after Latin
sidemen. Best accompanied with a mojito or ten.

## ★ Casa Panza

*1620 SW 8th Street, at SW 16th Avenue, Little
Havana (1 305 644 3444, www.casapanzacafe.
net). Bus 8, Little Havana Circulator.* **Open**
11am-11pm Mon-Thur, Sun; 11am-3am Fri,
Sat. **Admission** free. **Credit** AmEx, MC, V.
**Map** p283 C2.

The Tuesday and Thursday *fiestas* at this Spanish
tavern are legendary. A young professional crowd
eats, drinks and dances around the tables, while a
guitarist plays flamenco and sings, accompanied by
two stomping, costumed female dancers. Fridays
and Saturdays are also busy, but less frantic.

## Club Mystique

*7137 W Flagler Street, at Tamiami Canal Road,
Flagami (1-305 262 9500). Bus 8.* **Open** 8pm-
5am Wed; 6pm-5am Thur-Sun. **Admission** $10.
**Credit** AmEx, DC, MC, V.

Miami's long-standing salsa palace is packed on
weekends with serious dancers. You can observe
some incredible moves here; the atmosphere is akin
to a Latin version of *Saturday Night Fever*.

## Hoy Como Ayer

*2212 SW 8th Street, at SW 22nd Avenue, Little
Havana (1-305 541 2631, www.hoyocomoayer.us).
Bus 8, Little Havana Circulator.* **Open** 9pm-3am
Wed-Sun (phone ahead to check). **Admission**
$7-$25. **Credit** AmEx, DC, MC, V. **Map** p283 C1.

Dark and cheaply decorated, Hoy Como Ayer is not
a pretty spot, but it offers a crash course in Cuban
music. Artists perform *boleros* (ballads), *trova*
(folk music), *son* (traditional Cuban dance music)
and *timba* (a contemporary dance beat) from
Wednesday to Sunday.

## James L Knight International Center

*400 SE 2nd Avenue, at SE 4th Street,
Downtown (1-305 416 5970, www.jlkc.com).
Metromover Knight Center.* **Open** *Box
office* 10am-5.30pm; from noon before show.
**Admission** $25-$100. **Credit** AmEx, DC,
Disc, MC, V. **Map** p282 E3.

The James L Knight, which feels like a huge high
school auditorium, welcomes major Latin artists,
from rockers to crooners.

## Mango's Tropical Café

*900 Ocean Drive, at 9th Street, South Beach
(1-305 673 4422, www.mangostropicalcafe.com).
Bus C, H, K, W, South Beach Local.* **Open** 11am-
5am daily. **Admission** $5-$10. **Credit** AmEx,
MC, V. **Map** p280 E3.

A well-known pick-up joint in business for more
than 20 years, Mango promotes an island-fever
atmosphere with its sweet cocktails, Jello shots and
a house band playing perfunctory salsa and
merengue. Decorated with tropical murals, the bar
opens on to the street, with a good view of the
beach. The bar girls manage to make even Katy
Perry look overdressed.

**Casa Panza.**

**ARTS & ENTERTAINMENT**

# Performing Arts

*Miami's got talent – and some showstopping theatres to go with it.*

Long gone are the days when Miami's only productions were either political dramas or third-rate nursing-home productions of *Annie* and *Cats*. Theatre audiences have grown over the past decade, both in number and sophistication, and every season seems to outdo the last. Since its 2006 opening, the spectacular Adrienne Arsht Center – the second-largest performing arts centre in the country – has helped to put the city firmly on the cultural map. And the addition of the Frank Gehry-designed New World Center has kept the momentum going. These behemoths aside, each year brings a fresh crop of blockbusters, often Broadway hits such as *Les Misérables*, *Mary Poppins* and *Priscilla, Queen of the Desert*. Add to this the many big-hitting operatic productions, plus some great fringe shows, and you have a scene that's looking pretty healthy. Miami also offers audiences a vast variety of dance, from ballet to salsa, representing a broad range of styles and cultures.

## INFORMATION & TICKETS

For performance information, call the venues or companies directly or pick up a copy of the weekly *Miami New Times* (you can also find complete listings available online at www.miaminewtimes.com). The Performing Arts section of the *Miami Herald*'s print and digital editions is also a useful guide. The *Miami Herald* runs the comprehensive www.miami.com website too. Miami Beach has its own cultural website, www.mbculture.com, to keep visitors and residents abreast of what's happening around town on the performing arts front.

Tickets for major companies and venues can be purchased from **Ticketmaster** (1-800 745 3000, www.ticketmaster.com), while discount same-day theatre tickets to some shows can be purchased from the **Cultural Connection** (www.culturalconnection.org), a collaborative website created by WLRN Public Radio and Television and the Theatre League of South Florida. **Ticket Florida** (1-954 462 0222, www.ticketflorida.com) is the official box office division of the Broward Center for the Performing Arts (*see p190*) and its affiliated theatres.

### THE BEST THEATRES

For starchitect-designed Downtown digs
**Adrienne Arsht Center**. *See p190.*

To catch a rising star
**New Theatre**. *See p192.*

For cutting-edge acoustics
**New World Center**. *See p187.*

For first-class pliés
**Miami City Ballet**. *See p194.*

For salsa and socialising
**Salsa Mía**. *See p195.*

## Classical Music & Opera

### ORCHESTRAS & ENSEMBLES

**Florida Grand Opera**
*Various venues (1-305 854 1643, box office 1-800 741 1010, www.fgo.org).*

The 72-year-old Florida Grand Opera is a highly respected company. Its 2012/2013 season included performances of *La Bohème*, *The Magic Flute* and *La Traviata*. The company performs locally at the Adrienne Arsht Center (*see p190*) and at the Broward Center for the Performing Arts in Fort Lauderdale (*see p190*).

### Miami Lyric Opera

*Various venues (www.miamilyricopera.org).*
This company launched in 2004 with a mission to make opera more accessible; one of its greatest successes was *La Bohème* under the stars in a Miami Beach park. Other recent offerings have included *La Traviata* and *Carmen*. Performances take place at the Colony Theatre in South Beach (*see p193*) and the Olympia Theater at the Gusman Center for the Performing Arts (*see p185*).

### Seraphic Fire & Firebird Chamber Orchestra

*Various venues (1-305 285 9060, www.seraphicfire.org).*
Trivia: Seraphic Fire once sang on a Shakira album. Maybe the sultry songstress taught the chamber choir, which specialises in Baroque and Renaissance music, a thing or two about topping the charts; in 2010, Seraphic Fire's recording of Monteverdi's *Vespers of the Blessed Virgin* was the number one download on iTunes' classical music charts. And its Grammy-nominated recording of Brahms' *Ein Deutsches Requiem* debuted at number seven on *Billboard* magazine's classical charts.

## VENUES

### ★ New World Center

*500 17th Street, at Washington Avenue, South Beach (1-305 673 3330, box office 1-305 673 3331, www.newworldcenter.com). Bus A, C, G, K, L, M, R, S, W, South Beach Local.* **Open** Box office 10am-5pm Mon-Fri (10am-interval performance days); noon-interval Sat, Sun performance days. **Admission** free-$75. **Credit** AmEx, MC, V. **Map** p280 C3.
America's only full-time orchestral academy, the New World Symphony grooms graduates from conservatories for careers in the symphony and other high-profile posts. Concerts range from classical to experimental, and the quality is high: guest teachers have included Yo-Yo Ma and Itzhak Perlman, and past guest conductors have included Sir Neville Marriner and Paavo Järvi. Founder Michael Tilson Thomas of the San Francisco Symphony often lends a hand too. In 2011, the symphony opened this new home – a $200 million showpiece by Frank Gehry. *See also p188* **Perfect Pitch**.

# Theatre

## MAJOR VENUES

The **Adrienne Arsht Center for the Performing Arts** (*see p190*) is a sparkling venue and the place to catch touring Broadway shows and ballet. The **Fillmore Miami**

Florida Grand Opera.

# Perfect Pitch

*Frank Gehry's New World Center is a success inside and out.*

When it comes to cultural offerings, South Beach has always been better known for its mojitos than its classical music scene. But the addition of the **New World Center** (*see p187*) in 2011 (unveiled just five years after the Adrienne Arsht Center and a decade after Art Basel took up residence at the Miami Beach Convention Center around the corner) means Magic City's arts scene is, well, magic.

Like most things in Miami, the shiny new performance space – home to the New World Symphony, the country's only full-time orchestral academy – came with a good deal of fanfare. Particularly when NWS artistic director Michael Tilson Thomas persuaded renowned architect Frank Gehry to design it. (Gehry, it turns out, used to babysit Thomas when the two were growing up in Los Angeles.) Their goal in designing the space was a fairly straightforward one: to create a concert hall that would meld classic architecture and cutting-edge music capabilities to help lure younger audiences. From day one, the result has been a tremendous success.

Although the surprisingly simple style is a bit of a departure from Gehry's typically bold flourishes, reviews of the design have been overwhelmingly positive. 'This is a piece of architecture that dares you to underestimate it or write it off at first glance,' noted *Los Angeles Times* writer Christopher Hawthorne of the minimal (and rectangular) plaster and glass façade. But don't let the simplicity of the educational space-cum-performance hall fool you; no detail of the 133,000-square-foot facility has been left to chance.

The New World Center offers top-notch technical capabilities and a variety of distinct spaces that aim to inspire visitors. It starts at the entrance, where a two-storey atrium bathes in natural light during the day. The main concert hall holds an intimate crowd of just 756, with seating on a steep incline so that no seat is more than 13 rows from the stage. There's even a rooftop garden and lounge that makes the most of the Center's location just two blocks from the beach.

But the building's exterior is where things get really interesting. Dutch landscape design firm West 8 created a wonderful 2.5-acre front lawn and filled it with a plethora of plant life, including hurricane palms, royal poincianas and bougainvillea. The northern part of this green expanse is known as the Miami Beach Soundscape, with a 7,000-square-foot high-definition projection wall and 167 tiny speakers (each one individually tuned). Here, NWS showcases free 'wallcasts' of select events happening inside (or at another symphony hall); from October to May, the City of Miami Beach uses the space to screen hit movies to the public; and in 2012, Art Basel hosted a 12-hour video art installation. And none of it costs a single cent.

Adrienne Arsht Center for the Performing Arts of Miami-Dade County.

**Beach at the Jackie Gleason Theater**
(*see p182*) used to fulfill the same function as
the Arsht Center, and is still a good place to
see major concerts and comedy shows. Past
performers have included Jerry Seinfeld,
Tracy Morgan and Sarah Silverman.

## Actors' Playhouse at the Miracle Theatre
*280 Miracle Mile (SW 24th Street), at Salzedo
Street, Coral Gables (1-305 444 9293, www.
actorsplayhouse.org). Bus 24, 72, Coral Gables
Circulator.* **Open** *Box office* 10am-6pm Mon-Sat;
noon-6pm Sun. *Performances* 8pm Wed-Sat; 2pm
Sun. **Tickets** $35-$48. **Credit** AmEx, MC, V.
**Map** p284 C4.

### INSIDE TRACK
### ADRIENNE ARSHT CENTER

After 11 years and a $500 million bill,
Miami's spectacular Performing Arts
Center (*see right*) made its debut in
October 2006. Designed by César Pelli,
the striking stone and glass behemoth
looms large over Downtown, blending a
1929 art deco tower into the postmodern,
ship-like structure. Some critics say its
unorthodox shape is elegant; others
dismiss it as a drab monolith. But the
fact is that Miami now boasts the second-
largest performing arts complex in the US.

A prime location on Miracle Mile makes this a great
destination for theatregoers, who can enjoy a meal
and shopping before the show. This non-profit theatre presents a full season of staged productions for
adults, a children's theatre series, educational programming, acting classes and a wide array of community services.

## ★ Adrienne Arsht Center for the Performing Arts of Miami-Dade County
*1300 N Biscayne Boulevard, between NE 13th
& 14th Streets, Downtown (information 1-786
468 2000, box office 1-305 949 6722, www.
arshtcenter.org). Bus 3, 16, 32, 36, 48, 62, 95,
A, C, K, M, S, T.* **Open** *Box office* 10am-6pm
Mon-Fri. **Tickets** prices vary. **Credit** AmEx,
MC, V. **Map** p282 A3.
After many delays, a budget overrun and a few
name changes, this spectacular $500 million César
Pelli creation opened in 2006. The striking postmodern architecture alone makes it worth a visit. But the
fact that it's home to the Florida Grand Opera and
the Miami City Ballet, and occasionally hosts the
New World Symphony and Cleveland Orchestra,
doesn't hurt either. Touring Broadway shows, musicals, world music and children's shows also feature.

## Broward Center for the Performing Arts
*201 SW 5th Avenue, at W Las Olas Boulevard,
Fort Lauderdale (1-954 462 0222, www.broward
center.org).* **Open** *Box office* 10am-5pm Mon-Fri;
noon-5pm Sat, Sun. **Tickets** prices vary. **Credit**
AmEx, MC, V.

This $52 million theatre complex consists of the 2,700-seat Au-Rene Theater and the intimate 590-seat Amaturo Theater. Performances really do run the gamut: Broadway musicals, serious drama, modern dance, ballet, classical music, pop concerts and comedy all feature. It's also known for its children's theatre. Fort Lauderdale is a bit of a trek from Miami for a show, but if traffic is good you can be here in under 40 minutes. The centre is situated in the middle of the city's Riverwalk Arts & Entertainment District, with plenty of restaurants and cafés for pre- or post-theatre refreshment. *Photo p192*.

## SMALLER VENUES

### Aventura Arts & Cultural Center

*3385 NE 188 Street, off NE 29th Avenue, Aventura (1-305 466 8002, www.aventura center.org).* **Tickets** $3-$55. **Credit** AmEx, MC, V.

Believe it or not, there's more to Aventura than its mall. This 326-seat waterfront cultural centre, which is managed by the same people as the impressive Broward Center for the Performing Arts (*see p190*), offers spectacular views and a full lineup of events, from dramatic stage productions featuring well-known actors to Beatles tribute concerts.

### ★ GableStage

*Biltmore Hotel, 1200 Anastasia Avenue, at Granada Boulevard, Coral Gables (1-305 445 1119, www.gablestage.org).* **Bus** 52, 56, 72. **Open** *Box office* noon-5pm Mon-Wed; noon-8pm Thur-Sat; noon-7pm Sun; also 1hr before

performance. *Performances* 8pm Thur-Sat; 2pm, 7pm Sun. **Tickets** $37.50-$50. **Credit** AmEx, MC, V. **Map** p284 D2.

Offering an eclectic season of contemporary drama and comedy, with the occasional classic mixed in, GableStage productions are hand-picked by artistic director Joe Adler, who travels regularly to London and New York in search of the latest hits. This house is Miami's most reliable by far, turning out shows with solid production values and excellent acting.

### Manuel Artime Theater

*900 SW 1st Street, at NW 9th Avenue, Little Havana (1-305 575 5057, www.manuelartime theater.com).* **Metromover** *Miami Avenue.* **Open** *Office* 8am-5pm performance days. **Admission** prices vary. **Credit** AmEx, MC, V. **Map** p283 C3.

Shows at this elegant 839-seat theatre range from the Miami Lyric Opera to Latin stars, such as Maria Creuza, the Brazilian bossa nova diva, and José González, the Swedish-Argentinian folkie.

### Parker Playhouse

*707 NE 8th Street, at NE 7th Avenue, Fort Lauderdale (1-954 462 0222, www.parker playhouse.com).* **Open** *Box office* noon-5pm & 90mins before show Tue-Sat. **Tickets** $36.50-$47.50. **Credit** AmEx, MC, V.

Anything goes at Parker Playhouse, at least as far as its programming is concerned. In the same week you find yourself transfixed by an international modern dance company, you could also be slapping your knee as your favourite comedian cracks wise on the stage. Comedy, concerts and travelling talk shows happily mingle with classical music, ballet and off-Broadway productions of hit musicals. The 46-year-old neoclassical playhouse is also a feast for the eyes for fans of classic architecture.

### New Theatre
*Roxy Performing Arts Center, 1645 SW 107th Avenue, at SW 16th Street, University Park (1-305 443 5909, www.new-theatre.org). Bus 8, 11, 24, 71.* **Open** *Box office* 2-8pm Thur-Sat; noon-2pm Sun. *Performances* 8pm Thur-Sat; 1pm Sun. **Tickets** $35-$40. **Credit** AmEx, MC, V.

While the quality of theatre here is sometimes uneven, the mission is clear: a careful blend of modern classics and new, sometimes controversial, pieces by up-and-coming playwrights. In 2003, New Theatre put Miami on the performing arts map with the debut of Cuban-born, Miami-bred playwright Nilo Cruz's *Anna in the Tropics*, which received a Pulitzer Prize that year.

## OTHER COMPANIES & SERIES

### City Theatre
*Various venues (1-305 755 9401, www.city theatre.com).* **Performances** times vary. **Tickets** $20-$25. **Credit** AmEx, MC, V.

From an edgy short by Neil LaBute to a poignant piece by Shel Silverstein, City Theatre's Summer Shorts is an annual marathon of one-act plays. The festival selects from hundreds of national submissions, and also showcases the finest local talent. It takes place in early June at the Adrienne Arsht Center (*see p190*).

### M Ensemble Company, Inc
*404 NW 26th Street, at NW 5th Avenue, Wynwood (1-786 953 8718, www.themensemble. com). Bus 2, 6.* **Open** *Box office* 4-10pm Thur-Sat; 2-6pm Sun. *Performances* 8pm Thur-Sat; 3pm Sun. **Tickets** $25-$45. **Credit** AmEx, MC, V. **Map** p285 F2.

Founded in 1971, this is Florida's oldest-established black theatre company. The M Ensemble's primary goal is to revive classics by African-American playwrights, such as August Wilson's *The Piano Lesson*, and to venerate black icons, as seen in Bill Harris's *Robert Johnson: Trick the Devil*, a tribute to the legendary bluesman.

### Miami Light Project
*404 NW 26th Street, at NW 5th Avenue, Wynwood (1-305 576 4350, www.miami lightproject.com). Bus 2, 6.* **Open** *Box office* 10am-5pm Mon-Fri. **Tickets** prices vary. **Credit** AmEx, MC, V.

Miami Light Project is known for bringing both avant-garde and stalwart performers to Miami. Past visitors have included Laurie Anderson, Los Muñequitos de Matanzas and Danny Hoch. One annual favourite is February's Here & Now festival, when the group showcases cutting-edge works-in-progress by local performers.

## HISPANIC THEATRE

Updated weekly, www.teatroenmiami.com is an outstandingly comprehensive website dedicated to Spanish-language theatre. The website's creator, Cuban-born composer and writer Ernesto García, culls articles (mostly in Spanish, though some are in English) from

**Broward Center for the Performing Arts**. *See p190*.

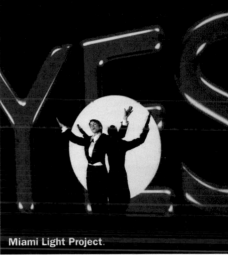

Miami Light Project.

Miami, New York, Latin America and Europe and posts them on the website, along with original articles and interviews. If there's something interesting going on in Miami's Hispanic theatre scene (and there usually is), you'll find it on this website. If you don't speak Spanish, though, you'll have little use for it.

### International Hispanic Theatre Festival of Miami

*Teatro Avante, 2nd Floor, 744 SW 8th Street, at SW 7th Ave (1-305 445 8877, www.teatro avante.com). Bus 6, 8, 208.* **Open** *9am-9pm Mon-Fri; 2-8.30pm Sat, Sun.* **Tickets** *$30.* **Credit** AmEx. **Map** p283 C4.

Held during July, this is the largest Hispanic theatre festival in the US and one of the most important Hispanic theatre events in the world. Classical, contemporary and experimental works are performed in Spanish, Portuguese and English by companies from across the globe. The main venue is Teatro Avante, but shows take place all over town, as do lectures and workshops. The festival is celebrating its 28th birthday in 2013.

# Dance

The city has an impressive grouping of home-grown dance companies, including the **Miami City Ballet** and the **Momentum Dance Company**. Many local companies have dedicated studio space, and all of them hold performances elsewhere in rented venues, as well as at the **Colony Theatre** and the **New World Dance Theater**. Plenty of touring companies also make appearances in town, so you may well catch something good while you're here.

## VENUES

### ★ Colony Theatre

*1040 Lincoln Road, at Lenox Avenue, South Beach (1-305 674 1040, www.colonytheatre miamibeach.com). Bus C, G, H, K, L, M, S, W, South Beach Local.* **Open** *Box office noon-5pm Tue-Sat & 1hr before performance. Performances times vary.* **Tickets** *prices vary.* **Credit** AmEx, MC, V. **Map** p280 C2.

There's something very theatrical about art deco architecture, and the Colony Theatre is a gem of a 1934 building, which has been faithfully refurbished in recent years. The Miami Lyric Opera stages productions here, but there is also comedy, dance and contemporary theatre, such as *Angels in America*, or one-off movies like *The Rocky Horror Picture Show*. It's at the western end of the Lincoln Road Mall (*see p39*), so you're surrounded by restaurants and bars for a little post-performance fun. *Photo p194.*

### New World Dance Theater

*25 NE 2nd Street, at N Miami Avenue, Downtown (1-305 237 3135, www.nwsa.mdc.edu). Metrorail Government Center.* **Open** *Box office 10am-4pm. Performances times vary.* **Tickets** *free-$50.* **No credit cards.** **Map** p282 D2.

The New World School of the Arts, a high school and college, has produced many a Miami artist, including Hernan Bas. Its theatre stages everything from Broadway musical revivals, such as *The Pajama Game*, to experimental dance.

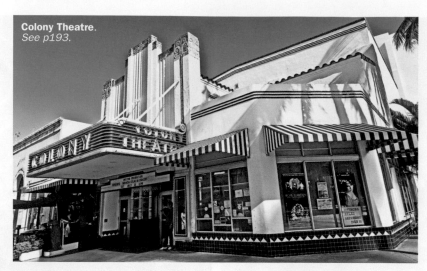

**Colony Theatre.**
See p193.

## COMPANIES
### Ballet

#### ★ Miami City Ballet
*2200 Liberty Avenue, at 22nd Street, South Beach (1-305 929 7000, box office 1-305 929 7010, www.miamicityballet.org). Bus C, G, H, L, M, S.* **Open** *Box office* 10am-5pm Mon-Fri. *Performances* times vary. **Tickets** $20-$175. **Credit** AmEx, MC, V. **Map** p280 C3.
The Miami City Ballet is one of the largest classical ballet companies in the US, with 40 dancers and an estimated annual budget of around $13.5 million. Former New York City Ballet principal Edward Villella founded the company almost three decades ago, in 1985; in more recent times he has moved beyond Balanchine classics to show off his own choreographic skills, with superb results. Productions take place at the Adrienne Arsht Center (*see p190*).

### Modern

#### Dance Now Miami
*Little Haiti Cultural Center, 212 NE 59 Terrace, at NE 2nd Avenue, Little Haiti (1-305 975 8489, www.dancenowmiami.org).*
This contemporary dance company, in residence at the Little Haiti Cultural Center, aims to make the art of dance accessible to as diverse an audience as possible. DNM pulls from various styles – including ballet, modern dance and jazz.

#### Karen Peterson & Dancers
*www.karenpetersondancers.org.*
South Florida's only self-proclaimed 'mixed ability' dance company, this unique troupe mixes able-bodied dancers and dancers in wheelchairs. It also has its own black box performance space. Check the website for a schedule of upcoming performances.

#### Miami Contemporary Dance Co
*www.miamicontemporarydance.net.*
Miami Contemporary Dance emerged on the modern dance scene in 2000 and has been producing provocative work ever since. Artistic director Ray Sullivan integrates traditional forms such as tango into his modern choreography. He often veers towards the political, as seen in his exploration of human rights in *If You Were in My Shoes, What Color Would They Be?*

#### Momentum Dance Company
*1-305 858 7002, www.momentumdance.com.*
Momentum Dance Company performs work by local choreographers, as well as pioneers such as Isadora Duncan. It also offers extensive programming for children. And it's educational, too, as each show is followed by a workshop. The group produces the annual Miami Dance Festival (*see p195*), which is held each April/May.

### World

#### IFÉ-ILÉ Afro-Cuban Dance & Music Ensemble
*1-305 476 0832, www.ife-ile.org.* **Tickets** prices vary. **Credit** AmEx, MC, V.
The IFÉ-ILÉ Afro-Cuban troupe is best known for Yoruba, Congo and Bantu dances. It also performs modern dance and popular Latin moves such as rumba, salsa and mambo. Founder Neri Torres danced with the National Ballet of Cuba before defecting in 1991.

## FESTIVALS

### Miami Dance Festival
*1-305 858 7002, www.momentumdance.com.*
**Date** early Apr-mid May.
The Momentum Dance Company hosts and performs – and invites other dance companies out to play – at this six-week celebration of movement. The event showcases a diverse menu of dance styles at venues throughout Miami, including an opening night soirée at the Colony Theatre (*see p193*), plus additional performances at the Miami Beach Botanical Garden (*see p40*) and Miami Beach Cinematheque (*see p168*).

## DANCE CLASSES

### Best of Dance
*Various venues (1-786 597 6458, www.bestofdance.com).* **Rates** vary.
Randy Pittman provides advanced and beginner classes in ballroom, Argentinian tango, hustle and swing at various locations throughout Miami.

### Bozenka's Bellydance Academy
*Various venues (1-305 788 0515, www.bozenka.biz).* **Rates** vary.
Bellydancing veteran Bozenka teaches her moves at all levels, at various locations throughout Miami and around the world. Visit her website to find out when she's next taking roll call.

### In Motion School of Classical Ballet
*2nd Floor, 1700 Biscayne Boulevard, at NE 47th Street, North Miami (1-305 751 2229, www.in motionmiami.com).* **Open** 9am-9pm Mon-Thur;

9am-7pm Fri; 8.30am-2.30pm Sat. **Rates** vary.
**No credit cards.**
Led by artistic director Renee Rich, a master of jazz and tap, In Motion has serious credentials, but the studio teaches dancers of all skills and ages. As the name attests, ballet is the most prominent offering. But classes are also offered in jazz, tap, modern and hip hop. In Motion was recently voted Miami's Best Dance Center by *New Times*.

### Kendall Dance Studio
*8838 SW 129th Street, off SW 87th Avenue, Kendall (1-305 233 8700, www.kendalldance.com).* *No public transport.* **Open** 9am-9pm Mon-Sat.
**Rates** vary. **No credit cards.**
Advanced and beginner classes for every type of dancing imaginable, including ballroom, formation, foxtrot, jitterbug, waltz, bolero and salsa. Friday nights are a must with group classes – advanced dancers at 7pm, beginners at 8pm (both $12) – followed by a weekly Dance Party at 9pm.

### ★ Salsa Mía
*Yuca Lounge, 2nd Floor, 501 Lincoln Road, at Drexel Avenue, South Beach (1-305 987 3033, www.salsamia.com).* **Open** 8.15-11pm Fri.
**Rates** $40 per class. **No credit cards.**
Boasting some of the best instructors in South Beach, Salsa Mía teaches dancers Latin style, confidence and fun. On Friday nights after class, Yuca Lounge becomes a steamy nightclub; students often stay behind and show off their new skills. On Wednesdays and Sundays at 8.15pm, you'll find Salsa Mía's movers and shakers at DAF Studio (2nd Floor, 1501 SW 8th Street, at SW 15th Avenue, Little Havana), with classes followed by a dance session.

**Miami City Ballet.**

**ARTS & ENTERTAINMENT**

# Sport & Fitness

*Get in on the action.*

Blessed with warm weather year-round, Miami is a prime d estination for outdoor activities. Whether you prefer a jog on the beach, a game of tennis, scuba diving or surfing, there are plenty of ways to elevate your heart rate on land and in the water. Working out is a way of life here, and gyms are more social than bars. If treadmills don't turn you on, there are many sports to watch live or while downing a few beers on Ocean Drive. In 2012, the city opened the gates to Marlins Park, a certified green professional baseball stadium, which, in true Miami style, boasts its own nightclub. Like its South Beach outpost, the ballpark version of the Clevelander (*see p105*) features live DJs, scantily clad female dancers and a swimming pool.

## SPECTATOR SPORTS

There are four pro sports teams in south Florida: the Dolphins (American football), the Panthers (hockey), the Heat (basketball) and the Marlins (baseball). The Panthers advanced to the Stanley Cup play-offs in 2012, and the Heat are one of the NBA's top teams, winning the World Championships in 2012. After a terrible 2007 season in which the Dolphins ended with a 1-15 win/loss record, the team is now heading in the right direction, and the Marlins remain competitive if somewhat inconsistent.

### TICKETS AND INFORMATION

Tickets can be purchased at venue box offices or through **Ticketmaster** (1-800 745 3000, www.ticketmaster.com). For ticket brokers, the most reputable is **Todd's Tickets** (1-800 784 8633, www.toddstickets.com).

## Baseball

For years the **Miami Marlins** (formerly the Florida Marlins) battled to get their own stadium, and that dream came true when Marlins Park opened in Little Havana in time for the 2012 baseball season. Miami also boasts two top-level college baseball teams, the **FIU Panthers** and the **University of Miami Hurricanes**.

### FIU Panthers

*FIU Baseball Stadium, Florida International University, 11200 SW 8th Street, at SW 112th Avenue, South Miami (1-305 348 4263, www. fiusports.com). Bus 8, 11.* **Open** *Box office 9am-5pm Mon-Fri.* **Season** *Jan-Apr.* **Tickets** *$5-$7.* **Credit** *AmEx, MC, V.*

### Miami Marlins

*Marlins Park, 501 Marlins Way, at NW 5th Street, Little Havana (1-305 480 1300, www. miami.marlins.mlb.com). Bus 6, 7, 11, 12, 17, 21, 51.* **Open** *Box office 9am-6pm Mon-Fri; 10am-4pm Sat.* **Season** *Apr-Oct.* **Tickets** *$20-$195.* **Credit** *AmEx, MC, V.*

### University of Miami Hurricanes

*Alex Rodriguez Park at Mark Light Field, University of Miami, 5821 San Amaro Drive, at Mataro Avenue, Coral Gables (1-305 284 4171, www.hurricanesports.com). Bus 48, 56/Metrorail University.* **Open** *Box office 8.30am-5pm Mon-Fri.* **Season** *Feb-May.* **Tickets** *$8-$10.* **Credit** *AmEx, MC, V.*

## Basketball

The **Miami Heat** have sizzled over the last few years. As Downtown Miami has revitalised, basketball games have become a place to see celebrities sitting courtside, enjoying the AmericanAirlines arena. FIU's **Panthers** and UM's **Hurricanes** are the college teams. Although the Hurricanes have performed well on court, they have been the subject of an NCAA investigation into athletic compliance practices.

**FIU Panthers**

*US Century Bank Arena, SW 8th Street & 107th Avenue, Sweetwater (1-305 348 4263, www.fiusports.com). Bus 8, 11.* **Open** *Box office* 9am-5pm Mon-Fri. **Season** Nov-Feb. **Tickets** $10-$100. **Credit** AmEx, MC, V.

**★ Miami Heat**

*AmericanAirlines Arena, 601 Biscayne Boulevard, at NE 6th Street, Downtown (1-786 777 1000, www.nba.com/heat). Metromover Freedom Tower.* **Open** *Box office* 10am-5pm Mon-Fri. **Season** Nov-May. **Tickets** $10-$350. **Credit** AmEx, Disc, MC, V. **Map** p282 C3.

**University of Miami Hurricanes**

*BankUnited Center, 1245 Dauer Drive, at William E Walsh Avenue, Coral Gables (1-305 284 2263, www.hurricanesports.com).* **Open** *Box office* 9am-5pm Mon-Fri. **Season** Nov-Mar. **Tickets** $15-$30. **Credit** AmEx, MC, V.

## Football

For decades football was the only sport in town, and the **Dolphins** and **Hurricanes** kept their fans enthralled with Super Bowl wins and National Title games. Recently, though, the Dolphins have suffered a dip in form. The Hurricanes continue their streak as a football powerhouse; as of the 2011 season, the team had produced the highest number of players-turned-pros in the NFL (42 in total).

**Miami Dolphins**

*Sun Life Stadium, 2269 NW 199th Street, at NW 27th Avenue, Miami Gardens (1-305 943 8000, www.miamidolphins.com). Bus 27, 297.* **Open** *Box office* 8.30am-5.30pm Mon-Fri. **Season** Sept-Dec. **Tickets** $24-$900. **Credit** AmEx, MC, V.

**University of Miami Hurricanes**

*Sun Life Stadium, 2269 NW 199th Street, at NW 27th Avenue, Miami Gardens (1-305 943 8000, www.hurricanesports.com). Bus 27, 297.* **Open** *Box office* 8.30am-5.30pm Mon-Fri. **Season** Sept-Dec. **Tickets** $30-$500. **Credit** AmEx, MC, V.

## Greyhound racing

Greyhound racing has been popular in Florida since the 1930s. Gambling enthusiasts still flock to the tracks; they also offer year-round poker and simulcasts of pari-mutuels.

**Flagler Greyhound Track**

*450 NW 37th Avenue, at NW 4th Terrace, West Flagler (1-305 649 3000, www.magiccitycasino. com). Bus 6, 7, 37.* **Season** Early June-late Nov. **Races** 1pm, 8pm Tue, Fri, Sat; 8pm Thur, Sun. **Admission** free.

**Mardi Gras Casino**

*831 N Federal Highway (US 1), at Pembroke Road, Hallandale (1-954 924 3200, www.mardi grascasinofl.com). Bus Broward County Transit 1, board at Aventura Mall.* **Season** Dec-Apr. **Races** 5pm, 7pm Mon, Thur-Sun. **Admission** free.

Miami Heat.

ARTS & ENTERTAINMENT

## Horse racing

Horse racing and south Florida have been an item for close to a century, since **Hialeah Park** (*see p70*) opened in 1921. The sport has waned in popularity in recent years, and Hialeah closed its doors in 2001. The historic park reopened in 2009, but not at full capacity; it offers regular simulcast racing now and is scheduled to reopen as a fancy new casino in summer 2013.

### Calder Casino & Race Course
*21001 NW 27th Avenue, at NW 215th Street, North Dade (1-305 625 1311, www.calder racecourse.com). Bus 27, 91.* **Open** from 10.30am daily. **Season** Apr-Dec. **Admission** free-$10. **No credit cards**.

### Gulfstream Park
*901 S Federal Highway (US 1), between Hallandale Beach Boulevard & Ives Dairy Road, Hallandale Beach (1-954 454 7000, www.gulfstreampark.com). Bus 3.* **Season** Jan-Apr. **Admission** free-$15. **No credit cards**.

## Ice hockey

The **Florida Panthers** are skating on thin ice with hockey fans. The team wowed the nation by making it to the Stanley Cup Finals in 1996, but have been plagued ever since by coaching disasters and inconsistencies.

### Florida Panthers
*BB&T Center, 1 Panther Parkway, at Sunrise Boulevard, Sunrise (1-954 835 7000, www.florida-panthers.com). 110 bus.* **Open** Box office 9am-5pm Mon-Fri. **Season** Oct-May. **Tickets** $15-$250. **Credit** AmEx, DC, Disc, MC, V.

## Jai-alai

Jai-alai (pronounced 'high-aligh') was for many years the unofficial sport of Miami. Hailing from the Basque Country, the blindingly fast game is played within a court with high walls, like a large squash court, and the object is to hurl a ball, called a *pelota*, against the wall with so much speed and spin that the opposition can't catch or return it.

### Dania Jai Alai
*301 E Dania Beach Boulevard (A1A), at US 1, Dania Beach (1-954 927 2841, www.dania-jai-alai.com). Bus Broward County Transit 1, board at Aventura Mall.* **Games** noon, 7pm Tue-Sat. **Admission** free. **No credit cards**.

### Miami Jai Alai
*3500 NW 37th Avenue, at NW 34th Street, near Miami International Airport (1-305 633 6400,* www.fla-gaming.com/miami). Bus 36, J. **Games** noon Mon-Fri; 1pm Sun. **Admission** free.

## Motorsport

### Homestead Miami Speedway
*1 Speedway Boulevard, Homestead (1-305 230 5000, www.homesteadmiamispeedway.com).* **Admission** $35-$120. **Credit** AmEx, MC, Disc, V. Hosts the Gainsco Auto Insurance Indy 300 in March and the NASCAR Sprint Ford 400 and Miami 300 in November.

## Polo

### Miami Beach Polo World Cup
*The Setai, 2001 Collins Avenue, at 20th Street (1-866 468 7630, www.miamipolo.com). Bus C, G, H, L, M, S.* **Date** Late Apr. **Admission** varies. **Credit** AmEx, MC, V. **Map** p280 C3. Polo might not be the first sport you associate with Miami, but it makes sense. The game is synonymous with money, socialites and Argentinians. Every April the cream of the international crop assembles for chukkas on South Beach.

# ACTIVE SPORTS & FITNESS
## Bowling

### Bird Bowl
*9275 Bird Road (SW 40th Street), at SW 92nd Avenue, South Miami (1-305 221 1221). Bus 40.* **Open** 8.30am-1am Mon-Thur, Sun; 8.30am-3am Fri, Sat. **Rates** $2.50-$4 per person per game; $21-$31/hr after 6pm Fri-Sun. *Shoe rental* $3.75. **Credit** MC, V.

### Lucky Strike
*1691 Michigan Avenue, at Lincoln Road, Miami Beach (1-305 532 0307, www.bowlluckystrike. com). Bus C, H, K, W, South Beach Local.* **Open** 11.30am-1am Mon-Thur, Sun; 11.30am-2am Fri; 11am-2am Sat; 11am-1am Sun. **Rates** $3.95-$5.95 per person per game or $45/hr. *Shoe rental* $3.95. **Credit** AmEx, MC, V. **Map** p280 C2.

## Cycling

For spectacular ocean views and a bit of uphill biking, try the **Rickenbacker Causeway**, an elevated bridge that links Virginia Key and Key Biscayne to the mainland. Ensure you have a good lock, as bikes often disappear in Miami.

### Fritz's Skate, Bike & Surf Shop
*1620 Washington Avenue, between Lincoln Road & 16th Street, South Beach (1-305 532 1954). Bus C, L, M, S, South Beach Local.* **Open** 10am-9pm Mon-Sat; 10am-8pm Sun. **Credit** AmEx, DC, Disc, MC, V. **Map** p280 D3.

**Miami Beach Polo World Cup.**

### Miami Beach Bicycle Center

*601 5th Street, at Washington Avenue, South Beach (305 674 0150). Bus C, H, K, W, South Beach Local.* **Open** 10am-7pm Mon-Sat; 10am-5pm Sun. **Credit** AmEx, DC, MC, V. **Map** p280 E3.

## Fishing

Line casting is widely available, with Florida Bay, Biscayne Bay, the Intracoastal Waterway, the Gulf Stream and the Everglades providing plenty of options.

For sport fishing, try a local charter service. **Mark the Shark** offers half-day and full-day deep-sea fishing trips for groups of up to ten; fishing for sailfish and marlin can be done from the boat **Therapy IV** at Haulover Marina; **Reel Time Charter** specialises in walleye, steelhead, yellow perch and smallmouth; and **L&H** offers fishing for sailfish and dolphin fish.

Charter boats are pricey, but there's always the option of party boats. These 60- to 90-footers carry up to 100 people and provide tackle, bait and instruction. The **Kelley Fleet** has two 65-footers and an 85-footer, and the **Reward Fleet** has a 70-footer and a 60-footer.

If money is really tight, join the locals fishing from the many bridges that connect the islands of Miami Beach to the mainland.

You don't need a saltwater fishing licence if you fish from a charter boat, but you do if you're renting your own boat. Neither do you need a saltwater licence if fishing from land or a structure tied to land. Freshwater and saltwater licences for non-residents cost $17 for three days, $30 for seven days and $47 for a year. To buy one, call 1-888 347 4356 or

visit www.floridaconservation.org. Tackle shops, such as **Crook & Crook**, also sell them.

### Crook & Crook

*2795 SW 27th Avenue, at US 1, Coconut Grove (1-305 854 0005, www.crookandcrook.com). Bus 27.* **Open** 7am-7pm Mon-Fri; 6am-7pm Sat; 6am-3pm Sun. **Credit** AmEx, DC, Disc, MC, V.

### Kelley Fleet

*Haulover Marina, 10800 Collins Avenue, at 108th Street, Bal Harbour (1-305 945 3801, www.miamibeachfishing.com). Bus H, K, S, T.* **Rates** (per person) $43/half day; $64/day. **Credit** AmEx, Disc, MC, V.

### L&H

*Crandon Marina, 4000 Crandon Boulevard, Key Biscayne (1-305 361 9318, www.landhsportfishing.com). Bus B.* **Rates** $800/half day; $1,200/day. **Credit** AmEx, MC, V.

### Mark the Shark

*Biscayne Bay Marriott Marina, 1633 N Bayshore Drive, at Venetian Causeway, Downtown (1-305 759 5297, www.marktheshark.com). Bus 48.* **Rates** $700/half day; $1,100/day. **Credit** AmEx, DC, MC, V.

### Reel Time Charters

*2560 S Bayshore Drive, at Aviation Avenue, Coconut Grove (1-305 856 5605, www.fishmiami.com). Bus 48.* **Rates** $350-$450/half day; $450-$550/day. **Credit** AmEx, DC, MC, V. **Map** p285 A4.

### Reward Fleet

*Dock A, Miami Beach Marina, 300 Alton Road, at 3rd Street, South Beach (1-305 372 9470, www.fishingmiami.com). Bus H, M, W.* **Trips** 9am-1pm, 1.45-5.30pm, 8pm-12.30am daily. **Rates** (per person) $50/half day. **Credit** AmEx, MC, V. **Map** p280 E2.

### Therapy IV

*Haulover Marina, 10800 Collins Avenue, at 108th Street, Bal Harbour (1-305 945 1578, www.therapy4.com). Bus H, K, S, T.* **Trips** 8am-noon, 1-5pm daily. **Rates** shared charter $180 per person/half day; private charter $750/half day, $1,400/day. **Credit** AmEx, DC, MC, V.

## Golf

### Biltmore Golf Course

*1200 Anastasia Avenue, at Granada Boulevard, Coral Gables (1-305 460 5364, www.biltmorehotel.com). Bus 52, 72.* **Open** 9.30am-6pm Mon; 7am-6pm Tue-Thur; 6.30am-6pm Sat, Sun. **Rates** $65-$209. **Credit** AmEx, MC, V. **Map** p284 D2. Located at the magnificent Biltmore Hotel (*see p157*), this historic 18-hole course was built in 1925.

Sport & Fitness

**ARTS & ENTERTAINMENT**

### Crandon Golf Course
*6700 Crandon Boulevard, Key Biscayne (1-305 361 9129). Bus B.* **Open** 6.30am-9.30pm daily. **Rates** $50-$225. **Credit** AmEx, MC, V.
Crandon has the world's largest tee, seven saltwater lakes and many holes overlooking Biscayne Bay.

### Doral Golf Resort
*4400 NW 87th Avenue, at NW 41st Street, Doral (1-305 592 2000, www.doralresort.com/golf). Bus 36, 87.* **Open** sunrise-sundown daily. **Rates** $75-$350. **Credit** AmEx, DC, Disc, MC, V.
One of the top courses in south Florida, the Doral is home to the PGA Ford Championship, held in March. It's nearly impossible for non-members to get a tee time, so book way in advance.

### ★ Miami Beach Golf Club
*2301 Alton Road, at W 23rd Street, Miami Beach (1-305 532 3350).* **Open** 6.30am-7.30pm daily. **Rates** $100-$200. **Credit** AmEx, MC, V. **Map** p280 B2.
Opened in 1923, the landmark Miami Beach Golf Club is now run by the City of Miami. It recently received a $10 million facelift and is seen as one of the finest public courses in south Florida.

## Gyms

For gyms catering to a gay crowd, *see pp170-175.*

### ★ Crunch Fitness
*1259 Washington Avenue, at 12th Street, South Beach (1-305 674 8222, www.crunch.com). Bus C, H, K, W, South Beach Local.* **Open** 6am-11pm Mon-Thur; 6am-10pm Fri; 8am-9pm Sat; 9am-8pm Sun. **Rates** *Day membership* $35. **Credit** AmEx, DC, Disc, MC, V. **Map** p280 D3.
Crunch works hard to take the tedium out of a gym session, offering weekly DJ sessions and imaginative classes based on dance, yoga and even surfing moves.

**Other locations** 1676 Alton Road, between Lincoln Road & 17th Street, South Beach (1-305 531 4743); 3505 W 20th Avenue, at W 35th Street, Hialeah (1-888 227 8624).

### David Barton Gym
*2377 Collins Avenue, at 23rd Street, South Beach (1-305 534 1660, www.davidbartongym.com). Bus C, G, H, L, M, S.* **Open** 5.30am-11pm Mon-Fri; 8am-8pm Sat, Sun. **Rates** *Day membership* $25; *weekly membership* $99. **Credit** AmEx, DC, Disc, MC, V.
This trendy gym is for people who want to be seen while on their machines, but the facilities are impressive too. Spread over 45,000 square feet, it features Pilates and yoga studios, a pool and spa, and DJs liven up evening workouts twice a week.

### Downtown Athletic Club
*200 S Biscayne Boulevard, at SE 3rd Street, Downtown (1-305 358 9988). Bus 3, 16, 48, C, S.* **Open** 5.30am-10pm Mon-Thur; 5.30am-9pm Fri; 8am-2pm Sat, Sun. **Rates** *Day membership* $25. **Credit** AmEx, DC, Disc, MC, V.
The place to go if you want to meet a banker, lawyer or executive. The gym also includes two racquetball courts, a basketball court, sauna and whirlpools.

## In-line skating

In South Beach, most stores, bars and eateries are so used to skaters that they don't even ask them to remove their wheels before they enter. For rentals, go to **Fritz's Skate, Bike & Surf Shop** (*see p198*).

## Pool & billiards

Pool purists disdain the lone table in the back of a bar. Instead, they prefer to patronise true pool halls such as **New Wave Billiards** (1403 SW 107th Avenue, Kendall, 1-305 220 4782). Tables

Miami Beach Golf Club.

cost about $9 to $15 an hour, depending on the time of day. You've got to be 21-plus to hit up **Chalk Miami** (1234 Washington Avenue, at 12th Street, 1-305 674 1712, www.chalkmiami. com), South Beach's pool hall/ping pong club/nightclub hybrid, with no cover charge.

## Swimming & watersports

### CANOEING, KAYAKING & ROWING
For details on canoeing and kayaking at **Shake-A-Leg**, *see below*. **South Beach Kayak** (1711 Purdy Avenue, 1-305 975 5087) also caters to everyone from first-timers to experienced paddlers. For rowing, try the **Miami Beach Rowing Club** (6500 Indian Creek Drive, Miami Beach, 1-305 861 8876), which meets regularly and offers sculling (two oars per person) and sweeping (one oar each) classes.

### SAILING
#### Club Nautico Boat Rental
*Crandon Park Marina, 4000 Crandon Boulevard, Key Biscayne (1-305 361 9217). Bus B.* **Open** 9am-5pm daily. **Rates** *Boat rental* from $399/half day; from $599/day. **Credit** AmEx, Disc, MC, V.

#### ★ Shake-A-Leg Miami Water Sports
*1711 Purdy Avenue, at South Beach (1-305 858 5550, www.shakealegmiami.org). Bus 42, 48.* **Open** 9am-5pm daily. **Rates** $80-$350 (boat rental); $15-$25/hr (kayak rental). **Credit** AmEx, MC, V. This is one of the city's most welcoming venues. Programmes run the gamut from recreational sailing, kayaking and canoeing to power boating.

### SCUBA DIVING
Some of Florida's best treasures are found underwater, but the rules for enjoying them are strict. If you're a beginner, you'll have to take lessons and get yourself certified. Most dive shops offer lessons as well as equipment rental. The best dives in the region are in Key Largo at the **John Pennekamp Coral Reef State Park** (*see p221*).

#### Austin's Diving Center
*10525 S Dixie Highway (US 1), at SW 105th Terrace, Kendall (1-305 665 0636, www.austins diving.com). Bus 104.* **Open** 9am-7pm Mon-Sat. **Rates** prices vary. **Credit** AmEx, DC, Disc, MC, V.

#### Divers Den
*12614 SW 88th Street, at SW 126th Avenue, Kendall (1-305 595 2010). Bus 88.* **Open** 9.30am-7pm Mon-Fri; 9am-5pm Sat. **Rates** prices vary. **Credit** AmEx, Disc, MC, V.

#### Divers Paradise
*Crandon Marina, 4000 Crandon Boulevard, Key Biscayne (1-305 361 3483, www.keydivers.com).*

---

### INSIDE TRACK SURF'S UP

Fancy catching a wave or two to complete your immersion into Miami beach life? **Florida Surf Lessons** (1-561 625 5375, www.floridasurflessons.com) offers group and private lessons for all skill levels, from beginners to competitive surfers. Sessions are held on the southern tip of Miami Beach, near Nikki Beach Club at 1st Street, and boards and wetsuits are provided. Prices range from $50 to $150 per person, depending on class length (1.5-2.5hrs) and the number of participants.

---

*Bus B.* **Open** 10.30am-5pm Tue-Fri; 8am-2pm Sat, Sun. **Rates** $300-$499 for certification classes. **Credit** AmEx, DC, Disc, MC, V.

### SWIMMING
If your hotel doesn't have a pool, it's worth the trek to the **Venetian Pool** (*see p55*). For other public pools, contact the Miami-Dade Park and Recreation Department on 1-305 755 7800 or go to www.miamidade.gov/parks/swimming.htm.

## Tennis & racquetball

Miami hosts one of the tennis world's biggest non-Grand Slam tournaments, the **Sony Open** (*see p22*). For information about public courts, call the Miami-Dade Park and Recreation Department at 1-305 755 7800 or go to www.miamidade.gov/parks/tennis.htm.

### Crandon Park Tennis Center
*7300 Crandon Boulevard, at Key Biscayne (1-305 365 2300). Bus B.* **Open** 8am-10pm Mon-Fri; 8am-7pm Sat, Sun. **Rates** $4-$11 per person per hr. **No credit cards.**
There are 18 hard courts, two European red clay courts, four American green clay courts and two grass courts. There are floodlights for night play on 13 of the hard courts.

### Salvadore Park Tennis Center
*1120 Andalusia Avenue, at Columbus Boulevard, Coral Gables (1-305 460 5333). Bus 24.* **Open** 7am-9pm Mon-Fri; 7am-7pm Sat, Sun. **Rates** $7.20-$10 per person per hr. **No credit cards.** **Map** p284 C2.

### Tropical Park Tennis Center
*7900 SW 40th Street, at SW 79th Avenue, South Miami (1-786 205 1006). Bus 40.* **Open** 2-10pm Mon-Thur; 2-9pm Fri; 7am-7pm Sat, Sun. **Rates** $2-$4 per person per hr. **No credit cards.**

**ARTS & ENTERTAINMENT**

# Escapes & Excursions

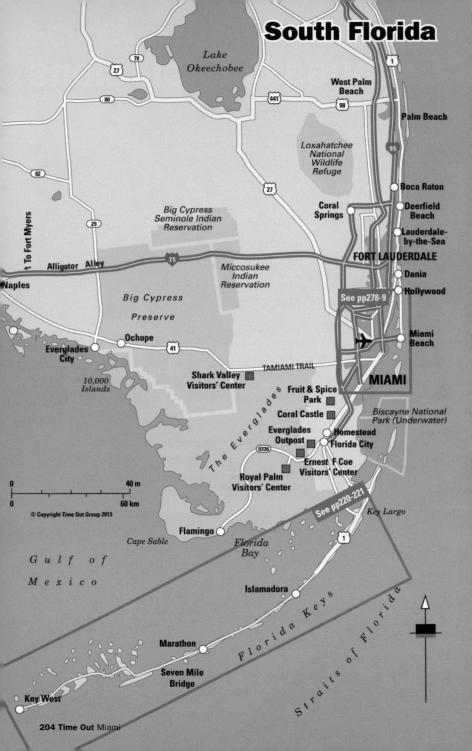

# South Florida

Lake Okeechobee

West Palm Beach

Palm Beach

Loxahatchee National Wildlife Refuge

Boca Raton

Deerfield Beach

Coral Springs

Lauderdale-by-the-Sea

Big Cypress Seminole Indian Reservation

**FORT LAUDERDALE**

Dania

Miccosukee Indian Reservation

Hollywood

Alligator Alley

See pp278-9

Naples

Big Cypress Preserve

Miami Beach

**MIAMI**

Ochope

Everglades City

10,000 Islands

Shark Valley Visitors' Center

TAMIAMI TRAIL

Fruit & Spice Park

Biscayne National Park (Underwater)

Coral Castle

The Everglades

Everglades Outpost

Homestead

Florida City

Ernest F Coe Visitors' Center

Royal Palm Visitors' Center

0        40 m
0        60 km
© Copyright Time Out Group 2013

See pp220-221

Key Largo

Flamingo

Cape Sable

Florida Bay

G u l f   o f

M e x i c o

Islamadora

Florida Keys

Marathon

Seven Mile Bridge

Straits of Florida

Key West

**204 Time Out** Miami

# Getting Started

*Leave the city behind.*

The trips you make out of Miami may well be the highlight of your visit. For locals, heading out of town on a regular basis is the only way to keep sane. While the Gold Coast resorts to the north, including Fort Lauderdale and Palm Beach, offer more of the same – with less of an ethnic element and far greater wealth – somewhere like the Everglades is simply unlike anywhere else on earth (except possibly subtropical Queensland in Australia). You can visit for half a day or lodge in the national park and spend days hiking, kayaking or boating. Likewise, driving down through the Florida Keys is a unique experience. To cross over the Seven Mile Bridge with nothing in sight except a thin sliver of silvery road that bisects a vast and alarmingly infinite canvas of blue is nothing short of trippy. Just remember to keep your eyes on the road.

## SIDE TRIPS

Beyond the trips described in this chapter, there are several other worthwhile destinations outside the scope of this book but still visitable from Miami. Chief among these are the sleepy towns and resorts of the **Gulf Coast**. Just a further half-hour's drive beyond Everglades City (*see p216*), **Naples** is the west coast version of Palm Beach, a ritzy resort of trendy boutiques and gourmet restaurants with 41 miles of public beach. It's a far cry from the dazzle of Miami, but if you're looking for powdery sand and to be in bed by 10pm, when most bars close, this is the place for you. A short drive north is **Fort Myers** and neighbouring **Fort Myers Beach** on Estero Island, which is like a downmarket version of Miami Beach.

We recommend keeping the foot on the gas and pushing on to the nearby island of **Sanibel** and its northern extension, **Captiva**. Sparsely populated but with mile upon mile of compacted seashell beaches, they are that rarity – beauty spots in which carefully controlled human intervention has permitted wildlife to flourish. To reach the islands from Miami is about a three-hour drive along US 75. Accommodation is plentiful, and there's a tourist information office right at the entrance to Sanibel to help with bookings.

## TIMING YOUR VISIT

As temperatures in Florida soar, the cost of a holiday plunges. From late April/early May, when the weather is usually gorgeous, hotel, car rental and other prices start to dip. As summer progresses, deals quickly become steals. Of course, you do have to consider your tolerance for steamily humid weather, as well as your enthusiasm for hurricanes, as the annual hurricane season runs from June to the end of November.

## INFORMATION

Tourist information

Check the local papers for information. One of the best sources for inspiration is the Sunday *Miami Herald*, which contains an impressive travel section.

### Visit Florida

*Suite 300, 661 E Jefferson Street, Tallahassee, FL 32301 (1-850 488 5607, 1-866 972 5280, www.visitflorida.com).*
A wide variety of guide books and leaflets can be downloaded, viewed as ebooks or ordered via the excellent Visit Florida website. You'll also find loads of essential information on restaurants, accommodation, activities and more.

## Camping & outdoors

### Florida Association of RV Parks & Campgrounds (FARVC)

*1340 Vickers Road, Tallahassee, FL 32303 (1-850 562 7151, www.farvc.org).* **Open** 9am-5pm Mon-Fri.
Call or write for a *Florida Camping Directory*.

### Florida Department of Environmental Protection

*Division of Recreation & Parks, MS 535, 3900 Commonwealth Boulevard, Tallahassee, FL 32399 (1-850 245 3029, www.dep.state.fl.us).* **Open** 8am-5pm Mon-Fri.
Contact the Department to request a free copy of the comprehensive *Guide to Florida State Parks*.

## GETTING AROUND

Further transport information is given in individual **Escapes & Excursions** chapters.

## By air

It's easiest to book any internal US flights through an agent in your home country, or as part of your international ticket. However, this is not always the cheapest way. Reduced-rate return fares are usually cheapest on weekdays, and often require seven-day advance booking and a Saturday stopover. Flights from Fort Lauderdale are often cheaper than from Miami.

Airlines running regular flights from Miami to various points in Florida include **American Eagle** (American Airlines' regional affiliate; 1-800 433 7300, www.aa.com), **Continental** (1-800 525 0280, www.continental.com), **Delta** (1-800 221 1212, www.delta.com), **United** (1-800 241 6522, www.united.com) and **US Airways** (1-800 428 4322, www.usairways.com).

## By bus

### Greyhound

*4111 NW 27th Street, at 41st Avenue, near Miami International Airport (1-800 229 9424, 1-305 871 1810, www.greyhound.com). Bus 7, 37, 42, J.* **Open** *Ticketing office* 24hrs daily.
**Credit** AmEx, Disc, MC, V.
The national long-distance bus service. Travel is cheaper Monday to Thursday, and buying a return ticket at the time of departure will save 5-15%.

## By car

For driving tips and car rental companies, *see p261*. The best Florida maps for drivers are Triple A or Rand McNally, and the official Florida Transportation Map. For the Keys, we recommend UniversalMAP.

### American Automobile Association (AAA/Triple A)

*1-800 596 2228, www.aaa.com.* **Open** 24hrs daily.
*Florida Division: 1000 AAA Drive, Member Services Department 68, Heathrow, FL 32746 (1-407 444 4240).* **Open** 8.30am-5.30pm Mon-Fri.
*South Miami office: 6643 S Dixie Highway, at SW 67th Avenue, Miami 33143 (1-305 661 6131). Bus 73, 500/Metrorail Dadeland North.* **Open** 9am-6pm Mon-Fri.
Triple A is the US road emergency and information company. It provides excellent – and free – maps, guidebooks, specific travel routes (TripTiks) and towing services to its members and to members of affiliated organisations (such as the British AA).

## By train

### Amtrak

*1-800 872 7245, www.amtrak.com.* *Station: 8303 NW 37th Avenue, at NW 79th Street, near Hialeah (1-305 835 1221). Bus 32, 79, L/Metrorail Tri-Rail.*
Long-distance train services. You can travel from New York to points on the east coast of Florida, including Miami. The connecting bus service (available only to rail passengers) provides a service to Orlando, Tampa, Key West, West Palm Beach and other points. Its bus service between Orlando and Fort Myers can be accessed by any traveller. If you travel by Amtrak, it's worth planning ahead, since return tickets are cheaper than two one-ways.

### Tri-Rail

*1-800 874 7245, www.tri-rail.com.*
A commuter rail line that runs the 70-plus miles between Miami and Fort Lauderdale and the Palm Beaches. It links with Miami's rapid transit system Metrorail and various Miami bus routes (for further details of city public transport, *see pp260-261*). Fares vary by zones. Flat-fare, all-day tickets that provide unlimited travel are available on weekends for $5 (adults) or $2.50 (reductions).

## By boat

The **Port of Miami** (1-305 371 7678) is one of the world's busiest passenger and freight ports, with millions of cruise-ship passengers passing through each year. Seven ultra-modern cruise terminals provide an easy check-in and boarding process.

You can book cruises to destinations as diverse as Mexico, Puerto Rico, France, Haiti, St Thomas, Jamaica, Key West, Colombia, the Panama Canal and most of the Caribbean islands. Try **Carnival Cruise Lines** (1-800 764 7419), **Norwegian Cruise Line** (1-866 234 7350) or **Royal Caribbean Cruise Lines** (1-866 562 7625).

# Fort Lauderdale & Palm Beach

*It's not all glitz on the Gold Coast.*

Anyone in search of a slice of 'old Florida' should head for the Gold Coast, a stretch of sand-fringed real estate running north from Miami that includes Palm Beach, Boca Raton and Delray Beach. Affordable, decidedly non-chic 1950s beachfront hotels still exist along the old Dixie Highway, offering top-notch service and a relaxed atmosphere. The further north you travel, the less urban clutter you'll find. Of course, the population here is also more homogeneous (which is to say, white) and less interesting for it, made up in large part by communities of spring-stepped retirees.

Palm Beach remains the preserve of the super-rich, while Fort Lauderdale has become the favoured destination for travellers in search of well-groomed beaches, golfing greens and shops.

## HALLANDALE, HOLLYWOOD & DANIA

Skip **Hallandale**, a condo-land for retirees, unless you fancy playing the horses at **Gulfstream Park**, a top thoroughbred horse track (*see p198*). The park markets itself as a family attraction, with activities for the kids. If you prefer old-fashioned pari-mutuels, **Mardi Gras Casino** (*see p197*) has dog racing from December to May, plus more than 70,000 square feet of gaming action, including poker tables and 1,300 slot machines.

Hollywood's main draw is **Hollywood Beach**, a quirky destination beloved by French Canadian snowbirds (winter residents). The **Broadwalk**, a two-and-a-half-mile beach promenade, is home to more than 25 hotels, dozens of restaurants and shops, three public parks and a regular schedule of free outdoor concerts at the Hollywood Beach Theatre.

Adding to the area's growing appeal is the **Seminole Hard Rock Hotel and Casino** (*see p208*), an all-in-one entertainment hub offering accommodation, dining, shopping, slot machines and gaming tables. The Hard Rock also lives up to its legendary name, attracting top-notch musical talents such as Eric Clapton.

Not far from the urban hubbub is the **Anne Kolb Nature Center** (*see below*), a mangrove estuary inhabited by wading birds, which you can explore on foot or by boat.

Quiet **Dania Beach**'s claim to fame is its antiques shops, which line several blocks of US 1 and Dania Beach Boulevard. There's also the dubious appeal of jai-alai (a variety of Basque pelota), reputedly the fastest game in the world. Games are held at **Dania Jai-Alai** (*see p198*). The city's beaches are clean and accessible, with a long fishing pier.

Dania's additional attractions include the **International Game Fish Association Museum** (*see p208*), which houses galleries, virtual reality fishing and a marina. Next door is **Bass Pro Shops Outdoor World** (*see p208*), a superstore for outdoorsy types.

Across the interstate is **Boomers** (*see p208*), with go-karts, bumper boats, batting cages, mini golf and the Flame Thrower, an upside-down tandem amusement park ride.

### Anne Kolb Nature Center

*West Lake Park, 751 Sheridan Street, Hollywood (1-954 357 6161, www.broward.org/parks).* **Open** 9am-5pm daily. **Admission** $1.50; free under-5s. **No credit cards.**

**Fort Lauderdale Beach**.

**Bass Pro Shops Outdoor World**
*220 Gulf Stream Way, Dania Beach (1-954 929 7710, www.basspro.com)*. **Open** 9am-10pm Mon-Sat; 10am-7pm Sun. **Credit** AmEx, Disc, MC, V.

**Boomers**
*1700 NW 1st Street, Dania Beach (1-954 921 1411, www.boomersparks.com)*. **Open** noon-10pm Mon-Thur; noon-1am Fri; 11am-1am Sat; 11am-10pm Sun. **Rides** Flame Thrower $6; other rides vary. **Credit** MC, V.

**International Game Fish Association Museum**
*300 Gulf Stream Way, Dania Beach (1-954 922 4212, www.igfa.org/museum)*. **Open** 10am-6pm Mon-Sat; noon-6pm Sun. **Admission** $10; $5 reductions; free under-2s. **Credit** MC, V.

## Where to eat & drink

For table dancing, plus good Greek food, head for **Taverna Opa**, which is on the Intracoastal Waterway. The laid-back **Le Tub Saloon**, also on the water, is popular with locals for decent seafood, gumbo and chilli. The **Rustic Inn** is renowned for serving garlic crabs on newspaper-covered tables, while **Jaxson's Ice Cream Parlour** is quintessential Americana, serving up gaudy ice-cream concoctions, burgers, hot dogs and steaks.

**Jaxson's Ice Cream Parlour**
*128 S Federal Highway, Dania (1-954 923 4445, www.jaxsonsicecream.com)*. **Open** 11.30am-11pm Mon-Thur; 11.30am-midnight Fri, Sat; noon-11pm Sun. **Main courses** $10-$14. **Credit** AmEx, Disc, MC, V.

**Rustic Inn**
*4331 Ravenswood Road (Anglers Avenue), Dania Beach (1-954 584 1637, www.rusticinn. com)*. **Open** 11.30am-10.45pm Mon-Sat; noon-

9.45pm Sun. **Main courses** $16-$33. **Credit** AmEx, Disc, MC, V.

**Taverna Opa**
*410 N Ocean Drive, at Hollywood Boulevard, Hollywood Beach (1-954 929 4010, www.taverna oparestaurant.com)*. **Open** 4pm-midnight Mon-Thur, Sun; 4pm-1am Fri, Sat. **Main courses** $13-$33. **Credit** AmEx, Disc, MC, V.

**Le Tub Saloon**
*1100 N Ocean Drive, Hollywood Beach (1-954 921 9425, www.theletub.com)*. **Open** 11am-1am Mon-Thur; noon-2am Fri-Sun. **Main courses** $7-$25. **Credit** MC, V.

## Where to stay

**Seminole Hard Rock Hotel & Casino**
*1 Seminole Way, Hollywood (1-866 502 7529, www.seminolehardrockhollywood.com)*. **Rates** $199-$599 double. **Credit** AmEx, Disc, MC, V.
Recently renovated, the Hard Rock invites guests to live like rock stars in one of its 500 spacious rooms and suites. There's plenty of on-site gambling, dining and entertainment, too, which means you'll never have to leave the joint.

**Westin Diplomat Hotel**
*3555 S Ocean Drive, Hollywood (1-954 602 6000, www.diplomatresort.com)*. **Rates** $229-$699 double. **Credit** AmEx, Disc, MC, V.
A behemoth that dominates the beach, the Diplomat is a sprawling, luxurious resort.

## FORT LAUDERDALE

Neat, clean and well-tended, Fort Lauderdale has shed its *Beach Blanket Bingo* image. Strict public ordinances have pushed the college kids and their bacchanalian spring break parties up north to Daytona and Panama City Beach or south to Cancún. In their absence,

Fort Lauderdale has become an upscale spot for dining, nightlife and culture (it's also a gay hotspot; *see p175* **Join the Party**).

Dubbed the 'Venice of America', it has 300 miles of waterways, from the New River in the centre to yacht-lined canals. And you can actually tour the city by water. One option is the **Water Taxi** (1-954 467 6677, www.watertaxi.com), which scoots along the Intracoastal Waterway and the New River, serving both as public transport and tour vessel. There are 15 stops, and an all-day, unlimited pass costs $20 ($13 under-12s; free under-fives). Sightseeing cruises are also offered on two Mississippi-style paddle wheelers: the **JungleQueen Riverboat**, operating from the Bahia Mar Yacht Center (801 Seabreeze Boulevard, 1-954 462 5596, www.junglequeen. com), and the **Carrie B**, which sails from the New River Docks at 444 N New River Drive East (1-954 768 9920, www.carriebcruises.com). Sightseeing trips on the *JungleQueen* are $20, or $23 on the *Carrie B*; evening cruises with dinner and a show on the *JungleQueen* are $43 per person.

**Fort Lauderdale Beach** is a wide and handsome sandy strip with a brick promenade for skaters, joggers and cyclists. Postcard-perfect, it comes complete with bronzed lifeguards and coconut palms. The nearby **Elbo Room** (*see right*), the bar made famous in the 1960s teen-lust classic *Where the Boys Are*, is a lone remnant of formerly giddy times. Today's more sedate beachgoers head to **Beach Place**, a shopping, dining and entertainment emporium located on A1A just north of the foot traffic-heavy Las Olas Boulevard. Other attractions include the **International Swimming Hall of Fame** (*see right*), with its two 50-metre pools and a theatre that screens the films of Esther Williams and Johnny Weissmuller, and **Bonnet House Museum & Gardens** (*see right*), a 35-acre tropical oasis and historical house.

Another big patch of green (linked to the beach via a tunnel) is the **Hugh Taylor Birch State Park** (*see below*), with nature trails, wildlife watching and canoe rentals.

It's worth strolling the **Riverwalk** (www.goriverwalk.com), a mile-long waterside promenade that leads to the Riverwalk Arts and Entertainment District, home to the **Fort Lauderdale History Center** (*see below*), as well as the **Museum of Art**, **Stranahan House**, the city's oldest structure (1901), and the interactive **Museum of Discovery & Science**, with an IMAX theatre (for all, *see p210*). There's also the excellent **Broward Center of Performing Arts** (*see p188*).

## Bonnet House Museum & Gardens
*900 N Birch Road (1-954 563 5393, www.bonnethouse.org).* **Open** 10am-4pm Tue-Sat; 11am-4pm Sun. **Admission** $20; free under-6s. **Credit** AmEx, Disc, MC, V.

## Elbo Room
*241 S Atlantic Boulevard (1-954 463 4615, www.elboroom.com).* **Open** 10am-2am Mon-Thur; 10am-3am Fri, Sat; 10am 2am Sun. **Credit** AmEx, Disc, MC, V.

## Fort Lauderdale History Center
*219 SW 2nd Avenue (1-954 463 4431, www.fortlauderdalehistorycenter.org).* **Open** noon-4pm Tue-Sun. **Admission** $10; free under-6s. **Credit** AmEx, MC, V.

## Hugh Taylor Birch State Park
*3109 E Sunrise Boulevard, at A1A (1-954 564 4521, www.floridastateparks.org/hughtaylorbirch).* **Open** 8am-sunset daily. **Admission** $6/car. **No credit cards.**

## International Swimming Hall of Fame
*1 Hall of Fame Drive (1-954 462 6536, www.ishof.org).* **Open** 9am-5pm daily. **Admission** $8. **Credit** AmEx, MC, V.

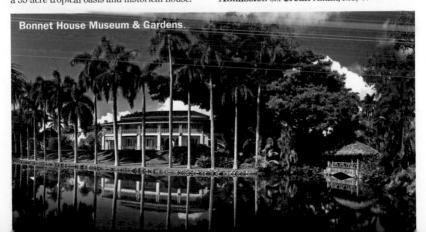

Bonnet House Museum & Gardens.

## Museum of Art

*1 E Las Olas Boulevard (1-954 525 5500, www.moafl.org)*. **Open** 10am-5pm Mon-Wed, Fri, Sat; 10am-7pm Thur; noon-5pm Sun. **Admission** $25-$30; free under-6s. **Credit** AmEx, Disc, MC, V.

## Museum of Discovery & Science

*401 SW 2nd Street (1-954 467 6637, www. mods.org)*. **Open** 10am-5pm Mon-Sat; noon-6pm Sun. **Admission** $14; $12-$13 reductions. **Credit** AmEx, MC, V.

## Stranahan House

*335 SE 6th Avenue (1-954 524 4736, www. stranahanhouse.org)*. **Open** 10am-4pm daily.

**Admission** $12; $7-$11 reductions. **No credit cards**.

## Where to eat & drink

The fresh seafood is a standout at the **Blue Moon Fish Company** (4405 W Tradewinds Avenue, 1-954 765 1950, www.bluemoonfishco.com, main courses $16-$37). As the name suggests, **Canyon** (1818 E Sunrise Boulevard, 1-954 765 1950, www.canyonfl.com, main courses $26-$38) does glorious Southwestern grub, but be prepared to queue. It may be in a mall, but Tuscan **Casa D'Angelo** (Sunrise Square Plaza, 1201 N

# Better in the Bahamas?

*Set sail on a day trip to paradise.*

Back in the 1980s, a catchy advertising jingle claimed it was 'better in the Bahamas'. But is it true? Now Florida tourists can find out for themselves on a day cruise to the islands, with Spanish cruise line Balèaria Bahamas Express making jaunts from Port Everglades in Fort Lauderdale to Freeport on Grand Bahama Island. The ship sails at 9am, docks in the Bahamas at noon, and sets off for Florida again at 6pm. Schedules change on a monthly basis (from daily to three times per week) and the fleet consists of two ships. The no-frills *Maverick* is pretty much just seating and a café, but the *Pinar del Río*, which can take approximately 500

passengers, has more to offer in the way of distractions, including first-class accommodation, café-bar, duty-free gift shop and on-board slot machines.

During the outward crossing, head up to the roof deck. With the Caribbean to the south and Bermuda to the north, you can watch the Bahamas sashay into view as the journey progresses. But just when you're starting to enjoy the peace, the industrial bleakness of Freeport harbour jolts you back to reality. Tourists are greeted with the sounds of Harry Belafonte – Day-O! – before being herded off in one of three directions: shops, casinos or beach. Choose the beach.

On the way, take in the island: distinguished by forests of Australian pine, it's less developed than Florida, but strip malls are creeping in. Most visitors head for Port Lucaya for a swim. Once you see the sugary sand, your cruise is made: the beaches alone are worth the price of the cruise. The water's startling turquoise hues are produced by a combination of shallow seas, fine white sand and the way the light is reflected. A day at the beach is over all too quickly and it's back on board, but there's more to come: the sunset on the roof deck. As the sun dips below the horizon, it's like a love scene from *Titanic*. The perfect end to an international day trip.

*Prices start at $50 for a one-way ticket (first-class accommodation is twice that). Longer stays are available. Balèaria also offers day trips between Miami and Bimini. Call 1-866 699 6988 or visit www.ferry express.com for information and bookings.*

Federal Highway, 1-954 564 1234, www.casa-d-angelo.com, closed lunch, main courses $14-$42) is the best Italian in town. Romantic **Casablanca Café** (3049 Alhambra Street, 1-954 764 3500, main courses $18-$27) serves a medley of Mediterranean fare in a Moroccan-style setting, while the slick **Johnny V's** (625 E Las Olas Boulevard, 1-954 761 7920, www.johnnyvlasolas.com, main courses $25-$39) does Floribbean fusion cuisine. Dinner at kitsch **Mai Kai** (3599 N Federal Highway, 1-954 563 3272, www.maikai.com, main courses $16-$49) is not gourmet, but it comes with a Polynesian revue. **Shula's on the Beach** (321 N Fort Lauderdale Beach Boulevard, 1-954 355 4000, www.donshula.com, main courses $22-$78), located within the Westin Beach Resort, is a shrine to former Miami Dolphins coach Don Shula, where Angus steaks come with ocean views. Himmarshee Village, in Downtown's Arts & Entertainment District, also has plenty of lively bars and restaurants.

## Where to stay

### Hyatt Regency Pier Sixty-Six
2301 SE 17th Street Causeway (1-954 525 6666, www.pier66.com). Rates $139-$400 double. **Credit** AmEx, MC, V.
This beachfront giant is among the more popular – and plush – chain hotels.

### Lago Mar Resort & Club
*1700 S Ocean Lane (1-954 523 6511, www.lagomar.com).* **Rates** $199-$600 double. **Credit** AmEx, DC, Disc, MC, V.
This lavish resort boasts its very own private beach, a huge spa and an upscale Italian restaurant.

### Pillars Hotel
*111 N Birch Road (1-954 467 9639, www.pillarshotel.com).* **Rates** $179-$549 double. **Credit** AmEx, DC, Disc, MC, V.
Small and luxurious, the Pillars Hotel is also distinguished by its waterway location and attractive colonial/plantation decor.

### Riverside Hotel
*620 E Las Olas Boulevard (1-954 467 0671, www.riversidehotel.com).* **Rates** $139-$449 double. **Credit** AmEx, DC, Disc, MC, V.
On chichi Las Olas Boulevard, this smart 1930s hotel is good for shopping and restaurants.

## Resources

Pick up a copy of the free *New Times*, or check out the *Sun-Sentinel* for dining and entertainment listings. Online, visit www.browardpalmbeach.com or www.sun-sentinel.com/citylink.

**Morikami Museum & Japanese Gardens.**

### Greater Fort Lauderdale Convention & Visitors Bureau
*Suite 200, 100 E Broward Boulevard (1-954 765 4466, www.sunny.org).* **Open** times vary.

## BOCA RATON & DELRAY BEACH

The largest county south-east of the Mississippi River, Palm Beach County encompasses a national wildlife refuge and the northern reaches of the Everglades, as well as part of Lake Okeechobee, the second-largest freshwater lake in the country. But the coast has always attracted visitors, from Spanish explorers in the 1500s to today's retirees and sun-seekers.

The southernmost city is **Boca Raton**, a sterile-looking enclave of upmarket gated communities. There is history here, visible in the exquisite **Boca Raton Resort & Club** (*see p212*). Designed by visionary Addison Mizner in 1926, at the time the fanciful property was the most expensive hotel ever built, furnished with Mizner's private collection of rare antiques. The land boom stifled Mizner's grand plans for Boca Raton, but his architectural style lives on: Boca's shopping and cultural district, **Mizner Park** (built in 1991), is home to the **Boca Raton Museum of Art** (*see p213*) plus more than 50 upscale shops and restaurants.

If you want to stop between Fort Lauderdale and Palm Beach, do so at **Delray Beach**, an intimate town with wide beaches, trolley tours and an impressive cultural scene. A one-mile walking trail connects the museums, galleries and historic sites. Local treasures include **Sundy House**, a splendid old inn with lush gardens and an outstanding restaurant (*see p212*); and **Morikami Museum & Japanese Gardens** (*see p212*), a tribute to the Japanese agricultural workers who came to Florida 100 years ago; it has lovely lakes, gardens and walking trails.

### Boca Raton Museum of Art
*Mizner Park, 501 Plaza Real, Boca Raton (1-561 392 2500, www.bocamuseum.org).* **Open** 10am-5pm Tue, Thur, Fri; 10am-9pm Wed; noon-5pm Sat, Sun. **Admission** $8; free under-12s. **Credit** AmEx, Disc, MC, V.

### Morikami Museum & Japanese Gardens
*4000 Morikami Park Road, Delray Beach (1-561 495 0233, www.morikami.org).* **Open** 10am-5pm Tue-Sun. **Admission** $10; $6 reductions. **Credit** AmEx, Disc, MC, V.

## Where to eat & drink

### Blue Anchor Pub
*804 E Atlantic Avenue, Delray Beach (1-561 272 7272, www.theblueanchor.com).* **Open** 11.30am-2am daily. **Main courses** $10-$24. **Credit** AmEx, DC, Disc, MC, V.
The owners, former editors of the *Daily Mirror*, were regulars at the old Blue Anchor on London's Chancery Lane. When the pub was demolished, they bought its façade and had it shipped over here.

### Sundy House Restaurant
*106 S Swinton Avenue, Delray Beach (1-877 439 9601, www.sundyhouse.com).* **Open** 11.30am-2pm, 6-9pm Tue-Sat; 10.30am-2pm, 6-9pm Sun. **Main courses** $24-$36. **Credit** AmEx, Disc, MC, V.
Get an outside table for splendid garden views.

## Where to stay

### Boca Raton Resort & Club
*501 E Camino Real, Boca Raton (1-888 543 1277, www.bocaresort.com).* **Rates** $199-$599 double. **Credit** AmEx, DC, Disc, MC, V.

### Crane's Beach House
*82 Gleason Street, Delray Beach (1-561 278 1700, www.cranesbeachhouse.com).* **Rates** $189-$499 double. **Credit** AmEx, MC, V.
A small and characterful inn, Crane's Beach House is decked out in tropical hues, with verdant gardens, two saltwater pools (each with a waterfall) and a fantastically fun tiki bar.

### Sundy House
*106 S Swinton Avenue, Delray Beach (1-561 272 5678, www.sundyhouse.com).* **Rates** $169-$399 double. **Credit** AmEx, Disc, MC, V.

## Resources

### Greater Delray Beach Chamber of Commerce
*64A SE 5th Avenue, Delray Beach (1-561 278 0424, www.delraybeach.com).* **Open** 8am-5pm Mon-Fri.

## PALM BEACH & WEST PALM BEACH

Unlike most of Florida, Palm Beach does little to encourage the average tourist. The only visitors this island town wants are those who would rather pick up a bauble from Tiffany's than a seashell from the beach. Palm Beach is still the winter playground of corporate heirs, obscure royalty and American bluebloods; the rest of the world must content itself with admiring the exteriors of its multi-million-dollar residences and doing a little window-shopping. Public beaches are rare; the few that do exist might as well be private, the parking is so bad. Tip: lodge elsewhere and make Palm Beach a day trip.

The town's most interesting attraction is the **Henry Morrison Flagler Museum** (*see p213*). Housed in Whitehall, the former luxury home of the railway magnate, it tells

CityPlace.

the fascinating story of Palm Beach's beginnings and explains how this oil tycoon was the catalyst for Florida's development. The **Breakers**, Flagler's sublime oceanfront hotel, rises above the palms and serves as charity ball central. Even if you're not staying here, make sure you take a stroll through the Florentine lobby, splurge on afternoon tea or try Sunday brunch.

Aptly named **Worth Avenue** is the town's main shopping street, and it is worth a look if only to get an eyeful of the Mediterranean architecture, tranquil courtyards and crassly displayed wealth.

Mansion-spotting is pretty tricky: most of the places are surrounded by high stucco walls covered with vegetation and guarded by retired CIA agents. Most impressive is **Mar-a-Lago** (1100 Ocean Boulevard, www.maralagoclub), the ultra-exclusive private club and part-time home to Donald and Melania Trump.

Henry Flagler 'persuaded' the black labourers who built Palm Beach to leave by offering them free land on the mainland; to make sure they did so, he torched their houses on the island. Thus, the town of **West Palm Beach** was born. It has since eclipsed its affluent neighbour in population and diversity and serves as the county seat.

Downtown's main **Clematis Street** begins at the waterfront with a public library and a fun fountain, and continues westwards with an array of theatres, bistros, clubs and boutiques. Nearby is **CityPlace** (*see below*), one of the country's biggest shopping/dining/residential conglomerations, with fountains and cobbled streets. A free trolley connects CityPlace and Clematis. Cultural attractions include the highly regarded **Norton Museum of Art** (*see below*), with its 19th- and 20th-century art and photography collections, including pieces by Miró, Picasso and Brancusi.

### CityPlace

*700 Rosemary Avenue, at Okeechobee Boulevard, West Palm Beach (1-561 366 1000, www.city place.com).* **Open** 10am-10pm Mon-Sat; noon-6pm Sun.

### Henry Morrison Flagler Museum

*1 Whitehall Way, Palm Beach (1-561 655 2833, www.flagler.org).* **Open** 10am-5pm Tue-Sat; noon-5pm Sun. **Admission** $18; $3-$10 reductions. **Credit** AmEx, DC, MC, V.

### Norton Museum of Art

*1451 S Olive Avenue, West Palm Beach (1-561 832 5196, www.norton.org).* **Open** 10am-5pm Tue, Wed, Fri, Sat; 10am-9pm Thur; 11am-5pm Sun. **Admission** $12; $5 reductions; free under-12s. **Credit** AmEx, DC, Disc, MC, V.

## Where to stay

### Breakers

*1 S County Road, Palm Beach (1-561 655 6611, www.thebreakers.com).* **Rates** $299-$899 double. **Credit** AmEx, DC, MC, V.

If you've got the bucks, this palatial hotel, set on 140 acres overlooking the sea, is the place to spend them.

## Resources

### Palm Beach Chamber of Commerce

*Suite 106, 400 Royal Palm Way, Palm Beach (1-561 655 3282, www.palmbeachchamber.com).* **Open** 8.30am-5pm Mon-Fri.

### Palm Beach County Convention & Visitors Bureau

*Suite 800, 1555 Palm Beach Lakes Boulevard, West Palm Beach (1-800 554 7256, www.palm beachfl.com).* **Open** 8.30am-5.30pm Mon-Fri.

## GETTING THERE & AROUND

### By car

From Miami, head north on I-95, the main freeway, or US 1 (Federal Highway). For Hollywood, exit at Hollywood Boulevard east. For Fort Lauderdale (about 30mins from Miami), from I-95 take I-595 east and follow signs for 'Fort Lauderdale US 1 North'; once on US 1, turn right on 17th Street. This leads to the beach and major hotels. From Fort Lauderdale to Delray Beach, the fastest route is via I-95; the most scenic is via A1A (Ocean Drive). Exit at Atlantic Avenue east (take care not to confuse this with the Atlantic Avenue exit in Pompano Beach). For both West Palm Beach and Palm Beach (a 90min drive from Miami), exit I-95 at Okeechobee Boulevard east.

### By train

**Tri-Rail** (1-800 874 7245, www.tri-rail.com) operates services between Miami and the Gold Coast. From Miami International Airport, trains depart daily (usually twice an hour) to points north, including Hollywood, Fort Lauderdale (40mins) and Palm Beach (2hrs). Miami–Fort Lauderdale is about $10; to get from Fort Lauderdale to Palm Beach costs $5.65.

### By bus

**Greyhound** (1-800 231 2222, www.greyhound. com) runs buses daily from its Miami terminal (4111 NW 27th Street, near Miami International Airport) to Fort Lauderdale (515 NE 3rd Street); round-trip fare is $14 and the journey takes about an hour. From Fort Lauderdale, buses run daily to West Palm Beach for a round-trip fare of about $24.

**ESCAPES & EXCURSIONS**

# The Everglades

*Wet and wild.*

Commonly and inaccurately thought of as swamp, the Everglades is actually more of a shallow, bankless river; a 'river of grass', as Florida environmentalist Marjory Stoneman Douglas termed it in her famous 1947 book of the same name. The Everglades occupies the southernmost 80 miles of the state of Florida, of which the Everglades National Park at the tip, on which this chapter focuses, is just a part. The natural course of the river flows the 100 miles from Lake Okeechobee to Florida Bay at a rate of 100 feet per day, with the water's depth varying from as much as three feet to as little as three inches.

The national park is the only one in the US to be recognised by the United Nations as both an International Biosphere Reserve and World Heritage Site, and is home to plant and animal life found both in the West Indian tropics and in more temperate northern zones. Nowhere is the idea of south Florida as a meeting point of north and south more true than here.

### FLORA AND FAUNA

'River of grass' is actually far too limiting a definition for the variety of plant life within the Everglades: saw palmetto (commonly called sawgrass) may be dominant, but there are more than 1,000 kinds of seed-bearing plants and 120 types of trees. Mangrove and various hardwood tree hammocks (islands) dot the expanses of sawgrass, and, during the summer, flowering plants add splashes of colour to the green canvas.

The park also teems with animal life. Deer roam, and the area is the only place in the world where alligators and crocodiles co-habit. The alligators (flat nose, raised nostrils) are far more abundant, with the more aggressive crocodiles (tapered snout, visible teeth) keeping to the saltier waters nearer the coast. During a walk along one of the park's trails, expect to see the aforementioned reptiles (don't get too close and definitely don't feed them), as well as snakes (some poisonous), turtles and frogs, along with less scary stuff such as rabbits, butterflies and some of the 350 species of birds that reside in the park or make it a migratory rest stop.

As full of wildlife as the Everglades may seem, it is, in fact, a troubled sanctuary of last resort for many species. The number of wading birds in the southern area has plummeted in the last half-century, as has its population of Florida panthers. Similarly, although the Everglades has never had a large population of black bears, they're more reluctant than ever to show themselves to visitors.

Although it's the country's second-largest national park, the Everglades (founded in 1947) is not as obviously stunning as its mountainous western cousins. As such, its beauty can't be appreciated from the windows of a speeding car. Even exploring the area on a noisy airboat climaxes when the driver turns off the engine and leaves you floating silently in the grass.

### PLANNING YOUR TRIP

In terms of access, the park can be divided into two main areas: the northern section, reached via the Tamiami Trail (aka SW 8th Street, aka US 41) and accessed by Shark Valley and Everglades City; and the southern section, accessed via Homestead and Florida City on US 1. Of the two access points, Shark Valley is the closer to central Miami; it's a journey of about 70 to 90 minutes. Getting down to the Ernest F Coe Visitors' Center, which marks the entrance to the southern part of the national park, can take closer to two hours. Unfortunately, there's no public transport into either area; renting a car is the only option.

It's advisable to bring sunscreen, a hat and sunglasses. During the wet season – June to October – mosquito repellent is absolutely essential, and it's not a bad idea in the drier months too. Mosquitoes are only half the problem; dawn and dusk in summer bring out the 'no-see-ums', tiny, near-invisible insects with a ferocious bite. The wet season also brings heavy rains that raise the water levels causing wildlife to disperse, with the result that animal sightings are less frequent. Parts of the Everglades can also flood, including the Shark Valley Trail.

Regardless of which access point you use, entrance to the park costs $10 per vehicle for a seven-day pass, or $25 for a year's access.

Coopertown Airboat Rides.

# Northern Access

Shark Valley, 25 miles west of the Florida Turnpike (SR 821), is the most accessible part of the Everglades from Miami and makes for a perfect day or half-day outing. The **Tamiami Trail** (US 41), which leads here, is the old, two-lane road across the southern part of the state, along the park's northern boundary. It's named after its end points, Tampa and Miami. Recent plans have called for the park's boundaries to be stretched to protect against encroaching development. To accomplish this would involve the government buying the tourist businesses that line the edge of the park, most of which are relics of a simpler, albeit tackier, era.

Beyond Shark Valley, the Tamiami Trail continues west, heading for the Gulf Coast. Before then, turn south on SR 29 for Everglades City and the Gulf Coast Visitors' Center (about a two-and-a-half-hour drive from Miami).

Airboat operators, tours of **Miccosukee Indian Village** (*see below*) and alligator wrestling shows along the Tamiami Trail are pleasantly worn at the edges, though generally lacklustre. It's only marginally impressive to watch a grown man wrestle a 'gator that looks more interested in sleeping; and, in truth, it's far less representative of traditional Indian culture than it is of Florida's voracious tourist industry.

At tiny **Coopertown**, airboat tours have been running for close to 60 years. The guides are knowledgeable, and this may be the best of several places to take a ride, if only so you can have a beer before or after in the **Coopertown Restaurant** (*see below*), where the walls are covered with decades' worth of Everglades memorabilia. Given the rarity of tourists lingering here, it's a good idea to indulge in only a quick snack with that beer.

### Coopertown Airboat Rides/Restaurant
*Tamiami Trail/US 41, 11 miles west of Turnpike, Miami (1-305 226 6048, www.coopertown airboats.com). Open 8am-6pm daily.* **Main courses** $9-$22. **Credit** AmEx, DC, MC, V.
Airboats are flat-bottomed skiffs powered by a great big fan at the back. They're loud and environmentally dubious, but a heap of fun. Rides depart every 20 minutes throughout the day, last around 40 minutes and cost $22 per person or $11 for children under 12. Under-sevens go for free.

### Miccosukee Indian Village
*500 SW 177th Avenue, off the Tamiami Trail/US 41, Miami (1-305 552 8365, www.miccosukeetribe.com).* **Open** *Museum* 9am-4pm daily. *Restaurant* 8am-5pm daily. **Admission** *Museum* $10; $6 reductions; free under-6s. **Credit** (restaurant only) AmEx, MC, V.

Shark Valley Tram Tours.

A bridge between old and new lifestyles, the Village presents Miccosukee arts and crafts (patchwork sewing, doll making, basket weaving), a museum of Indian heritage, airboat tours, alligator wrestling and an ultra-modern casino.

## SHARK VALLEY

Shark Valley features a 15-mile paved road leading to an observation tower overlooking the heart of the Everglades. You can walk or cycle it (bikes can be rented at the park entrance for $8.50 per hour; the last rental is at 4pm). Alternatively, the **Visitors' Center** (*see below*) offers two-hour ranger-guided tram tours, though you might need to book up to three weeks in advance (call 1-305 221 8455 for reservations). There are also briefer trails, including the third-of-a-mile **Bobcat Boardwalk** and the slightly longer **Otter Cave Trail**. Even these walks are likely to bring encounters with the park's inhabitants, including many alligators, which delight in napping on the road with near (if not absolute) indifference to visitors. Remember, though: this isn't Disney World, so keep your wits about you and be careful where you tread.

### Shark Valley Visitors' Center
*36000 SW 8th Street (Tamiami Trail/US 41), Miami (1-305 221 8776, www.nps.gov/ever).* **Open** 9.15am-5.15pm daily. **Tram tours** $20; $12.75-$19 reductions. **No credit cards**.
Tram tours run on the hour (9am-4pm Dec-Apr; 9am, 11am, 2pm, 3pm May-Nov). They last around 90 minutes.

## Where to stay

There is no accommodation and no camping at Shark Valley. The closest accommodation is in Everglades City, which lies about 40 miles further west.

## TO EVERGLADES CITY

Less than ten miles west after Shark Valley on the Tamiami Trail, the road passes through **Big Cypress National Preserve**, its cypresses and pines growing in swampy terrain. Main access is via **Big Cypress Welcome Center** (*see p217*), starting point for a couple of trails and scenic drives. Some 20 miles further along the Tamiami, the tiny town of **Ochope** boasts the smallest post office in the US, little more than seven by eight feet. The 'panther crossing next five miles' sign is worth a snapshot.

South of SR 29 from the Tamiami Trail is **Everglades City**, the gateway to the **Ten Thousand Islands**. This is where the Glades meet the Gulf of Mexico, the coastline fracturing into thousands of islands, many thick with mangroves. The town isn't much to write home about, although it has a remote, quaint feel and a handful of colourful shops aimed at visitors. Outside, of course, Mother Nature's version of reality may not be air-conditioned, but the environment is incredibly lush and rich in wildlife. For information, as well as permits for camping within the park, visit the **Gulf Coast Visitors' Center** (*see p217*), which is three miles south of the Tamiami Trail on SR 29.

Porpoises and some of Florida's remaining 1,200 manatees can be found here, as well as bald eagles. The easiest way to get on the water is with **Everglades National Park Boat Tours** (*see p217*). Ninety-minute tours of the islands start at 9am and leave every half-hour until 4.30pm. Canoes and kayaks can be rented by the hour or day, and overnight camping trips along the Wilderness Waterway trail south to the Flamingo Visitors' Center are also offered.

### Big Cypress Gallery
*52388 Tamiami Trail, Ochopee (1-239 695 2428, www.clydebutcher.com).* **Open** 10am-5pm daily. **Credit** AmEx, MC, V.

Florida's answer to Ansel Adams, Clyde Butcher photographs the state's vanishing wilderness, with poetic and haunting results. Recommended.

### Big Cypress Swamp Welcome Center
*HCR 61, Tamiami Trail/US 41, Miami (1-239 695 4758, www.nps.gov/bicy).* **Open** 9am-4.30pm daily. **Admission** free.

### Everglades National Park Boat Tours
*Gulf Coast Ranger Station, SR 29, Everglades City (within Florida 1-800 445 7724, outside Florida 1-239 695 2591, www.nps.gov/ever).* **Open** 9am-5pm daily. **Rates** *Canoes* $24/day 8.30am-4.30pm; $48 overnight. *Boat tours* $32-$42.50; $16-$21.50 reductions. **Credit** AmEx, MC, V.

### Gulf Coast Visitors' Center
*SR 29, Everglades City (1-239 695 3311, www.nps.gov/ever).* **Open** *Mid Apr-mid Nov* 9am-4.30pm. *Mid Nov-mid Apr* 8am-4.30pm.

## Where to stay

In Everglades City, near the Gulf Coast Visitors' Center, there are a limited number of hotels. Local recreational vehicle (RV) sites permit camping, but they're not designed to make you feel at one with nature. Along the Wilderness Waterway are a number of chickees – covered wooden platforms elevated above the open water – that also offer camping. During the winter, campsites ($16) on the islands and chickees must be reserved in person at the Gulf Coast Visitors' Center (*see above*).

### Captain's Lodge & Villas
*102 E Broadway, Everglades City (1-239 695 4211, www.captains-lodge.com).* **Rates** $60-$170 double. **Credit** Disc, MC, V.
All rooms at this English-owned hotel have private bathrooms. There's also an Olympic-sized pool.

### Ivey House
*107 Camellia Street, Everglades City (1-239 695 3299, www.iveyhouse.com).* **Rates** $89-$289 double. **Credit** MC, V.
This family-run accommodation includes an inn, cottage and lodge. When the weather gets a bit steamy, guests can retreat to the shared pool, complete with waterfall. The owners also run North American Canoe Tours, offering canoe rentals and eco tours.

### Rod & Gun Club Lodge
*200 Riverside Drive, Everglades City (1-239 695 2101, www.evergladesrodandgun.com).* **Rates** $95-$140 double. **No credit cards.**
An erstwhile hunting club, this charming lodge is now a small hotel. It has always attracted an august crowd: past guests have included no fewer than five US presidents and assorted other notables.

# Southern Access
## ERNEST F COE, ROYAL PALM & FLAMINGO VISITORS' CENTERS

The main southern access point to the park is just south-east of Homestead and Florida City off SR 9336 (*see p218* **Getting there**).

Rod & Gun Club Lodge.

It's here that you'll find the main **Ernest F Coe Visitors' Center** (*see below*), which was expanded after the original buildings were damaged by Hurricane Andrew in 1992. It now houses educational exhibits, a small cinema screening orientation films, and a bookshop. No trails start from the Coe, but four miles inside the park is the **Royal Palm Visitors' Center** (*see right*), a sub-centre serving as the head of both the Gumbo Limbo and Anhinga walking trails. The animals and birds here are well known for their ease around humans, and the Royal Palm area presents some of the best wildlife photo opportunities in the whole park.

Though swampy in places, the Everglades here is more wooded than it is in the northern part of the park. At **Long Pine Key** there are picnic areas within the slash pine forests and on the banks of numerous small lakes. Just under 13 miles west of the Coe Center is **Pa-hay-okee Overlook** (Pa-hay-okee is the Indian name for the Everglades; it means 'Big Water'); a quarter-mile boardwalk leads to an observation tower where you can watch some of the park's larger birds, such as vultures and hawks, fly over their domain.

The road dips south from here, first passing some small hammocks of stately mahogany trees, then on to the mangrove forests that signal the approaching shoreline of Florida Bay. Around 38 miles from the park entrance is **Mrazek Pond**, noted as a prime viewing spot for some of the park's more exotic waterfowl.

Beyond Mrazek, at the very end of SR 9336, is **Flamingo**, site of a small (and not terribly good) visitors' centre and a busy marina. This is very much the jewel of the Everglades. The scenery is straight out of Robinson Crusoe, with walking and canoe trails wandering off through dense mangrove forests and along the calm, island-filled waters of Florida Bay. Flamingo is also the gateway for boat trips to campsites up and down the coast, and unspoiled beaches such as Cape Sable. Local concessions rent canoes, kayaks, motorboats and even houseboats, and there are daily sightseeing cruises; *see right*. Fishing is permitted, but check with the ranger's office for licensing requirements and restrictions, which are seasonal and fluctuating.

### Ernest F Coe Visitors' Center
*40001 SR 9336, Homestead (1-305 242 7700, www.nps.gov/ever).* **Open** 9am-5pm daily. **Credit** MC, V.

### Everglades Alligator Farm
*40351 SW 192nd Avenue, off Palm Drive, Homestead (1-305 247 2628, www.everglades. com).* **Open** 9am-6pm daily. **Rates** $23; $15.50 reductions; free under-4s. **Credit** AmEx, DC, MC, V.

Not officially part of the Everglades park, this is a distilled version of the Florida wilderness, complete with 2,000 alligators, airboat rides, local and exotic snakes, and a couple of Florida panthers pacing their cages. An observation deck gives a sweep of the landscape, while an airboat ride gives you a real feel of the Everglades. Alligator wrestling (11am, 2pm, 5pm) and feeding (noon, 3pm) thrill the kids.

### Flamingo Marina
*1 Flamingo Lodge Highway, Flamingo (1-239 695 3101, www.evergladesnationalparkboattours flamingo.com).* **Open** *Rental desk* 7am-5.30pm Mon-Fri; 6am-5.30pm Sat, Sun; last rental 4pm. **Rates** *Canoes* $4-$10/hr; $22-$30/half-day; $32-$40/day. *Kayaks* $11-$15/hr; $35-$45/half-day; $45-$55/day. **Credit** AmEx, DC, MC, V.
A Backcountry Cruise aboard the *Pelican* departs hourly from 9am to 4pm from mid December to mid April (reduced tours the rest of the year; see website for details). The round trip takes two hours and costs $32.25, or $16.25 for children (free under-5s). Note that boat rentals require a $100-$675 credit card deposit.

### Royal Palm Visitors' Center
*40001 SR 9336, Homestead (1-305 242 7700, www.nps.gov/ever).* **Open** 8am-4.15pm daily. **Credit** MC, V.

## Getting there

From Miami, head west on I-395 to SR 821 south, aka the Florida Turnpike. The Turnpike ends in Florida City, where you take the first right through the centre of town and follow the signs to the park entrance on SR 9336; take a left at **Robert is Here** (19200 SW 344th Street, Homestead), a legendary fruit stand.

## Where to stay

Outside the park, there are numerous motels and hotels in Homestead and Florida City, although these are both charmless, highway-side developments. Inside the park, there are managed campsites at Long Pine Key, Flamingo and Chekika; during the winter, though, you must book campsites ($16) in person at the Flamingo Visitors' Center.

### Best Western: Gateway to the Keys
*411 Krome Avenue, Florida City (1-305 246 5100, www.bestwestern.com).* **Rates** $80-$150 double. **Credit** AmEx, DC, MC, V.
Clean, simple rooms. Minimum stay at peak season.

### Days Inn of Homestead
*51 S Homestead Boulevard (US 1), Homestead (1-305 245 1260, www.daysinn.com).* **Rates** $63-$108 double. **Credit** AmEx, DC, MC, V.
A pretty standard Days Inn with 100 rooms.

# The Florida Keys

*Go island-hopping by car.*

Just as any Floridian will tell you that their state
is unlike the rest of the US, inhabitants of the
Keys are proud to claim the Keys are unlike the
rest of Florida. And they're right. This group
of 45 islands south of Miami trails the rounded
mainland coast like a procession of tadpoles.
There's a 113-mile road that links the Keys
(from the Spanish '*cayo*', meaning small island)
to the bottom of the mainland, but that's where
any ties with Miami's frenetic pace end.

The isles, flanked by the Atlantic Ocean to
the south and the Gulf of Mexico to the north, are
shadowed on both sides by the Florida Reef, a vast strip of living coral a few
miles off the coast rich in marine, bird and plant life. Some of the islands are
monstrously overpopulated and lure tourists with vulgar neon and nasty T-shirts.
But the further south west you travel, the more peaceful the backdrop. Many
visitors head straight to Key West, skipping the islands en route. Aside from the
fact that Key West is too touristy for some tastes, it's foolhardy to drive straight
through the rest of the Keys. Some hold worthwhile attractions, others offer
unique natural beauty, while others still are just wonderfully peaceful.

## KEY FACTS

It's not clear when the islands were first
inhabited, but it's believed Native American
Indians made their home here long before white
settlers staked their claim in the 19th century.
At first, farming communities made a living
with fruit orchards, and on Big Pine Key
a thriving shark processing factory was
established, butchering up to 100 of the
creatures a day for their hides and oil-rich
livers. Cubans, who only had to sail 90 miles
from Havana, soon joined the white Americans.
Today, their influence is still felt across the
islands, albeit less so than in Miami.

Tourism struck in the early 1900s, when
Henry Flagler built his ambitious railway
to Key West. Pinned as 'Flagler's Folly', the
mammoth project was originally designed to
open up trade routes. But the 1935 Labor Day
Hurricane put an end to Flagler's 20-year vision
when 40 miles of line were washed out to sea.
Just three years later, though, the first Overseas
Highway (US 1) was completed, linking the
islands to the mainland forever. Parts of
Flagler's Folly became fodder for Hollywood

when they were blown up for scenes in a
number of movies, including the Sylvester
Stallone, er, bomb, *The Specialist*.

Key West is the driest city in Florida and
sunny nearly all year round. Temperatures
during summer can reach the mid-thirties, but
cool winds sweeping across the Atlantic to
the Gulf keep the heat bearable. In December,
meanwhile, temperatures can drop to the low
teens. Throughout the year, afternoon showers
are possible and will soak you to the skin in
minutes, but they rarely last more than a couple
of hours. Mosquitoes are no more of a problem
here than in Miami. A 24-hour hotline (1-305
229 4522) gives a pre-recorded Florida weather
report, as well as tide times.

Bicycle theft excepted, crime is pretty much
non-existent in Key West. Walking around the
place at night is far safer than in many areas
of the United States, but it's advisable to stay
clear of the area around Bahama Village after
dark. The further north-east you travel, the
more alert you should be; in Key Largo you'll
need to revert to savvy traveller mode.

During peak season – January to April,
especially at weekends – the Keys get

John Pennekamp Coral Reef State Park. *See p222.*

extremely busy. Prices rise in hotels, and availability plummets: the Keys, and Key West in particular, are even more lacking in affordable accommodation than Miami. In other words: book early.

## Tourist information

### Florida Keys & Key West Tourist Development Council
*(1-800 352 5397, www.fla-keys.com).*

### Islamorada Visitor's Center
*MM 83.2. Postal address: PO Box 915, Islamorada, FL 33036 (1-800 322 5397,*

*1-305 664 4503, www.islamoradachamber.com).* **Open** 9am-5pm Mon-Fri.

### Key Largo Chamber of Commerce
*MM 106. Postal address: 10600 Overseas Highway, Key Largo, FL 33037 (1-800 822 1088, 1-305 451 4747, www.floridakeys.org).* **Open** 9am-6pm daily.

### Key West Chamber of Commerce
*1st Floor, 510 Greene Street, Key West, FL 33040 (1-305 294 2587, www.keywestchamber.org).* **Open** 8am-6pm Mon-Fri; 9am-6pm Sat, Sun.

### Lower Keys Chamber of Commerce
*MM 31. Postal address: PO Box 430511, Eight Pine Key, FL 33043 (1-800 872 3722, 1-305 872 2411, www.lowerkeyschamber.com).* **Open** 9am-5pm Mon-Fri; 9am-3pm Sat.

### Marathon Chamber of Commerce & Visitors Center
*MM 122. Postal address: 12222 Overseas Highway, Marathon, FL 33050 (1-800 262 7284, 1-305 743 5417, www.floridakeysmarathon.com).* **Open** 9am-5pm daily.

## GETTING THERE

### By car

The simplest way to get to the Keys is to head south on I-95, which leads into US 1 (Overseas Highway), and keep going straight. However, a more pleasant detour can be had by ducking off US 1 a little south of Homestead and taking a left on to **Card Sound Road** (SR 905-A). Taking this route, you avoid most of the tourist

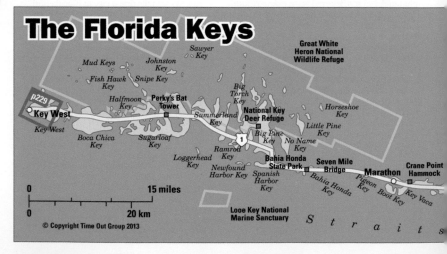

# The Florida Keys

Sawyer Key
Great White Heron National Wildlife Refuge

Mud Keys
Johnston Key

Fish Hawk Key
Snipe Key

Big Torch Key

p229
Halfmoon Key
Perky's Bat Tower

**Key West**
Summerland Key
National Key Deer Refuge
Horseshoe Key

Key West
Boca Chica Key
Sugarloaf Key
Big Pine Key
Little Pine Key

Loggerhead Key
Ramrod Key
No Name Key

Newfound Harbor Key
Bahia Honda State Park
Seven Mile Bridge
Crane Point Hammock

Spanish Harbor Key
Bahia Honda Key
Pigeon Key
**Marathon**
Key Vaca
Boot Key

0 _____ 15 miles

0 _____ 20 km

© Copyright Time Out Group 2013

Looe Key National Marine Sanctuary

S t r a i t s

traffic and get to go over **Card Sound Bridge**, which soars a stunning 65 feet above Barnes Sound. You also get to stop at **Alabama Jack's** (58000 Card Sound Road, 1-305 248 8741), a wonderful bar and eaterie built on a couple of barges and frequented by a great mix of boaters, boozers, bikers, downhome country folk and vaguely boho Keysians. It's only open during the day (11am-7pm daily), with weekend afternoons being particularly lively.

The journey from Miami to Key West takes three to four hours, depending on traffic, and can take even longer on holiday weekends. When you reach the Keys, US 1 becomes a narrow, two-lane highway with a speed limit of 55mph, often less. **Mile Markers** (MM), small green signs beside the road, start in South Miami at MM 126 and end at Key West with MM 0. Addresses along the route are followed by – and in some cases, consist solely of – their mile marker location. These signs are not always easy to spot.

In places, the Florida Keys make for a gloriously scenic drive. The **Seven Mile Bridge** (MM 40-47), in particular, offers the terrifically weird illusion of driving on water as it soars endlessly into the distance. But several other stretches, while not as spectacular, are no less lovely. It's worth buying a detailed Keys map that shows which side roads are worth a detour.

### By bus

The **Keys Shuttle** (1-888 765 9997, 1-305 289 9997, www.keysshuttle.com) is a door-to-door service from Fort Lauderdale and Miami International Airports to Key Largo and other points in the Keys. Call 24 hours ahead to make reservations. **Greyhound** (*see p206*) operates two buses a day to Key West from Miami International Airport and Downtown Miami. There are several scheduled stops along the Keys, but you can flag the bus down at any point. The journey from Miami to Key West takes four to five hours and costs about $40-$60 each way.

### By air

There are a number of daily services to Marathon and Key West airports from Fort Lauderdale and Miami. Prices start at $125 one-way. Like any airline reservation, the earlier you book your flight the better deal you're likely to find. Contact **United** (1-800 854 8331, www.united.com), **US Air** (1-800 428 4322, www.usairways.com) or **American Airlines** (1-800 433 7300, www.aa.com).

# The Upper Keys

Entering the Keys by road is an underwhelming experience. None of the Keys' famed character is at all visible, with US 1 lined on either side by faded T-shirt shops, seen-better-days motels, raggedy billboards and next to no scenery. Don't be too disheartened, though, it does get better.

## KEY LARGO & TAVERNIER

Before it gets better, though, you'll have to pass through **Key Largo**, which couldn't be less like the film if it tried. Where the 1948 flick reeked of glamour, exoticism and intrigue, Key Largo

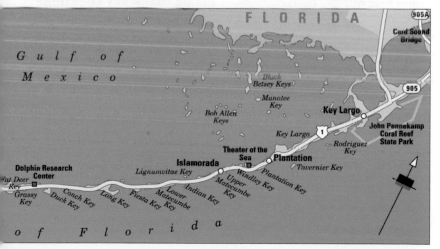

just reeks. It's the longest, largest and easternmost of the Keys islands (the name comes from the Spanish for 'Long Island'), and every other building seems to be a cheap motel, sandal shop or T-shirt retailer. On this evidence, you'd be forgiven for thinking the population of the Keys can be split into two groups: those who sell T-shirts and those who buy them.

That said, tucked away here is one of the Keys' treasures: the mostly underwater **John Pennekamp Coral Reef State Park** (*see below*), which takes in a vast 54,000 acres, stretching into the Atlantic. **Dolphin Cove** (*see below*) and **Dolphins Plus** (MM 99.5, 1-305 451 1993, www.dolphinsplus.com) offer dolphin encounters. Dolphins Plus specialises in therapeutic dolphin swimming.

South of Key Largo, at MM 93, you'll find **Tavernier**, a small town that's notable chiefly for its protected strip of architecturally intriguing wooden buildings dating from the turn of the 19th century – that and the impressive **Florida Keys Wild Bird Center** (*see below*).

### Dolphin Cove

*MM 101.9, Key Largo (1-877 365 2683, 1-305 451 4060, www.dolphinscove.com).* **Open** 9am-6pm daily. **Admission** prices vary. **Credit** AmEx, MC, V.
One of many watery attractions in the Keys, Dolphin Cove is set in a natural lagoon and offers a mixture of entertainment and education, including ecology and kayak tours around the Florida Bay, snorkel trips and, of course, opportunities to swim with the dolphins (be sure to book ahead).

### Florida Keys Wild Bird Center

*MM 93.6, Tavernier (1-305 852 4486, www.fkwbc.org).* **Open** sunrise-sunset daily. **Admission** by donation. **No credit cards**.
The Laura Quinn Wild Bird Sanctuary is a heart-warming, not-for-profit spot whose role in helping to preserve bird life on the Keys shouldn't be under-estimated. It isn't an attraction as such, but the centre does welcome visitors – and donations.

### ★ John Pennekamp Coral Reef State Park

*MM 102.6, Key Largo (1-305 451 6300, www.pennekamppark.com).* **Open** 8am-5pm daily. *Boat tours* 9.15am, 12.15pm, 3.15pm daily. **Admission** $8/vehicle; $2/pedestrians. *Boat tours* $24; $17 reductions. **Credit** Disc, MC, V.
The land-based portion of this vast park is pleasant, encompassing hammock trails and beachy areas, but the main attractions are underwater. This is the most accessible portion of the coral reef that runs the length of the Keys. No array of pictures or brochure flim-flam can prepare you for the beauty

of the reef, which can be seen from the comfort of a glass-bottomed boat. Garish fish and exotic sea creatures glide around, and can be viewed up close by snorkelling or diving (tours also available, along with equipment rental). The much-photographed Christ of the Abyss statue is within the boundaries of the park, submerged in 25ft of water six miles east-north-east of Key Largo's South Cut. *Photo p220.*

## Where to eat

Unfortunately, dining in Key Largo suffers from its proximity to Islamorada (*see p223*), where the eating options are better and more varied. But there is one local institution that draws in people from far and wide: the **Fish House** (MM 102.4, 1-305 451 4665, www.fish house.com) may be done up in kitsch nautical motifs (ropes, nets, fish murals), but the abundant array of local seafood is fresh and beautifully prepared with simple sauces and seasonings. Get there early to avoid the queues. Another local highlight is the home-style cooking at **Mrs Mac's Kitchen** (MM 99.4, 1-305 451 3722, www.mrsmacskitchen.com).

## Where to stay

There are plenty of independent motels in and around Key Largo. Among the chains around these parts are **Holiday Inn** (MM 100, 1-305 451 2121, www.holidayinnkeylargo.com) and **Hampton Inn** (MM 102, 1-305 451 1400, www.hamptoninnkeylargo.com), along with large and pricey **Marriott** (MM 103.8, 1-305 453 0000, www.marriott.com) and **Hilton** (MM 97,

Florida Keys Wild Bird Center.

1-305 852 5553, www.keylargoresort.com)
resorts. There's also camping at the **John
Pennekamp Coral Reef State Park**, with
47 spaces for tents or RVs costing about $30-
$50 per night (for reservations call 1-800 326
3521; for more on the park, *see p222*).

### Bay Harbor Lodge
*97702 Overseas Highway (MM 97.7), Key Largo
(1-305 852 5695, www.bayharborkeylargo).*
**Rates** $95-$205. **Credit** AmEx, MC, V.
One of the more pleasant budget spots on Key Largo,
with a 40ft heated pool.

### Jules' Undersea Lodge
*51 Shoreland Drive (MM 103.2), Key Largo
(1-305 451 2353, www.jul.com).* **Rates** $300-
$400/person. **Credit** AmEx, Disc, MC, V.
A unique and understandably pricey hotel that sleeps
up to six people 30ft underwater. Surprisingly, it has
mod cons such as air conditioning and WiFi, and
other bonuses include unlimited diving. You'll need
to scuba dive your way to the hotel's entrance, of
course; if you're not already certified, the hotel offers
a three-hour course for $95.

### Kona Kai Resort
*97802 Overseas Highway (MM 97.8), Key Largo
(1-800 365 7829, 1-305 852 7200, www.konakai
resort.com).* **Rates** $199-$419 room; $259-$1038
suite. **Credit** AmEx, Disc, MC, V.
An impressive, cosy independent resort with more
amenities and attractions than you'd expect of a 13-
unit operation, including an art gallery and hundreds of species of orchid.

## ISLAMORADA
The name prepares you for a reality that's
possibly more idyllic than the one you'll find.
That said, the group of islands known as
**Islamorada** – Plantation, Windley, Upper
Matecumbe, Shell Lignumvitae, Indian and
Lower Matecumbe Keys, running from MM 90
to MM 74 – does offer the first glimpse of a
quieter Keys existence. Whereas Key Largo is
a dive centre, here it's fishing that dominates –
or, as the T-shirts put it, 'Islamorada, a quaint
little drinking town with a fishing problem'.

Classic sights along this 16-mile stretch are
few, with the **Theater of the Sea** (*see below*)
being the main attraction. However, the
**Lignumvitae Key Botanical State Park**
and **Indian Key Historic State Park** (for
both, *see below*) are both pleasant diversions,
while the small but splendid beaches that sit
by the roadside offer the first validation of the
Keys' reputation as an idyllic, restful stop. The
Chamber of Commerce at MM 83.2 (*see p220*)
has a wealth of local information.

### FREE Indian Key Historic State Park
*Accessible from MM 85.5 (1-305 664 2540,
www.floridastateparks.org/indiankey).* **Open**
8am-sundown daily. **Admission** free.
An island with a rich history (the Indian tribe that
once lived here was booted out by fishermen from
the Bahamas, and then by wreckers), Indian Key is
now uninhabited. The tours are worth taking,
though you'll have to go by boat from Robbie's
Marina (1-305 664 8070, www.robbies.com) at MM
77.5, where you can also see and feed huge tarpon
fish. Booking is recommended as the island isn't
always accessible.

### Lignumvitae Key Botanical State Park
*Accessible from MM 78.5 (1-305 664 2540,
www.floridastateparks.org/lignumvitaekey).*
**Open** 9am-5pm Mon, Thur-Sun. *Ranger tours*
10am, 2pm Fri-Sun. **Admission** *Ranger tours*
$2, $1.50 children. **Boat tours** $29. **Credit** AmEx,
DC, Disc, MC, V.
Tours to this lovely preserve of tropical forests and
rare birds, which are paired with tours of Indian
Key, can also be taken from Robbie's Marina. Book
ahead, and don't forget your insect repellent and
good walking shoes.

### Theater of the Sea
*84721 Overseas Highway (MM 84.5) (1-305 664
2431, www.theaterofthesea.com).* **Open** 9.30am-
5pm daily. **Admission** $29.95; $20.95 reductions;
free under-3s. **Credit** MC, V.
If Miami's Seaquarium is a poor imitation of
SeaWorld in Orlando, then the Theater of the Sea is
a poor imitation of the Seaquarium. After all, this

venue is more than 60 years old. But kids will still enjoy the performing animal shows, and, if you book ahead, the chance to swim with dolphins, sea lions and stingrays.

## Where to eat

Perhaps the second best of all the Keys in terms of dining options, Upper Matecumbe Key crams several fine eateries into its four or so miles. The **Green Turtle Inn** (MM 81.2, 1-305 664 2006, www.greenturtleinn.com) has been offering fine seafood (including turtle chowder) at fine prices since 1947. Another old stager is the **Islamorada Fish Company** (MM 81.5, 1-305 664 9271, www.ifcstonecrab.com), which has a lovely bayside deck for consumption of fish sandwiches. Keep your eyes peeled for manatees, which are aplenty here. **Marker 88** (MM 88, 1-305 852 9315, www.marker88.info) is a pricey gourmet option with fans and detractors in about equal numbers; it's open for lunch and dinner from 11am until 10pm daily. Alternatively, the **Holiday Isle Tiki Bar** (MM 84, 1-305 664 2321), located within the Postcard Inn (*see right*), is a very tacky but fun frozen drink outpost on the water, where getting drunk is pretty much a requirement. There's also **Woody's** (MM 82, 1-305 664 4335, www.woodysinthekeys.com), a strip club-cum-hard rock joint, which is not the place for anyone who shies away from audience participation.

## Where to stay

There are branches of **Days Inn** (MM 82.5, Upper Matecumbe Key, 1-305 664 3681, www. daysinnflakeys.com) and **Hampton Inn** (MM 80, Upper Matecumbe Key, 1-305 664 0073, www.hamptoninn.com).

### Casa Morada
*136 Madeira Road, off MM83 (1-305 664 0044, www.casamorada.com).* **Rates** $259-$699. **Credit** AmEx, DC, Disc, MC, V.
Owned and run by protégés of Ian Schrager, this is one of Florida's first 'boutique motels'. The dowdy old motel has been spruced up in a tropical, minimalist style, and the grounds are a lush Shangri-La. The pool, deck and bar overlook the Gulf of Mexico; grab a kayak and paddle into the sunset.

### Cheeca Lodge & Spa
*MM 82, Upper Matecumbe Key (1-305 664 4651, www.cheeca.com).* **Rates** $189-$599 double. **Credit** AmEx, DC, Disc, MC, V.
Cheeca Lodge is a huge, popular and pricey resort that sprawls across 30 acres of waterfront property with practice links, tennis courts, a heliport and a 5,000sq ft spa.

### Moorings Village & Spa
*123 Beach Road (off MM 82), Upper Matecumbe Key (1-305 664 4708, www.themooringsvillage. com).* **Rates** $349-$1,500 cottages. **Credit** AmEx, DC, Disc, MC, V.
Set on a former coconut plantation, the Moorings boasts a romantic and luxuriant setting. The 18 quaint houses and cottages are nestled amid rich bougainvillea and palms, as are the swimming pool and tennis court. The beach is superb for the Keys.

### Postcard Inn at Holiday Isle
*MM 84 (1-800 327 7070, 1-305 664 2321, www.holidayisle.com).* **Rates** $139-$639 double. **Credit** AmEx, Disc, MC, V.
A vast four-resort complex of 176 rooms, studios, cottages and suites. Less smart than Cheeca Lodge, it's a bit cheaper, too, but still features plenty of amenities, fine beaches and cheesy (in a good way) Tiki-style bars.

# The Middle Keys

## LONG KEY

The original Spanish name was Cayo Vivora, or Rattlesnake Key – not because the island was particularly snake-infested but because its sinuous shape reminded early settlers of a striking rattler. It's now largely taken up by the 965-acre state recreation area (*see below*).

### Long Key State Park
*MM 67.5 (1-305 664 4815, www.florida stateparks.org/longkey).* **Open** 8am-sunset daily. **Admission** $5/car; $2/pedestrians. **No credit cards**.
There's some beautiful nature to be enjoyed here, including mangroves harbouring a variety of birds. The water is very shallow, and from the beach you can safely wade way, way out into the Atlantic Ocean – a great bonus for kids. You can also go snorkelling or canoeing.

## CONCH KEY TO FAT DEER KEY

There are few points of interest on the short drive from Long Key to Marathon, through Conch Key, Grassy Key and the assorted smaller Keys. Some are home to fishermen, especially at **Tom's Harbor Cut**, while others offer super-swanky resorts: Duck Key, reached via a bridge at MM 61, is where you'll find the Morris Lapidus-designed **Hawk's Cay Resort** (1-305 743 7000, www.hawkscay.com). The high point for visitors is without doubt the **Dolphin Research Center** (*see p225*), but aside from that you're best off pushing on to Marathon.

### ★ Dolphin Research Center

*MM 59, Grassy Key (1-305 289 1121,*
*www.dolphins.org).* **Open** 9am-4.30pm daily.
**Admission** $20; $15-$17 reductions; under-3s
free. *Dolphin encounters* $199. **Credit** AmEx,
Disc, MC, V.

This non-profit spot is part research facility, part
education organisation and part tourist attraction,
and it fulfils all three of its roles with aplomb. Those
after a cutesy dolphin show will be disappointed, but
that's not the point: staff here are more concerned
with the benefits of dolphin-related therapy on hand-
icapped kids, although anyone can swim with the
dolphins by booking in advance. The giant statue of
a bottlenose dolphin in front of the centre is of Mitzi,
the star of the original *Flipper* movie.

## KEY VACA & MARATHON

**Marathon**, on the island of **Key Vaca** (named
after the manatees, or sea cows, that once
thrived in these waters), is the last major
settlement before Key West. It's an odd mix
of delicious beaches (the lively **Sombrero
Beach**, off Sombrero Road at the south side),
subtropical forests (**Crane Point**; *see right*),
cheap motels, variable restaurants and seamy
bars. The result is an indelicate mish-mash of
a place, neither natural nor urban, neither quiet
nor loud, neither great nor lousy. Appropriate,
then, that it should sit at the halfway mark
between Key Largo and Key West.

Most of the locals who work here (as opposed
to the many retirees) are involved in fishing
or the tourist industry. At times, it seems as

Seven Mile Bridge.

if everyone who isn't running a motel is out
fishing, and those who aren't doing either are
taking the motel guests out on a boat to watch
the fishermen.

### Crane Point

*5550 Overseas Highway (MM 50.5), Marathon
(1-305 753 9100, www.cranepoint.net).* **Open**
9am-5pm Mon-Sat; noon-5pm Sun. **Admission**
$12.50; $8.50-$11 reductions; under 4s free.
**Credit** AmEx, Disc, MC, V.

This extraordinary 63-acre subtropical forest, the
last remaining virgin palm hammock in the US, is
named after philanthropists Francis and Mary Crane,
who lived here for years. The property includes
the Museum of Natural History and a compact
Children's Activities Center. Adderley House, built
by a Bahamian immigrant in 1904, offers a glimpse
into how things used to be. But the real attraction is
the steamy nature trail leading to the water. All in
all, it's a splendid, undervalued spot, and a lovely
way to pass a few hours.

## Where to eat

The **Island Fish Co** (MM 54, 1-305 743 4191,
www.islandfishco.com) serves up reasonable
seafood, and the **Cracked Conch Café** (MM
49.5, 1-305 743 2233, www.conchcafe.com) is
an enjoyable half-bar, half-grill.

## Where to stay

Chain-wise, try the **Holiday Inn Express**
(MM 54, Marathon, 1-305 289 0222, www.ihg.
com/holidayinnexpress). Most other options
are cheap 'n' cheerful motels.

### Conch Key Cottages

*62250 Overseas Highway (MM 62.3), Conch Key,
Walkers Island (1-800 330 1577, www.conchkey
cottages.com).* **Rates** $149-$375. **Credit** AmEx,
Disc, MC, V.

If you want to stay in a luridly coloured studio or
pleasant cottage on your own island with your own
private beach, head here. No smoking allowed.

## PIGEON KEY & THE SEVEN MILE BRIDGE

**Pigeon Key** was once home to the labourers
on Flagler's railroad. These days it's all but
deserted, although it merits a visit for the
peaceful atmosphere, its informative museum
and for the chance to ride by train on the old
**Seven Mile Bridge**. The island is accessible
only by train, bike or on foot. Head for the
**visitors' centre** (located, appropriately, in
a red railway carriage at MM 47, right before
the bridge, 1-305 289 0025, www.pigeonkey.
net), where you can leave your car.

Right by the visitors' centre begins the **Seven Mile Bridge** (actually only 6.7 miles long), a soaring structure opened in 1982 to replace the original bridge, which was built 70 years earlier. When the first bridge was completed in 1912, newspapers proclaimed it the Eighth Wonder of the World; now it's the world's longest guano-spattered fishing pier. Thinking about its construction makes the mind boggle; this is also the Keys' most spectacular stretch of highway.

# The Lower Keys

By the time they've crossed the Seven Mile Bridge and realised their ultimate destination is only 35 or so miles away, many visitors hurry through the Lower Keys and head straight for Key West. But though traditional Keys sights and activities – read: T-shirt shops and glass-bottomed boat tours – are few and far between, the Lower Keys offer some truly lovely scenery and a couple of effortlessly enchanting stops.

## BAHIA HONDA & BIG PINE KEYS

Bahia Honda is home to the beautiful and tranquil **Bahia Honda State Park** (*see right*). More typical signs of life arrive in **Big Pine Key**, the Keys' second-largest island after Key Largo. For visitors, the place's main attraction are the Key Deer. There are fewer than 300 of these pint-sized deer left on the island, and those that remain are protected by the 2,251-acre **National Key Deer Refuge**, set up in the 1950s. They're reclusive creatures, and only come out in force around dawn and dusk. However, look out while you're driving: more than 50 deer are killed each year by careless drivers. For more information, stop at the **National Key Deer Refuge Headquarters** (*see right*); to get to the refuge, turn west off the highway just south of MM 31 on to Key Deer Boulevard (940), from where signs point the way to the headquarters. A right turn off Key Deer Boulevard on to Watson Boulevard leads to a concrete bridge across Bogie Channel and on to **No Name Key**, a tiny cul-de-sac of an island that once hosted a clandestine training base for anti-Castro Cuban guerrillas. Today, it's famous for the **No Name Pub** (N Watson Boulevard, 1.5 miles north of US 1, 1-305 872 9115, www.nonamepub.com). The oldest pub in these parts, this rustic 1936 shack is decorated with dollar bills and clutter. The service is similarly shambolic, but the pizzas are great; sandwiches and smoked fish served on paper plates also hit the spot.

## ★ Bahia Honda State Park

*MM 37, Bahia Honda Key (1-305 872 2353, www.bahiahondapark.com).* **Open** 8am-sunset daily. **Admission** $8/car. **Credit** AmEx, Disc, MC, V.

Perhaps the prettiest of all the parks in the Keys, Bahia Honda offers something for everyone: there are nature trails for explorers, good diving and snorkelling for aquatic adventurers (equipment rental is available from the marina), camping for outdoor types (as well as cabins for more indoorsy outdoor types) and the loveliest white sand beaches in the Keys.

## National Key Deer Refuge Headquarters

*179 Key Deer Boulevard (MM 31), Big Pine Key (1-305 872 0774, www.fws.gov/nationalkeydeer).* **Open** 8am-5pm Mon-Fri.

The place to come for information about the Key deer that roam these parts, and where to see them.

## THE TORCH KEYS TO BOCA CHICA KEY

After Big Pine, the rest of the Keys serve as the home straight into Key West. However, there are a few stops you can make. The **Torch Keys** – Little, Big and Middle – which are named after the sappy torchwood trees found around here, are missable, unless you have the cash for **Little Palm Island Resort & Spa** (*see below*) on Little Torch Key, a luxury retreat whose restaurant is consistently rated as one of the best dining spots on the Keys. Otherwise, at MM 17 on **Sugarloaf Key** is what appears to be a sail-less windmill: this is **Perky's Bat Tower**. In the 1920s, a man named Richter C Perky, a property developer from Miami, had plans to turn Sugarloaf Key into a private holiday and fishing retreat. Before he could do that, he needed to clear the area of the viciously bloodthirsty local mosquitoes. Perky read that bats could help get rid of the insects, so he built a 35-foot tower in a bid to lure them. But the bats never showed up, the mosquitoes stayed and Perky went bust, leaving the tower as a monument to his entrepreneurial dreams.

## Little Palm Island Resort & Spa

*28500 Overseas Highway (accessible from MM 28.5), Little Torch Key (1-305 872 2524, www.littlepalmisland.com).* **Rates** $590-$990 bungalow suite. **Credit** AmEx, Disc, MC, V.

Private Little Palm Island, accessible only by boat or seaplane, is as exclusive as the Keys get. Accommodation is in beachfront bungalows set among the palms. There are endless activities above and below water. But, blissfully for some, there are no phones, TVs, alarm clocks – or children under 16. A world-class spa adds to the tranquil atmosphere.

# The Young Man and the Sea

*Hemingway's stint in Key West proved a pivotal chapter in his life.*

Ernest Hemingway arrived in Key West in April 1928 with his second wife, Pauline. In 1931, Pauline's rich Uncle Gus provided the couple with the grand home that continues to draw in the tourists on Whitehead Street (*see p230*). Hemingway had a fine old time here – in the mornings he worked on his novels, including *A Farewell to Arms*, and in the afternoons he went deep-sea fishing and hung with the boys at Sloppy Joe's (*see p233*), where he ran up a monthly tab on his whisky and sodas. Then, one day in 1936, a journalist named Martha Gellhorn walked into the bar on assignment to interview the writer. Almost immediately, the two began an affair. His marriage ended in 1939 when, almost eight years to the day that he'd moved into Whitehead Street, Hemingway moved out. The following year, 13 days after divorcing Pauline in Miami, he married Martha (wife number three of four) and they moved to Havana. Pauline, meanwhile, stayed on in Key West and ran an interior design shop on the corner of Caroline and Ann Streets. She occupied the Whitehead Street house until her death in 1951.

For all the time he spent here, Key West only made it into one of Hemingway's novels, the indifferent *To Have and Have Not*. Howard Hawks used the tale as source material for the far superior movie starring Humphrey Bogart and Lauren Bacall, in which he transferred all the action to the French Caribbean island of Martinique.

# Key West

Settlers came to Key West in the early 1800s, a mix of farmers, wreckers and opportunists. By 1860, Key West was the largest and richest city in Florida – and the country's wealthiest town per capita – thanks to its thriving wrecking industry, a practice in which individuals salvage fine furnishings and other valuables from shipwrecks (and there were plenty of them). Many of today's modern-day settlers will admit they never intended to live here, but somehow couldn't bear to return across the bridge to the mainland. As one local said: 'In the 1970s came the hippies, followed by the gays and the cruise ship brigade.'

Key West suffered a slump in the 1940s, several years after the wrecking, sponge and cigar industries had collapsed or departed and the 1935 hurricane had destroyed the bridge linking it to the mainland. It took a long while for the island to recover its economic footing, but recover it certainly has.

Key West is a strange place, but it's not quite as strange as the locals like to think it is. The island is the last of the Keys – it's closer to Havana than Miami – and is home to a population of just 30,000, but it's visited by thousands more tourists each year, drawn by thoughts of eccentric charm, lively nightlife and quirky individuality. All of those characteristics still exist, but they've been overwhelmed by the chase for the tourist dollar.

There's no doubt that the town badly needed regenerating a few decades ago, and the tourist industry was a worthwhile buck to pursue. But the pursuit has gone too far, and much of the spirit that gave Key West its reputation has vanished. It's been replaced by a weird kind of good-time hippie theme park in and around Old Town, the westernmost area of Key West, and the centre of the action. Worse, the locals, while keen to play up their quirks and mannerisms – they once tried to secede from the US and rename Key West the Conch Republic – and happy to take the money, can also be outwardly disparaging about the tourists that make them

**Key West.**

ESCAPES & EXCURSIONS

Mallory Square.

their living. Walking down main Duval Street, you can't help but feel like the joke's on you.

That said, there is some of the old Key West that remains: you just have to look beyond Old Town to uncover it. The architecture here is pretty – a collection of Caribbean and New England-style homes on narrow streets – and some of the attractions are genuinely decent. A pair of good beaches – at **Fort Taylor** and the artificial, rocky **Smathers Beach** – provide quality chill-out time, while snorkellers dive in at various points along the coast.

## OLD TOWN

Waterfront **Mallory Square** is where American sailors raised the US flag in 1822 to mark the purchase of Florida from Spain. Boy, what did they start – it's now the crassest place in the Keys, particularly in the hour or two before sunset, when the plaza fills with street entertainers and expensive food stands taking advantage of the hundreds who gather each evening to watch the big orange ball dip below the horizon. That said, Mallory Square is an obvious place to begin exploring, not least because just off it is the **Key West Chamber of Commerce** (*see p220*), which distributes free tourist information, maps and brochures. The building housing the chamber was owned in the 1800s by one of the town's wealthiest citizens, wrecking master Asa Tift; his story, and the background to the business that made Key West rich, is told in the **Key West Shipwreck Treasures Museum** (*see p230*), which is located one block west of the chamber.

West of the museum, at the end of Wall Street, is the old red-brick **Custom House Museum** (*see p229*), now home to the Key West Art & Historical Society. The well-tended triangular park in front of the Custom House is Clinton Square, with a monument to the Union soldiers and sailors who lost their lives here during the Civil War (taken by yellow fever; no shots were fired down here). South of Union Square is the excellent **Mel Fisher Maritime Heritage Museum** (*see p230*); if you only visit a couple of Key West attractions, this should be one of them.

## WHITEHEAD STREET

Running south from Union Square is Whitehead Street, and at no.205 is **Audubon House & Tropical Gardens** (*see p229*). Across the street is an old Navy cistern, one of several on the island that were at one time used to collect rainwater for drinking supplies (Key West only got running water in 1942). Beyond the cistern are the Presidential Gates, originally designed to be opened for US presidents only. The last sitting president to pass through was JFK, who came here in 1962 during the Cuban Missile Crisis. The gates now give public access to the **Truman Little White House** (*see p230*). Across Whitehead Street, what is now **Kelly's Caribbean Bar, Grill & Brewery** (*see p231*) was formerly the first home of PanAm Airlines; the first round-trip ticket to Havana was sold here in 1927. Three blocks down, on the corner with Southard, is the **Green Parrot** (*see p233*), Key West's best bar and one of the few in town not connected to the island's best-known boozer, who is commemorated a further three blocks up the street at the **Hemingway Home & Museum** (*see p230* and *p227* **The Young Man and the Sea**). Opposite is the eminently missable **Lighthouse & Keeper's Quarters** (*see p230*) – although at one time the lighthouse keeper must have enjoyed incomparable views into Ernest's bathroom.

Whitehead ends at the **Southernmost Point of the USA**, marked by a great big bottle-recycling bin. This is Key West's prime 'I was here' photo op. But beware of the men who offer to take your picture and then demand a tip.

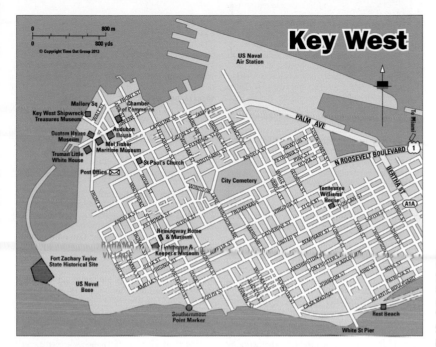

## DUVAL STREET

Key West's main street boasts more souvenir
outlets than Disney World, alongside a bar
scene unrivalled in its hideousness. But it's not
all bad, particularly towards the southern end.
At the junction with United Street, one of a row
of pleasingly dilapidated wooden residences
houses the splendid **Banana Café** (*see p230*).
Hemingway's old drinking haunt **Sloppy
Joe's** (*see p233*) is on Duval at the corner with
Greene Street, but the coach-party atmosphere
makes boozing here depressing.

### EAST OF DUVAL

One block east of Duval Street is Simonton
Street; at no.314 are the **Casa Antigua
Apartments**, Hemingway's first lodgings
when he arrived in Key West in 1928. **William
Kerr House** at no.410 is particularly gorgeous,
executed in 1880 in a style known locally as
'carpenters' Gothic'.

Six blocks away (passing 608 Angela
Street en route, where Elizabeth Taylor was
a frequent visitor to the house of her father-
in-law, Shakespearean scholar Philip Burton),
at the junction of Margaret and Angela, is the
small but neatly kept **City Cemetery**, with
its collection of strange and witty gravestones
(most famously, 'I told you I was sick'). Tours

are offered by the Historic Florida Keys
Foundation (1-305 292 6718, www.historic
floridakeys.org) twice a week. Call ahead
for schedule and reservations.

### Audubon House & Tropical Gardens

*205 Whitehead Street, at Greene Street (1-305
294 2116, www.audubonhouse.com).* **Open**
9.30am-5pm daily. **Admission** $12; $5-$7.50
reductions; free under-6s. **Credit** AmEx, MC, V.
John James Audubon, pioneering ornithologist
and painter of *Birds of America*, never lived in this
house; it merely commemorates his visit here. The
self-guided audio tours preserve the tranquillity of
the lovely building, while the rare Audubon prints
and the calming gardens are a delight.

### Custom House Museum

*281 Front Street, at Greene Street (1-305 295
6616, www.kwahs.org).* **Open** 9.30am-4.30pm
daily. **Admission** $7; $5 reductions; free under-6s.
**No credit cards**.
A grand old building that originally housed the customs office, postal service and district courts, this
Mallory Square landmark is now home to the Key
West Art & Historical Society. The collection
includes a miscellany of artworks by local painters,
old PanAm memorabilia, painted woodcarvings by
local luminary Mario Sanchez, as well as exhibits on
pirates and a young Ernest Hemingway.

### ★ Hemingway Home & Museum

*907 Whitehead Street, at Olivia Street (1-305 294 1575, www.hemingwayhome.com)*. **Open** 9am-5pm daily. **Admission** $13; $6 reductions; free under-5s. **Credit** (shop only) MC, V.
Relentlessly hyped – especially when you consider that Ernest only lived here for eight years – and often busy, this is nonetheless one of Key West's most appealing sights. The stories related by the laconic guides (they set off every 15 minutes) bring the place to life. And it's a must for fans of six-toed cats named after celebrities. Nearly 50 polydactyl (six-toed) cats roam the museum grounds, many of them descendants of Snowball, Hemingway's own multi-toed ball of fur, which lived with him on the property. Today, all of the cats are named after famous figures such as Rudolph Valentino or Tennessee Williams, as a nod to Hemingway's own tradition. In late 2012, the US Department of Agriculture won a decade-long battle against the Hemingway Home, claiming that the animals shouldn't be allowed to simply roam the property. Nothing has been confirmed on how the cats' free-wheeling ways might change, but it's best to catch them now.

### Key West Shipwreck Treasures Museum

*1 Whitehead Street, at Front Street (1-305 292 8990, www.keywestshipwreck.com)*. **Open** *Shows* every 30mins 9.45am-4.45pm Mon, Wed-Sun; 9.45am-5pm Tue. **Admission** $12; $5 reductions. **Credit** AmEx, Disc, MC, V.
A lively actor-led presentation on the wreck of the *Isaac Allerton*, told from the perspective of wrecker Asa Tift. Good fun, and a decent counterpart to the Mel Fisher Maritime Heritage Museum (*see below*).

### Lighthouse & Keeper's Quarters

*938 Whitehead Street, at Olivia Street (1-305 295 6616, www.kwahs.org)*. **Open** 9.30am-4.30pm daily. **Admission** $10; $5 reductions; free under-6s. **Credit** AmEx, DC, MC, V.
A small lighthouse museum is only half the attraction here: if you can walk 88 steps to the balcony, you'll be rewarded with spectacular views.

### Mel Fisher Maritime Heritage Museum

*200 Greene Street, at Whitehead Street (1-305 294 2633, www.melfisher.org)*. **Open** 8.30am-5pm Mon-Fri; 9.30am-5pm Sat, Sun. **Admission** $12.50; $6.25-$10.50 reductions. **Credit** AmEx, MC, V.
An assortment of impressive and rare artefacts at this museum commemorate the work of Mel Fisher, an old-school salvager who used snazzy new-school technology to unearth $400 million of treasure from wrecks in 1985.

### Truman Little White House

*111 Front Street, at Caroline Street (1-305 294 9911, www.trumanlittlewhitehouse.com)*. **Open** *Tours* 9am-4.30pm daily. **Admission** $16; $5.50-$14 reductions; free under-5s. **Credit** AmEx, Disc, MC, V.
The building where President Harry Truman, a big fan of the Keys, retreated for rest and recreation after World War II is now a pleasant museum. If you don't fancy the full tour, a small section is open for free.

## WHERE TO EAT & DRINK

The Key lime, a small yellow fruit resembling a roundish lemon, is sold on every corner in a variety of guises – not least the world-famous Key lime pie. And no visitor should leave without trying conch (pronounced 'conk'), a shellfish; best deep-fried and sampled as a fritter.

## Restaurants & cafés

### Banana Café

*1215 Duval Street, at Louisa Street (1-305 294 7227, www.bananacafekw.com)*. **Open** 8am-3pm Mon, Sun; 8am-3pm, 6-10pm Tue-Sat. **Main courses** $6-$12 breakfast; $21-$30 dinner. **Credit** AmEx, DC, Disc, MC, V.
This gorgeous little French-inspired place down at the southern end of Duval is a great spot for breakfast. Join the queue waiting for a table in the varnished hardwood interior or, better yet, out on the deck. The menu is brief and to the point – sweet and savoury crêpes, omelettes, salads and sandwiches – but it's all excellent stuff. Dinner is served as well and is equally good.

### Blue Heaven

*729 Thomas Street, at Petronia Street (1-305 296 8666, www.blueheavenkw.com)*. **Open** 8am-10.30pm daily. **Main courses** $17-$34. **Credit** AmEx, Disc, MC, V.
A perennial favourite, Blue Heaven is a former bordello. It now serves excellent Caribbean cuisine (barbecue shrimp, jerk chicken, surf 'n' turf) in laid-back surroundings. Note the slate billiard table bases in the sandy floor of the rear yard, where Hemingway used to attend cockfights. There's also a fine little beach bar.

### Café Marquesa

*600 Fleming Street, at Simonton Street, next to Marquesa Hotel (1-305 292 1244, www.marquesa.com)*. **Open** 6.30-10pm daily. **Main courses** $23-$43. **Credit** AmEx, DC, MC, V.
One of the classier restaurants in Key West, Café Marquesa is a softly lit, elegant room with a low-key bar that serves chi-chi martinis. The menu, created by chef Susan Ferry based on seasonal availability, is similarly sophisticated. Porcini-dusted diver sea scallops are served with truffle butter, saffron risotto and Swiss chard, while a smoked salmon appetiser comes with blue corn cakes, crème fraîche and trout roe. It also has one of the most comprehensive wine lists in town.

# Essential Key West Festivals

*Kitsch happenings and gastro gatherings dot the town's eclectic calendar.*

### Fantasy Fest
*www.fantasyfest.com*
Book early if you want to catch Key West at its wackiest during this over-the-top ten-day event when outrageously costumed characters rule the town. If nonstop parties, parades, street fairs and horseplay are not your speed, steer clear in mid-October.

### Hemingway Days
*www.fla-keys.com/hemingwaymedia*
Papa is everywhere you look at this long-running July celebration, which commemorates his favourite activities with plenty of drinking, writing, drinking, fishing and drinking. The Hemingway Look-Alike Contest, hosted by Sloppy Joe's (*see p233*), is one of the most popular events.

### Kelly McGillis Classic International Women's & Girls' Flag Football Championship
*www.iwffa.com/kmc22.html*
For more than 20 years, the star of *Top Gun* has invited all-female teams from around the world to get physical in this February flag football tournament.

### Key West Conchfest
*www.conchfestkeywest.com*
This one-day tribute to sea snails takes place in March. The Conchfest has been

Hemingway Days.

celebrated for more than 50 years and includes a conch shell-blowing contest.

### Key West Food & Wine Festival
*www.keywestfoodandwinefestival.com*
Held in January, just weeks before the South Beach Wine & Food Festival (*see p27*), this culinary extravaganza isn't quite ready to compete with its counterpart to the north. But it's only four years old, so give it time.

### Key West Pride
*www.keywestpride.org*
Revellers from all over the world gather for five days in June for dance parties, drag shows, film screenings, street fairs, pool parties, pageants and a massive parade down Duval Street.

---

### El Siboney
*900 Catherine Street, at Margaret Street (1-305 296 4184, www.elsiboneyrestaurant.com).* **Open** 11am-9.30pm daily. **Main courses** $10-$17. **No credit cards.**
Located off the beaten track, El Siboney is an unpretentious single-storey, red-brick shack offering the finest Cuban food in town. It's also really cheap.

### Half Shell Raw Bar
*231 Margaret Street (1-305 294 7496, www. halfshellrawbar.com).* **Open** 11am-10.30pm daily. **Main courses** $6-$34. **Credit** AmEx, Disc, MC, V.
A local institution, this seafood canteen is located in an old shrimp factory and still has a pleasingly blue collar feel. Situated right on the wharf, it offers a few highly prized waterside tables, from which you can throw bread and watch as the surface is churned up by shoals of hungry fish. For your own meal, go for one of the excellent shrimp, oyster or grouper po' boy sandwiches.

### Kelly's Caribbean Bar, Grill & Brewery
*301 Whitehead Street, at Caroline Street (1-305 293 8484, www.kellyskeywest.com).* **Open** 11am-10pm daily. **Main courses** $16-$30. **Credit** AmEx, DC, Disc, MC, V.
The Kelly in question is *Top Gun* actress Kelly McGillis, while the food is surprisingly decent, if not especially Caribbean. Fans claim the kitchen does the best conch fritters – and they're certainly big and meaty. There's also an attached microbrewery.

### Louie's Backyard
*700 Waddell Street, at Vernon Street (1-305 294 1061, www.louiesbackyard.com).* **Open** 11.30am-3pm, 6-10.30pm daily. **Main courses** $36-$40. **Credit** AmEx, DC, MC, V.
The Floribbean cuisine here is outstanding, but the real winner is the setting – smack on a prime slab of the Gulf. Reservations are hard to come by, but there's always the outdoor bar, where you can drift away on pina coladas and an Eden-style ambience.

**ESCAPES & EXCURSIONS**

# Island Queens

*Welcome to pink paradise.*

In case you're wondering about all the rainbow flags, Key West is a gay mecca. This is slightly perturbing to the fiftysomething tourists from the American Midwest, who disembark from their cruise ships and gawk at the drag queens through the windows of Duval Street's gay bars. They'd do well to go inside; these are the liveliest venues in town.

**Bourbon Street Pub** (no.724, 1-305 293 9800, www.bourbonstpub.com) is party central, with a lively bar, muscly go-go boys and a 'clothing optional' pool party from noon to 5pm on Saturdays. The **801 Bourbon Bar** (no.801, at Petronia, 1-305 294 4737, www.801bourbon.com) has drag queens named Sushi and Kylie, and deafening disco beats. Out the back, the adjoining **Saloon One** bar, entered separately, is pure sleaze. With a dungeon, wooden paddles for spanking and grim porno films, this leather bar is not the place for cosmos. **Aqua** (no.711, 1-305 294 0555, www.aquakeywest.com), by contrast, is a cheesy dance club where you might see more drag queens singing torch songs.

Away from the main drag, **La-Te-Da** (no.1125, 1-305 296 6706, www.lateda.com), the former Key West home of Cuban exile José Martí, is great for martinis by the pool, but skip the food. Upstairs is the **Crystal Room** (1-305 296 6706), where life is, indeed, a cabaret. There's also an on-site hotel plus the 'By George' piano bar, an outdoor terrace bar and the marble crystal bar.

You'd be hard-pressed to find a homophobic hotel in Key West. But **Island House** (1129 Fleming Street, 1-305 294 6284, www.islandhousekeywest.com, $99-$499) is the queen of the scene. Here, amid lush foliage and gingerbread architecture, guests shed their clothes and inhibitions. Bronzed Muscle Marys glisten under the mist spray system on the sun deck or bare all by the pool; bashful types cover up and sneak a peek. At night the place is a garden of Eden, with Adam and Steve giving in to temptation at every turn. If lurking by the jacuzzi is not your style, take refuge in conversation by the poolside bar. Despite all the hanky-panky, the decor is comfortable and the service professional.

Most of the guesthouses follow a similar formula: a sultry pool setting and a 'clothing optional' policy for optimum body-watching. The recently renovated **Equator** (818 Fleming Street, 1-305 294 7775, www.equatorresort.com, $140-$275 double) is another voyeur's paradise, though it's less cruisey than Island House. In an 1892 Bahamian-style house, there's also **Tranquility Guesthouse** (817 Fleming Street, 1-305 296 2131, www.tranquility guesthouse.com, $169-$375 double).

The Lebanese, as Blanche Devereaux called them, join forces at **Pearl's Rainbow** (525 United Street, 1-305 292 1450, www.pearlsrainbow.com, $99-$329 double), a clothing optional, adults-only resort that's welcoming to all persuasions, but is particularly popular among women. **Alexander's Guesthouse** (1118 Fleming Street, 1-800 654 9919, www.alexanders keywest.com, $155-$90 double) is also mixed, and probably the classiest queer guesthouse in town. The gardens are resplendent with banana trees and hibiscus, and the decor approaches boutique standard. There's a nudist sun deck, but the rest of the resort is covered up and positively restrained compared to many of the gay options around town.

Finally, if you're not too embarrassed to ride in a trolley car with Judy Garland blaring from loudspeakers, the **Gay and Lesbian Historic Trolley** tour gives a queen's-eye view of Key West (tours leave from the corner of Angela and Duval Streets at 4pm Sat, 1-800 535 7797).

For more information on all of Key West's various gay goings-on, visit www.gaykeywestfl.com.

ESCAPES & EXCURSIONS

### Nine One Five

*915 Duval Street (1-305 296 0669, www.915 duval.com).* **Open** 6-11pm daily. **Main courses** $24-$36. **Credit** Am Ex, Disc, MC, V.
On the quiet part of Duval, this cool restaurant-wine bar is a hit with locals. Set in a Victorian house, with tables on the veranda and twinkly lights strewn everywhere, it's a lovely spot. There are 20 wines by the glass and a tapas-style menu.

### Pepe's

*806 Caroline Street, at William Street (1-305 294 7192, www.pepescafe.net).* **Open** 7.30am-10pm daily. **Main courses** $11-$29. **Credit** Disc, MC, V.
Opened in 1909, Pepe's is a ramshackle place, but that doesn't stop the throngs of people waiting in line to dive into Gulf oysters and creamed chipped beef on toast at low prices.

### 7 Fish

*632 Olivia Street, at Elizabeth Street (1-305 296 2777, www.7fish.com).* **Open** 6-10pm Mon, Wed-Sun. **Main courses** $17-$29. **Credit** AmEx, MC, V.
Hidden down a quiet backstreet, 7 Fish has all the makings of a best-kept secret. The only trouble is, the seafood is so good here that word has got out; reservations are recommended. The setting remains simple, classy and candlelit. The menu features just-caught mahi-mahi, gorgeous ceviche and seasonal local fish such as wahoo. Even the non-seafood items, such as a signature banana chicken with caramelised walnuts, have a local flavour. The staff are friendly and knowledgeable.

### Bars

As with the food culture, the epicentre of drinking culture on Key West is Duval Street, which at night turns into a heaving, wretched mass of overexcited, boozed-up fun-seekers.

### Green Parrot

*601 Whitehead Street, at Southard Street (1-305 294 6133, www.greenparrot.com).* **Open** 10am-4am daily. **No credit cards.**
The Parrot, here since 1890, can get as loud and lairy as some of the Duval Street spots, but at least it's mostly locals doing the shouting. It's got a great divey atmosphere and a decent range of beers (about ten of them on draught).

### Sloppy Joe's

*201 Duval Street, at Greene Street (1-305 294 5717, www.sloppyjoes.com).* **Open** 9am-4am Mon-Sat; noon-4am Sun. **Credit** Disc, MC, V.
The most famous bar in south Florida, and all the worse for it. If you really must visit, go during the day before the insipid live music starts and everyone gets hammered on the Slush Puppie-style house cocktails. One thing's for sure: if Hemingway were alive today he wouldn't be drinking here.

## SHOPPING

Key West is a town with a classy literary pedigree. It has acted as a retreat, haven or hideaway not just for Hemingway, but also for John Dos Passos in the 1920s; poet Robert Frost, who spent 16 winters beginning in 1934; and Tennessee Williams, who arrived in 1941 and stayed because he 'liked to swim'. More recently, the island has harboured James Leo Herlihy, author of *Midnight Cowboy*; Pulitzer Prize-winning novelist Alison Lurie; and sexologist Nancy Friday. Pick up their work at the superb **Key West Island Books** (513 1/2 Fleming Street, 1-305 294 2904, www.key westislandbooks.com, open 10am-9pm Mon-Sat, 10am-6pm Sun), just off Duval.

Otherwise, everything in Key West is expensive, and decent shops are few and far between (T-shirt shops breed far more successfully than the beleaguered manatee). However, there are some unusual shops worth checking out. At the **Cuban Leaf Cigar Factory** (310 Duval Street, 1-305 295 9283), you can watch cigars being made before buying them. **Capricorn Jewelry** (706B Duval Street, 1-305 292 9338, www.keywestlovebracelet.com) has a good selection of unique gold and silver charms plus the Key West Love Bracelet, a custom-designed key-clasp bracelet. The **Key West Kite Company** (408 Greene Street, 1-305 296 5483, www.keywestkitecompany.com) is worth a visit to see all the colourful designs, while **Glass Reunions** (825 Duval Street, 1-305 294 1720, www.glassreunions.com) sells locally made, hand-blown art and household items that are unlikely to make it home in one piece. For a bit of luxe shopping, **Besame Mucho** (315 Petronia Street, 1-305 294 1928) sells classy gifts, chocolates and fine linens.

If you're self-catering, don't shop at the small supermarkets along the main strips, where tourists are charged more than natives. **Key Plaza** on N Roosevelt Boulevard has decent stores, include an outpost of local supermarket chain Publix. If you get the munchies at night, head for the 24-hour **Sunbeam Groceries & Deli** (500 White Street, 1-305 294 8993). Otherwise, the best food shopping of all is at **Fausto's Food Palace** (522 Fleming Street, 1-305 296 5663 & 1105 White Street, 1-305 294 5221, www.faustos.com), a superb deli-cum-supermarket.

## WHERE TO STAY

During the high season in Key West (Nov-Apr), accommodation prices soar and early booking is advised. Both the **Westin Key West Resort & Marina** (245 Front Street, 1-305 294 4000, www.westinkeywestresort.com) and the

**Reach**, a Waldorf Astoria resort (1435 Simonton Street, 1-305 296 5000, www.reach resort.com) are right in the heart of Key West. However, most of the chains are clustered on N Roosevelt Boulevard, away from the Old Town. They include **Best Western** (no.3755, 1-305 296 3500, www.bestwestern.com), **Days Inn** (no.3852, 1-305 294 3742, www.daysinn.com) and **Quality Inn** (no.3824, 1-305 294 5739, www.qualityinn.com).

Off-season, you can find deals at guesthouses and B&Bs, which can be very cost-effective if four people share a room with two beds. Budget accommodation can be found at the youth hostel near the centre of town or at the chain motels. Alternatively, stay in one of the old gingerbread-style family homes. Prices start at $40 per night off-season and run to $200-plus.

## Ambrosia House

*622 Fleming Street, at Elizabeth Street (1-305 535 9838, www.ambrosiakeywest.com).* **Rates** $189-$469 double. **Credit** AmEx, MC, V.
Near touristy Duval Street, but tucked away on a leafy back road, Ambrosia House is a little haven. Comprising two quaint inns, it's dotted with comfy suites, but most of its standard rooms have fridges too. Many rooms boast French doors that open on to porches, terraces, gardens or the pool. Wicker and wood furniture and hammocks create a cottagey feel.

## Duval Gardens

*1012 Duval Street, at Truman Street (1-800 867 1234, 1-305 292 3379, www.duvalgardens. com).* **Rates** $165-$755 double. **Credit** AmEx, Disc, MC, V.
A mid-priced, family-run B&B up at the quieter end of Duval, with a small pool and free off-street parking. Rooms are small but comfortable, some with sensual gauzy curtains around the beds.

## Gardens Hotel

*526 Angela Street, at Simonton Street (1-800 526 2664, 1-305 294 2661, www.gardenshotel.com).* **Rates** $165-$775 double. **Credit** AmEx, MC, V.
The Gardens Hotel was named the 'prettiest hotel in Key West' by the *New York Times*, and it's easy to see why. Built in 1875, this romantic inn is set in an idyllic shady garden, where orchids, bamboo and palms flourish amid fountains, ponds and a heated swimming pool. An aviary completes the picture. Rooms are decked out with Bahamian-style plantation furniture fashioned from yew and mahogany.

## Heron House

*512 Simonton Street, at Fleming Street (1-800 294 1644, 1-305 294 9227, www.heronhouse.com).* **Rates** $169-$399 double. **Credit** AmEx, MC, V.
Built in 1856, Heron House is one of Key West's oldest buildings and located in the heart of the historic district. The ambience is typically tropical, with an orchid-filled garden, a pool fringed with plants and balconies bursting with greenery. Inside, rattan furniture and Key West watercolours continue the lush feel.

## Island City House

*411 William Street, at Eaton Street (1-800 634 8230, 1-305 294 5702, www.islandcityhouse. com).* **Rates** $150-$420 double. **Credit** AmEx, Disc, MC, V.
The oldest guesthouse on the island consists of three lovely balconied houses ranged around a semi-tropical courtyard, with 24 luxurious suites with colonial-style furnishings and hardwood floors. There's a large swimming pool and four cats, two of which have six toes.

## Key West International Youth Hostel

*718 South Street, at William Street (1-305 296 5719, www.keywesthostel.com).* **Rates** from $44 per person. **Credit** MC, V.
Cheap dorm rooms down near the Southernmost Point, a five-minute walk from central Old Town. There are full kitchen facilities, bike rentals, free parking, pool table, picnic area and complimentary wireless internet access. Another bonus is 24-hour access. Booking is essential in winter.

## Marquesa Hotel

*600 Fleming Street, at Simonton Street (1-305 292 1919, www.marquesa.com).* **Rates** $170-$520. **Credit** AmEx, DC, MC, V.
Key West's – and, some say, the country's – finest old hotel is a small complex of four historic buildings set around a lush garden with two pools. The place has won countless awards, and it's not hard to see why: this is a classy option.

## Paradise Inn

*819 Simonton Street, at Petronia Street (1-800 888 9648, 1-305 293 0807, www.theparadise inn.com).* **Rates** $149-$409 double. **Credit** AmEx, MC, V.
When a hotel calls itself Paradise, that's usually your cue to run a mile. Not this time. Here, you'll get a whiff of jasmine sitting on your vine-covered porch. Or breathe in the perfume from the ylang-ylang tree, the same plant used to make Chanel No.5. There's a pond filled with Japanese carp and a fountain-fed swimming pool. Inside, the beige and gold rooms are equally serene.

## Simonton Court

*320 Simonton Street, at Eaton Street (1-800 944 2687, www.simontoncourt.com).* **Rates** $169-$399 double. **Credit** AmEx, Disc, DC, MC, V.
Looking like something straight out of a southern Gothic novel, Simonton Court makes a lovely, sultry setting amid subtropical foliage. Old-fashioned gingerbread cottages are centred around a main house

with the kind of veranda that calls to mind southern belles and mint juleps. Take a morning dip in the pool and then have breakfast in the gardens.

### Southernmost Point Guest House

*1327 Duval Street, at South Street (1-305 294 0715, www.southernmostpoint.com).* **Rates** $100-$300 double. **Credit** AmEx, MC, V.
This family-run establishment is a rambling old colonial villa in lush gardens down at the classier end of Duval. It has gorgeous hardwood verandas with wicker chairs and ferns, and a small pool.

## GETTING AROUND

Key West's streets are narrow, and the island is small, so don't plan on using a car while you're here. However, if you do have one, you're best off parking it at the garage on the corner of Caroline and Grinnell Streets. Walking is the most sensible way to get around, although bikes, mopeds and scooters can be hired for between $7 and $30 a day; most firms insist on a credit card for vehicle rentals. Shop around for the best deal. Large rental firms include the **Bike Shop** (1110 Truman Avenue, 1-305 294 1073, www. thebikeshopkeywest.com) and **Adventure Rentals** (1-305 293 8883, www.keywest-scooter.com), which hires out scooters, bikes and motorcycles from five locations, including 503 Greene Street across from Sloppy Joe's. Many firms that rent scooters offer one- or two-seater vehicles. Try **Pirate Rentals** (401 Southard Street, 1-305 295 0000, www. piratescooterrentals.com) or **Paradise Rentals** (112 Fitzpatrick Street, 1-305 292 6441, www.paradisescooterrentals.com).

## Tours & excursions

The most popular trips are the 90-minute **Conch Tour Train** (1-305 294 5161, www. conchtourtrain.com) and **Old Town Trolley** (1-888 910 8687, www.trolleytours.com/key-west), which give similar – they're owned by the same firm – guided tours of the town's main attractions. Reckon on about $30 per person.
For twilight touring, try **Original Ghost Tours** (1-305 294 9255, www.hauntedtours.com) or **Ghosts & Legends of Key West** (1-305 294 1713, www.keywestghosts.com), both of which lead nightly excursions ($15-$18 per person, $10 for kids); call to make reservations.
Sunset cruises, tours to the coral reefs and glass-bottomed boat trips are touted from the numerous booths strung out along Duval Street.

# The Dry Tortugas

The Dry Tortugas are a group of islands 70 miles off the coast of Key West ('*tortuga*' means turtle in Spanish). The **Dry Tortugas National Park** (1-305 242 7700, www.nps. gov/drto) is home to the **Fort Jefferson** Civil War monument and a wildlife sanctuary. The park makes a perfect day trip from the bustle of Key West and is excellent for snorkelling and fishing. Visitors must bring all food, water and supplies. Free camping is allowed at ten sites. You can get to the park via the **Yankee Freedom** ferry service (1-305 294 7009, www.yankeefreedom.com) or **Sunny Days Catamaran** (1-866 878 2223, www.sunny dayskeywest.com). All services run daily.

**ESCAPES & EXCURSIONS**

**Fort Jefferson.**

# In Context

# History

*The American dream in action.*

Since Miami was officially incorporated as a city in 1896, its prosperity has seemed to ebb and flow with the tides of its famous beach. Affluent enclaves, years in the making, can be decimated in minutes if one of those notorious south Florida hurricanes makes landfall, and record-breaking land booms have repeatedly been halted by economic recessions. Even today, the disparity between the city's wealthiest residents (who casually tool around town in their shiny new Ferraris and Bentleys) and its struggling immigrant population is immediately visible. And yet it's this same economic disconnect that has made Miami the kind of aspirational city where seemingly anything can happen – the American dream in action. Perhaps *Scarface*'s Tony Montana – the city's most famous fictional resident – summed it up best: 'The world is yours'.

## MYTHICAL BEGINNINGS

Florida has been inhabited for at least ten centuries, but little is known about the lives of the earliest settlers, descendants of Central and South American Indians. Thanks to the 1998 discovery of artefacts in Downtown Miami, they are known to include the Calusa (or Tequesta) tribe, whose origins date back 2,000 years.

Yet detailed records only began with the arrival of one of Spain's greatest explorers. Juan Ponce de León sailed with Columbus on his second voyage to the Americas in 1493 and later conquered Puerto Rico for Spain. His reward was to be made governor of the island in 1510, but his wanderlust never died.

During Ponce de León's term as governor, he heard tales from Puerto Rico's Native American inhabitants about a mythical island called Bimini, believed to be somewhere north of Cuba. Bimini was said to be teeming with gold and to possess a magical spring whose waters restored youth and healed the sick. Seduced by the tales, de León repeated them to King Ferdinand V of Spain in 1512. He was instantly ordered to find, conquer and colonise Bimini.

When his expedition eventually sighted land on 27 March 1513, de León believed he had succeeded. Landing north of what is now St Augustine, on Florida's north-eastern coast, he claimed the place in the name of the king. As he had first seen land on Easter Sunday, known in Spanish as Pascua Florida ('Festival of Flowers'), he named the region Florida. Believing that he had found an island, de León tried to circumnavigate it and search for the fountain and the gold; finding neither, he gave up and returned to Puerto Rico in 1514.

Many Indian tribes inhabited Florida and the surrounding area. Some, like those in Cuba, had welcomed the Spanish colonists with open arms, but other tribes fiercely resented the invaders, and when de León returned to Florida in 1521 with two shiploads of horses, cattle, tools, seeds and people to start a new Spanish settlement, he came under attack. Badly wounded, he was forced to flee. He died in Cuba soon after.

The legend of Florida, however, lived on. During the next few years, a host of young Spaniards tried and failed to establish a permanent settlement, chiefly in the hope of finding gold. All were beaten back, and by the 1560s interest was starting to wane. But when a massive French force, led by Jean Ribaut, arrived in 1562 to claim the new territory for France, the Spanish realised they had to take action or lose Florida altogether.

## THE FIGHT FOR FLORIDA

Pedro Menéndez de Avilés, captain-general of the Spanish fleet, was ordered to destroy the French colony of Fort Caroline. In 1565, Ribaut and his followers were captured and executed, leaving Menéndez free to establish St Augustine, the oldest continuous European settlement in the US. The French tried but failed to retake the town, and it became a key trading centre. But the bloodshed didn't stop. In 1586, Britain attempted to get in on the act, sending Sir Francis Drake on a naval bombardment that razed St Augustine. For the next 150 years, the English, Spanish and French all vied with the Indians for control of the 'New World'. Spain had the upper hand until the Seven Years War (1757-63, also known as the French and Indian War) between Britain and France, in which Spain sided with France. In the First Treaty of Paris, which

**Pedro Menéndez de Avilés.**

ended the war, the Spanish ceded Florida in return for the port of Havana, which the British had captured in 1762.

Under British rule, Florida was divided into two separate colonies: East and West. But the central inland area was populated by the surviving Indian tribes, who had joined forces with the Creek Indians that had been pushed down into Florida by the American army. Collectively, the new Indians called themselves the Seminole (meaning 'wild one' or 'runaway') – and would prove a force to be reckoned with. The British held on to the area during the American War of Independence (1775-83), but the Second Treaty of Paris, which brought peace, handed Florida back to Spain.

## COLONISTS AND INDIANS

From 1814, American troops made a series of raids into Florida, claiming they were trying to capture escaped slaves from the neighbouring state of Georgia. They left the Spanish alone, but killed hundreds of Indians, who regularly gave refuge to escaped slaves and had begun to intermarry. The scale of the slaughter matched that seen elsewhere in the newly united States, with the Indians slowly

---

# Stormy Weather

*Considering a visit during hurricane season? You've been warned.*

Florida may be known as the Sunshine State, but it's also a hurricane magnet. Of the 170 hurricanes that struck the US during the 20th century, more than a third landed here. Floridians are resigned to the fact. Every year, during hurricane season – from June to November – locals board up their windows, tie up their boats and get out of the way.

Indeed, the curious phenomenon of naming storms adds a frisson of excitement. When forecasters describe the ferocity of Wilma or Sandy, the personification of mother nature adds to the drama, giving new meaning to the phrase 'Hell hath no fury like a woman scorned' (in the name of equality, storms are now named after men too). The process of ranking storms in categories of severity – from 1 (winds of 74-95mph) to 5 (winds of more than 155mph) – is also soundbite-friendly. But while it may be exciting for weather-channel surfers, the storms have taken a tragic toll.

On 18 September 1926, a Category 4 hurricane killed 800 people and left 50,000 homeless in Miami. Without radios, most people were oblivious to warnings; many died when they went outside during the lull of the storm's eye, only to be killed when the rear of the storm whipped in from behind.

On the night of 16 September 1928, 2,000 people died when a Category 3 roared into Lake Okeechobee and swamped local villages.

On Labor Day 1935, the most powerful hurricane in American history flattened the Keys. One of only three Category 5 storms to ever hit the US, it generated winds of 200mph. Anyone caught outside had their clothes ripped off by the sheer force of the gusts; every tree in Matecumbe Key was felled. The hurricane also destroyed Henry Flagler's Overseas Railroad – of the storm's 408 fatalities, 259 were World War I vets working on the tracks.

In September 1965, Hurricane Betsy confounded forecasters – and science – with its byzantine trajectory. After bypassing Florida and taking aim at South Carolina, the Category 3 storm suddenly reversed direction and slammed into a bewildered Miami.

But Hurricane Andrew was truly biblical in its rage. Miami had gone for 27 years without a direct hit, and the 1992 storm made up for it: a Category 5 hurricane, it made landfall near Homestead on 24 August with 165mph winds and proceeded to destroy Dade

being wiped out. The Americans' true intention, of course, was to remove the Indians completely and take control of the region in order to wrest it from the Spanish. The conflict became known as the First Seminole War. Led by General (later President) Andrew Jackson, the US troops captured the city of Pensacola in May 1818 and deposed the Spanish government. Spain formally ceded Florida to the US in 1819.

Thousands of colonists soon arrived from the north, pushing the native Indians further south. In 1830, the US Congress passed the Removal Act, a piece of legislation that is described in TD Allman's *Miami: City of the Future* as being reminiscent of apartheid in South Africa or Nazi Germany. In accordance with this new law, the Indians were ordered to move to a new territory in the barren lands west of the Mississippi. Their chief, Osceola, refused, thrusting his knife into the unsigned treaty as a show of defiance. A few weeks later, 110 US soldiers on patrol were killed by the Indians and some runaway slaves, sparking the Second Seminole War.

The cost to both sides, financially and in lives, was enormous. In 1837, the US

IN CONTEXT

County, wrecking trailer parks and leaving 150,000 homeless. With damage estimated at $30 billion, it was one of the most costly natural disasters in US history.

After Andrew, the storms kept coming. In 2004, four hurricanes hit south Florida; Miami was affected by Frances, a Category 2, and Jeanne, a Category 3. In 2005, the worst season on record, Miami was hit by a fledgling Katrina on its way to New Orleans, and was then clobbered by the freakish Wilma. Not only did it form in late October, but the Category 2 storm hit Miami from behind, sneaking in from the Gulf Coast to kill 25 people. In October 2012, Hurricane Sandy bypassed south Florida as it made its way up the Atlantic Coast; New York and New Jersey were not so lucky.

The season is not, perhaps, the ideal time to book a trip, but adventure tourists are not daunted. Just as millions of people evacuate, storm chasers arrive en masse, video cameras at the ready.
*Free tours of the National Hurricane Center (Florida International University, 11691 SW 17th Street, 1-305 229 4404, www.nhc.noaa.gov) are available (Jan-mid May) by appointment only.*

# 'The Seminole (meaning 'wild one') would prove a force to be reckoned with.'

agreed to negotiate, and Osceola entered one of their camps under a flag of truce. It was a ruse. He was captured and imprisoned, but still the war raged on. In the end, the US spent $40 million and lost 2,500 soldiers before the majority of the Seminoles (around 4,000) relented and moved to Arkansas. But a few refused to leave, and fled to the Everglades, where they remain today.

## SOUTHERN SYMPATHIES

In 1845, Florida became the 27th state to join the Union and, for a short time, there was peace. Miami also began to take shape. During the war the US had established Fort Dallas, a limestone fortress on the north bank of a river that flowed through southern Florida. When the soldiers left, the fort became the base for a tiny village established by William H English, which he called Miami (from the Indian word 'mayami', meaning 'big water'; the main Tequesta Indian settlement was by the Miami River).

In the meantime, railroads and steamboats had appeared in the north of the state, bringing prosperity and better links with the rest of the Union. William D Moseley was elected state governor and took control of a population that numbered 87,445, of which 39,000 were black slaves. The majority of the white population considered slavery acceptable, and the newly accepted state began to feel isolated as dissent about the use of slaves led to the formation of the Republican Party (trading in slaves had already been abolished in 1808).

When Abraham Lincoln became the first Republican president in 1860, Florida responded by withdrawing from the Union and joining other southern slave states in the Confederacy. Though the Civil War hardly touched south Florida, most of the towns in the north – with the exception of Tallahassee – were captured by the Union. There was only one major engagement: the Battle of Olustee in February 1864, which proved to be one of the last Confederate victories. But on 10 May 1865, federal troops entered Tallahassee and the US flag flew once more. Slavery was abolished, a new state constitution adopted, and Florida was readmitted to the Union in 1868.

## RAILROAD TO PARADISE

The 1862 Homestead Act promised 160 acres of land free to any citizen who would stay for five years and effect improvements. One taker was Edmund Beasley who, in 1868, moved to the bayside area now called Coconut Grove. Two years later, William Brickell bought land on the south bank of the Miami River; Ephraim Sturtevant acquired the area now known as Biscayne. In 1875, his daughter, Julia Tuttle, visited and became smitten. She didn't return for 16 years, but would eventually change the area's history.

Yet Miami would never have become a major city had it not been for one of America's great entrepreneurs. Henry Flagler, who made a $50 million fortune with John Rockefeller in the Standard Oil company, first came to Florida in the 1880s, thinking the warm climate would help his wife's frail health. After moving south, he entered the railroad and hotel business and, starting in St Augustine, built a new railroad. Flagler and his teams slowly worked their way down the east coast, building a plush hotel in each town. With the newspapers extolling Florida's weather – so warm that citrus fruits could be grown there – it soon became a tourist destination for the wintering rich. When another railway magnate, Henry Plant, built the Atlantic Coastline Railroad, which linked Jacksonville to Tampa on the west coast, a deluge of investors and visitors followed.

## THE MOTHER OF MIAMI

At the end of the 1880s, Miami was comprised of nothing more than a few plantations and trading posts. The first proper community, south of the Miami River, was Coconut Grove. But it was only after Julia Tuttle's husband died, in 1886, and she relocated from Cleveland to a plot of land north of the river, that things picked up. Tuttle approached Plant and asked him to extend his railroad to Miami. When she was turned down, she went to Flagler, whose own line stopped at Palm Beach, 66 miles north. He, too, refused, saying there was nothing in Miami.

Tuttle knew that without a railroad, the tiny settlement would be too isolated to prosper. Even the simple act of sending a letter from Palm Beach to Miami took two months: the letter went to a lighthouse at Jupiter, then by Indian river steamer to the railway at Titusville, then by train to New York, then by steamer to Havana, and finally by a trading schooner that docked at the Miami River – a total journey of 3,000 miles. Nature, though, soon intervened.

In the winter of 1894-5, a killer frost devastated the orange crop in the north of the state, but Miami, being further south, escaped the freeze. According to legend, Julia Tuttle sent Flagler a handful of orange blossoms to show that her crop was unaffected. When she agreed to give Flagler half her land (300 acres), along with some of William Brickell's, the hard-nosed businessman agreed to extend his railway.

When the first locomotive arrived in Miami on 15 April 1896, all 300 residents turned out to greet it. But some of the old-timers had never seen a train before and fled to the woods in fright. Thousands of new settlers and investors flocked down in anticipation of a boom. Ralph Munroe, a yacht designer, was one of them. His 1891 Coconut Grove house, the Barnacle, is the last vestige of pioneer architecture, and the oldest house in Dade County.

**Seminole Indians.**

## THE CITY TAKES SHAPE

The shallowness of Biscayne Bay had hindered the growth of the area, but the extension of the railroad meant that machines, supplies and people could easily get to Miami now. A month after the railroad arrived, Miami's first paper, the *Miami Metropolis*, rolled off the presses; in July 1896, Miami was granted city status; in September the first school opened. Flagler built the enormous, luxurious Royal Palm Hotel. Tourists began to visit, lured by advertisements that described Miami as 'the sun porch of America', 'where winter is turned to summer'.

To ensure growth took place in an organised fashion, the city's founders laid out a basic grid plan to the north and south of the river, only to see most of the wooden buildings destroyed in a fire in December 1896. Perhaps it was the shock of seeing her dream go up in flames, but Julia Tuttle died unexpectedly soon afterwards, at just 48 years of age. Miami's founding mother was gone, but the city was quickly rebuilt and the tourists kept coming. However, they were joined by some less welcome visitors.

During the ten-week Spanish-American War in 1898, 7,000 US troops were stationed in Miami waiting to be shipped down to Cuba. They amused themselves by using coconuts for target practice and swimming naked in the bay, much to the chagrin of locals. Tensions between the army and the churchgoing black community were rife and occasionally escalated into violence. Between the residents and the mosquitoes, the soldiers were miserable. One wrote home: 'If I owned both Miami and Hell, I'd rent out Miami and live in Hell.'

## MIAMI VICE

With the new century came new settlers. Both the population and the town grew rapidly; a business district, banks, movie theatres and a rival newspaper, the *Miami Evening Record*, were set up. There were so many drinking dens and gin houses that the main thoroughfare became known as Whiskey Street, prompting the arrival of Carry Amelia Moore Nation, 'the

Kansas Cyclone'. A giant of a woman, and the wife of a chronic alcoholic, she had a mission to banish all booze, seeing her name – Carry A Nation – as divine providence. She stormed into Miami in 1908 and sold copies of her newsletter, 'Smasher's Mail', but to no avail.

Even then, law enforcement was hardly Miami's strong point. The city's first marshall was Young F Gray, a bandy-legged Texan who was frequently so drunk that he needed help to mount his bicycle. As well as being the city's first cop, he was also the first to be suspended for drunkenness.

## CASTLES ON THE SAND

Governor Napoleon Bonaparte Broward, in office from 1905 to 1909, was the first to begin drainage of the Everglades in order to reclaim land for development. By 1913, 142 miles of canals had been constructed, and Henry Flagler had extended his railroad all the way to Key West. Government Cut, later known as the Port of Miami, was dug across the lower end of the future Miami Beach to improve access to the harbour, creating Fisher Island in the process.

John Collins, a visionary rather than a businessman, saw potential in the area and borrowed money to build a bridge from Miami to the beach. His money ran out halfway through, but he was bailed out by Carl Fisher, who had made a fortune inventing a new kind of car headlight; in return, Fisher was given much of the land on the beach. By the start of World War I, Miami was booming.

Fisher saw the potential of the beach and began removing trees and dredging the sea to realise his vision. In a year, the area had its first hotels, swimming pools, restaurants and casinos. It was a playground for the rich, many of whom moved to Miami permanently, building lavish waterfront estates such as James Deering's opulent Vizcaya (*see p59*).

## BOOM, BUST...

Miami's population doubled between 1920 and 1923. Many newcomers were drawn by slick advertising campaigns promoting equally slick community developments, such as the 3,000-acre Coral Gables. Described by its developer George Merrick as the City Beautiful, the Gables was designed as a vision of paradise on earth and regulated by an array of local laws – still in place today – to stay that way. The lavish Biltmore Hotel, built in 1926, typified the area's European feel and air of exclusivity. But not all new residents were so well-to-do.

Prohibition and its 'anti-saloon laws' never worked in Miami. With rum runners able to smuggle freely along the vast coast, the city soon became overrun by mobsters and illegal liquor, earning itself the nickname 'the leakiest spot in America'. Things got so bad that the old courthouse, once the venue for public hangings, had to be replaced in 1926 by a larger building (the Dade County Courthouse would hold the title of Miami's tallest building for 50 years).

Meanwhile, Miami enjoyed a building boom. Prices rocketed as speculators rushed in (the boom was satirised in the Marx Brothers' first movie, The Cocoanuts). Hotels and airports sprang up. Miami Beach alone suddenly found itself with more than 15,000 residents.

Everyone was so busy making money that when the Miami Tribune warned, in September 1926, of an impending tropical storm, few people paid attention. How they wished they had. A hurricane hit in the middle of the night in September, when winds of up to 128 miles per hour pounded the city. More than 100 people died and thousands were left homeless.

The hurricane damage was just being mended when the Great Depression and a state-wide recession brought on by the 1929 Wall Street Crash descended. As if that weren't enough, the northern part of Florida was invaded by Mediterranean fruit flies, which destroyed 60 per cent of the citrus groves. It seemed that the city was finished, a sentiment echoed by newspaper headlines that screamed: 'Miami is wiped out!'

### ...AND REBUILDING

Many of the millionaires who had profited during the boom years, including George Merrick and one-time mayor John 'Ev'

Sewell, were destroyed by the fall in real estate prices. But the mix of beautiful beaches, warm climate and endless potential remained, so new money soon began to flow in.

A group of mostly Jewish developers began building small, Moderne-style hotels on Miami Beach along Collins Avenue and Ocean Drive, adding to Miami's fast-growing Jewish community and creating what would later become the Art Deco District. With the hotels came tourists, and with the tourists came renewed prosperity. Pan American Airways launched a service connecting Miami with dozens of other major cities, including many in South America. Miami was soon established as one of the country's key 'gateways to Latin America' and the population grew steadily.

After Franklin D Roosevelt came to power in 1933 – just weeks after he survived an assassination attempt in Miami's Bayfront Park, in which Chicago mayor Anton Cermak was killed – he launched the New Deal, a package of reconstruction programmes designed to better the lives of Americans. Young men and war veterans were drafted to build parks and new public buildings, which, in Miami, included fire stations, highways, public housing and social clubs. A hurricane struck on Labor Day 1935, killing 400 people and wiping out much of the new construction work, but, once again, Miami found the will to rebuild. There was, however, resentment about Jewish involvement in southern Miami Beach. Slowly, the Beach became segregated: 'Gentiles Only' signs appeared in the northern part, just as the tide of anti-Semitism began to rise across the Atlantic.

### THE WAR AT HOME

The battles in Europe and the Far East seemed a long way off until the US naval base at Pearl Harbor was bombed without warning by the Japanese on 7 December 1941. The US entered the war, and no one was sure what would happen next. Florida's coastline was seen as a weak link in the US's defence, and tourism, by then the mainstay of Miami's economy, dropped off dramatically. Everyone's worst fears were confirmed in February 1942 when, in full view of thousands of horrified Miami residents, a fleet of German submarines attacked and sank four tankers in a torpedo attack just off the main harbour. More attacks quickly followed: with most of the US Navy's major ships out in the Pacific Ocean, German U-boats found they could attack Florida virtually at will. While the US never had to face the equivalent of the Blitz, the submarines ensured that Miami residents would never feel safe, and what little tourism remained quickly died away.

Ironically, the war would later save Miami. The warm climate was deemed perfect for training new soldiers, and by the end of 1942, nearly 150 hotels had been converted into barracks, with others turned into temporary hospitals for the wounded. By the time World War II was over, one-quarter of all officers and a fifth of enlisted men in the US Army Air Corps had passed through Miami.

The shortage of manpower brought about by the war improved the lot of Miami's growing black community. In the late 1940s, the first black police officer was appointed to patrol the

IN CONTEXT

## Beatles on the Beach

*How the Fab Four rocked Miami.*

Miami is frequently hit by hurricanes that blow in from the Caribbean. But in February 1964, a storm swept in from Britain: Beatlemania. The Fab Four's visit to Florida launched the Beatles' first US tour, and it marked a pivotal moment – when they morphed from Brit boy band into global superstars.

During the previous year, the Beatles had scored three number ones in the UK, but had bombed across the pond. 'I Want to Hold Your Hand', released in the US in December 1963, changed all that, reaching number one on the

Billboard charts. And after triumphant appearances on *The Ed Sullivan Show* in New York, the band flew to Miami for the sequel. On 13 February, the group's plane – a National 11 DC-8 flown by a pilot wearing a mop-top wig – landed at Miami International Airport, and pandemonium ensued. 'Do you think anybody will be here to meet us?' Paul McCartney asked a stewardess. Some 7,000 screaming teenagers answered his question.

The band stayed at the Deauville Beach Resort (*see p151*): John Lennon

'coloured district', and an all-black municipal court was set up. The city's first black judge was also appointed, and blacks were finally allowed into the Orange Bowl Stadium, albeit confined to sitting in the end zone.

Beaches remained segregated, however, adding to the underlying racial tensions that occasionally exploded into violence. In 1951, Carver Village, a black housing project in a formerly white neighbourhood, was repeatedly bombed. Several synagogues and a Miami Shores church were attacked because of their pro-black sympathies and activities.

## WELCOME TO VACATIONLAND

In the 1950s, southern Florida, and Miami in particular, became America's playground. Air travel made the place accessible to New Yorkers for quick weekends. Miami Beach gained a new strip of fabulous hotels, notably the Diplomat, Eden Roc and Fontainebleau. Designed by architect Morris Lapidus, the Fontainebleau was a stage set of a hotel. It gave its patrons everything they'd ever dreamed of, and was the celebrity magnet of its day. The entertainment manager, Joe Fischetti, was a cousin of Al Capone and a friend of Frank Sinatra,

hid in room 1211 with his then secret wife, Cynthia; the others split rooms 1218 and 1219, Paul and Ringo sharing one room, George Harrison crashing in the other with Murray the K, a New York DJ. Though the boys were photographed frolicking in the surf next to bemused matrons, mostly they were holed up inside, as fans wrote 'I love you, John' in the sand. Ruth Regina, their make-up artist, recalls the roar of the fans on the beach drowning out the roar of the surf. Two fans tried to get into the boys' rooms by posting themselves inside giant parcels. Trapped indoors, Paul McCartney fed the seagulls from his balcony.

On the evening of 16 February, wearing blue silk suits with black velvet collars, the band took to the stage in the Deauville's Napoleon ballroom in front of 3,000 hysterical fans. The gig was broadcast on *The Ed Sullivan Show* and 70 million Americans watched them sing 'She Loves You', 'This Boy', 'All My Loving', 'I Saw Her Standing There', 'From Me to You', 'Til There was You' and 'I Want to Hold Your Hand'.

After the concert, there was time for fun. 'Miami was like paradise,' said Paul McCartney. 'We had never been anywhere where there were palm trees. We were real tourists; we had our Pentax cameras and took lots of pictures.' Ringo Starr went to his first drive-in (in a Lincoln Continental) and watched *Fun in Acapulco* starring Elvis Presley. Buddy Dresner, their security guard, taught the boys how to fish and invited them home for a roast beef dinner ('Ringo cut my son's potato,' his wife, Dottie, told a local paper). He even lent the boys his speedboat, which Ringo promptly crashed into a pier. 'They didn't seem to mind,' Starr recalled.

The lads saw Don Rickles perform a stand-up gig and watched The Coasters in concert at the Mau Mau Room. Most famously, they met Muhammad Ali – then Cassius Clay – at the Fifth Street Gym, where he was training for a match against Sonny Liston, the world heavyweight champion. The Beatles entered the ring singing 'Yeah, yeah, yeah' and pretended to attack Ali, who jokingly responded 'No, no, no'. When John Lennon crooned, 'Listen, do you want to know a secret?' Ali pretended to knock him out. Then the boxer, who won his first world title later that week, told the boys: 'The whole world is shook up about you.'

**IN CONTEXT**

The 1980 Mariel Boatlift brought 125,000 Cuban refugees to Miami.

who played a series of engagements at the hotel. Sinatra and the hotel also hosted Elvis Presley's first post-army performance, an hour-long special made for ABC. The Fontainebleau was also the setting for *The Bellboy*, directed by and starring Jerry Lewis. By the mid '50s, two and a half million tourists were coming to Miami every year. Tourism chiefs claimed that more hotels had been built on Miami Beach since the end of World War II than in the rest of the world combined.

When Havana, the East Coast's premier party spot, was closed down by revolution in 1959, Miami cleaned up, offering a new mecca of surf, sun, flesh and flash. Chat show host Ed Sullivan moved down to broadcast from the Beach and secured the first performance by the Beatles on their US tour (*see p246* **Beatles on the Beach**).

## CUBAN MIGRATION

The 1959 Cuban revolution changed Miami in other, more significant ways. The city became home to thousands of anti-Castro immigrants. What started as a trickle became a flood as daily flights brought 100,000 Cubans to the city within a few months. Although the first wave was from Cuba's affluent middle classes, later arrivals were far less wealthy and found themselves competing with Miami's poorest residents for jobs and housing. When a recession hit in the 1970s, unemployment soared and violent, race-related confrontations became the norm, though this did little to stop the flow of Cubans. By 1973, there were more than 300,000 in Miami. The Jewish community also grew rapidly in the mid 1970s, becoming one of the largest concentrations of Jews in the US outside New York. Miami was very attractive to the older Jewish generation: 75 per cent of those living there were aged over 60.

Racial tensions, however, remained. In the summer of 1980, an all-white jury in Tampa, on the west coast of Florida, acquitted a white policeman of beating black insurance agent Arthur McDuffie to death. The anger of Miami's African-American community boiled over into a riot that claimed 18 lives and levelled parts of Liberty City. The disruption lasted three days and caused damage estimated at $80 million. The next week – as thousands of 'boat people' arrived from Haiti, fleeing their dictator and attracted by the success of the Cuban immigrants – *Time* magazine ran a cover story about Miami headlined 'Paradise Lost?'

The Mariel Boatlift in 1980 brought 125,000 Cuban refugees to Miami, including thousands of criminals and mental patients, part of a plan by Castro to unload the dregs of society. Cubans established themselves as the premier drug dealers in the area, not hesitating to shoot rivals out of business. Miami became Murder Capital USA, with 621 violent deaths in the city in 1981 alone, most of them narcotics related.

## DOWNTOWN COOL

Local councillors realised something had to be done to prevent Downtown and South Beach from being overrun by dealers and down-and-outs. The Art Deco District received federal protection, a new transport network was developed, and fashion photographers began staging shoots in South Beach, sparking its transformation in the 1980s and '90s into a hipster hangout buzzing with clubs, restaurants and bars. Xavier Suarez became Miami's first Cuban-born mayor in 1985, and worked to reduce racial tensions. Two years later, the city had become safe enough for the Pope to visit.

## ON THE UP

In 2007, what became known as 'Miami Manhattanisation' was in full swing, with construction beginning on some of the tallest buildings ever erected in the city's history. A year later, the boom burst in the wake of the subprime mortgage crisis, resulting in scores of empty and unfinished apartment buildings. But recent numbers have shown increased real estate sales and prices, and the sound of construction can be heard as projects that were put on hold when the bust hit are revving back up again. The Port of Miami Tunnel, a project that will widen the MacArthur Causeway by one lane in each direction (at an estimated cost of $1 billion) is back on and due to be completed in 2014. The city's dining and cultural scenes are heating up, too, and visitors are arriving in droves – in 2012, the hotel occupancy rate reached a 12-year high. As has happened so many times in the past, Miami is rebounding.

## Key Events

**1513** Juan Ponce de León lands in Florida, claiming it for Spain.
**1763** Spain cedes Florida to Britain.
**1783** The Spanish gain control again.
**1817-9** The First Seminole War.
**1819** Spain hands Florida to the US; it becomes a US territory in 1821.
**1835-42** The Second Seminole War.
**1845** Florida joins the Union, then withdraws during the American Civil War. It's eventually readmitted in 1868.
**1855-8** The Third Seminole War.
**1896** Henry Flagler's railroad arrives in April. Miami is granted city status in July.
**1905-13** The Everglades are drained to provide land for building; Miami Beach grows.
**1921** George Merrick begins building the city of Coral Gables.
**1926** A hurricane destroys much of the city, and Miami slides into recession, exacerbated by the Wall Street Crash of 1929.

**1930s** Hundreds of art deco hotels are built on Miami Beach.
**1935** A Labor Day hurricane wrecks the city, killing 400.
**1941** US joins World War II; thousands of US troops train in Miami.
**1959** Fidel Castro takes power in Cuba; 100,000 Cubans flee to Miami.
**1961** Kennedy attacks the Bay of Pigs.
**1962** The Cuban Missile Crisis.
**1980** The Liberty City riots tear the city apart; the Mariel Boatlift backfires.
**1984** *Miami Vice* begins on US TV.
**1992** Hurricane Andrew hits south Florida, leaving 150,000 people homeless.
**2000** Bush wins the presidential election, but only after multiple recounts in Florida.
**2003** The Florida Marlins win the baseball World Series.
**2008** The subprime mortgage crisis triggers a drop in property prices.
**2010** Construction begins on the Port of Miami Tunnel.

IN CONTEXT

# Architecture

*Eye candy abounds, from flamboyant palazzos to MiMo motels.*

If you build it, they will come. The phrase may call to mind Kevin Costner's baseball film *Field of Dreams*, but it's also an apt summary of Miami's architecture. Of course, the city is known for its peerless art deco legacy – Miami Beach has the highest concentration of deco buildings in the world, and their preservation has saved the South Beach skyline from becoming a canyon of condos. Yet there's a lot more to local architecture than pastels and portholes, and high-profile firms are creating a new wave of architectural landmarks. Miami's myriad styles have one thing in common, though: a feeling of fantasy and innovation.

## A SIMPLE START

The exception to the rule is Miami's earliest architecture, whose plain stylings stood in stark contrast to the later glitz. Dubbed 'frame vernacular', the pioneer homes of the late 1800s were built from local lumber and adapted for the hot climate: there were deep eaves and porches for shade, ample doors and windows for ventilation, and stilts for protection from flooding. The **Barnacle** (*see p58*) is a fine example: in yuppie Coconut Grove, it looks like a shack from *Little House on the Prairie* blew on to the set of *CSI: Miami*.

The Royal Palms, Miami's first hotel, was also wooden, but it was not spartan. Built by railway magnate Henry Flagler in 1897, it was a riverfront palace that hosted the likes of the Rockefellers, Carnegies and Vanderbilts. With starry guests and, for the time, opulent features (lifts, electricity, ballrooms, a pool and a gigantic veranda), it was a disaster movie waiting to happen. And in 1926 disaster did strike: a hurricane destroyed it.

## THE AGE OF OPULENCE

By then, wood-framed buildings were out of fashion and Mediterranean Revival was all the rage anyway. Its champion was Addison Mizner, a high society architect

*'Opa-Locka, which was modelled on the Middle East, was billed as the Baghdad of Dade County.'*

who grew up in Central America and was captivated by its exuberant buildings. In the 1920s, his lavish blend of Spanish, Moorish, Italian and Venetian styles transformed Palm Beach into a fantasy land for the rich and famous. The Mediterranean Revival style was ideal for the steamy climate: Mizner's buildings stayed cool thanks to wide balconies, cloistered walkways, terraces, courtyards and open loggias. Not only did the pale pastel colours look pretty in the Florida sun, they deflected heat.

The exotic pastiche also gave the Sunshine State a distinctive look and started a local trend for pushing the architectural envelope: 'The landscape gives you no help in Florida,' said Mizner. 'You must make your own.' Building in virgin territory certainly unleashed

**IN CONTEXT**

**The Barnacle**.

Mizner's creativity, according to Frank Lloyd Wright, one of the architect's fans. 'Many architects have imagination,' said Wright, 'but only Mizner had the courage to let his out of the cage.' One of his most famous remaining works is the luxurious **Boca Raton Resort & Club** (501 East Camino Real, Boca Raton, 1-888 543 1277, www.bocaresort.com), which the *New York Times* described as 'a palazzo masquerading as a hotel'.

In Miami, Mediterranean Revival reached gaudy new heights with **Vizcaya** (*see p59*), a 1922 Italianate palace built by industrial magnate James Deering. The 70-room showpiece blended together Renaissance, Baroque, rococo and neoclassical styles in a ten-acre Eden of jasmine and live oaks.

But Vizcaya had nothing on Coral Gables, also built in the 1920s. Billed as the 'most beautiful garden city in the world' by developer George Merrick, the plush district melded Spanish, Moorish and Italianate architecture in a 10,000-acre Shangri-La graced with classical fountains and squares. To make up for the lack of beaches, Merrick built winding waterways complete with gondolas, and fashioned the spectacular **Venetian Pool** out of an old quarry (*see p55*).

The marketing matched the architecture. Streets were given Spanish names: Ponce de León, Santa Maria and Alcazar. To attract the rich, Merrick imported foxes for hunting and Tahitian boys to shuck coconuts. At the **Biltmore Hotel** (*see p157*), the jet set gathered for polo matches and tea dances.

Other developers used a similar marketing technique and sold romantically named fantasies: Hollywood, Olympia, Mecca Gardens, Aladdin City. Opa-Locka, which was modelled on the Middle East, was billed as the Baghdad of Dade County; developer Glenn Curtiss sent his architect a copy of the *Arabian Nights*, resulting in domes, spires, parapets and minarets. Miami Springs, meanwhile, paid homage to the American south-west.

## TROPICAL DECO

The Depression brought an end to the showy Spanish style – excess was out. But art deco suited austerity. Functional replaced fussy, and the streamlined look

IN CONTEXT

Vizcaya.

was optimistic and futuristic. After the 1926 hurricane destroyed Miami Beach, deco architects such as L Murray Dixon and Henry Hohauser had a blank canvas.

Art deco was also a bit of fun in the gloom, especially once local architects had given the style a Miami twist. Buildings were embellished with flowers, flamingos and nautical touches (porthole windows, deck-style balconies). White exteriors were accented with bright colours: blue to evoke the sea, green to reflect the palms, pink as a nod to the sunset. In addition, the sharp aerodynamic angles and geometric shapes were contrasted with sensual textures: mother of pearl, exotic woods, frosted glass, limestone and terrazzo. To keep out the sun, 'eyebrows' were added to windows.

### FABULOUS '50S

Art deco gets all the glory, but Miami also has a rich legacy of Mid-century Modern buildings (MiMo). Shaped by the International Style, Bauhaus and Frank Lloyd Wright, MiMo in its purest form is austere: all concrete slabs and strict rectangles. But Miami architects fashioned a more flamboyant version. Local motifs included undulating walls, asymmetrical lines and vibrant colour. Kitsch cheesecake cut-outs and kidney-shaped pools also came into play, as did space-age details (weird fins and boomerangs). The god of MiMo was Morris Lapidus, whose work critics described as everything from 'the architecture of joy' to 'stark raving mad'. His motto was 'less is a bore' and 'too much is never enough'.

A true crowd pleaser, Lapidus said: 'My buildings are the crazy hat for women, the bright tie for men.' His most fabulous examples are the **Fontainebleau** (*see p150*) and Eden Roc hotels, but the funky **Deauville Beach Resort** (*see p151*), built by Lapidus protégé Melvin Grossman, is another gem: it looks like something from *The Jetsons*. The **Days Inn Thunderbird Beach Resort** in Sunny Isles Beach (*see p154*), the work of another MiMo star Norman Giller, is a 1955 monument to kitsch Americana, while the 1963 **Bacardi**

**Biltmore Hotel.**

**Building** (*see p50*) a masterpiece of Latin Modernism by Puerto Rican architect Enrique Gutierrez, mixes brutalism with florid murals. Roy France's 1949 **New Casablanca on the Ocean Resort Hotel** (6345 Collins Avenue, North Miami Beach) has a campy entrance featuring Arabian genie statues holding up the car port. The seedy motels in the MiMo district (*see p00*) also offer a glimpse of faded glory.

### BUILDING THE FUTURE

Miami's great architecture is not all in the past. The bold skyscrapers of the Arquitectonica firm are being copied from Dubai to Shanghai. Arquitectonica's first claim to fame was the 1982 **Atlantis condo** (2025 Brickell Avenue, Downtown; *photo p257*). Seen in the opening credits of *Miami Vice*, it's a flashy glass tower with a hole in the middle, accented by Lego-like trim. Dubbed 'Beach Blanket

# Walk Deco District

*Step back to the glory days along Ocean Drive.*

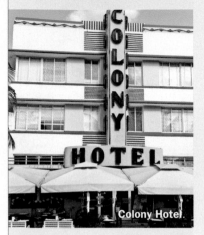

Colony Hotel.

Forget the sand: the best thing about South Beach is its sleek, streamlined, iridescent architecture, easily explored on foot. Unlike the grandiose power-tripping of its New York or Chicago relatives, Miami art deco is as giddy as a 1920s flapper decked out in beads and baubles. More than 800 buildings from the 1930s and early '40s survive in the city's historic Deco District, between 5th Street to the south and Dade Boulevard to the north. There's no single masterpiece, but the high concentration of flamboyant styles makes for a theatrical streetscape.

It's incredible to think that these buildings were almost destroyed by developers in the early 1970s. Their survival is due to a handful of activists who, in 1976, founded the Miami Design Preservation League (MDPL) and ensured South Beach was listed on the National Register of Historic Places.

The boom in South Beach deco is the result of two key events: the 1925 Paris Exposition Internationale des Arts Décoratifs et Industriels Modernes, and the hurricane of 1926. With most of the Beach's buildings destroyed by the latter, architects had a free hand to capitalise on the decorative and industrial trends sweeping the design world. Ship portholes and streamlined wings were incorporated into building designs; angular shapes and geometric patterns became predominant; while whimsical decorative touches, such as bas-reliefs, began to incorporate tropical themes including palm trees and flamingos.

### OCEAN & 5TH

The greatest haul of deco is concentrated in the ten blocks north of 5th Street, particularly along Ocean Drive. The principal architects of deco South Beach were New Yorkers Henry Hohauser and L Murray Dixon. **Park Central Hotel** (630 Ocean Drive) is one of Hohauser's best efforts, dating back to 1937 and featuring bold vertical bands and window 'eyebrows'.

The mauve, green and white colour scheme isn't authentic. The buildings of South Beach were originally painted white with subtle pastel trim. The postcard-friendly candy colours came along in the 1980s when Leonard Horowitz, an interior designer and MDPL preservationist, devised a palette of tones to draw attention to the architecture – and away from the squalor.

Jerry's Famous Deli.

In the early 1980s, this area was a bad crime spot, a natural setting for the gory violence in Brian De Palma's movie *Scarface*, which was shot at 728 Ocean Drive, as well as much of the action in hit crime show *Miami Vice*. The **Colony Hotel** at 736 Ocean Drive is one of Hohauser's first hotels (1935), and it's worth slipping into the lobby for a look at the original green Vitrolite fireplace with mural. More murals can be found at the 1939 **Breakwater Hotel** (940 Ocean Drive), signposted by a soaring pylon; the lobby paintings here feature a group of politicians and preservationists turning away a wrecking ball hovering over Ocean Drive.

Just over the road, the lone building in the park is the **Art Deco Welcome Center** (*see p256*). The centre is run by the MPDL, which first sprang into action when it tried to save two blocks of Ocean Drive, from 12th to 14th Streets. The focus was the deco triumvirate of the **Leslie** (no.1244), **Carlyle** (no.1250) and **Cardozo** (no.1300) hotels, built by different architects between 1937 and 1941. The Carlyle is classic Miami Beach deco: a flashy ensemble of striking vertical piers, horizontal lines, visor-like sunshades and curvaceous corners. Pure camp, it was a natural for the role of gay nightclub in *The Birdcage* (1996).

## COLLINS & ESPAÑOLA

The inspiration for the drag queens at the Birdcage was the Warsaw. Now closed, it was a legendary 1990s centre of debauchery housed in the striking **Hoffman's Cafeteria Building** (1450 Collins Avenue), a deco gem with central turret and sweeping 'angel wings' designed by Hohauser in 1939. From a cafeteria it became a ballroom, then a series of clubs, including the Warsaw; now it's **Jerry's Famous Deli**.

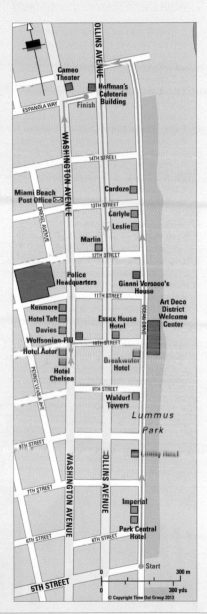

► **Walk** Deco District **(continued)**

Collins Avenue is less of a unified architectural set piece than Ocean Drive. Nonetheless, a handful of gems survive, notably the **Marlin** (no.1200), a 1939 design by Dixon that recalls sci-fi serials of the era such as *Flash Gordon*. Two blocks south of the Marlin is another beauty – Hohauser's 1938 **Essex House Hotel** (no.1001), where the porthole windows and smokestack-like neon tower call to mind a land-locked ocean liner. Collins also looks great at night, as the light fades to a bruised purple and the neon is switched on.

**WASHINGTON & 10TH**
Walk one block west and the money suddenly stops. While there are a handful of beautifully polished places on Washington Avenue, such as the **Hotel Chelsea** (no.944) and the **Hotel Astor** (no.956), most of the deco back here – such as the Wyndham Garden (no.1050) – looks like it's missed the party. Though there's some pretty gilt deco design in the foyer of the **Wolfsonian-FIU** (no.1001).

Three blocks up on the left is the **Miami Beach Post Office** (1300 Washington Avenue), dating from 1939 and designed in a style termed 'deco Federal'. It has a classical central rotunda and a minimalist façade, but the interior is busy with a cowboys-and-Indians frieze, a starburst ceiling and bits of shiny brass detailing.

On grim Washington, it's best to look up, particularly at no.1445, the old **Cameo Theater**, now the Cameo nightclub; above the chrome canopy and glass-block panel is a pretty carved keystone with a flourish of palm fronds.

Take a right on Española and you're back on Collins at Jerry's Famous Deli. But you don't have to stop: there's more fine deco north on Collins, particularly around 21st Street.

**Art Deco Welcome Center**
*1001 Ocean Drive, at 10th Street (1-305 672 2014, www.mdpl.org/welcome-center).* Bus C, H, K, W, South Beach Local. **Open** 9.30am-7pm daily. **Admission** free. **Credit** AmEx, MC, V. **Map** p280 D3. Guided deco walking tours 10.30am daily; Thursday evening tours 6.30pm ($20; $15 reductions). Self-guided audio tours 9.30am-5pm ($15).

Miami Beach Post Office.

Adrienne Arsht Center for the Performing Arts.

Bauhaus' and 'ecstatic modernism', the high-tech style blends the purity and panache of deco and MiMo with sci-fi. The surreal **Miami Children's Museum** (*see p161*) is another fine example.

**AQUA** (www.aqua.net), a gated community on Allison Island, also merges past and present. But this postmodern blend of deco and MiMo townhouses is also notable for its New Urbanist philosophy, which values high density and a pedestrian-friendly, village feel. It was developed by Craig Robins (who revived SoBe and the Design District) and planned by Duany Plater-Zyberk (DPZ), the Miami architects who created Seaside, a New Urbanist pastiche of small town USA in the Florida Panhandle (its clapboard cottages and front porches starred in *The Truman Show*).

If the new architecture is the stuff of fantasy and film sets, well, that's the Florida way. Over the years, local architects have fashioned a landscape of escape. No wonder the star architects are coming too. Argentine Cesar Pelli designed the dramatic **Adrienne Arsht Center for the Performing Arts** (*see p188*), Frank Gehry built the **New World Center** (*see p187*), a box-like concert hall for the New World Symphony whose simple style harks back to the world-renowned architect's earliest designs, and Swiss firm Herzog & de Meuron is working its magic on the **Pérez Art Museum Miami (PAMM)**, scheduled to open in December 2013. The blockbuster buildings go hand in hand with the revitalisation of Downtown. In Miami, if you build it, they will indeed come.

# Essential Information

# Getting Around

## ARRIVING & LEAVING

### By air

#### Miami International Airport (MIA)
*1-305 876 7000, www.miami-airport.com.* **Maps** pp278-279.
MIA is north-west of Downtown Miami. Unless you're planning to rent a car, the easiest way to get from the airport is the **SuperShuttle** (1-305 871 2000, www.supershuttle.com), a shared-ride van service. You'll find dispatchers waiting on the curb wherever you exit on the lower level of the arrivals building. Fares are $20 ($10 additional passengers) to a South Beach hotel or private residence; and $12-$31 to Coral Gables or Coconut Grove. You can arrange for the SuperShuttle to take you back to MIA by calling or making an online reservation 24 hours in advance.

You'll find **taxis** waiting outside MIA's arrival terminals. There's a $32 flat rate (not including tolls or tip) to South Beach – be sure to ask for it. The fare to Coral Gables is about $14-$34, or about $22 to Coconut Grove, both without tip.

You can also take the **Miami Beach Airport Flyer** from MIA to and from Miami Beach; it's a WiFi-equipped bus that costs just $2.35 each way. The Flyer runs every 30 minutes, offering an express service to and from the airport from 6am to 11.40pm, seven days a week. The service runs between the MIA Metrorail station (which can easily be reached by the MIA Mover, a 1.25-mile-long automated people mover that runs between the airport and Miami Rental Car Center) and Miami Beach (from 41st Street to South Pointe Drive). For more information, call 1-305 891 3131 or visit www.miamidade.gov/transit.

Launched in 2010, the MIA Rental Car Center (RCC) is a convenient, one-stop shop where visitors have their pick from 16 car rental agencies. Travellers arrive at the RCC via the MIA Mover; be sure that the rental agency gives you a map, so you can easily find your way out of the parking lot. The RCC's Quick Turnaround Area is equipped with 120 petrol pumps, though there are also several petrol stations along Le Jeune Road (NW 42nd Avenue) that are handy for pre-return refills.

#### Fort Lauderdale-Hollywood International Airport
*1-954 359 1200, www.fll.net.*
From Fort Lauderdale Airport you have several options on how to make the 30-mile trip to Miami. The best is to rent a car at the airport and drive south on either I-95 or the Florida Turnpike. Otherwise, take a shuttle bus from the lower level at the western end of Terminal 1 or between Terminals 2 and 3 or 3 and 4 to the Tri-Rail station and then take a commuter train south to Miami. Note, however, that the **Tri-Rail** schedule is very limited, running every two hours at the weekend.

There is also a shared-ride van service, **Go Airport Shuttle** (1-954 561 8888, www.go-airport shuttle.com), which will take you to your hotel in Miami or Miami Beach. Fares are $21 per person to South Beach, $34.50 to Coral Gables.

When it comes to returning to Fort Lauderdale Airport, there's another shared-ride option: you can book the **SuperShuttle** (1-305 871 2000, www.supershuttle.com) 24 hours in advance for $43 ($14 additional passengers) from South Beach, $46 from Coconut Grove and Coral Gables. Unfortunately, it doesn't pick up from the airport.

### By bus or rail

**Greyhound** and **Amtrak** run, respectively, bus and rail services into and out of Miami. For details and station addresses, *see p206.*

## PUBLIC TRANSPORT

Miami's public transport system is run by **Miami-Dade Transit**. For information and detailed transit maps, log on to www.miamidade. gov/transit or call 1-305 891 3131 (7am-8pm Mon-Fri, 8am-5pm Sat, closed Sun). Alternatively, try the Transit Information Center at Government Center Station, where you can pick up route maps or, if you're very lucky, the Miami-Dade County Transit Map, a schematic plan showing the various transport services and their connections. Guard it with your life.

### Buses

Buses – called **Metrobuses** in Miami – are for the unlucky. Only the poor or very elderly don't drive in this town. The vehicles are clean, air-conditioned and comfy, but they travel congested routes and often don't readily serve the places where visitors might want to go. (On South Beach itself, however, there's the South Beach Local shuttle bus; *see p32*). For more on specific, useful routes, see the individual Explore chapter introductions. Frequency of service varies by route, time and day of the week: as often as every 10 or 15 minutes or as far apart as every 45 minutes.

#### Fares & bus stops
A one-way bus fare is $2; children up to 3ft 6in tall travel free. Express buses cost $2.35. Transfers cost an extra 50¢; you must ask and pay for a transfer when you get on the bus. You'll need the exact fare, but the machines do take silver, crisp dollar bills and EASY tickets (*see below*). Bus stops are marked by a rectangular white sign with a blue and green metal marker bearing specific bus route(s), and often by a yellow kerb stripe. Sometimes they're not marked at all. Shelters are uncommon, so take a hat.

#### Tokens & passes
For frequent bus use, purchase an EASY Card, a reloadable transport pass that lets you pre-pay up to $150 on to a one-day, seven-day or one-month pass. EASY Cards can be purchased online (www.easycard. miamidade.gov) or at any Metrorail ticket vending station. If you're in town for a while and planning to do some major schlepping on public transport, the EASY Card can save you money, time and the annoyance of carrying change at all times.

### Rail

There are three train lines in Miami-Dade – **Metromover**, **Metrorail** and **Tri-Rail**.

#### Metromover
Miami's Metromover, an elevated, electric monorail that runs two very short loops – one inner, one outer – around Downtown from 5am to

ESSENTIAL INFORMATION

midnight seven days a week, is free to travel and offers fine views. Sadly, that's about all it offers as it goes nowhere useful.

### Metrorail

A 24.4-mile elevated train system that runs from Palmetto (north) to Dadeland (south), with stops around every mile, Metrorail is another of Miami's expensive and underused transit systems. As on the bus, a trip costs $2, plus 50¢ for a transfer. Trains run about every 15 minutes from 5am until midnight and every 30 minutes on weekends. If you plan to use Metrorail you must purchase an EASY Card or ticket; cash is not accepted. Visitors might find Metrorail useful for trips to Coconut Grove, Coral Gables and Vizcaya. Metrorail also connects to **Tri-Rail**, the Gulf Coast's intercity commuter system (*see p206*).

## TAXIS

Taxi meters start at $2.50 for the first one-sixth of a mile and click away at $2.40 per additional mile, plus waiting time charges ($24 per hour). For short distances, they're affordable; for long distances, they can cost a fortune. The meter racks up $10 just travelling the length of the MacArthur Causeway. On top of hefty fares, you're also expected to tip 15 per cent; cabs carry a handy tip calculation chart pasted on the passenger windows. Visit www.taxifarefinder.com before reserving a trip to get an estimated price. Cabs are usually radio-dispatched, but on South Beach and Downtown you can flag one down. Restaurants and hotels will call cabs for patrons. Note that drivers often speak little or no English. Some reliable companies are **Best Yellow Taxi Service** (1-305 444 4444), **Central Cabs** (1-305 532 5555) and **Metro Taxi** (1-305 888 8888).

Limos are a dime a dozen in some areas, especially South Beach. Rates start at $50 per hour for a Lincoln Town Car and escalate to $100-$125 per hour for a ten-passenger stretch limo. Nearly all companies require a 3hr minimum rental time, and many tack on a 20 per cent 'gratuity'. Ask your hotel to recommend a service.

To make a complaint about a taxi, call 1-305 375 3677.

## DRIVING

Like most Americans, Miamians regard driving as their birthright. But because such a large segment of the population was neither born

nor raised here, many residents drive without knowledge of local traffic rules. In addition to the usual big-city problems, you'll encounter some uniquely local driving issues, such as drivers who change lanes without signalling, stop suddenly at the top of freeway on-ramps in merging lanes and/or ignore stop signs. Then there are the many elderly drivers who drive in a kind of panic but at a snail's pace, always refusing to give way. Not to mention those with their mobile phones clamped to their ears. Don't forget, too, that several major highways change names with mysterious frequency.

The potentially lethal driving dangers for which Miami became notorious in the early 1990s – carjackings – have subsided to normal (for the US) levels, although you still wouldn't want to get lost in many neighbourhoods. (Generally speaking, Miami's easternmost communities are safer than the central and western sectors).

If you do find yourself lost and in need of directions, stay calm. Always stop at well-lit commercial outlets for directions, and take into account who's around. Another option is to call your hotel or your destination for directions. Don't leave valuable items visible in your car, even while you're in motion, as 'smash-and-grab' robbers approach idling cars at traffic lights.

If you break down, use your judgement about whether to leave the car and phone for help. The AAA recommends you wait until a police car passes and flag it down. If you're a member of the AAA or have affiliated membership through a similar foreign group, always call the organisation rather than a towing service, as rates for the latter can be extortionate. Emergency phones are provided on freeways. If you have a mobile phone, dial *FHP for the highway patrol. *See also p267* **Safety & security**.

Two last points: during rush hours (7-9am, 4-6pm Mon-Fri), only vehicles carrying at least two people including the driver can travel in lanes marked 'HOV' ('high-occupancy vehicles'); and Florida law allows you to turn right on a red light if the road is clear, unless a sign says otherwise.

### Car hire

There are many car rental companies to choose from as long as you have a major credit card and are over 25 years of age. (Some local

car rental agencies will rent to people without credit cards if they are over 25, produce a licence and a round-trip air ticket, and pay a deposit of several hundred dollars, or to persons aged 21-25 with a major credit card.) Remember that the prices companies quote you do not include state sales tax or either collision damage or liability insurance. If your home policy or credit card doesn't cover you, grit your teeth and hand over the cash, even though it may almost double the rental bill. Driving without coverage can prove to be financially ruinous should the unlikely happen.

### Car rental companies
**Alamo** 1-800 462 5266, www.alamo.com.
**Avis** 1-800 331 1212, www.avis.com.
**Budget** 1-800 527 0700, www.budget.com.
**Dollar** 1-800 800 4000, www.dollar.com.
**Enterprise** 1-800 261 7331, www.enterprise.com.
**Global Rent a Car** 1-305 635 3060, www.globalrac.com.
**Hertz** 1-866 654 3131, www.hertz.com.
**National** 1-800 227 7368, www.nationalcar.com.
**Thrifty** 1-800 847 4389, www.thrifty.com.

### Parking

Parking on South Beach is an ordeal, and an expensive one at that. Invariably, you will have to use meters, parking lots (many of which have meters), garages or valet parking. For meters, you'll need tons of quarters (they cost $1.75 per hour but are free from 3am to 9am). For garages and valet services, you'll need tons of money, full stop. Additionally, there are 64 municipal lots scattered throughout the Miami Beach area. Rates are generally about $1-$2 per hour. See also www.miamibeachfl.gov or www.miamiparking.com.

## CYCLING & SCOOTERS

Cycling is a great way to get around; so is in-line skating. For more information, *see pp198-200*.

### Beach Scooter Sales & Rentals
*1341 Washington Avenue* (1-305 532 0977); *213 6th Street, Miami Beach* (1-305 6041718, www.beachscooter.com). **Open** 10am-8pm daily. **Credit** AmEx, DC, MC, V. **Map** p280 D3.

# Resources A-Z

**ESSENTIAL INFORMATION**

## ADDRESSES

On long, narrow Miami Beach, the east–west thoroughfares are numbered (the lower the number, the further south the street), with most taking the suffix 'Street'; the north–south thoroughfares all take proper names, with the majority using the suffix 'Avenue'. Figuring out cross-streets for Avenue addresses on Miami Beach is done by removing the last two digits of the street number. So, the cross-street for 1601 Collins Avenue is 16th Street, and the cross-street for 18215 Collins Avenue is 182nd Street.

Miami itself takes a more typical grid system, albeit one with quirks. It mostly divides into four quadrants: NW, NE, SE and SW. Point zero is Downtown at Flagler Street (the north–south divider) and Miami Avenue (the east–west divider) junction. East–west thoroughfares are numbered and take the suffix 'Street', while their numbered north–south counterparts use the suffix 'Avenue'. Again, cross-streets are simple to figure: they go in hundreds, so 3555 SW 8th Street is at SW 35th Avenue; 360 NW 8th Street is at NW 3rd Avenue.

## AGE RESTRICTIONS

**Buying/drinking alcohol** 21.
**Driving** 16.
**Sex** 18.
**Smoking** 18.

## ATTITUDE & ETIQUETTE

Hot weather and an overriding reliance on the tourist industry combine to make south and central Florida generally friendly. Casual dress is a necessity, thanks to weather that's usually hot and steamy, and the overall feel of the place is appropriately relaxed. However, this comes with several caveats. On a fairly trivial level, workers in the service industries on South Beach can be surly: many see themselves as 'resting' models/ musicians/whatevers, and they're not afraid to let customers know they think they're too handsome/ cool/talented to be doing their job.

More seriously, although the crime situation isn't as bad as it was in the early 1990s, parts of Miami are still unsafe; for more details, *see p266* **Safety & security**. Also, despite appearances, this is still the South. While Miami Beach is relaxed on race and sexuality, other parts of Florida – including the Keys before you reach Key West – are far less liberal. So choose your local bar carefully.

## BUSINESS

### Conventions & conferences

**Miami Beach Convention Center**
*1901 Convention Center Drive, between Dade Boulevard & 17th Street, South Beach (1-305 673 7311, www.miamibeachconvention.com). Bus C, G, H, K, L, S, W, South Beach Local.* **Map** p280 C3.
One of the best-designed convention centres in the US, this massive structure takes up four blocks in South Beach's Deco District. It can handle four major events at one time.

### Couriers & shippers

**DHL**
*1-800 225 5345, www.dhl.com.*
**FedEx**
*1-800 463 3339, www.fedex.com.*
**UPS**
*1-800 742 5877, www.ups.com.*

### Office services

**FedEx Office**
*1617 Alton Road, between 16th Street & Lincoln Road, South Beach (1-305 532 4241, www.fedex.com). Bus M, S, W.* **Open** 24hrs daily. **Credit** AmEx, MC, V. **Map** p280 C2. There are outposts of this efficient computer and copy centre all over the city (see website for locations).
**ProTranslating**
*2850 S Douglas Road, between Palermo & Sevilla Avenues (1-888 532 7887, 1-305 371 7887, www. protranslating.com). Metromover Miami Avenue.* **Open** 8.30am-5.30pm Mon-Fri. **Credit** AmEx, Disc, MC, V. **Map** p284 C4.

## CONSUMER

If you encounter a problem with a company, contact the Miami Lakes-based **Better Business Bureau** (1-305 827 5363, www.seflorida. bbb.org), an admirable non-profit public service organisation dedicated to monitoring the quality of businesses in many fields. The south-east Florida office serves the Miami region.

## CUSTOMS

A high volume of air traffic means that getting through Customs and Immigration at Miami International Airport might take an hour or more. Travellers from countries on the Visa Waiver Program (*see p268* **Visas & immigration**) can speed the process up by correctly filling in the two forms that you should have been given by your flight attendant, one for Customs, the other for Immigration. However, the popularity of the city among drug smugglers means searches are common. If you're stopped, just be polite co-operative; there's no point being otherwise, as you're only likely to be detained longer.

US Customs allows foreigners to bring in $100 worth of gifts (the limit is $800 for returning Americans) without paying duty. One carton of 200 cigarettes (or 100 cigars, as long as they're not Cuban) and one litre of liquor (spirits) are allowed. Plants, meat and fresh produce of any kind can't be brought into the country. You'll have to fill out a form if you carry more than $10,000 in currency. You'll be handed a white form on your inbound flight to fill in, confirming that you haven't exceeded any of these allowances. If you need to bring prescription drugs into the US, make sure the container is clearly marked, and bring your doctor's statement or a prescription.

## DISABLED

As in most of the US, disabled travellers to Miami are likely to find it relatively easy to get around. The exception may be South Beach's Deco District, where the 1930s architecture offers some tight angles and tiny lifts that can plague wheelchair users. However, even the smallest hotels often have ramps and lifts fitted, and by federal law all public buildings – including museums and libraries – must have wheelchair access and suitable toilet facilities.

Miami-Dade Transit buses are equipped with lifts or special low entrances, set spaces and grips, and both the Tri-Rail and Metromover (for both, see p257) are fully wheelchair-accessible.

On the beaches, there's wheelchair access at 10th Street and Ocean Drive on South Beach, at Crandon Park on Key Biscayne and at the North Shore State Recreation Area. You can also borrow Beach Chairs, wheelchairs specially designed to access sandy areas, at Haulover Beach and Crandon Park Beach (see www.miamidade.gov/parks/fun-beach_wheelchairs.asp for more information). All public pools in Miami-Dade County are equipped with lifts.

The New York-based **Society for Accessible Travel and Hospitality** (1-212 447 7284, www.sath.org) can offer information and services for disabled travellers in all parts of the United States.

## DRUGS

Miami's fun-in-the-sun ethos doesn't extend to the drug laws, which are enforced with the same rigour as anywhere else in the US. Those convicted of possessing any controlled substance face penalties of up to a year in prison and fines ranging from $1,000 to $100,000. Those found in possession of crack cocaine face from five to 20 years in prison. Stick to mojitos.

## ELECTRICITY

The US uses a 110-120V, 60-cycle AC voltage rather than the 220-240V, 50-cycle AC used in Europe. Except for dual-voltage, flat-pin plug shavers, you'll need to run any appliances you bring via an adaptor. Most US videos and TVs use a different frequency from Europe: you won't be able to play back footage during your trip, but you can buy and use blank tapes.

## EMBASSIES & CONSULATES

Miami is a major point of entry into the US, and many nations have consulates in the area. Details of the UK consulate in Miami are given below; search online for others. If your country isn't listed, call directory information for Washington, DC (1 202 555 1212) to find the consular section of your embassy there.

**UK Consulate**
*Suite 2800, 1001 Brickell Bay Drive, at SE 8th Street, Downtown (1-305 400 6400, www.ukinusa fco.gov.uk). Bus 24, 48, 95, B/ Metrorail 8th Street.* **Open** 9am-4.30pm Mon-Fri.

## EMERGENCIES

In an emergency, call **911** for an ambulance, the fire service or the police. This number is free from all phones. For the **US Coast Guard**, you can either call 911 or 1-305 535 4472. For the **Poison Information Center** call 1-800 222 1222.

For a list of helplines, *see p264* **Helplines**; for hospitals in the Miami region, *see right* **Hospitals**; and for details on police stations in the area, *see p266* **Police**.

## GAY & LESBIAN

Information is available from the **Miami-Dade Gay & Lesbian Chamber of Commerce** (1130 Washington Avenue, at SW 11th Street, 1-305 673 4440, www.gogay miami.com). The website has daily events and comprehensive listings of community resources, dining and accommodation.

For general information on organisations serving the gay community, call **Switchboard of Miami** (1-305 358 1640, www.switchboardmiami.org), a 24-hour crisis and information line. **YES Institute** (5275 Sunset Drive, at SW 52nd Avenue, 1-305 663 7197, www.yesinstitute.org) and **Pridelines** (9526 NE Second Avenue, Miami Shores, 1-305 571 9601, www.pridelines.org) co-ordinate services for gay youth.

**Miami Gay & Lesbian Yellow Pages** has a website with listings at www.glyp.com. A list of forthcoming events, as well as articles on current news in Florida, can be found at the *Miami Herald* website at www.miamiherald.com, under the Gay South Florida link.

## HEALTH

### Accident & emergency

All the hospitals we list (*see below*) have emergency rooms.

### Contraception & abortion

**Jean Shehan Health Center**
*3119A SW 22nd Street, between SW 31st Avenue & SW 31st Court, South Miami (1-305 285 5535, www.plannedparenthood.org). Bus 24.* **Open** 0.30am-6pm Tue; 11am-7pm Wed; 1-5pm Thur; 9am-3pm Fri; 10am-3pm Sat.
Care for men and women, including birth-control supplies, testing and treatment for sexually transmitted diseases and pregnancy testing.

### Dentists

The **South Florida District Dental Association** (1-305 667 3647, www.sfdda.org) has a search facility on its website that will help you find a local dentist who's a member of the American Dental Association.

### Hospitals

In Miami, as in other parts of the US, you'll be charged a fortune for even basic medical care. Having full insurance cover, preferably with a low excess, is the only way to feel at ease; keep the details with you and leave a copy with someone at home.

If it's not an emergency, walk-in clinics are cheaper, friendlier and more numerous than hospitals. **Miami Beach Community Health Center** at the Stanley C Myers Center (710 Alton Road, at 7th Street, 1-305 538 8835, www.miamibeachhealth.org, 7.30am-6pm Mon, Wed; 7.30am-5pm Tue, Thur, Fri) is a public clinic that charges according to what you earn.

For emergencies, dial 911 or head for the nearest emergency room. **Mount Sinai Medical Center** in Miami Beach is considered the best but also charges the most.

### Children's Hospital
*3100 SW 62nd Avenue, off Red Road (SW 57th Avenue), at Devonshire Boulevard, South-West Miami (1-305 666 6511, www.mch.com). Bus 72.*
A specialist emergency room and good outpatient services.

### Coral Gables Hospital
*3100 S Douglas Road (SW 37th Avenue), at Santander Avenue, Coral Gables (1-305 445 8461, www.coralgableshospital.com). Bus 37.*
A 24-hour emergency department and a high-capacity outpatient unit with same-day surgery.

### Jackson Memorial Hospital
*1611 NW 12th Avenue, at NW 16th Street, Downtown (1-305 585 1111, www.jacksonhealth.org). Metrorail Civic Center.*
The main county hospital.

### Mount Sinai Medical Center
*4300 Alton Road, at 43rd Street, North Beach (1-305 674 2020, www.msmc.com). Bus C, M, R.*
A well-equipped hospital, and pricey.

### University of Miami Hospital
*1400 NW 12th Avenue, at NW 14th Street, Downtown (1-305 689 5511, www.umiamihospital.com). Bus 12, 22, 95, M/Metrorail Civic Center.*

## Opticians

*See p129.*

## Pharmacies

**Walgreens** (www.walgreens.com) and **CVS** (www.cvs.com) are the most prevalent chains, with branches all over town, several of which are open 24 hours a day.

## STDs, HIV & AIDS

### CARE Resource
*Suite 300, 3510 Biscayne Boulevard, at 35th Street, Design District (1-305 576 1234,*
*www.careresource.org). Bus 9, 10, J.* **Open** 8.30am-5pm Mon, Tue, Thur, Fri; 8.30am-7.30pm Wed.

### South Beach AIDS Project
*306 Lincoln Road, between Collins & Washington Avenues, South Beach (1-305 5532 1033, www.sobeaids.org). Bus C, G, H, K, L, R, S, W, South Beach Local.* **Open** 9am-7pm daily. **Map** p280 C3.

## HELPLINES

All lines are open 24 hours. For emergency services, *see p263.*

### Alcohol & Drug Abuse Hotline
*1-800 784 6776.*
### Alcoholics Anonymous
*1-305 461 2425.*
### Crisis & Suicide Counselling Service
*1-305 358 4357.*
### Rape Hotline
*1-305 585 7273.*

## ID

If you want to drink, carry photo ID with your date of birth (driving licence or passport), no matter how old you are.

## INSURANCE

Baggage, trip cancellation and medical insurance should be taken care of before you get on the plane. Of these, the big one is health. At the majority of medical centres you must prove you have insurance – by producing something with the company name and policy number on it – before they'll treat you. The alternative is to give your credit card. *See also p263* **Hospitals**.

## INTERNET

All but the cheapest hotels offer internet connection in the rooms, be it dataport or WiFi (for which a fee is sometimes charged, and it's sometimes hefty). The City of Miami Beach does maintain its own WiFi network, which can be accessed for free – yes, even on the beach – but the connection is often slow. Many libraries offer free internet access (including the main Miami-Dade Public Library; *see right*), although sessions are limited to 45 minutes. Many FedEx Office locations (*see p262*) have pay-to-use computers and printing facilities.

### CybrCaffe
*1574 Washington Avenue, at 15th Street, South Beach (1-305 534 0057). Bus C, H, K, W, South*
*Beach Local.* **Open** 9am-midnight daily. **Cost** $3/30mins, $5/hr. **Credit** AmEx, MC, V. **Map** p280 D3.

## LANGUAGE

Miami is virtually a bilingual city. You'll hear Spanish spoken almost everywhere; in areas such as Little Havana and Hialeah, it's the lingua franca. You can get by with just English, especially in the major tourist areas, but if you've ever picked up any kind of holiday Spanish, dust off that phrasebook now (for some basic Spanish vocab, *see p265* **¿Hablas español?**). That said, the only places you're really likely to need Spanish are small mom-and-pop-style businesses in Little Havana.

## LEFT LUGGAGE

**Miami International Airport** (*see p260*) has storage rooms at Central Terminal E, level 2, open 5am-9pm daily. Prices vary depending on the size of the bags stored. Short-term lockers are located beyond the security checkpoint to the gates.

## LEGAL HELP

Most Florida police officers are tourist-friendly. However, if you're challenged by a police officer, be sure to do exactly as you're told and don't make any sudden movements. If you find yourself arrested and accused of a serious crime, you'll be permitted one phone call, in which case your best bet is to call your consulate (*see p263*). If you don't have a lawyer or can't afford one, the court will appoint one for you. Otherwise, you can call the **Florida Bar Association** (1-850 561 5600) for a referral.

## LIBRARIES

### Miami-Dade Public Library
*101 W Flagler Street, at NW 1st Avenue, Downtown (1-305 375 2665, www.mdpls.org). Bus 3, 16, 95, C, K, S/Metromover Government Center.* **Open** 10am-6pm Mon-Sat. **Map** p282 D2.
Part of the Miami-Dade Cultural Center and the main branch of Miami-Dade's library system. It offers free internet access.

### Coconut Grove Branch
*2875 McFarlane Road, at S Bayshore Drive, Coconut Grove (1-305 442 8695). Bus 48.* **Open** 10am-6pm Mon, Wed, Thur, Sat; noon-8pm Tue. **Map** p285 B3.

## ¿HABLAS ESPAÑOL?

| | |
|---|---|
| **Good morning/afternoon** Buenos días | **seven** siete |
| **Good evening/good night** Buenas noches | **eight** ocho |
| | **nine** nueve |
| **Hello** Hola | **ten** diez |
| **Goodbye/see you later** Adiós/hasta luego | **eleven** once |
| | **twelve** doce |
| **Please** Por favor | **thirteen** trece |
| **Thank you** Gracias | **fourteen** catorce |
| **Excuse me** Perdóneme | **fifteen** quince |
| **Do you speak English?** ¿Habla usted inglés? | **sixteen** dieciséis |
| | **seventeen** diecisiete |
| **Sorry, I don't speak Spanish** Lo siento, no hablo español | **eighteen** dieciocho |
| | **nineteen** diecinueve |
| **I don't understand** No entiendo | **twenty** veinte |
| | **twenty-one** veintiuno |
| **How much is... ?** ¿Cuánto cuesta? | **thirty** treinta |
| | **forty** cuarenta |
| **Please can I have the bill?** La cuenta, por favor | **fifty** cincuenta |
| | **sixty** sesenta |
| **one** un, uno (m), una (f) | **seventy** setenta |
| **two** dos | **eighty** ochenta |
| **three** tres | **ninety** noventa |
| **four** cuatro | **one hundred** cien |
| **five** cinco | **five hundred** quinientos |
| **six** seis | **one thousand** mil |
| | **one million** un millón |

### Coral Gables Branch
*3443 Segovia Street, at Aledo Avenue, Coral Gables (1-305 442 8706). Bus 72.* **Open** 10am-6pm Mon, Thur-Sat; 1-9pm Tue, Wed. **Map** p284 D3.

### South Shore Branch
*131 Alton Road, at 1st Street, South Beach (1-305 535 4223). Bus H, M, W.* **Open** 10am-6pm Mon, Tue, Thur, Sat; noon-8pm Wed. **Map** p280 F2.

## LOST PROPERTY

For items lost on **Miami-Dade Transit**, call 1-786 469 5564 (8am-noon, 1-5pm Mon-Fri). If you've lost something at **Miami International Airport**, call 1-305 876 7377 or visit the Lost and Found office at North Terminal D, level 4. Otherwise, call your nearest police station (for a list of local ones, *see p266*).

## MONEY

The US dollar ($) divides into 100 cents (¢). Denominations for coins are: the penny (1¢), the nickel (5¢), the dime (10¢), the quarter (25¢) and the less common half-dollar (50¢). You may come across the smaller 'Susan B Anthony' dollar coin, which, though not common, is valid.

Paper bills are, confusingly, all the same size and colour (green). Denominations are $1, $5, $10, $20,

$50 and $100 (Benjamin Franklin). Older bills have smaller portraits, while newer bills have bigger, more cartoonish portraits.

### ATMs

Automated Teller Machines (ATMs) are commonplace: all banks have them, of course, but so do many convenience stores and gas stations. The main two globally recognised card networks are **Cirrus** (1-800 424 7787 for a list of locations) and **Plus** (1-800 843 7587); if your bank card displays either of these two symbols, you should be able to withdraw cash from ATMs. However, you'll be charged for the privilege: $1.50-$3 is common for US cardholders, while holders of foreign cards should check with their banks for details. Some machines also have annoying upper limits to how much you can withdraw at any one time (it can be as little as $60).

Most ATMs also dispense cash advances on credit cards, with MasterCard and Visa the most widely accepted. Again, prepare to be charged handling fees.

### Banks

Bank hours are usually 9am to 4pm Monday to Friday, and sometimes 6pm or 7pm on Thursdays, with drive-in windows open until 6pm.

Larger branches open on Saturday mornings. Below are some of the larger banks in Downtown Miami. All have branches elsewhere in the city; for your nearest, check the *Yellow Pages*, search online or call the 1-800 numbers listed by each bank.

### Bank of America
*1 SE 3rd Avenue, at E Flagler Street, Downtown (1-800 299 2265, 1-305 350 6350, www. bankofamerica.com). Bus 3, 16, 95, C, S.* **Open** 8.30am-4pm Mon-Thur; 8.30am-5pm Fri. **Map** p282 E2.

### Chase
*150 SE 2nd Street, at Brickell Avenue, Downtown (1-877 242 7372, 1-786 425 0559, www.chase.com). Bus 24, 48, 95, B/Metromover 8th Street.* **Open** 9am-6pm Mon-Fri; 9am-3pm Sat. **Map** p282 E3.

### Wells Fargo
*1395 Brickell Avenue, at SE 13th Street, Downtown (1-800 869 3557, 1-305 789 3900, www. wellsfargo.com). Bus 24, 48, 95, B/Metromover 8th Street.* **Open** 9am-5pm Mon-Thur; 9am-6pm Fri.

### Bureaux de change

Bureaux de change are less common in the US than Europe, but you'll find them in tourist areas. They generally charge higher commission and offer lower rates than banks, which all offer currency exchange.

**Lincoln Currency Exchange**
*1633 Washington Avenue, at Lincoln Road, South Beach (1-305 672 1633, www.lincolncurrency exchange.com). Bus C, H, K, W, South Beach Local.* **Open** 8am-10pm Mon-Sat; noon-8pm Sun. **Map** p280 C3.

### Credit cards

Credit cards are essential for renting cars and booking hotels, and handy for buying tickets over the phone and the internet. The five major cards accepted in the US are American Express (abbreviated as AmEx throughout this book), Diners Club (DC), Discover (Disc), MasterCard (MC) and Visa (V). MasterCard and Visa are the most popular; American Express is also widely accepted. Thanks to a 2004 deal between MasterCard and Diners Club, all businesses that accept the former can now in theory accept the latter, though in practice many businesses are unaware of this and may not comply.

If your cards or travellers' cheques are lost or stolen, call the following numbers:

**American Express**
*1-800 992 3404, 1-800 221 7282 travellers' cheques.*
**Diners Club**
*1-800 234 6377.*
**Discover**
*1-800 347 2683.*
**MasterCard/Maestro**
*1-800 627 8372, 1-800 223 9920 travellers' cheques.*
**Thomas Cook travellers' cheques**
*1-800 223 7373.*
**Visa/Cirrus**
*1-800 847 2911.*

## Tax

Sales tax in Florida is at least six per cent, but it varies by county: in Miami-Dade it's seven per cent. Be aware that hotels levy a further 13 per cent hotel room tax.

## NATURAL HAZARDS

### Mosquitoes

Although Miami itself has an effective control programme that ensures mosquitoes are rarely a pest, be prepared to be eaten alive the moment you leave the city limits. The Everglades and other wooded areas are the worst affected, so buy an insect repellent you like the smell of, and use it.

### Weather

Hurricane season in Florida runs from June to November, and during the year there may be as few as two or as many as 20 blowing in. The majority blow themselves out or remain at sea rather than striking the mainland. Devastated several times in the past (including a direct hit from Hurricane Wilma in 2005), Miami now has a highly sophisticated early warning system ensuring that when the 'big one' arrives, it's unlikely to be a surprise. The National Hurricane Center in Miami can give 24 hours' warning of a possible hit, and public radio and most TV stations then give out the latest information and evacuation plans. Be prepared to evacuate your hotel, even if the weather doesn't appear threatening when the warning is issued.

Tornadoes are part of the same weather system, but despite looking so dramatic, they're considerably less destructive.

They're also less predictable, so there's no warning. Most of Miami's buildings are robust enough to suffer only minor damage, even when directly in the path of a tornado, so stay inside and you're probably safest.

For weather updates, you can call the **National Weather Service Forecast Office** on 1-305 229 4522. For more information on storm and hurricane seasons, as well as a climate chart, *see p268*.

## OPENING HOURS

Office hours in Florida are usually 9am to 5pm, give or take half an hour. Shop hours vary considerably according to location: businesses in malls and pedestrian areas often open until 9pm or later, even on Sundays. Some Miami clubs and restaurants take a breather after the weekend: the occasional restaurant closes on Sunday and/or Monday, while many clubs are dark on Monday and Tuesday.

## POLICE

For emergencies, dial **911**. The numbers given below are non-emergency numbers.

**Coral Gables Police Dept**
*2801 Salzedo Street, at Sevilla Avenue, Coral Gables (1-305 442 1600). Bus 24, 72.* **Open** 24hrs daily. **Map** p284 C4.
**Miami Beach Police Dept**
*1100 Washington Avenue, at 11th Street, South Beach (1-305 673 7900). Bus C, H, K, W, South Beach Local.* **Open** 24hrs daily. **Map** p280 D3.
**Miami Police Dept**
*400 NW 2nd Avenue, at NW 4th Street, Downtown (1-305 603 6640). Metromover Government Center.* **Open** 24hrs daily. **Map** p282 C1.
**North Miami Beach Police Dept**
*16901 NE 19th Avenue, at NE 169th Street, North Miami Beach (1-305 662 7654). Bus E, H, V.* **Open** 24hrs daily.

## POSTAL SERVICES

First-class mail costs 46¢ within the US for letters up to one ounce, and 20¢ for each additional ounce. Postcards sent within the US require a 33¢ stamp. Overseas mail costs vary from country to country, but a postcard and a one-ounce letter both cost $1.10.

### Post offices

**Coconut Grove Post Office**
*3191 Grand Avenue, at Matilda Avenue, Coconut Grove, FL 33133 (1-800 275 8777, 1-305 529 6700). Bus 42, 48.* **Open** 8.30am-5pm Mon-Fri; 8.30am-2pm Sat. **Map** p285 B2.
**Coral Gables Post Office**
*251 Valencia Avenue, at Salzedo Street, Coral Gables, FL 33134 (1-305 441 0381, 1-305 443 2532). Bus 24, 42, J.* **Open** 8.30am-6pm Mon-Fri; 8.30am-1.30pm Sat. **Map** p284 C4.
**Downtown Miami Post Office**
*500 NW 2nd Avenue, at NW 5th Street, Downtown, FL 33101 (1-305 374 3216). Metromover Government Center.* **Open** 8am-5pm Mon-Fri; 9am-1.30pm Sat. **Map** p282 D2.
**Main Post Office**
*2200 NW 72nd Avenue, Miami International Airport, FL 33159 (1-800 275 8777). Bus 73.* **Open** 7.30am-9pm Mon-Fri; 8.30am-2pm Sat.
**Miami Beach Post Office**
*1300 Washington Avenue, at 13th Street, South Beach, FL 33139 (1-305 599 1787). Bus C, H, K, W, South Beach Local.* **Open** 8am-5pm Mon-Fri; 8.30am-2pm Sat. **Map** p280 D3.

### Poste restante

You can have mail sent to you c/o General Delivery at any post office, provided you use the correct zip code and collect it within 30 days using photo ID (a passport or driver's licence is preferred).

## SAFETY & SECURITY

South Florida acquired a nasty reputation for tourist crime in the late 1980s to mid '90s. Sometimes tourists were the targets, sometimes they got in the way of the crime wave that was sweeping the state. These days, tourist areas are visibly policed, and precautions have been taken to reduce car crime: signage has been improved, rental cars are not marked and rental agencies are required to provide maps and directions. These measures have had the desired result: tourist crime has been falling.

There's absolutely no need for paranoia, but don't leave your street sense at home. Barring random occurrences, you're fine on South Beach, but elsewhere in the city the usual urban crime thrives, and you could easily run into trouble by crossing an invisible line only locals are wise to. We've tried to give safety information for all the areas we discuss, but if in doubt, stay away.

## Safety tips

If your hotel has a safe, keep your valuables there. If you do carry them with you, do so discreetly and don't flash large amounts of cash around. Don't leave anything on the beach you want to keep, while you swim. Keep a note of your travellers' cheque and credit card numbers separately. It's a good idea to leave a note of these with someone at home, along with other emergency information, such as your insurers' contact number and passport number.

Keep all credit card slips, including receipts from credit sales at petrol stations, and don't let anyone overhear your card number. If your hotel asked for an imprint when you checked in, insist it be destroyed when you leave. Don't let anyone you don't know into your hotel room. Call the front desk if you need to check someone is a member of staff.

If somebody threatens you and demands money or goods, quietly give them what you have. Then go straight to the nearest phone or police station to report the crime. Make sure you get a reference number for any crime you report; you will need it for your insurance.

Finally, try not to look like a tourist. Grifters target tourists with elaborate cons, and purse-snatchers look for anybody not paying attention. Awareness is the key to safety in Miami.

For more on driving safety, *see p261* **Driving**.

## SMOKING

Following similar action by other states, in 2003 Florida adopted legislation that essentially banned smoking indoors in airports, offices, hotel lobbies, restaurants and bars. The exception to the rule: smoking is allowed in standalone bars designated hotel rooms and select outdoor seating areas in restaurants.

## TELEPHONES
### Dialling & codes

Most Miami numbers still take the code 305, but a recent reorganisation has added the 786 code into the Miami mix.

Numbers prefaced by 1-800, 1-888 or 1-877 are free – but if you dial them from your hotel you incur a flat fee (usually 50¢-$1). You can dial most (but not all) 1-800 numbers from outside the United States, but they will be charged at international rates, as will premium-rate 1-900 numbers.

## Making a call

For all calls – both local and long distance – dial 1 + [area code] + [the seven digit number].

For international calls, dial 011 followed by the country code (Australia 61; Germany 49; Republic of Ireland 353; Japan 81; New Zealand 64; UK 44; see the phone book for others) and the number, dropping the first zero of all UK numbers. For Canada, you just need to dial the area code.

In hotels, you may have to dial 0 or 9 before all these numbers to get a line. You'll also pay a surcharge; ask how much at your hotel, as using a phone card (*see below*), credit card or payphone can work out far cheaper, especially for long distance/international calls.

## Operator services

For collect (reverse charge) calls, dial the operator on 0. For police, fire or medical emergencies, dial 911. For local directory information, dial 411. For national long-distance directory information, dial 1 + [area code] + 555 1212 (if you don't know the area code, dial 0 for the operator).

## Public phones

To use a public phone, pick up the receiver, listen for a dialling tone and feed it change before dialling. The majority of call boxes charge 50¢. Make sure you have lots of change, as pay phones take only nickels, dimes and quarters. 911 calls are free.

## Phone cards

Hotels charge a lot for long-distance and international calls; a phone card, sold at delis, news kiosks, vending machines, pharmacies and other shops, is one solution.

It's worth shopping around for the longest talk-time for the lowest price. Examples include **AT&T** (1-800 225 5288), **MCI** (1-800 888 8000) and **Sprint** (1-800 366 2255), although there are plenty of smaller companies touting for custom. Don't just look at the price per minute to

the area you'll be calling most: also pay close attention to the small print detailing connection charges.

## Mobile phones

In Europe and much of the rest of the world, mobile phones work on the GSM network at either 900 or 1800 MHz, but in the US GSM operates in the 800 and 1900 MHz bands; visitors should check with their service providers whether their phones will work in Miami. Visitors from other countries will need a tri-band phone and a roaming agreement. Also check the price of calls made (and received) while roaming, as these can be very expensive. Renting may be a better bet. The International Currency Exchange (ICE) Business Center at Miami International Airport, located in the South Terminal between Concourses H and J, rents cell phones and sells prepaid SIM cards for travellers to use with their own mobile devices.

## TIME

Florida operates on Eastern Standard Time, which is five hours behind Greenwich Mean Time (London), one hour ahead of Central Time (Chicago), two hours ahead of Mountain Time (Denver) and three hours ahead of Pacific Standard Time (the West Coast). Daylight Saving Time runs almost concurrent with British Summer Time from the second Sunday in March (clocks go forward) to the first Sunday in November.

## TIPPING

Tipping is standard practice. In fact, many restaurants add the tip on to the bill before you get it; always check unless for some reason you want to tip twice. If the bill doesn't already contain a tip add 15-20 per cent in restaurants.

Bartenders and food delivery workers should get a tip of 15 per cent. Cloakroom attendants, doormen and the like should be tipped a dollar or so. Bellhops and baggage attendants merit $1-$2 a bag, while hotel maids should be left $1-$2 per night. Cab drivers, too, expect to be tipped 15 per cent, plus $1 per bag. Foreign visitors should note, that, almost without exception, staff in the service industries in the US are paid next to nothing as a basic wage, and rely heavily on gratuities. In other words, they feel

ESSENTIAL INFORMATION

they've got a genuine gripe if you don't cough up – and they're likely to let you know about it.

## TOURIST INFORMATION

Visitor guides, including maps, are available free from the following.

**Coconut Grove Chamber of Commerce**
*2820 McFarlane Road, at S Bayshore Drive, Coconut Grove (1-305 444 7270, www.coconut grovechamber.com). Bus 48, Coconut Grove Circulator.* **Open** 10am-6pm Mon-Fri. **Map** p285 B3.

**Greater Miami Convention & Visitors' Bureau**
*Suite 2700, NationsBank Building, 701 Brickell Avenue, at SE 7th Street, Downtown (1-305 539 3000, www.miamiandbeaches.com). Bus 24, 48, 95, B/Metromover 8th Street.* **Open** 8.30am-5pm Mon-Fri. **Map** p282 F3.

**Visit Miami Beach Visitors Center, Miami Beach Chamber of Commerce**
*1901 Convention Center Drive, at 17th Street, South Beach (1-786 276 2763, www.miamibeachguest. com). Bus A, M, L, S.* **Open** 10am-4pm daily. **Map** p280 C3.

## VISAS & IMMIGRATION

### Visas

Currently, 36 countries participate in the Visa Waiver Program (VWP; www.cbp.gov/esta), including Australia, Ireland, New Zealand and the UK. Citizens of these countries do not need a visa for stays in the US shorter than 90 days (business or pleasure) as long as they have a machine-readable passport (e-passport) valid for the full 90-day period, a return ticket, and authorisation to travel through the ESTA (Electronic System for Travel Authorization) scheme. Visitors must fill in the ESTA form at least 24 hours before travel (72 hours is recommended) and pay a $14 fee; the form can be found at www.cbp.gov/xp/cgov/travel/ id_visa/esta/). If you don't qualify for entry under the VWP, you'll need a visa; leave plenty of time to obtain one before travelling. For information about visas, see www.travel.state.gov or call 1-202 663 1225 (8.30am-5pm Mon-Fri; recorded information at other times).

UK citizens can find information at www.usembassy.org.uk or by calling the embassy's Visa Information Hotline (09042 450100).

### Immigration

Your airline will give all visitors an immigration form to be presented to an official when you land. Fill it in clearly and be prepared to give an address where you're staying (a hotel is fine). Upon arrival, you may have to wait an hour or longer in Immigration. You may be expected to explain your visit; be polite and prepared. Note that all visitors to the US are now photographed and electronically fingerprinted on arrival on every trip.

## WEIGHTS & MEASURES

America operates on the US standard system, which is similar to the imperial system (miles, gallons, pounds).

## WHEN TO GO

Like many subtropical places, Miami has two seasons: rainy and dry (not to mention hot and hotter). Miami's average temperatures run from 61-73°F (16-23°C) in January to an uncomfortably hot 75-88°F (24-31°C) in July and August, the height of summer.

The winter air is warm, dry and pleasant, though you may need a sweater in the evening, and the sea is still warm enough for swimming.

Summer, meanwhile, gets very hot and unpleasantly humid during the day, and sultry in the evening, with morning and late afternoon the best times for going to the beach for a dip in the jacuzzi-warm sea. June to November is hurricane season: winds are high and storms rush in during the afternoon. Most are brief, but sometimes tropical rains set in. Weather-watchers will find the dramatic display of clouds and lightning, with the possibility of a

stray tornado, intoxicating. The Season runs from the end of November to May. This is when hotel and car rental rates shoot up and most major events occur. November/December and late April/early May are good times to visit: the weather's usually good, but prices aren't at their peak.

For phone forecasts, dial 1-305 511 then 4400 for Florida, 4020 for Miami, 4374 for Orlando and 4998 for hurricanes.

### National holidays

**New Year's Day** 1 Jan.
**Martin Luther King Jr Day** 3rd Mon in Jan.
**Presidents Day** 3rd Mon in Feb.
**Memorial Day** last Mon in May.
**Independence Day** 4 July.
**Labor Day** 1st Mon in Sept.
**Columbus Day** 2nd Mon in Oct.
**Veterans' Day** 11 Nov.
**Thanksgiving Day** 4th Thur in Nov.
**Christmas Day** 25 Dec.

## WORKING IN THE US

For foreigners to work legally in the United States, a US company has to sponsor your application for an H-1 visa. For this to be approved, your prospective employer is obliged to convince the Immigration Department that there is no American citizen qualified to do the job as well as you. Students have an easier time: UK students can contact the **British Universities North America Club** (BUNAC) for help in arranging a temporary job and the requisite visa (Priory House, 6 Wrights Lane, London W8 6TA, 020 7251 3472, www.bunac.org/uk).

Another good resource is www. foreignborn.com. Local jobs are also posted at www.miamiherald.com.

## CLIMATE

|  | Average high (°F/°C) | Average low (°F/°C) | Average rain (in) |
|---|---|---|---|
| **Jan** | 73 (23) | 61 (16) | 2.8 |
| **Feb** | 75 (24) | 61 (16) | 2.1 |
| **Mar** | 79 (26) | 64 (18) | 2.5 |
| **Apr** | 81 (27) | 66 (19) | 3.2 |
| **May** | 84 (29) | 72 (22) | 6.8 |
| **June** | 86 (30) | 73 (23) | 7.0 |
| **July** | 88 (31) | 75 (24) | 6.1 |
| **Aug** | 88 (31) | 75 (24) | 6.3 |
| **Sept** | 88 (31) | 75 (24) | 8.0 |
| **Oct** | 82 (28) | 72 (22) | 9.2 |
| **Nov** | 79 (26) | 66 (19) | 2.8 |
| **Dec** | 75 (24) | 63 (17) | 2.0 |

# Further Reference

## BOOKS

For more on Miami crime fiction, *see pp17-20*.

### Fiction

**Russell Banks** *Lost Memory of Skin* (2012) An observation on the stark differences between Miami's haves and have-nots. Also see part-time resident Banks's *Continental Divide* (1985), about a showdown in Little Haiti as the American Dream implodes.
**Christine Bell** *The Perez Family* (1991) Mariel refugees use their sizeable talents to get a sweet immigration deal.
**Edna Buchanan** *Miami, it's Murder* (1995) A tough female reporter investigates bizarre and dangerous crimes.
**James W Hall** *Tropical Freeze* (1989) A pacey, readable Miami-set thriller.
**Ernest Hemingway** *To Have and Have Not* (1937) Hemingway is Key West's mascot, but this is his only book set there.
**Carl Hiaasen** *various novels* All Hiaasen's crime novels are set in Florida, and all are sharp, satirical and deliriously off the wall. As good a holiday primer as a shelf of non-fiction.
**Marjorie Kinnan Rawlings** *The Yearling* (1938) Pulitzer Prize winner about a boy growing up in central Florida.
**Elmore Leonard** *various novels* Not all Leonard's books are set in south Florida. Those that are include *La Brava, Gold Coast, Maximum Bob, Pronto* and *Riding the Rap.*
**Peter Matthiessen** *Killing Mister Watson* (1991) The settlement of the Everglades, and how it led to some of south Florida's current problems.
**Thomas McGuane** *Ninety-Two in the Shade* (1995) A cult favourite about the quest for self-discovery of an aspiring Key West fishing guide.
**Sean Rowe** *Fever* (2005) A 21st-century 'tropical noir' set in south Florida.
**John Sayles** *Los Gusanos* (1991) The noted indie film director's take on Cuban Miami.
**Charles Willeford** *Miami Blues* (1984) Superior to the better-known film in all ways.

**Tom Wolfe** *Back to Blood* (2012) A slate of over-the-top characters – including a sex addiction specialist and a wealthy porn addict – are set loose on Magic City.

### Non-fiction

**TD Allman** *Miami: City of the Future* (1987) Hugely colourful biography of the city.
**Barbara Baer Capitman** *Deco Delights* (1988) A photo-tour of Miami Beach's deco buildings, by the woman who helped ensure their survival.
**Edna Buchanan** *The Corpse Had a Familiar Face* (1987) Pulitzer Prize-winning journo's in-your-face account of her years covering one of the world's edgiest crime beats.
**David Leon Chandler** *Henry Flagler* (1986) Lowdown on the robber baron largely responsible for establishing Miami's infrastructure.
**Joan Didion** *Miami* (1987) Compelling impressions of the meltdown pot.
**Howard Kleinberg** *Miami Beach: A History* (1994) How the Beach got the way it is today. Kinda.
**Morris Lapidus** *Too Much is Never Enough* (1996) Autobiography of the architect who reinvented Miami glamour in the 1950s.
**Stuart B McIver** *Dreamers, Schemers & Scalawags: The Florida Chronicles* (1994) The underground history of Florida's mobsters, gamblers and risk-takers.
**Gary Monroe** *Life in South Beach* (1989) B&W photos of the pre-renaissance Beach
**Arva Moore Parks** *Miami, The Magic City* (1981) The 'official' history of the city.
**David Rieff** *Going to Miami: Exiles, Tourists and Refugees in the New America* (2000) Controversial vision of Miami alienated from the US.
**Marjory Stoneman Douglas** *The Everglades: River of Grass* (1947) A personal testament to the vulnerable beauty of the Everglades that kick-started conservation in the 1940s.
**Alexander Stuart** *Life on Mars* (1996) Moving, observant and funny essays on the heart and souls of Florida.
**Alfredo Triff** *Miami Arts Explosion* (2006) A chronicle of Miami's burgeoning visual arts scene from the former *Miami New Times* art critic.
**John Viele** *The Florida Keys* (1996) A multi-volume history.

## FILM

For more on Miami in film, *see p169* **Essential Miami Films**.

**Bad Boys** *dir. Michael Bay* (1995) Best friends/cops Will Smith and Martin Lawrence switch places and attempt to clean up the streets of Miami in this watchable enough buddy action/comedy. (The same cannot be said for its 2003 sequel.)
**The Bellboy** *dir. Jerry Lewis* (1960) Lewis plays the bellboy in this riotous flick filmed in the luxurious Fontainebleau Hotel.
**The Birdcage** *dir. Mike Nichols* (1996) Worth watching for the opening tracking shot in from the sea to the neon-lit party scene of Ocean Drive alone.
**A Hole in the Head** *dir. Frank Capra* (1959) Comedy starring Frank Sinatra as a widower struggling to save his Miami motel. Ol' Blue Eyes won an Oscar for the song 'High Hopes'.
**Key Largo** *dir. John Huston* (1948) The movie that named the island – not vice versa.
**Miami Blues** *dir. George Armitage* (1990) Another Miami-set crime flick, boasting one of Alec Baldwin's best performances.
**Miami Vice** *dir. Michael Mann* (2006) Vice detectives Crockett and Tubbs are back at it, taking on the Florida drug world – this time on the big screen.
**Scarface** *dir. Brian de Palma* (1983) Pacino gives a terrifying performance as a Cuban Marielito razoring rivals and nose-diving into mounds of cocaine. A Miami period piece.
**There's Something About Mary** *dir. Peter and Bobby Farrelly* (1998) Geeky Ben Stiller tracks high-school love Cameron Diaz (the titular Mary) to Miami. Cue crude, offensive, sexist set pieces – and gut laughs.

**True Lies** *dir. James Cameron* (1994) Arnold does his Schwarzeneggerian thing. As flashy and shallow as Miami Beach itself.

## TV

**Burn Notice** A former government spy uses his special ops training to help everyday citizens in one of the few Miami-set shows actually shot in Miami. Premièred in 2007 and still going strong.

**Dexter** Sickeningly funny psycho-drama about a vigilante serial killer. Premièred in 2006, ending in the autumn of 2013.

**The Golden Girls** Hilarious series about four co-habiting, cheesecake-munching retirees, which ran from 1985 to 1992.

**Miami Vice** Created by Michael Mann, this 1980s series focused on the lives and loves of Sonny Crockett and Ricardo Tubbs. Big hair, even bigger shoulder pads – and huge fun.

**Nip/Tuck** Christian Troy and Sean McNamara are partners in a top plastic surgery firm, making Miamians more beautiful one boob job at a time from 2003 to 2010.

## MUSIC

**Bacilos** *Caraluna* Catchy Spanish tunes with intelligent lyrics from a group of diverse Latin rockers who met at the University of Miami.

**Celia Cruz** *Regalo del Alma* The patron saint of Miami's Cuban community left a gift for her fans with her final, perfect album, supported by some great young musicians from Havana. (She passed away in 2003.)

**Flo Rida** *Mail on Sunday* 'Low', the first single off the rapper's debut album, spent ten weeks as the country's number one song and broke all sorts of records (at the time) for its number of digital downloads.

**Gonzalo Rubalcaba** *Supernova* Acclaimed jazz pianist Rubalcaba gets a chance to shine.

**Gloria Estefan** *Greatest Hits* She's hokey, yes, and her new albums are forgettable, but the Miami diva's early hits remain classics of crossover.

**Iggy Pop** *Skull Ring* The godfather of punk brought the Stooges to his Miami Beach home for a reunion album, which also features Sum 41 and Green Day.

**Los Van Van** *Live at the Miami Arena* Police in riot gear were called in to protect concert-goers from the wrath of Cuban exile demonstrators at this 1999 performance of Cuba's most popular band. As this two-CD set attests, art triumphed over politics on that historic night.

**Manolin Puente** *Live in the US* The 'salsa doctor' attempts to cure political ills with his booty-shaking music at this Miami concert.

**Pitbull** *M.I.A.M.I.* The rapper/producer's 2004 debut album is an abbreviation for 'Money is a Major Issue', but don't try telling his hordes of hometown fans that.

**Ricky Martin** *Ricky Martin* If you'd like to live *la vida loca*, this is the soundtrack.

**Siete Rayo** *Descemer* The debut album from this Afro-Cuban funk band is a knock-out.

**Spam Allstars** Any one of the CDs (including an excellent live album) from Miami's most loved dance/funk band is worth a listen.

**Trick Daddy** *www.thug.com* The new generation of Miami rap. Not for the easily offended, and much the better for it.

**Trina** *Diamond Princess* Eve, Missy Elliot and more hip hop luminaries join Miami's 'Baddest Bitch' for some dirty rhyming.

**Various** *Heart of Stone: The Henry Stone Story* Disco king Henry Stone ignited Miami's dance scene in the 1970s, sowing the seeds for the *Saturday Night Fever* sensation. This two-CD compilation features artists ranging from legendary KC & the Sunshine Band to funky R&B diva Betty Wright.

## WEBSITES

**City of Coral Gables** *www.citybeautiful.net* Official portal to the City Beautiful.

**City of Miami** *www.miami.gov/home* Official link to civic and visitor information.

**Citysearch** *www.miami.citysearch.com* Pretty generic lifestyle and ents information with locals' ratings. Strong music section.

**Critical Miami** *www.criticalmiami.com* Concentrates on political and cultural commentary and 'hedonistic pursuits', plus listings for the week. Good links to other sites too.

**Curbed** *www.miami.curbed.com* Who knew that real estate news could be so hugely interesting?

**Daily Candy** *www.dailycandy.com/miami* Hipsters' guide to local culture, eating, shopping and nightlife.

**Eater** *www.miami.eater.com* Up-to-the-minute news on the openings (and closings) on the city's restaurant and bar scene.

**Florida Keys History Museum** *www.keyshistory.org* Complete Keys archive from 120,000 BC – when the reef started forming – to now.

**Greater Miami Convention & Visitors' Bureau** *www.miamiandbeaches.com* The glitz big-up, followed by useful information.

**City of Miami Beach** *http://web.miamibeachfl.gov* City administration's site with the all-important official beach temperature.

**MB Culture** *www.mbculture.com* Offers a full lineup of the latest cultural happenings in and around Miami Beach, from music to movies to theatre.

**Miami Herald** *www.miami.com* Even with the *Miami Herald's* daily publishing schedule, there's still plenty more to talk about, which is where this excellent site comes in.

**Miami New Times** *www.miaminewtimes.com* Spruce and savvy writing on Miami's hot topics and places in this online version of the city's main free alt paper.

**Ocean Drive magazine** *www.oceandrive.com* Monthly glossy entertainment and lifestyle magazine featuring fashion, culture and celebrity interviews galore.

**South Beach Magazine** *www.southbeach-usa.com* The Miami 'scene': shopping, dining, real estate and so on.

**State of Florida** *www.myflorida.com* Everything from the email address of the Governor to a hospital services guide.

**Yelp** *www.yelp.com* Everyday citizens share their opinions (the good, the bad and the very, very ugly) on any area business or service.

# Index

INDEX

**INDEX**

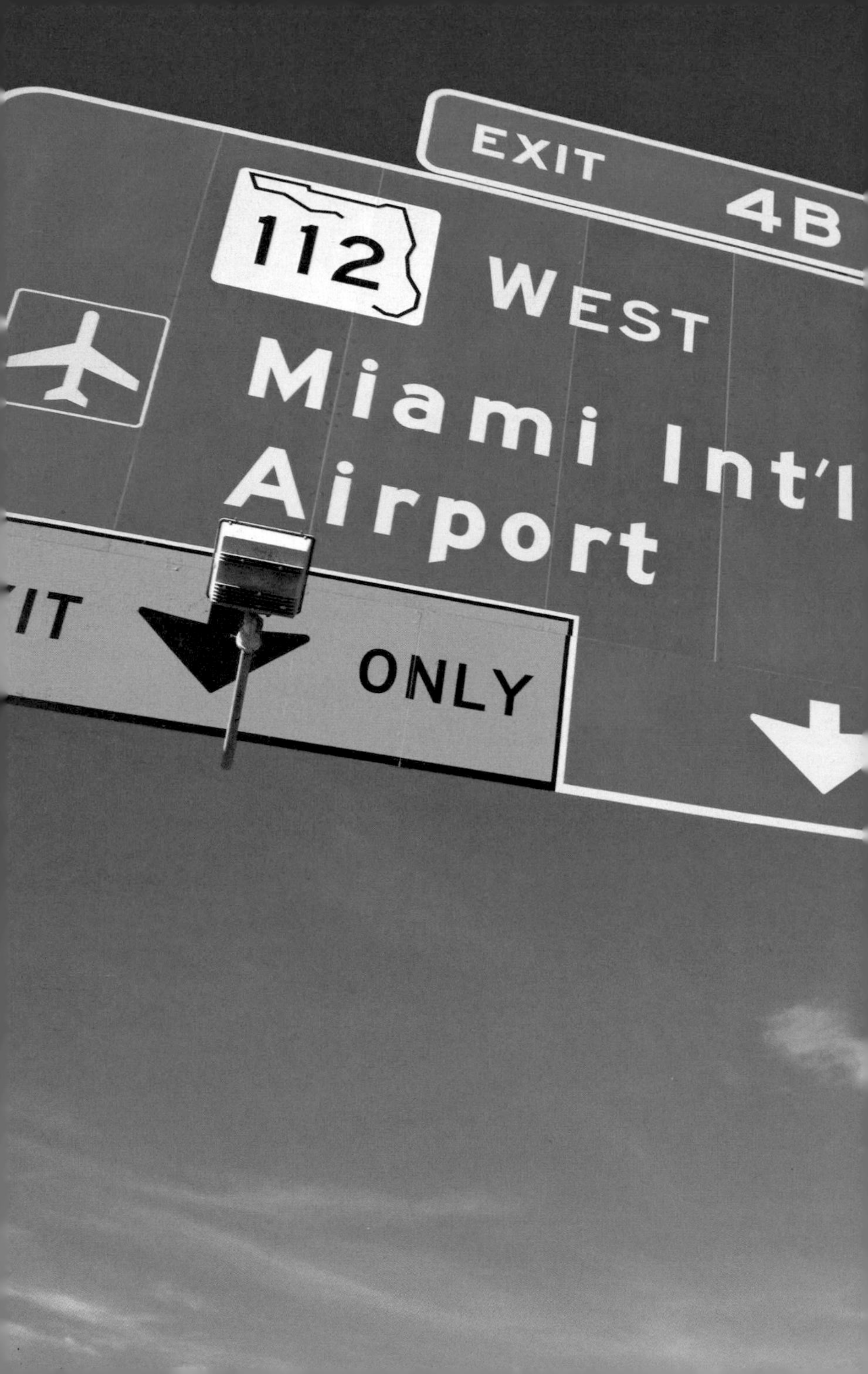
EXIT
4B
112
WEST
Miami Int'l
Airport
ONLY

# Maps

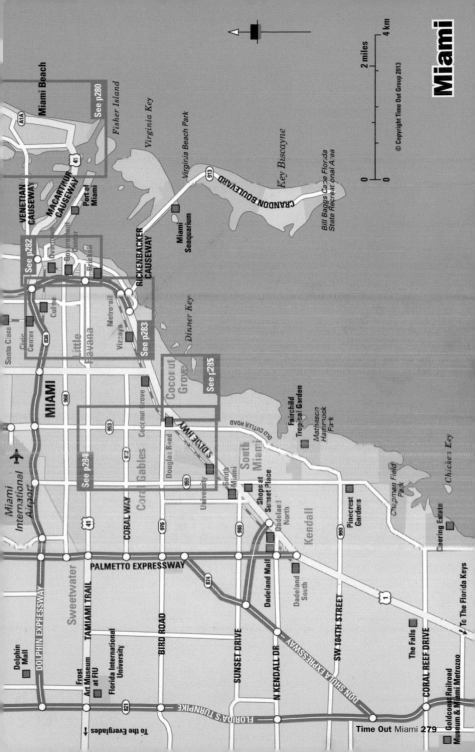

# Miami

Miami Beach

See p280

Fisher Island

Virginia Key

Virginia Beach Park

Key Biscayne

Bill Baggs Cape Florida State Recreational Area

© Copyright Time Out Group 2013

0 — 2 miles
0 — 4 km

VENETIAN CAUSEWAY

MACARTHUR CAUSEWAY

Port of Miami

RICKENBACKER CAUSEWAY

913

CRANDON BOULEVARD

Miami Seaquarium

See p282

Overtown

Government Center

Brickell

See p283

Metrorail

Vizcaya

Dinner Key

Santa Clara

Civic Center

836

Culmer

Little Havana

MIAMI

836

Coconut Grove

See p285

Coconut Grove

953

S DIXIE HWY

Old Cutler Road

Fairchild Tropical Garden

Matheson Hammock Park

Chicken Key

Miami International Airport

See p284

Coral Gables

972

Douglas Road

959

University

South Miami

Coral Way

CORAL WAY

976

Shops at Sunset Place

Dadeland North

South Miami

986

Kendall

Pinecrest Gardens

990

Chapman Field Park

Deering Estate

Sweetwater

PALMETTO EXPRESSWAY

TAMIAMI TRAIL

41

US 1

Dolphin EXPRESSWAY

Dolphin Mall

Frost Art Museum at FIU

Florida International University

BIRD ROAD

874

SUNSET DRIVE

Dadeland Mall

Dadeland South

N KENDALL DR

DON SHULA EXPRESSWAY

SW 104TH STREET

The Falls

CORAL REEF DRIVE

1

Goldcoast Railroad Museum & Miami Metrozoo

To The Florida Keys

821

FLORIDA'S TURNPIKE

To the Everglades

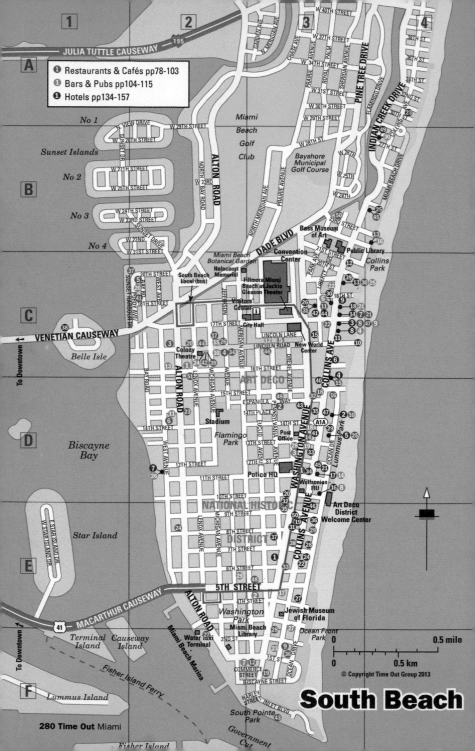

South Beach

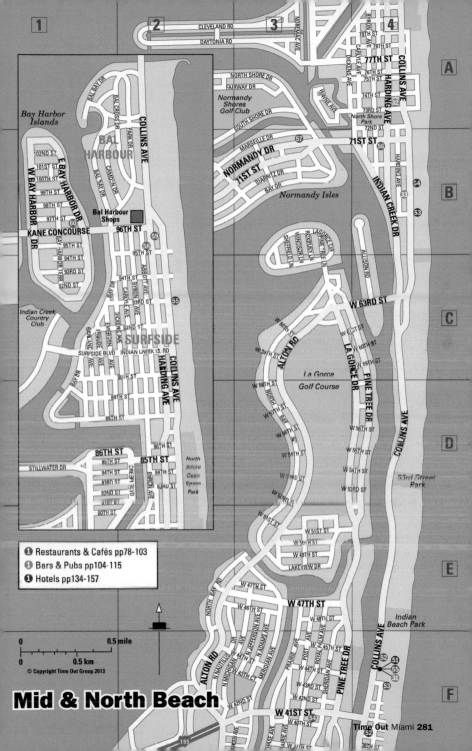

# Mid & North Beach

**❶** Restaurants & Cafés pp78-103
**❶** Bars & Pubs pp104-115
**❶** Hotels pp134-157

0.5 mile
0.5 km
© Copyright Time Out Group 2013

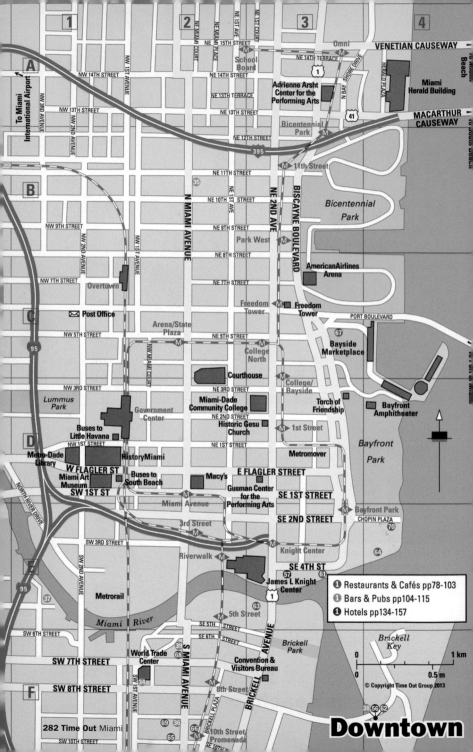

## Downtown

# Little Havana

1  2  3  4

A

B

C

D

E

F

Miami River

NORTH RIVER DRIVE

395

58

95

SW 22ND AVENUE

SW 17TH AVENUE

SW 12TH AVENUE

SW 7TH AVENUE

SW 8TH AVENUE

NW 7TH STREET

NW 6TH STREET
NW 5TH STREET
NW 4TH STREET
NW 3RD STREET
NW 1ST STREET

NW 6TH STREET
NW 5TH STREET
NW 4TH STREET
NW 3RD STREET
NW 2ND STREET
NW 1ST STREET

Marlins Park

W FLAGLER STREET
SW 1ST STREET

W FLAGLER STREET
SW 1ST STREET

SW 2ND STREET
SW 3RD STREET
SW 4TH STREET
SW 5TH STREET
SW 6TH STREET
SW 7TH STREET

SW 21ST AVENUE
SW 3RD STREET
SW 4TH STREET
SW 5TH STREET
SW 6TH STREET
SW 7TH STREET

SW 8TH AVENUE

SW 6TH AVENUE
SW 15TH AVENUE
SW 14TH AVENUE
SW 13TH AVENUE
SW 11TH AVENUE
SW 10TH AVE.

Brigade 2506 Memorial

SW 8TH STREET (CALLE OCHO)

SW 8TH STREET

Máximo Gómez Park

Bay of Pigs Museum

Tower Theatre

SW 9TH STREET
SW 10TH STREET
SW 11TH STREET

SW 9TH STREET
SW 10TH STREET
SW 11TH STREET

SW 12TH STREET
SW 13TH STREET
SW 14TH STREET
SW 15TH STREET
SW 16TH STREET
SW 16TH TERRACE
SW 17TH STREET
SW 17TH TERRACE
SW 18TH STREET
SW 19TH STREET
SW 20TH STREET
SW 21ST STREET

SW 12TH STREET
SW 13TH STREET
SW 14TH STREET
SW 15TH STREET
SW 16TH STREET
SW 17TH STREET
SW 18TH STREET
SW 19TH STREET
SW 20TH STREET

SW 12TH AVE.
SW 13TH AVE.
SW 14TH AVE.

SW 16TH AVENUE
SW 17TH AVENUE

SW 21ST AVENUE

SW 22ND AVENUE

SW 17TH AVENUE

SW 12TH AVE (MEMORIAL BLVD)

SW 13TH AVE.

SW 12TH COURT

SW 22ND STREET
SW 23RD STREET
SW 24TH STREET
SW 25TH STREET

NW 7TH AVENUE
NW 8TH AVENUE
SW 24TH ROAD
SW 25TH ROAD
SW 26TH ROAD
SW 27TH ROAD
SW 28TH ROAD
SW 21ST ROAD
SW 22ND ROAD
SW 23RD ROAD

SW 3RD AVENUE
SW 1ST AVENUE

Vizcaya Metrorail Station

Miami Science Museum

Vizcaya Museum & Gardens

SAMANA DRIVE

SHORE DRIVE

ALASKA DRIVE

BAYSHORE DRIVE

TIGERTAIL AVENUE

RICKENBACKER CAUSEWAY

To Downtown Miami

To Downtown

To Key Biscayne

To Coconut Grove

400 m
400 yds

© Copyright Time Out Group 2013

# Coral Gables

© Copyright Time Out Group 2013

❶ Restaurants & Cafés pp78-103
❶ Bars & Pubs pp104-115
❶ Hotels pp134-157

# Street Index